THE DOLLAR TRAP

THE
DOLLAR
TRAP

How the U.S. Dollar Tightened Its Grip
on Global Finance

ESWAR S. PRASAD

PRINCETON UNIVERSITY PRESS

Princeton and Oxford

Copyright © 2014 by Princeton University Press

Published by Princeton University Press, 41 William Street, Princeton, New Jersey 08540
In the United Kingdom: Princeton University Press, 6 Oxford Street, Woodstock,
Oxfordshire OX20 1TW

press.princeton.edu

Library of Congress Cataloging-in-Publication Data
Prasad, Eswar S.
The dollar trap: how the U.S. dollar tightened its grip on global finance / Eswar S. Prasad.
pages cm
Includes bibliographical references and index.
ISBN 978-0-691-16112-9 (hardback : alk. paper)
1. Dollar, American.   2. Dollarization.   3. Capital movements.
4. International finance.   I. Title.
HG540.P73   2014
332.4'973—dc23   2013023902

British Library Cataloging-in-Publication Data is available

This book has been composed in Adobe Garamond Premier Pro with DIN display
by Princeton Editorial Associates Inc., Scottsdale, Arizona.

Printed on acid-free paper. ∞

Printed in the United States of America

3   5   7   9   10   8   6   4   2

To Basia, Berenika, and Yuvika

My inspiration, my love, my everything

CONTENTS

FIGURES AND TABLES

PREFACE

The U.S. dollar reigned supreme in global finance for most of the twentieth century. In recent years, its position on that pedestal has seemed increasingly insecure. The creation of the euro in 1999 constituted a major challenge to the dollar, but that challenge has faded. Now the Chinese renminbi is seen as a rising competitor.

The global financial crisis, which had its epicenter in the U.S., has heightened speculation about the dollar's looming, if not imminent, displacement as the world's leading currency. The logic seems persuasive. The level of U.S. government debt relative to gross domestic product (GDP) is at its highest point since World War II and could soon be back on an upward trajectory. America's central bank, the Federal Reserve, has taken aggressive actions to prop up the economy by injecting massive amounts of money into the U.S. financial system. Moreover, it is apparent to the entire world that political dysfunction in the U.S. has stymied effective policymaking. All these factors would be expected to set off an economic decline and hasten the erosion of the dollar's importance.

Contrary to such logic, this book makes the argument that the global financial crisis has *strengthened* the dollar's prominence in global finance. The dollar's roles as a unit of account and medium of exchange might well erode over time. Financial market and technological developments that make it easier to denominate and conduct cross-border financial transactions directly using other currencies, without the dollar as an intermediary, are reducing the need for the dollar. In contrast, the dollar's position as the foremost store of value is more secure. Financial assets denominated in U.S. dollars, especially U.S. government securities, are still the preferred destination for investors interested in the safekeeping of their investments.

The dollar will remain the dominant reserve currency for a long time to come, mostly for want of better alternatives. In international finance, it turns out, everything is relative.

Structure of the Book

The book intersperses analytical and narrative elements and is divided into four parts.

Part One: Setting the Stage

The first part summarizes the arguments that underpin the book's thesis. The Prologue (Chapter 1) describes how certain dramatic developments in global financial markets since 2008 have played out in a curious and unanticipated manner. The sequence of economic events runs directly counter to the expected course for a country whose financial markets were imploding and whose economy was heading into a deep and prolonged recession.

The main themes of the book are laid out in Chapter 2. It explains the origins and resilience of the dollar's status as the principal reserve currency in the post–World War II era. The dollar has survived various threats to its dominant role in the global monetary system, allowing the U.S. to continue exploiting its "exorbitant privilege" as the purveyor of the most sought-after currency in global finance. Foreign investors are keen to invest in financial assets denominated in U.S. dollars, allowing the U.S. government and households to maintain high levels of consumption through cheap borrowing.

The large scale of borrowing from abroad, signified by massive U.S. current account deficits, is in fact a relatively recent phenomenon. It coincides with the latest wave of financial globalization—the surge in international financial flows—that got under way in earnest in the early 1990s. These phenomena turn out to be interrelated. Rising cross-border capital flows, particularly to and from emerging market economies, play a central role in the story told in this book.

Part Two: Building Blocks

The second part provides a guided tour through some key analytical concepts that are necessary to underpin any analysis of the international monetary system. I identify various paradoxes in the present structure of international finance that serve as the ingredients for the book's main thesis.

Chapter 3 sketches out the main elements of a standard framework that economists use to study international capital flows, and illustrates how and why the data refute it in many ways. For instance, the theory predicts that capital should flow from richer to poorer economies, whereas the reality has been the opposite. Even though one of its main predictions is refuted by the data, the framework provides a useful benchmark for exploring deficiencies in the present setup of global finance. This necessitates a more careful investigation of the direction, composition, and volatility of capital flows. These topics have taken on greater significance as financial markets around the world continue to become more tightly linked to one another.

Indeed, the global financial crisis has not deterred even the emerging market economies, which once had extensive restrictions on capital flows, from allowing freer movement of financial capital across their borders. Chapter 4 analyzes how rising integration into global financial markets has affected these economies' external balance sheets (i.e., their asset and liability positions relative to the rest of the world). Emerging markets have been able to alter the profile of their external liabilities away from debt and toward safer forms of capital inflows, such as foreign direct investment. Still, even as their vulnerability to currency crises has declined, these economies face new dangers from rising capital flows, including higher inflation as well as asset market boom-bust cycles fueled by those flows.

In Chapter 5, I turn to the growing importance of "safe assets," investments that at least protect investors' principal and are relatively liquid (i.e., easy to trade). Rising financial openness and exposure to capital flow volatility have increased countries' demand for such assets even as the supply of these assets has shrunk. Emerging market economies have a stronger incentive than ever to accumulate massive war chests of foreign exchange reserves to insulate themselves from the consequences of volatile capital flows. The global financial crisis shattered conventional views about the level of reserves that is adequate to protect an economy from the spillover effects of global crises. Even countries that had a large stockpile found their reserves shrinking rapidly in a short period during the crisis, as they strove to protect their currencies from collapse. So now the new cry of policymakers in many emerging markets seems to be: We can never have too many reserves.

Additionally, many of these countries, as well as some advanced economies like Japan, have been intervening heavily in foreign exchange markets in order to limit appreciation of their currencies, thereby protecting their export competitiveness. Exchange market intervention results in the accumulation of reserves, which need to be parked in safe and liquid assets, generally government bonds. Moreover, at times of global financial turmoil, private investors add to the demand for safe assets.

With its deep financial markets, the U.S. has become the primary global provider of safe assets. Government bonds of many other major economies—such as the euro zone, Japan, and the U.K.—look shakier in the aftermath of the financial crisis, as these economies contend with weak growth prospects and sharply rising debt burdens. As a result, the supply of safe assets has fallen even as the demand for them has surged.

Official and private investors around the world have become dependent on financial assets denominated in U.S. dollars, mainly because of the lack of viable alternatives. U.S. Treasury securities, representing borrowing by the U.S. government, are still seen as the safest of financial assets worldwide. Therein lies the genesis of the dollar trap.

Does it make sense for other countries to buy increasing amounts of U.S. public debt, when the amount of that debt is ballooning rapidly and could threaten U.S. fiscal solvency? In Chapter 6, I make the case that foreign investors, especially the central banks of China and other emerging markets, are willing participants in an ostensible con game set up by the U.S. Foreign investors hold about half of the outstanding U.S. federal government debt. The high share of foreign ownership should make it a tempting proposition for the U.S. to cut its debt obligations simply by printing more dollars, thus reducing the value of that debt and implicitly reneging on part of the obligations to its foreign investors. Of course, such an action is unappealing, as it would push up inflation and affect U.S. investors and the U.S. economy as well.

I argue that there is a delicate domestic political equilibrium that makes it rational for foreign investors to retain faith that the U.S. will not inflate away the value of their holdings of Treasury debt. Domestic holders of U.S. debt constitute a powerful political constituency that would inflict a huge political cost on the incumbent government if inflation were to rise sharply. This gives foreign investors some reassurance that the value of their U.S. investments will be protected.

But China and other countries are still frustrated that they have no place other than dollar assets to park most of their reserves. This frustration is heightened by the disconcerting prospect that, despite its strength as the dominant reserve currency, the dollar is likely to fall in value over the long term. China and other key emerging markets are expected to continue registering higher productivity growth than the U.S. Thus, once global financial markets settle down, the dollar is likely to return to the trend of gradual depreciation that it has experienced since the early 2000s.

In other words, foreign investors stand to get a smaller payout in terms of their domestic currencies when they eventually sell their dollar investments. This is a price foreign investors seem willing to pay to hold assets that are otherwise seen as safe and liquid. Financing continued fiscal profligacy in the U.S. stings.

Part Three: Inadequate Institutions

As national economies become more closely connected with one another, there is greater potential for both conflict and cooperation. Which of these two paths is taken has implications for the global configuration of reserve currencies. The third part of the book illustrates how existing frameworks for international economic cooperation have not worked well, leaving conflict rather than cooperation as the more typical state of affairs. This part of the book takes the reader on a behind-the-scenes tour of some of the intrigue in international financial diplomacy, using a variety of sources and even drawing on unconventional sources, such as Wikileaks cables.

Economic tensions among countries are being heightened by the proclivity of the U.S. and other advanced countries to use unconventional monetary policies aggressively—in effect, printing large amounts of money—to prop up their economies and financial systems. These measures have the side effect of depreciating their currencies. Currency depreciation is a zero sum game—if one currency depreciates, some other currency has to appreciate. Hence, actions taken by some major central banks have set off a spate of currency wars as other countries take steps to prevent their own currencies from appreciating. In Chapter 7, I examine the rhetoric and substance behind currency wars. Ironically, when countries resist currency appreciation through intervention in foreign exchange markets, which adds to their foreign exchange reserves, they end up reinforcing the dollar's prominence as a reserve asset.

One concern is that currency wars could end up becoming a more destructive negative sum game in which all players get hurt. If countries' actions aimed at promoting their own short-term interests end up impeding international trade and financial flows, no country will escape from the negative consequences. Coordinated collective action is therefore in the long-term interest of all countries. In Chapter 8, I trace out how one attempt to mediate a global truce on currency tensions—during an episode that preceded the global financial crisis—fell apart. For all their positive rhetoric, national leaders were unable to put collective interest before the parochial interests of their own countries. This episode illustrates that although global coordination of certain economic policies seems desirable in principle, it has proven elusive in practice.

The goal of coordinating policies was revived during the worst of the global financial crisis through the efforts of the Group of 20, comprising the major advanced and emerging market economies. Chapter 9 describes how this large and diverse group did manage some notable accomplishments in the crucible of the crisis, but the spirit of cooperation ultimately proved fleeting. To break free of the dollar, emerging markets have tried various forms of coordination among themselves, but success has been elusive on that front as well.

With their backs against the wall, some emerging markets have tried to use temporary capital controls—legal restrictions on inflows of capital into and outflows of capital from their economies—to protect themselves from the onslaught of volatile capital flows. Chapter 10 provides a survey of how the debate on capital controls has shifted. Such controls have become more palatable, as they are no longer seen as violating international norms if there are extenuating circumstances, such as fears that a country's banking system or equity markets are in danger of being overwhelmed by inflows of foreign capital. However, this self-defense mechanism turns out not to work very well in practice. This leaves emerging markets with few options to protect themselves other than building up ever-larger stocks of foreign exchange reserves that can be deployed as buffers against capital flow and currency volatility.

In Chapter 11, I review some attempts to create global safety nets that would offer protection from crises and other episodes of extreme volatility, thereby reducing countries' incentives to self-insure by accumulating foreign exchange reserves. The International Monetary Fund (IMF) has created new lending programs, with guaranteed access to money in bad times. These programs are meant to function more like insurance schemes, rather than as traditional loan programs that require countries to meet tough policy conditions. There have been few takers for these insurance schemes, perhaps because there is a stigma attached to pre-emptively seeking the IMF's assistance.

Of course, the IMF is not the only game in town. During the financial crisis, the U.S. Federal Reserve offered a few foreign central banks access to dollars. Those central banks were then able to provide dollars to commercial banks in their countries that suddenly found themselves deprived of dollar funding. But such ad hoc lines of credit are nowhere near enough to meet the global demand for dollars.

Because these attempts at obviating the need for self-insurance by individual countries have not proven successful, I briefly summarize a proposal for a simple global insurance scheme that would solve many conceptual problems that have bedeviled other collective approaches. However, the world does not yet appear ready for a proposal that is technically simple but could shake up existing institutional structures. The clutches of the dollar trap remain sticky.

Part Four: Currency Competition

The final part of the book evaluates potential competitors to the dollar and sums up the dollar's prospects. Countries' desire for insurance through accumulation of safe assets, and the ability of the U.S. to provide purportedly safe assets in prodigious amounts that meet the demand, suggest that the dollar's position is secure. Still, there are competitors to the dollar that are beginning to flex their muscles.

Chapter 12 critically evaluates the much-hyped prospects of China's currency, the renminbi, displacing the dollar. China is already the second-largest economy in the world and is on track to become the world's largest economy within the next decade. The Chinese government is taking aggressive steps to promote the international use of its currency. This chapter makes the case that the renminbi is on its way to becoming a viable reserve currency. However, the limited financial market development and structure of political and legal institutions in China make it unlikely that the renminbi will become a major reserve asset that other countries turn to for safekeeping of the bulk of their reserve funds.

The renminbi is hardly the only currency with aspirations of playing a more prominent role on the world stage. Chapter 13 reviews the prospects for other currencies, as well as alternatives such as gold and bitcoins, to threaten the dollar. With greater integration of global financial markets and rapid technological advancements, it will become easier to settle cross-border trade and financial transactions in currency pairs that do not include the dollar. The main conclusion from Chapters 12 and 13 is that the dollar is likely to become less important as a medium of exchange for intermediating international transactions. But its position as a store of value remains secure for the foreseeable future.

Although this book presents more reasons to be sanguine than concerned about the dollar's future, the global monetary system is at a fragile equilibrium. Chapter 14 analyzes various tipping point scenarios that could cause the dollar to come tumbling down from its pedestal. A few such scenarios are plausible, but there is no easy escape route from the

"We've set aside this particular room for those who still worship the almighty dollar."

Source: Michael Maslin / The New Yorker Collection / www.cartoonbank.com.

dollar, as financial turmoil even in its home country will simply drive investors back into its arms.

Chapter 15 points out that, in addition to its size and the strength of its financial markets, the U.S. enjoys advantages that most other countries can only aspire to. These advantages include the robustness of its public, political, and legal institutions, along with a strong and self-correcting system of checks and balances among these institutions.

The threads of argument in the book converge to a conclusion that the dollar will continue to reign as the leading reserve currency for many years to come. This dollar-centric equilibrium seems to be unstable, with big risks for the entire world economy. The very fear of the devastation that would be wrought if it were to fall apart might, paradoxically, serve to make this equilibrium a stable one.

I leave it to the reader to decide whether the book's conclusion is a comforting or disturbing one.

PART ONE

Setting the Stage

Prologue

Truth is stranger than fiction,
but it is because Fiction is obliged to stick to possibilities;
Truth isn't.

Pudd'nhead Wilson's New Calendar, Mark Twain

International finance has come to resemble a morality play, but one mostly featuring government mandarins and assorted knaves, with few heroes to speak of. The moral is ultimately that virtue is not necessarily its own reward; rather, an excess of virtue may be harmful. Do pay careful attention to all the twists and turns in the plot—reality turns out to be stranger than anything the fevered imagination of a playwright could muster.

Let us pick up the plot from not too long ago.

Stage Set for Dollar Collapse

In 2007, the U.S. recorded a third successive year of current account deficits of over $700 billion, roughly equivalent to 5 percent of annual U.S. gross domestic product (GDP). The current account deficit represents the amount a country borrows from abroad to finance its consumption and investment. Fears that foreign investors would stop lending to the U.S., precipitating a plunge in the dollar's value, were palpable. This was also the year the U.S. housing market began to unravel after a prolonged period of rising housing prices, accentuating fears about prospects for the U.S. economy and the dollar. Financial market bigwigs, prominent academic economists, government officials, the press, and international financial institutions were all warning of a looming dollar collapse.

Jim Rogers, the co-founder of the Quantum Fund with George Soros, was quoted as saying, "If [Federal Reserve Chairman] Ben Bernanke starts running those printing presses even faster than he's already doing, we are going to have a serious recession. The dollar's going to collapse, the bond market's going to collapse." Many financial analysts joined the chorus warning of a dollar crisis, with that phrase appearing increasingly frequently in their reports and interviews. An editorial in the leading German magazine *Der Spiegel* warned of nothing less than an economic Pearl Harbor, noting that "an attack on the US economy is probably the most easily predictable event of the coming years."

Paul Krugman of Princeton University wrote that "Almost everyone believes that the US current account deficit must eventually end, and that this end will involve dollar depreciation ... there will at some point have to be a 'Wile E. Coyote moment'—a point at which expectations are revised, and the dollar drops sharply." Kenneth Rogoff of Harvard University pointed to "a greatly increased risk of a fast unwinding of the U.S. current account deficit and a serious decline of the dollar. We could finally see the big kahuna hit." Eisuke Sakakibara, a former top Japanese finance ministry official, warned that a dollar plunge was coming in 2008. The International Monetary Fund (IMF) and the World Bank both sounded the alarm that, if the U.S. did not reduce its reliance on foreign capital, a disorderly decline in the dollar's value was likely and that there would be devastating consequences worldwide.

The drumbeat of warnings intensified as 2008 dawned. Then, the economic picture in the U.S. took a sharp turn for the worse, and financial markets braced for the dollar crash prophecies to be validated. That is when the drama surrounding the dollar began to diverge from the script.

Act One

In October 2008, U.S. financial markets were reeling. The meltdown of the housing market earlier in the year and the fall of the financial giant Lehman Brothers in September were sending waves of panic through every part of the financial system. The corporate paper market had nearly frozen, the stock market was collapsing, and a major money market fund, the Reserve Primary Fund, had "broken the buck" (its net asset value had fallen below par) and was threatening to take the entire money market down with it. Shock waves from the crisis were reverberating around the world.

Historical precedent made clear what was coming. When other countries have been hit by financial or currency crises, the outcomes have been similar—investors, both domestic and foreign, run for the exits, pull capital out, and dump the currency. Surely, the financial crisis would not just be a gentle fall from grace but rather the coup de grâce for the dollar's dominance in global finance.

Then something remarkable happened. A wave of money flooded *into* the U.S., the very epicenter of the crisis. U.S. investors pulled their capital back home from abroad, while foreign investors in search of a safe haven for their money added to the inflows. From September to December 2008, U.S. securities markets had net capital inflows (inflows minus out-flows) of half a trillion dollars, nearly all of it from private investors. This was more than three times the total net inflows into U.S. securities markets in the first eight months of that year. The inflows largely went into government debt securities issued by the U.S. Treasury (finance ministry). In contrast, many other advanced economies, including Germany and Japan, experienced overall net outflows of capital in that period.

The dollar, which should by all rights have plunged in value, instead rose sharply against virtually every other currency. It even rose against other major advanced economy currencies except for the Japanese yen.

Prices of U.S. Treasury securities increased as demand for them soared. As a consequence, interest rates stayed low even after the government instituted a massive fiscal expenditure program to stave off the collapse of financial markets and the economy. This was the opposite of the typical response of interest rates, which tend to rise when the government borrows more to finance its spending. In fact, yields on three-month Treasury bills even turned slightly negative on certain days that December —nervous investors were in effect willing to pay the U.S. government for the privilege of holding those securities.

Act Two

In November 2009, as global financial markets were slowly getting back on their feet, concerns about Greece's debt situation began to grow. Greek officials admitted that their fiscal books had been cooked and that the country's government debt amounted to 113 percent of GDP, nearly double the upper limit of 60 percent that euro zone members had agreed to abide by at the time of the euro's inception a decade earlier. In January 2010, the European Commission issued a scathing report concluding that Greece's budget deficit for 2009 was likely to be even higher than the government's estimate of 12.5 percent of GDP and well over the euro zone limit of 3 percent.

As it became clear that Greece was facing an economic collapse, concerns began to mount about fiscal and banking problems in other economies on the euro zone periphery. Ireland and Portugal were seen as especially vulnerable, and there were even concerns about Spain and Italy. On May 2, 2010, the European Commission, the European Central Bank (ECB), and the IMF agreed to a bailout package for Greece. In November, the Irish government also signed up for a bailout package, and concerns intensified that the other periphery economies of the euro zone might start reneging on their debt and would need bailout packages as well.

Once again, troubles abroad drove money into the U.S. From December 2009 to November 2010, as the debt crisis cascaded across the euro zone and built up to catastrophic proportions, yields on U.S. ten-year Treasury notes fell by more than 1 percentage point, from 3.6 percent per year to 2.5 percent. In the third quarter of 2010, when the euro zone debt crisis seemed in danger of spiraling out of control, the U.S. had net inflows of nearly $180 billion into its securities markets. In the first two quarters of that year, net inflows into those markets had averaged just $15 billion. Foreign private investors accounted for about two-thirds of these net inflows in the third quarter; the remainder was from central banks and other official investors.

Act Three

Even as centrifugal forces were threatening to tear the euro zone apart, there was more drama to come in the U.S. In 2011, political brinksmanship led to a standoff between President Obama's administration and the Republican-controlled U.S. House of Representatives over the debt ceiling. If the ceiling was not raised, the U.S. Treasury would lose the authority to raise money from financial markets, and the government would essentially run out of money to pay its bills and meet repayment obligations on its debt.

The Treasury Department made it clear that failure to raise the debt ceiling would be devastating and that patchwork solutions like "prioritizing" payments on the national debt above other obligations would not prevent default. It released a document laying out the consequences:

Failing to increase the debt limit would have catastrophic consequences . . . [it] would precipitate another financial crisis and threaten the jobs and savings of everyday Americans . . . it would call into question the full faith and credit of the United States government—a pillar of the global financial system.

The fear of a technical debt default by the U.S. government cast a pall over financial markets as the deadline drew near. Neither side—President Obama or the Republicans—blinked until the very end. On July 31, 2011, a Sunday, the two parties finally reached an agreement to raise the debt ceiling and trim government expenditures by about $2.4 trillion over the next decade. The agreement was signed into law on August 2, 2011, the day before the government would in principle have hit its borrowing limit. By all counts, this deal was nowhere near enough to tackle the long-term deficit problem.

On August 5, the rating agency Standard & Poor's (S&P) did the unthinkable—it cut the rating on U.S. government debt from AAA to AA+ and kept the outlook on the long-term rating at "negative." According to S&P, the safest financial instrument in the world was no longer as safe as it had been thought to be. In a statement accompanying its downgrade, S&P had this to say:

The downgrade reflects our opinion that the fiscal consolidation plan that Congress and the Administration recently agreed to falls short of what, in our view, would be necessary to stabilize the government's medium-term debt dynamics . . . we believe that the prolonged controversy over raising the statutory debt ceiling and the related fiscal policy debate indicate that further near-term progress containing the growth in public spending, especially on entitlements, or on reaching an agreement on raising revenues is less likely than we previously assumed and will remain a contentious and fitful process.

In other words, the deal had kicked the proverbial can down the road and done nothing to change the trajectory of U.S. debt, which would continue its inexorable rise beyond levels that some economists thought were already too high and unsustainable. The S&P statement then went on to excoriate the politics surrounding the debt ceiling and fiscal negotiations:

> The political brinksmanship of recent months highlights what we see as America's governance and policymaking becoming less stable, less effective, and less predictable than what we previously believed.

This action by S&P was expected to be the wake-up call for financial markets. Finally, reason would prevail. The dollar would have its come-uppance and fall in value, the absurdly low interest rates on U.S. government bonds would finally spike up, and capital would flee from the U.S.

Or not. What effect did the ratings downgrade have on U.S. debt markets? The effect was indeed big, only it was exactly the reverse of what had been expected. Yields on ten-year Treasury notes, which should have risen now that U.S. government debt had been deemed riskier, instead fell by 1 full percentage point from July to September of that year. Net capital inflows into U.S. securities markets jumped to nearly $180 billion in August and September, again driven mostly by private inflows. The dollar spiked up in value once more, repeating its pattern over the past decade of falling gradually in normal times and rising sharply in perilous times—even when the peril originated in the U.S. economy.

Act Four

The political debate in the U.S. had gotten increasingly rancorous in the lead-up to the presidential elections in 2012. Democrats and Republicans were at loggerheads on economic and social policies, as Barack Obama and Republican nominee Mitt Romney laid out very different (if not very specific) visions of how the country ought to be run. With the economy still sputtering, economic issues dominated the elections.

The biggest concern in financial markets was the gun the U.S. Congress had put to its own head. Unless a budget agreement could be reached by December 31, 2012, a set of automatic tax increases and government expenditure reductions would kick in, holding down the budget deficit but dealing a body blow to the U.S. economy. The estimated size of the fiscal contraction—a combination of across-the-board spending cuts and an expiration of the Bush tax cuts—was about $500 billion. If nothing were done, the economy would face a drag of about 4 percent of GDP relative to optimistic forecasts of 2.5 percent GDP growth in 2013. In other words, the economy could be headed for another recession.

The Republicans were hoping to capture the White House, displace the Democrats as the majority party in the Senate, and retain their majority in the House of Representatives. Whatever the outcome, most analysts were betting that rationality would return to the U.S. political scene in the lame duck session of Congress, the period between the elections and the start of the next legislative session. Once the election season was out of the way, surely the bitter partisanship would recede, and both parties would work together to avoid fiscal and financial doom.

On November 5, 2012, the day after the elections, Americans woke up to a political outcome that left the balance of power virtually unchanged. The days wore on and December arrived, with budget negotiations going nowhere as positions on both sides hardened. Emboldened by his new mandate, President Obama indicated there would be no deal without an increase in tax rates for the wealthy. The Republicans referred to the Administration's proposals as "not serious" and noted that "we're almost nowhere" in making progress toward a deal. With no resolution in sight, the economy trudged inexorably toward the "fiscal cliff." Christmas and New Year's Day came and went with no deal. It was only on January 2, 2013—technically, the day after the economy had gone over the cliff—that a deal was reached.

While these events were playing out in the fall of 2012, stock markets in the U.S. rose and fell, as every surge of optimism that a deal would be reached was almost invariably followed by some other obstruction to a compromise. As for bond markets, however, the yield on ten-year Treasury notes stayed in the narrow range of 1.6–1.9 percent through this entire period. The dollar barely moved against other major currencies. Yields on ten-year notes started to drift back above 2 percent in January 2013, raising concerns that interest rates were now on their way up. But there was little further increase in the ten-year Treasury note yield, leaving it at a far lower level than in any period since the 1960s.

The Drama Goes On

The U.S. fiscal drama continued into 2013, with the budget "sequester" taking effect in March. The sequester took a blunt hatchet to public expenditures, cutting them by about $100 billion per year through 2021 and hurting the tenuous economic recovery. Anticipation of further rounds of the debt ceiling fight raised concerns about continued economic and political gridlock. Through all this, the yield on ten-year U.S. Treasuries remained stable in a narrow range around 2 percent. Even minor increases in interest rates raised concerns about the tide turning and Treasuries falling out of favor with investors. But these panicky reactions to small perturbations have proved to be overhyped.

It is of course unlikely that such low rates will last for long. Indeed, by early September 2013, the yield on ten-year notes was creeping toward 3 percent. Yields on U.S. Treasuries are likely to rise further as economic conditions in the U.S. and the rest of the world normalize. But such increases should be considered in their proper context—relative to the average ten-year bond yield of about 4.5 percent during 2000–2007, the period of the "Great Moderation," when the U.S. economy was growing at an average rate of roughly 2.6 percent per year and annual inflation averaged 2.8 percent. In other words, even a significant increase in interest rates from their low levels as of mid-2013 might signal a return to normalcy rather than an exodus from U.S. Treasury debt and the dollar.

It is hardly surprising if turmoil in other financial markets causes money to flow into the U.S. in search of safe investments, thus keeping U.S. interest rates low and pushing up the dollar's value. But, as the episodes described in this chapter have illustrated, the dollar also tends to strengthen even when its home economy gets pounded with financial and fiscal problems.

How did we end up in such a topsy-turvy Bizarro World, where everything seems inverted or backward (as in the American comic series of that name)? How do we make sense of a world in which money flows into the U.S. in search of a safe haven from the fallout of financial market troubles, even if those troubles originate in U.S. financial markets themselves? Therein lies a tale.

What Is So Special about the Dollar?

In the Country of the Blind, the One-eyed Man is King.
The Country of the Blind, H. G. Wells

The tale of how the dollar came to have a central role in the world economy is a fascinating one. Why the global financial crisis fortified the dollar's stature is even more intriguing. This story is not an arcane one relevant merely to financial market players (and academic economists picking over the carnage) but also one that will have repercussions for ordinary people from Beijing to Johannesburg to São Paulo. Truly, much of the world has been drawn, willingly or otherwise, into the web of the dollar, and there is no easy way out. The story has implications not just for the world we live in today but also for the future stability of the world economy.

The essence of the story can be distilled into one question: *If not the dollar, then what?* The fact that there is no good answer to this question has been the bane of the global monetary system for many decades. This system, if it can be called that, is characterized by capital flows across national borders, exchange rates between national currencies, financial markets that facilitate international transactions, and institutions that manage the framework of rules and conventions that underpin these activities.

Surprisingly, the wave of global financial integration that started about two decades ago has only sharpened the question about why this system is so dollar-centric, rather than providing any viable answers. When investors need to find a safe place to put their money during a time of financial upheaval, they ultimately end up turning to the U.S. When the world is scrambling for cash, as it was during the worst of the financial crisis, the clamor around the world is for more dollars. The reality is that, in an imperfect world, the dollar still stands out as a paragon of strength, relatively speaking.

11

Demand for Safe Assets Rises and Supply Shrinks

Paradoxically, the global financial crisis, which was triggered by the U.S. housing market meltdown and then quickly infected financial markets in the U.S. and around the world, has cemented the dollar's dominant role. The reason for this strange outcome is that the crisis has increased the demand for safe financial assets even as the supply of such assets from the rest of the world has shrunk, leaving the U.S. as the main provider. It is instructive to analyze why the demand for and supply of safe assets has shifted.

Investors around the world remain on edge as the world lurches from one crisis to another, with the euro zone debt crisis following on the heels of the financial crisis. More trouble is anticipated in global financial markets: their weak underbellies and lack of effective regulation have been exposed, and steps taken by governments and financial regulators to deal with these problems are hardly reassuring. This has raised the demand for safe financial assets that at least protect investors' principal, can easily be converted to other currencies, and are liquid—easy to trade even in large quantities. Typically, only government bonds of the major advanced economies meet these criteria. Financial institutions that are now being told by their regulators to hold larger amounts of liquid securities as a safety buffer are adding to the demand for safe assets.

Moreover, emerging market economies continue to contribute to the strengthening of the dollar's leading role in global finance through their accumulation of dollar assets as foreign exchange reserves. Officials in these countries are concerned that, with their capital accounts becoming more open to cross-border capital flows, they are increasingly vulnerable to volatility of those flows. These countries view international investors as fair-weather friends who proffer more capital than needed in good times, creating problems of domestic inflation and asset market booms. At the first sign of trouble, however, these investors tend to turn tail, often precipitating asset market and currency crashes. Large stocks of foreign exchange reserves give emerging market policymakers some reassurance that they can better cope with capital flow and currency volatility.

China may have enough foreign exchange reserves—$3.5 trillion as of June 2013—to cope with everything but an apocalypse. Other emerging markets are not in quite so sanguine a position and still have a strong incentive to add to their reserve stockpiles. They do this by intervening in foreign exchange markets, which involves purchasing hard currencies —currencies such as the dollar and the euro that are widely used and easy to trade—in return for domestic currencies.

Central banks around the world also have another motive to intervene in foreign exchange markets. They do this to prevent their currencies from appreciating in value, as that would adversely affect the competitiveness of their exports. Some emerging markets like China have been driven by such "mercantilist" motives for a long period. These interventions result in a buildup of hard currency assets that need to be invested in relatively safe and liquid financial instruments, adding to the clamor for safe assets.

While the demand for safe assets is surging, their supply has shrunk after the financial crisis. The crisis dealt fatal blows to many large firms and banks, some with long and rich histories. Consequently, the notion of privately issued securities being safe has evaporated, even when they are issued by rock-solid corporations or financial institutions. For many years to come, government securities that are highly liquid and backed up by credible central banks and national governments are going to be perceived as the only reliable safe assets. With its rising level of public debt, the U.S. government stands out as the leading provider of assets that satisfy these criteria.

The U.S. is hardly the only economy that can provide safe assets denominated in a reserve currency. But now, even some advanced economy central banks, like the Bank of Japan and the Swiss National Bank, are engaged in monetary operations that will weaken their currencies. They are also intervening directly in foreign exchange markets to prevent currency appreciation. So they are adding to the demand for safe assets instead of helping to satisfy demand from the rest of the world.

It's All Relative

This is not a story about American exceptionalism. Rather, it is one about weaknesses in the rest of the world and deep problems in the structure of the global monetary system. The reason the U.S. appears so special in global finance is not just the size of its economy but also the fact that it has fostered a set of institutions—democratic government, public institutions, financial markets, a legal framework—that, for all their flaws, are still the ones that set the standard for the world.

U.S. debt markets, where debt securities issued by corporations and the government can be traded, remain unrivaled in terms of both depth (the volume of securities available for trading) and liquidity (the amount of trading or turnover of those securities). In particular, by any measure of size and turnover, the U.S. Treasury bond market dwarfs government bond markets of other major economies.* Domestic and foreign investors continue to put their faith in these investments despite the high and rising level of U.S. federal government debt.

What accounts for this faith? The system of checks and balances among the different arms of government, together with an open and transparent democratic process, has created a sense of confidence in U.S. public institutions. The rule of law is firmly established, with even the executive branch being subject to the dictates of the law. This adds to the confidence among foreign investors that they will be treated fairly if they invest in the U.S. and that the debt owed to them will not be arbitrarily written off at the whim of politicians.

Even if investments in the U.S. are safe from expropriation, there remains the question of how to reconcile the continued prominence of the U.S. dollar with ongoing shifts in the balance of global economic power. Emerging market economies, especially China and India, weathered the crisis better than the advanced economies did. These economies are catching up to the U.S. in some respects, including size, and are eroding many of the advantages it has enjoyed for a long time. Nevertheless, the emerging markets will not easily be able to overcome the enormous lead that the U.S. has built up for itself through its financial markets and robust public institutions. China may soon exceed the U.S. in sheer economic size, but its financial markets are unlikely to match up to those of the U.S. any time soon. More importantly, with its present institutional and political setup, and also its weak legal framework, China will not command the faith of international investors the way the U.S. does.

---

* In this book, I use "government bonds" as a generic term referring to government debt securities of all maturities. For the U.S., the term covers Treasury bills (with a maturity of one year or less), Treasury notes (with maturities ranging from two to ten years), and Treasury bonds (with maturities longer than ten years). The terms "U.S. Treasuries" and "U.S. Treasury securities" have the same connotation as U.S. government bonds.

No Room for Comfort

The dollar's dominance persists even as its home economy looks increasingly vulnerable on account of its high and rising level of public debt. Deep political schisms in the U.S. are blocking solutions that would help tackle the long-term deficit and debt problems in a rational manner. That its main anchor is drifting in shallow and shifting sands ought to raise red flags about the stability of the global monetary system.

Of course, one could argue equally well that matters would be far worse in the absence of a common reserve currency that was widely and uniformly accepted and in which investors around the world had confidence. Such a currency needs to be backed by a trusted and respected institution. The U.S. central bank, the Federal Reserve (Fed), is now seen as an institution that has the ability to single-handedly forestall a meltdown of the global financial system. Its ability to issue dollars in unlimited quantities when financial markets need them has transformed the Fed into a credible lender of last resort not only to the U.S. financial system but also to the world at large. Perhaps the dollar has become the indispensable glue holding the international monetary system together.

The story told in this book is not an encouraging or reassuring one. The world is mired in a fragile equilibrium that presages even greater financial instability, and there are many shocks that could cause the global monetary system to come apart at the seams. Some paths to greater stability exist, and, as is the case with many other difficult problems in economics, the solution involves a complicated mix of sorting out incentives and collective action problems. The first part of the solution requires getting incentives right for countries to implement tough but sound choices on fiscal and structural reforms, rather than relying on the crutch of easy money. The second part is to fix coordination problems that, if left unresolved, lead countries to focus on their perceived short-term interests and employ policy tools that could cause collective harm. Here, too, a contemporary example is the excessive reliance on activist monetary policies rather than more fundamental reforms to revive or increase growth.

None of these solutions is easy. Indeed, one of the main messages of this book is a sobering one. Given how difficult it is to get the politics of reforms right at the national level, coordination of policies at the international level might be a chimera. So, without being too Panglossian about it, a dollar-centric system might actually be the best of the available alternatives.* It gives all countries an incentive to maintain the stability of what ought to be an unstable equilibrium.

To examine the genesis of this situation, history is a good place to start.

A Brief History of the U.S. Dollar's Road to Dominance

The U.S. dollar has been the principal global currency for most of post–World War II history. In fact, the U.S. economy is estimated to have become the largest in the world in the 1870s. By the early 1900s, it also accounted for the largest share of global trade. However, without a central bank and with many restrictions on cross-border capital flows, the dollar was far behind the British pound in terms of prominence in global financial markets. A hodgepodge of currency notes was being issued by U.S. private banks, and even after the production of currency notes was taken over by the government, the instability of the U.S. banking system did little to build confidence in the dollar.

The Federal Reserve Act of 1913 created the nation's central bank, with the objective of providing a more elastic supply of currency and more effective bank supervision. The creation of the Fed generated substantial impetus to expand the dollar's use in international trade and financial transactions. Other factors outside of U.S. economic policy also contributed to the dollar's rising prominence. For example, the onset of World War I led other reserve currency competitors to suspend their currencies' convertibility to gold so they could finance their war efforts by printing money, giving an added boost to the dollar's status as a reserve currency.

Ever since it surpassed the British pound—which some scholars argue happened as early as the 1920s, whereas others describe it as a post–World War II phenomenon—the dollar has been at the center of the global monetary system. The dollar's prominence was cemented under the Bretton Woods system of fixed exchange rates that was put in place in 1945 to obviate the intense currency competition that had hampered

---

* In Voltaire's satirical novel *Candide,* the title character views the world through the prism of his mentor, Dr. Pangloss: " all is for the best in this world . . . in this best of all possible worlds."

world trade in the aftermath of the Great Depression. Under this system, other key currencies were pegged to the dollar, which in turn was convertible into gold.

The end of the gold standard in the early 1970s did not affect the dollar's leading role in global finance. As the gap in economic size between the U.S. and other economies grew wider, and as U.S. financial markets came to be the largest in the world, the dollar grew increasingly powerful. Most of the world's transactions related to trade and financial flows across national borders are now settled in dollars. It remains the currency in which a major proportion of global foreign exchange reserves is held, and the dollar is recognized and accepted worldwide.

This has created a bounty for the U.S., often disparagingly referred to as an exorbitant privilege. The U.S. has lived beyond its means for an extended period, with its consumption and investment substantially exceeding the output it produces. The country has been able to borrow from the rest of the world, and the dollar's status has allowed it to finance this debt at cheap interest rates. What is more, because this debt is all denominated in dollars, the U.S. can in principle reduce its debt burden to other countries simply by printing more dollars and reducing the value of that debt in inflation-adjusted terms. Other countries have chafed at this privilege and yearned to move to a less dollar-centered system.

Under Attack

The introduction of the euro was expected to shift the balance of power by unifying the economic power of the euro zone bloc, whose GDP now rivals that of the U.S. Until the euro came into being, there had been no serious competitor to the dollar in the postwar era—other currencies, such as the British pound, German deutsche mark, and Japanese yen, came in a distant second or further behind. The euro was created on January 1, 1999, and euro coins and notes started circulating in 2002, replacing the national currencies of the 12 initial member countries of the euro zone. Monetary union was seen as an essential step in the unification of Europe, so that its economic power and influence in the world economy could be resurrected.

Events followed the expected trajectory in the early years of the euro, with the U.S. dollar quickly losing ground to the new currency. The European Union's expanding trade, both among countries within the Union and across the Union's borders, helped elevate the euro into a major currency for settling international trade transactions.

The share of global foreign exchange reserves held in dollars, an important indicator of the dollar's prominence as a global reserve currency, fell by 6 percentage points in just a four-year period from 2000 to 2004. The euro's share went up by a corresponding amount. For all the excitement this engendered, it turned out that this shift was mainly the result of expressing all reserve holdings in dollar terms. The apparent rise in the euro's share was largely driven by an increase in its value relative to the dollar rather than a durable shift in reserves from dollars to euros.

In any event, the euro's drive to dominance stalled soon thereafter, with its share of global foreign exchange reserves unable to break through the 30 percent threshold. The dollar's share has remained stable at around 62 percent in recent years, whereas the euro's share has fallen back to 24 percent. And now, of course, the euro zone has enough problems to contend with merely to keep itself together, let alone challenge the dollar's position.

By the latter half of the past decade, the U.S. dollar was coming under attack on other fronts as well. With China and other emerging markets growing rapidly in the early years of the new millennium, emerging market currencies appeared to be positioning themselves to take over another slice of the dollar's domain.

It looked like the dollar's days were numbered. But this tale took some unexpected twists during and after the global financial crisis.

Coup de Grâce Turns into Moment of Grace

The financial crisis ought to have been the last straw that sealed the dollar's fate and displaced it from its preeminent role in global finance. After all, the crisis was precipitated by the near-breakdown of U.S. housing and financial markets.

Then, on the way to its dethroning, a funny thing happened to the U.S. dollar. As described in Chapter 1, right when U.S. financial markets seemed on the verge of collapse, taking global markets down with them, money kept flowing into rather than out of America. Viewed through the prism of world economic history, what happened during the financial crisis stands out as a big conundrum. At a time of financial panic triggered by the U.S., the dollar was still regarded as the ultimate safe haven.

In fact, what happened during the crisis was just an extreme example of how the dollar has fared in recent years. Consider one indicator of global risk—the Chicago Board Options Exchange Market Volatility Index, better known as the VIX. This is a measure of the implied volatility of index options on the S&P 500 index. In plainer language, it represents the market's expectation of the degree of stock market volatility over the next 30 days. Although the VIX captures expectations of volatility in the U.S., the index covers most major U.S. firms, including many multinationals that have extensive global operations. So the VIX has come to be known as a gauge of the amount of fear in global financial markets.

This fear gauge tends to spike upward when there is financial market distress in any major economy or economic region that is likely to have global consequences. In October 2008, when there was a serious prospect of U.S. financial collapse, the VIX hit an all-time high. In June 2010, when the euro zone debt crisis was heating up, and then again in September 2011, when the U.S. debt ceiling standoff had ended but with no real resolution to the U.S. fiscal problems, the VIX rose sharply.

Remarkably, whether a jump in the VIX is due to concerns about U.S. or foreign financial markets, the net result has always been the same. In the months around the spike, money gushes into the U.S. Typically, this money is parked in U.S. Treasury bonds, driving down Treasury bond yields (when bond prices go up because of stronger demand, yields on those bonds—i.e., interest rates—go down). And despite low interest rates in the U.S., the monetary inflows imply increased demand for dollars, propping up the dollar's exchange rate relative to other major currencies.

In short, the dollar remains the preferred refuge from troubled financial markets, even if its home country is the source of those troubles. This seems a curious situation given the long-held view that the U.S. has relied on the generosity of foreign investors to finance its high consumption levels. The reliance on foreign capital ought to make the U.S. vulnerable rather than being seen as a haven of safety.

The Relatively Short History of U.S. Profligacy

Notwithstanding its long-standing reputation as a spendthrift nation, the history of U.S. profligacy financed by the rest of the world is a rather short one. It coincides with the recent wave of financial globalization,

19

which picked up steam in the latter half of the 1980s. Indeed, it is only since the early 1990s that the U.S. current account has registered a sizable and persistent deficit. Figure 2-1 shows that the U.S. current account was in surplus or roughly balanced for most of the 1900s. Between 1945 and the early 1970s, the U.S. did sometimes face a balance of payments deficit. Even though its current account was roughly balanced, it was losing gold reserves (the dollar was then convertible into gold at a fixed price under the Bretton Woods system of fixed exchange rates).

In absolute terms, massive and protracted U.S. current account deficits are a relatively recent phenomenon. Figure 2-2 shows that the U.S. started running a large deficit in the 1980s, led by a rise in the government budget deficit. The current account deficit was eliminated by 1990, even though budget deficits remained large. Starting in 1990, however, the current account deficit rose sharply, reaching a level of $800 billion by 2006. This happened even though the U.S. budget balance turned into a surplus during 1998–2001 under President Bill Clinton (who was in office 1993–2001). In 2002, the budget balance turned back into a defi-

FIGURE 2-1. U.S. Current Account Balances: A Historical Perspective

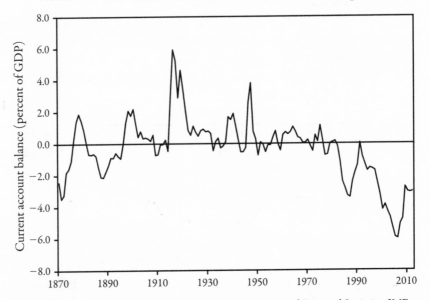

Data sources: Taylor (2002) for data until 1960; IMF International Financial Statistics; IMF World Economic Outlook.

FIGURE 2-2. U.S. Current Account and Government Budget Balances, 1960–2012

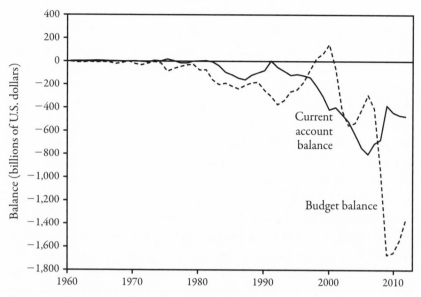

Data source: U.S. Bureau of Economic Analysis.

Note: A negative number indicates a current account deficit or a budget deficit.

cit, and the deficit continued to increase during the years of the George W. Bush administration (2001–09). The budget deficit then exploded after the financial crisis, averaging $1.4 trillion in each year during 2009–12. During this four-year period, U.S. public debt rose by nearly $6 trillion. Thus, the substantial increase in the production of safe assets by the United States and the willful acquisition of these assets by the rest of the world really picked up pace only over the past decade. This is precisely the period during which financial globalization took off, with surging cross-border capital flows among countries.

A Delicate Political Equilibrium

As of June 2013, $10 trillion of U.S. federal government debt was owed to private and foreign investors. Of this amount, more than half— $5.6 trillion—represents obligations to foreign investors, including central banks, institutional investors like pension funds, and retail investors. Adding in debt owed to the Social Security trust funds (which are considered part of the government) and the Federal Reserve raises the total level of U.S. federal government debt to $16.8 trillion, roughly equivalent to U.S. annual GDP.

One would think there is an enormous temptation to inflate away the value of U.S. debt, as a significant amount of the burden of such an implicit "default" would be borne by the rest of the world. Nevertheless, there seems to be a shared faith among foreign and domestic investors that the U.S. Federal Reserve is unlikely to let inflation get out of hand and will do whatever it takes to keep inflation down. One reason for such restraint is that about two-fifths (44 percent) of U.S. Treasury debt, excluding debt held by the Social Security trust funds and the Federal Reserve, is domestically owned.

This fraction strikes a nice balance. It may be sufficient to reassure the rest of the world that the temptation to inflate away some of the debt will be held in check by domestic political economy considerations. Potent voting blocs—such as retirees, who hold a large part of their retirement portfolios in fixed-income investments—would be hurt by inflation. Moreover, a burst of inflation would raise interest rates, increasing the government's borrowing costs, and also increase government payments on social security and other items indexed to inflation.

So perhaps it is in fact rational for foreign investors interested more in safety than in high returns to invest in U.S. government bonds.

Paradoxes Proliferate

This leads to another paradox. The major advanced economies are building up massive levels of public debt, with the U.S. leading the way. At the same time, their central banks have pumped large amounts of money into their economies to try to kick-start growth. Some of this money has found its way to emerging market economies, causing their currencies to appreciate. This has set off currency wars, with emerging markets' central banks intervening in foreign exchange markets to forestall currency appreciation, as that would hurt their export competitiveness.

Emerging markets are not too unhappy about building up foreign exchange reserves in this process, as reserves protect them from the financial instability that might be in prospect, because the fiscal and monetary policies of the U.S. are heightening global risks. And where is this protection money held for safekeeping? Largely in U.S. dollar assets!

The dollar's strength as the principal global reserve currency should not be mistaken for a prediction that the value of the dollar will remain strong relative to other major currencies. Despite upward spikes in its value during periods when global financial markets are unsettled, the dollar has been gradually falling in value over the past two decades. This is a natural and necessary part of the adjustment to bring down large U.S. trade and current account deficits, and this trend is likely to resume once financial markets settle down. The currency depreciation is necessary to raise U.S. exports relative to imports, reducing the trade deficit. Higher productivity growth in emerging markets relative to the U.S. also indicates that the dollar should depreciate against those countries' currencies in the long term.

This prognosis for the dollar only heightens the anomalous situation of foreign investors, especially emerging market central banks, who are accumulating dollar assets as stores of value. For it means that, measured in their own currencies, these investors face the prospect of a significant loss on their dollar assets. Even measured in dollar terms, the returns on U.S. Treasury securities are at historical lows, implying a high price for safety when one considers the opportunity cost of other uses for those funds, where they could earn a higher return. When inflation-adjusted interest rates on Treasuries are negative, as has been the case for an extended period, investors are practically paying the U.S. government to hold their money.

Is life imitating art, in this case the Bizarro World of comic books? In one episode, a salesman enthusiastically peddles rather unique bonds with this sales pitch: "Buy Bizarro bonds! Guaranteed to lose money for you!" From a long-term perspective, some foreign investors (including central banks) appear to be falling for this odd sales pitch. Much like in the comic, where an enthusiastic buyer of Bizarro bonds exclaims: "What a bargain!"

The Dollar's Dominance Weakens—Except as a Store of Value

The dollar is not immune to shifts in the global economic landscape. Among the many fundamental realignments taking place in the world economy, the one with the biggest economic and political impact could be the battle for dominance among major currencies. Emerging market economies are growing by leaps and bounds and catching up to the size of advanced economies. Some emerging market currencies, which had stood on the sidelines for a long time, are gradually beginning to move to center stage. These developments, along with the greater integration of global financial markets, will result in a decline in the dollar's role in international finance in two dimensions—as a unit of account and as a medium of exchange.

The dollar's primacy as a "vehicle" currency for the denomination and settlement of trade transactions is bound to become less essential over time. Many countries are signing agreements with each other to facilitate settlement of trade transactions directly in their own currencies. With the development of deeper and more sophisticated financial markets around the world, there will be more trading and hedging of foreign exchange risk in bilateral currency pairs that exclude the dollar. There will be less need to denominate trade in commodities such as oil in just one currency.

Some Reserves Lose Their Luster

The dollar's roles as a unit of account and a medium of exchange are increasingly less secure, but its true forte is as a store of value. Dollar-denominated securities, especially U.S. Treasuries, are still seen by investors worldwide as the safest of financial assets. There are of course other currencies that are backed by trusted central banks. These economic areas, including the euro zone, Japan, the United Kingdom, and Switzerland, all provide high-quality government bonds that investors regard as safe assets.

Many of these bonds are now on somewhat shakier ground. In January 2012, the rating agency S&P cut by one notch the ratings of two of the euro zone's hitherto AAA-rated countries—Austria and France. The rating on France's sovereign debt was also taken down a notch below AAA by another ratings agency later that year. The statement accompanying the downgrade by Moody's was biting, noting that the French economy had "deteriorating economic prospects" and that its "long-term economic growth outlook is negatively affected by multiple structural challenges including its gradual, sustained loss of competitiveness and the long-standing rigidities of its labour, goods and service markets."

In February 2013, the top rating of another major reserve currency bit the dust when Moody's downgraded U.K. sovereign debt by one notch, noting the country's weak growth prospects and its high and rising debt burden. The same could be said of the prospects of many other advanced economies. Such downgrades of the sovereign credit of major advanced economies often seem to cause only limited damage in the form of higher borrowing costs, at least initially, as they do not contain much new information and are widely expected by market participants. However, such actions chip away at the investor confidence that is needed to anchor an expanding role for reserve assets denominated in these currencies. In contrast, as illustrated in Chapter 1, investor perceptions about the riskiness of U.S. sovereign debt seem immune to the views of rating agencies.

In terms of sheer size and liquidity, it is hard to match the U.S. Treasury bond market. Adding in other debt securities only widens the gap between the U.S. and other economies. The combined size of U.S. domestic debt securities markets, as measured by the market value of outstanding bonds issued by different levels of government and by private corporations, was nearly $33 trillion in 2012. This was slightly more than the sum of the domestic debt securities markets of the euro zone, Japan, Switzerland, and the U.K. combined. Even this picture doesn't fully convey the size of the gap between the debt securities markets of the U.S. and the rest of the world.

Euro zone bond markets have become fragmented. It is now apparent that a German government bond, or bund, is not quite the same thing as a Greek government bond. The size of the "safe" part of the euro zone bond market is smaller than it appears once one takes into account only bonds issued by the core euro zone economies, such as Austria, Germany, France, and the Netherlands. Even some of those, as noted above, are regarded as safe only because the European Central Bank (ECB) has implicitly signaled it will stand behind those bonds. The stock of Japanese bonds is massive, but the amount of those bonds that are actively traded is small, as Japanese banks, pension funds, and other institutional investors hold most of those bonds. All of this implies that none of the other major advanced economy currencies is in a position to substantially reduce the dollar's prominence as a reserve asset.

Newer, Nimbler Competitors

Could new reserve currencies challenge the dollar even in its role as an international store of value? Are there other safe havens that international investors can retreat to at times of global financial turmoil?

China's renminbi is well on its path to internationalization, meaning a broader use in global trade and financial transactions, and is likely to become a significant reserve currency within the next decade.* Even as the renminbi attains this status, and even if the size of the Chinese economy overtakes that of the U.S., it is a reasonably safe bet that the U.S. dollar will by far remain the key reserve currency.

The reason is simple—it comes down to trust. Although China has economic strength and dynamism on its side, it has yet to develop a strong framework of public and political institutions. For all its economic heft and its low level of debt, China is unlikely to be entrusted by foreign investors with large sums of their money. Money that goes into China—and undoubtedly there will be increasing amounts in the years ahead—is likely to be driven by the motives of investors in other countries to diversify their portfolios and the desire of foreign governments to befriend a rising economic power. It is unlikely that money will flow to China because of investors' eagerness to take refuge from troubled financial markets elsewhere, especially as China's financial markets themselves are relatively underdeveloped and beset by considerable risks.

As China and other emerging market economies grow larger and account for more of global GDP and trade, and as their financial markets develop, these countries' currencies will no doubt start playing more prominent roles in international finance. Nevertheless, they will not displace the dollar.

Shifting Patterns of Capital Flows

There are many compelling and logical reasons why, in principle, the dollar's dominance in global finance should be under siege. These include rising levels of U.S. public debt and obligations to the rest of the world, ineffectual U.S. macroeconomic policies, and the emergence of new currencies. The reality, however, is that the dollar has faced numerous threats in recent decades but has withstood them all. It may be somewhat the

---

* *Renminbi* literally means "people's money" and is the name of the Chinese currency. The unit of account is the yuan. For an analogy, consider the British currency, which is the pound sterling, whereas the unit of account is the pound. I use the terms renminbi and yuan interchangeably in this book.

worse for wear from all of these battles, but there is no viable challenger to the dollar's status as the definitive safe haven currency.

The U.S. has put together a winning combination that no other country comes close to matching—not just a large economy but also deep financial markets, rock-solid public institutions, and an effective legal framework—that other countries have faith in. The consequence is that the U.S. dollar is likely to remain the world's main port for shelter from financial storms for a long time to come. The enduring faith in the U.S. as a sanctuary for investments is abetted rather than eroded by the enormous and rising level of its public debt.

A disconcerting corollary to the "depth" of the Treasury bond market is that the massive level of public debt engenders concerns about macroeconomic instability and uncertainty about the future of the dollar. Moreover, there is a widely held view that the capital flows that financed rising U.S. debt levels at cheap interest rates provided the tinder for the financial crisis and facilitated its rapid spread to all corners of the world. This view about the deleterious effects of capital flows has created a clamor for fundamental changes to the global monetary system. The dollar's central role in this system has also come under critical scrutiny.

Even though the U.S. remains at the center of global finance, there have been massive shifts in the nature and patterns of international capital flows that have implications for the present status and future prospects of the dollar. Capital flows, both short-term and long-term, tend to drive fluctuations in currency values. To get a handle on currency movements, it is necessary to better understand what drives these flows. The rise of emerging markets also has implications for the structure of global financial flows, as this group of fast-growing economies has come to play an increasingly prominent role in the world economy. In the next chapter, I review some of these developments. This will lead us deeper into the convoluted world of international finance, seething with paradoxes and lurking dangers.

PART TWO

Building Blocks

The Paradox of Uphill Capital Flows

INSPECTOR JACQUES CLOUSEAU: *Welcome. We can always use an extra mind. Now, let me bring you up to speed. We know nothing. You are now up to speed.*

The Pink Panther 2

Virtually every economist is familiar with Bob Lucas's work. Bob, or Robert E. Lucas, Jr., is a Nobel Prize–winning economist at the University of Chicago. He was also my Ph.D. thesis supervisor, and my fondest memories of graduate school involve meetings in his smoke-filled room (he no longer smokes!), where I learned how to do economics. The genius of Lucas is not just that he found elegant answers to some difficult questions in economics but also that he was able to frame important questions in a simple and clear manner, providing fertile ground that waves of future researchers could then plough in search of answers.

About the time I was getting ready to leave Chicago for my first job, Lucas was working on an important paper that tied together the fields of macroeconomics and international finance. That paper, by asking a simple but profound question, would set off a massive wave of research that continues to this day.

The question posed in the title of Lucas's five-page paper, published in 1990 in the *American Economic Review,* was "Why Doesn't Capital Flow from Rich to Poor Countries?" The logic of the standard economic theories that Lucas used to postulate his question is simple and persuasive. Wealthier countries like Japan and the U.S. have more physical capital—plant and equipment, machinery, computers—and less labor compared to less wealthy economies like China and India. Because the amount of labor relative to physical capital is much higher in developing countries, each additional unit of capital can be combined with more labor and ought to be more productive in those countries. Therefore, financial capital ought to flow from capital-rich countries to capital-poor ones.

Robert E. Lucas, Jr., University of Chicago. Nobel Prize in Economics, 1995.

Financial flows that are transformed into physical capital investment in poorer economies should make everyone better off. Investors from rich countries would earn higher returns on their savings than they would by investing in their own countries. Poor countries would benefit from getting additional capital, allowing them to boost investment and growth. Eventually, these flows would taper off as the ratio of capital to labor became roughly equal across countries.

Theory Meets Reality

The reality, as Lucas pointed out, was quite different from those predictions. Back in the 1980s, the amount of capital flowing from rich to poor countries was small, far smaller than could be explained by any reasonable version of the theory. In his paper, Lucas proposed one explanation —that the quality of labor in developing countries was inferior because of lower literacy and training rates. In other words, once you adjusted for quality, the difference in the amount of labor in poor countries relative to rich countries was not as great as the difference based on just counting up the number of working-aged persons.

Another possible explanation was "political risk," a broad term encompassing political instability and other factors that might make it difficult for foreign investors to repatriate profits or even retain control of their investments in less developed economies. Lucas had framed the question elegantly, but his answers were not entirely persuasive, as they could not possibly account for more than a small part of the difference between theory and facts.

Academic economists are loath to give up elegant theories without a fight simply because the facts do not match them. We tend to first quarrel with the facts, worrying whether they are as clean as our theoretical models. Lucas's paper set off a wave of research trying to explain why the observed pattern of international capital flows was not a violation of theory but simply required better data or a few tweaks to the model. For instance, over the years, researchers have argued that emerging markets have a number of problems that make capital less productive than in advanced economies. These problems include ramshackle infrastructure, unstable governments that could turn around and confiscate foreign-owned companies, high levels of corruption, and so on. The implication of this line of argument is that looking at ratios of physical capital relative to the stock of labor is far from sufficient to determine how much financial capital should be flowing from rich to poor countries.

Even as this research was under way, private capital flows to emerging markets picked up in the 1990s, as advanced economy investors looked abroad for higher returns than they could earn in their home countries. Many developing countries in Latin America and Asia took full advantage and started pulling in more inflows, mostly in the form of debt. This debt was mainly from loans provided by foreign banks but also included foreign investors' purchases of bonds issued by governments and corporations in emerging markets. Some of these funds went to finance extravagant government expenditures and household consumption booms

Country Classification

In most of the analysis in this book, I focus on economies that meet a minimum size threshold and are reasonably well integrated into global trade and finance. I classify countries that meet these criteria into two groups—the advanced industrial economies and the emerging market economies.

One should not make too much of the distinction between these two groups, as the distinction has become blurred over time. Many former emerging markets like Korea, Hong Kong, and Singapore have now become advanced economies as their per capita incomes have risen sharply over the past couple of decades. Indeed, as many have noted, landing at the airport terminals even in Beijing or Shanghai—let alone Hong Kong or Singapore—after departing from any of the terminals in New York often makes one wonder which is the richer and more advanced economy. Of course, the major cosmopolitan areas in many emerging market economies are hardly representative of the standard of living enjoyed by the broader population in those countries.

To distinguish between the two groups of countries, I adopt a cutoff of annual per capita income of $16,000 in 2012, with each country's income converted to dollars using market exchange rates. Countries with per capita incomes above $16,000 are considered as advanced, although I leave Saudi Arabia in the group of emerging markets, because its economy is largely driven by oil rather than industry (this designation is also consistent with the convention adopted by international institutions). Emerging markets typically have annual per capita incomes in the range of $1,000–$16,000. Using purchasing power parity exchange rates, which adjust for differences in costs of living across countries, yields a similar breakdown of the two groups, but at a different income cutoff of $21,000.

The sample I use for my analysis contains 29 advanced economies and 29 emerging markets. Together, they account for about 95 percent of world GDP, trade, and financial flows. The list of countries that I use for most of the empirical analysis in this book is as follows:

> Advanced economies: Australia, Austria, Belgium, Canada, Czech Republic, Denmark, Estonia, Finland, France, Germany, Greece, Hong Kong, Iceland, Ireland, Israel, Italy, Japan, Korea, Netherlands, New Zealand, Portugal, Singapore, Slovak Republic, Slovenia, Spain, Sweden, Switzerland, United Kingdom, United States.

> Emerging markets: Argentina, Brazil, Bulgaria, Chile, China, Colombia, Hungary, India, Indonesia, Jordan, Kazakhstan, Kenya, Latvia, Lithuania, Malaysia, Mexico, Morocco, Nigeria, Pakistan, Peru, Philippines, Poland, Romania, Russia, Saudi Arabia, South Africa, Thailand, Turkey, Ukraine.

rather than being directed to investment (e.g., in infrastructure or plant and equipment) that would improve long-term productivity.

Other countries invested the foreign capital unwisely, partly as a consequence of weak financial systems, often aided and abetted by cronyism and corruption that led to the funds being channeled to firms with good political connections rather than to the most productive ones. When foreign investors started getting nervous about the policies in some of these countries, they stopped lending to them and eventually pulled out their money. There followed a series of financial crises that wracked many economies, especially in Asia and Latin America.

Once the dust settled from the Mexican Tequila crisis (1994) and the Asian and Russian financial crises (1997–98), investors from rich countries started renewing their interest in emerging markets. Meanwhile, as the new millennium got under way, something curious began to happen to overall international capital flows that would be an even starker refutation of conventional theories about the direction of those flows.

Uphill Flows

Just like water, capital is supposed to flow downhill, from richer to poorer economies, as posited by Lucas. Of course, countries receiving this capital would eventually have to pay back their obligations to international investors. They could do this by using the foreign capital to increase investment, grow faster, and become richer, thereby generating enough resources to pay off foreign investors. Only *net* inflows of capital matter from the perspective of this theory. A country could be investing abroad but receiving larger inflows, so on net it would be a capital importer. In contrast, a net exporter of capital would be exporting more capital than it imports. Capital imports and exports can be carried out by private investors or by official institutions, such as central banks.

A country's current account balance is a summary measure that reflects net capital flows through all channels—official and private. A current account deficit signals net imports of capital from the rest of the world, whereas a current account surplus signifies that a country is a capital exporter (see Figure 3-1).

FIGURE 3-1. The Current Account and Capital Flows

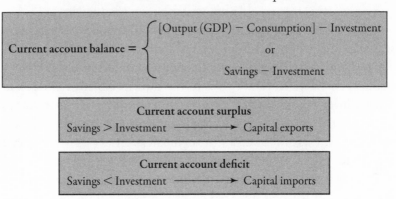

In research that I conducted with Raghuram Rajan and Arvind Sub-ramanian in 2006 when we were at the IMF, we confirmed something that other researchers had started noticing—that capital had in fact been flowing "uphill" during the 2000s. As a group, the advanced economies were running a current account deficit. This is exactly counter to theory —richer advanced economies should be lending to poorer developing economies rather than borrowing from them.

Private capital flows have certainly been moving downhill from the advanced economies, but these have been more than offset by official flows going in the other direction. The distinction between private and official flows will turn out to matter in many important ways later in the book, but from the point of view of the standard theory, only the sum of these two types of flows matters for growth.

China and the U.S. are the canonical examples of this upside-down world. Americans are on average about eight times richer than the Chinese. Yet, it is the U.S. that has been running a massive current account deficit for many years now, meaning that its consumption and investment together exceed its output (see Figure 3-1). Another way of looking at it is that savings (which is output minus consumption) is less than investment in the U.S. Someone has to finance that deficit, and it turns out that countries like China are doing exactly that. China has been running a current account surplus every year since 2000, meaning that it produces more than it consumes and invests. To put it another way, savings exceeds investment in China. Over this period, China has received large capital inflows from private investors in advanced economies, but these have been swamped by its official outflows.

Capital Exporters and Importers

A country's current account balance can shift from surplus to deficit, or the other way around, from year to year, although in practice these surpluses and deficits tend to be persistent. Rather than looking at current account balances year by year, a different way of looking at overall capital exports and imports is to look at these balances summed up over a number of years. A positive sum indicates that a country is a net exporter of capital over the relevant period. A negative sum indicates that it is a capital importer.

Figure 3-2 shows the main importers of capital during 2000–2012. The U.S. stands out as the major importer of capital, absorbing about

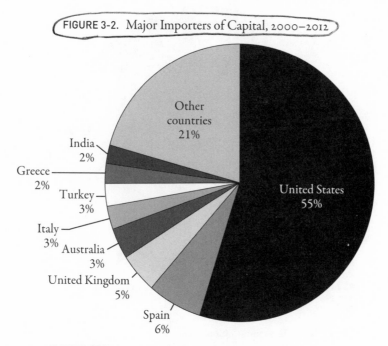

FIGURE 3-2. Major Importers of Capital, 2000–2012

Data source: IMF World Economic Outlook, April 2013.

Notes: For each country, current account balances (in billions of dollars) are summed up over 2000–2012. Countries that have a negative total balance over that period (a cumulative current account deficit) are categorized as capital importers. Summing up these total balances across all capital importers yields total world capital imports. This combined total is then apportioned among the capital-importing countries.

$7.1 trillion, or more than half of the overall net inflows of this group of countries. There are a few other advanced economies—Spain, the United Kingdom, Australia, Italy, and Greece—and two emerging markets—Turkey and India—that are significant capital importers.

Figure 3-3 shows that China is the main exporter of capital in the world, accounting for about 16 percent of global capital exports, or roughly $2.2 trillion, during 2000–2012. Germany and Japan are also substantial exporters of capital. It is interesting to note that the euro zone as a whole ran a nearly balanced current account over this period, with the surpluses of countries like Germany and the Netherlands offset

FIGURE 3-3. Major Exporters of Capital, 2000–2012

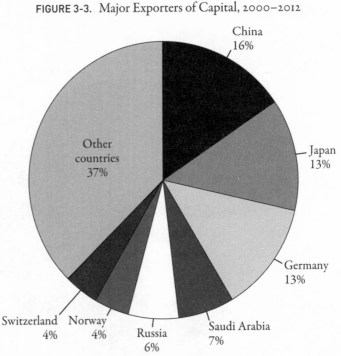

Data source: IMF World Economic Outlook, April 2013.

Notes: For each country, current account balances (in billions of dollars) are summed up over 2000–2012. Countries that have a positive total balance over that period (a cumulative current account surplus) are categorized as capital exporters. Summing up these total balances across all capital exporters yields total world capital exports. This combined total is then apportioned among the capital-exporting countries.

by deficits of countries like Spain, Italy, Greece, and Portugal. Oil exporters like Saudi Arabia, Russia, and Norway are also major exporters of capital, as is Switzerland.

These figures present a more nuanced picture of global capital exports and imports, and add some wrinkles to the portrayal of uphill capital flows. During 2000–2012, emerging markets as a group exported about $3 trillion, whereas advanced economies as a group imported $4 trillion. The difference is made up mainly by oil-exporting countries—such as Algeria, Iran, Kuwait, Libya, Qatar, and the United Arab Emirates— that are not included in the group of emerging markets that I consider. Of course, the data in Figures 3-2 and 3-3 could include capital exports from advanced economies like Germany and Japan to other advanced economies like the U.S., as the destinations for net capital outflows from any given country are not identified.

It is fairly clear from these figures that advanced economies are much bigger net importers of capital, whereas emerging markets are net exporters. The U.S. is a key driver of this phenomenon. Thus, the basic story of uphill flows of capital is preserved. China, a fast-growing but still middle-income economy, is exporting vast amounts of capital to the rest of the world, while the U.S., one of the richest countries in the world, imports hundreds of billions of dollars of capital each year.

Are Uphill Flows a Problem?

A positive or negative current account balance is not a bad thing per se. It depends on a country's circumstances, especially its level of development. For a poor country constrained by a low level of domestic savings, higher investment financed through foreign capital—implying a current account deficit—may be a path to rapid economic development. For the U.S., where the household savings rate out of disposable income has been low and government saving is negative, it is not as pretty a picture, as the deficits have mainly been used to fuel consumption.

Current account deficits leave a country vulnerable to a situation wherein foreign investors are no longer willing to invest in it. This could happen if those investors start having doubts about whether they will continue to earn good returns on their investments or, in some cases, worry about getting paid back at all. When that happens, and it often happens abruptly, the country has no choice but to cut consumption and investment drastically to make up for the loss of foreign financing.

The U.S. has not faced this problem yet—as discussed in Chapter 2, it is special in many ways—but many emerging markets, such as India and Turkey, are at risk because of their current account deficits. India has a high savings rate but invests even more than it saves. The high rate of investment is good for its economic growth but does mean that the country could suffer when it falls out of favor with foreign investors.

Current account surpluses create no such vulnerability, but surpluses are not always a good thing. If a capital-poor country is saving more than it invests, the implication could be that the country's financial markets are simply unable to handle the intermediation of domestic savings into domestic investment.

China in fact has one of the highest rates of investment in the world—about 45 percent of annual output is reinvested, with a large chunk of that investment going into infrastructure and housing. The savings rate is even higher, as households, corporations, and the government all save a lot. A high national savings rate is usually considered a good thing, but in China's case there is some evidence that the high savings rates might actually reflect problems, such as the lack of a good safety net and deficiencies in the financial system. There are also many concerns about whether the Chinese financial system, which is dominated by state-owned banks, is doing a good job of channeling domestic savings into the most productive domestic investments. So, in the case of China, the current account surplus might be a symptom of deeper problems.

This leads to another empirical puzzle related to uphill capital flows.

Another Growth Conundrum

One side effect of uphill capital flows is that those capital-poor economies that are exporting capital should be growing slower than their counterparts who are getting net inflows of capital and, therefore, investing more than they could based on their limited domestic savings. Well, not quite. In our paper, Rajan, Subramanian, and I documented another noteworthy empirical fact—developing countries that have borrowed less from other countries or even sent capital abroad (in net terms) have actually grown faster than countries that have relied on foreign capital. It turns out that higher investment is certainly good for growth, but economic outcomes are a lot better when this investment is financed through domestic savings rather than by importing capital from abroad.

China is a poster child for this empirical finding—it is a big capital exporter as reflected by its current account surplus, yet it has grown at a remarkable pace. In fact, the result turns out to hold across a large group of developing countries. In research done in parallel with ours, Pierre-Olivier Gourinchas at the University of California, Berkeley, and Olivier Jeanne of the Johns Hopkins University showed that the puzzle went even deeper—when they looked at productivity growth, they found that more capital tends to flow to developing economies that have *lower* productivity growth.

Thus, among developing countries, those that rely less on foreign capital or even export capital on average have better output and productivity growth compared to those that borrow more from abroad and should, according to theory, enjoy faster growth. The implication of this research is that uphill capital flows are not intrinsically a problem. Still, there was a pervasive sense in the policy community that something was not quite right, as capital-poor economies were financing rising current account deficits in advanced economies that, in principle, needed the capital less than poorer economies did.

Rajan (who is now the governor of India's central bank) presented an early version of our research at the Jackson Hole conference in 2006. This annual conference, organized by the Federal Reserve Bank of Kansas City, has become famous for attracting top central bankers from around the world. The central bankers let down their hair—at least figuratively speaking—for a couple of days as they listen to a handful of academic presentations and then go off to hike, bike, or take rafting trips at the base of the majestic Grand Teton mountains. The research presented at this conference tends to be less technical than at standard academic conferences but more innovative and relevant to policies. That year's conference theme was "The New Economic Geography." Our paper in effect showed how the geography of capital flows had shifted during that decade.

Following the presentation, there was the usual spirited floor discussion involving conference participants. Even though most participants found the correlations that we reported to be interesting, they were not persuaded that the phenomenon amounted to much of a puzzle. Allan

Meltzer of Carnegie-Mellon University, for instance, argued that our results simply reflected emerging markets' mercantilist policies—keeping
their currencies undervalued by shipping more capital out of the country, thereby making their exports of goods and services more competitive
in international markets. This was very much the prevailing view in the
U.S., where policymakers were formalizing the view that uphill capital
flows reflected problems in other countries.

Deficits as a Sign of Virtue

The intellectual case for the U.S. perspective on this issue was spear-
headed by Ben Bernanke. On March 10, 2005, Bernanke, who by then
had become one of the more influential members of the board of governors at the Federal Reserve, gave a speech in Richmond, Virginia. His
speech was about the U.S. current account deficit, and he was clear that
the deficit was primarily the consequence of domestic policies and economic developments in the U.S. itself. But a central thesis of his speech
was that foreign factors—specifically, economic developments in emerging market economies—were necessary to explain why this deficit had
persisted and even grown. He deftly coined a phrase that would come to
encapsulate his views on what was driving uphill flows:

> I will argue that over the past decade a combination of diverse
> forces has created a significant increase in the global supply of
> saving—a global saving glut—which helps to explain both the
> increase in the U.S. current account deficit and the relatively low
> level of long-term real interest rates in the world today.

Bernanke's argument was that the high level of saving relative to investment in emerging markets was distorting the international financial system. In other words, the capital inflows into the U.S. represented the
consequences of (1) poor policies in emerging markets that caused their
households and corporations to save too much and (2) underdeveloped
financial markets that prevented those savings from being absorbed
domestically into investment in those economies.

Being an academic at heart, Bernanke was of course more balanced in
his views, recognizing that U.S. budget and current account deficits were

largely the result of his own government's bad policies. But his remarks had the undeniable air of assigning a fair amount of blame to emerging market economies for preventing natural adjustment mechanisms, such as a depreciation of the dollar, that would have forced the U.S. to adjust its deficits by increasing borrowing costs and the prices of imported goods. Many American economists, such as John Taylor of Stanford University, rejected this view, and the pushback was even stronger from emerging markets that were dismissive of the blame that was being ascribed to them for permitting the U.S. to live beyond its means.

Meanwhile, the George W. Bush administration deftly turned a negative into a positive in the 2008 Annual Economic Report of the President, which was released early that year. Breaking with tradition, the report did not fret about the current account deficit, the amount that the U.S. borrows from the rest of the world to fill the financing gap for its consumption and investment. Rather, it talked in gushing terms about the capital account surplus—the amount the rest of the world is willing to invest in the U.S.—and how that was a reflection of the productivity and strength of the U.S. economy. The current account deficit and capital account surplus are two sides of the same coin, but this was certainly a more encouraging and positive spin of the data.

Thus, the U.S. succeeded in developing two parallel narratives about global imbalances, both of which cast its own economy in a virtuous light. The underpinning of these narratives was that mercantilist policies and financial market weaknesses in emerging markets were causing them to save too much and export their savings. Given the sheer size of its economy and its current account surplus, China of course was and remains the most prominent exhibit in any debate about mercantilist policies.

In the broader policy and academic communities, rising current account deficits in the U.S. and expanding current account surpluses in China began to be seen as typifying the problem of "global imbalances." The negative connotation was intentional, capturing the view that capital was flowing in a direction opposite to that predicted by conventional theoretical models and that blame for those flows was to be assigned to inappropriate policies in both advanced and emerging market economies.

Do Current Account Imbalances Matter?

Even if persistently large current account deficits or surpluses are benign at the level of individual countries, they could have deleterious consequences from a global perspective. In the lead up to and right after the global financial crisis of 2008–09, the discussion about capital flows centered on global macroeconomic imbalances and their implications. To this day, there is a raging debate about whether these current account imbalances are an "equilibrium" phenomenon rather than a serious problem in themselves, and about how much they contributed to precipitating the financial crisis.

This debate goes back even further to the view espoused by policymakers in some countries, such as Australia, Chile, and the United Kingdom, that current account deficits should not be a concern so long as they do not reflect public sector budget deficits. This view came to be known as the "Lawson doctrine," in honor of the U.K. Chancellor of the Exchequer Nigel Lawson, who articulated it in the late 1980s. The logic is that current account deficits that stem from private sector borrowing and that are willingly financed by foreign investors should not be a cause for alarm. Australian economist John Pitchford put it more colorfully, arguing that the behavior of "consenting adults" that may result in current account deficits should not be subject to policy interference unless they stem from clearly identifiable problems in the functioning of markets that need to be fixed.

The 1992 sterling crisis seemed like fitting comeuppance for Lawson's perspective. The British pound came under attack, had to be devalued, and was forced off the European Exchange Rate Mechanism. Other events—ranging from Chile's 1982 crash after a few years of running massive current account deficits to the recent global financial crisis—show that private sector debts often end up becoming socialized, so even private sector–driven current account deficits should be cause for concern. Moreover, for economies like the U.S., large public budget deficits have gone hand in hand with low levels of private saving. The desire for private agents and governments in advanced economies to borrow from other countries needs to be accompanied by an explanation of why poorer economies are willing to finance those deficits. Hence, an explanation of these imbalances must also deal with the puzzle of uphill capital flows.

What Explains Persistent Current Account Imbalances?

There is no dearth of theories. For instance, Dani Rodrik of Princeton University has argued that the reason for uphill flows is that emerging markets are not savings-constrained, as is assumed in standard theories, but investment-constrained. In other words, lack of funds is not the problem, as many emerging markets have high savings rates. His contention is that various weaknesses in policies and institutions make it difficult for emerging markets to invest those funds productively within their own borders. China may be seen as a counterexample to this theory, because its ratio of investment to GDP is very high, as noted earlier. In a roundabout way, concerns about China's investment patterns do fit in with this story—the very rapid growth of investment financed by an inefficient banking system could be leading to a large amount of misallocated and unproductive investment.

Other economists, such as Ricardo Caballero at the Massachusetts Institute of Technology, have formalized the argument that financial systems in emerging markets are not able to channel capital effectively to productive investments. Hence, emerging markets in effect send capital to advanced economies and then hope that investors from those economies will invest this money back in their countries and channel capital to good investment opportunities. This is one way of working around weaknesses in the domestic financial system.

Of course, the financial crisis has rendered somewhat dubious the proposition that the advanced economies have more robust and better-regulated financial markets. Based on standard measures of financial market development, such as the amount of credit provided by the banking system relative to the size of the economy, advanced economies certainly appear to have better financial markets. But whether they are in fact more efficient at allocating capital and managing risks, either within their countries or abroad, remains open to question.

Advanced economy financial systems look more sophisticated but are not necessarily more robust and stable than those in emerging market economies. Indeed, the crux of the concern about current account imbalances is that the saving glut in emerging market economies fueled financial market mayhem in the U.S. The logic is that, in the absence of uphill official flows of capital, interest rates in the U.S. would have risen as the demand for credit rose in the mid-2000s. There might still have been some asset market bubbles, but they would have popped without causing major damage. Instead, the inflows from emerging market economies kept long-term interest rates in the U.S. low, even when the Fed raised short-term policy rates. Those low rates and the search for higher yields fueled larger levels of speculative investments financed with cheap money, ultimately resulting in a disastrous crisis that ended up harming not just the U.S. but also the emerging markets themselves.

Global current account imbalances have abated after the crisis, but some of the issues raised in the debates about those imbalances are relevant for evaluating the ongoing risks from international capital flows. These issues remain pertinent to this day—while the ebbs and flows of current account balances have garnered much of the attention, emerging markets have continued their integration into global financial markets. As we will see in the next chapter, for these economies the financial crisis proved to be just a road bump in the process.

4

Emerging Markets Get Religion

Let me not pray to be sheltered from dangers but to be fearless in facing them.
. . .
Let me not look for allies in life's battlefield but to my own strength.
Fruit-Gathering, Rabindranath Tagore

The concept of financial globalization—rising capital flows among countries and closer integration of their financial systems into global capital markets—has been tarnished by the financial crisis. Multinational banks have significantly curtailed their international operations. Many of them were badly damaged and some even went belly-up as a result of the crisis. This has led to a retrenchment of financial globalization among the advanced economies, as their banks had been the biggest players in mediating cross-border flows. In contrast, emerging markets have continued to remove restrictions on capital flows across their borders and are experiencing rising flows both into and out of their economies.

To some extent, this reflects the confidence among emerging market policymakers that their economies are now less vulnerable to crises sparked by external factors. Ayhan Kose of the IMF and I have documented that these economies have improved their fiscal and monetary policy frameworks, with most of them bringing inflation and fiscal deficits under control. These policy shifts have not only made most of these economies more resilient to adverse shocks but also have paid off in terms of a better profile of capital inflows. As a result, over the past decade and a half, there has been a remarkable transformation in the nature of emerging markets' external balance sheets. Even though these economies have reduced their exposure to risks that resulted in many of them experiencing crises in the past, they now face an entirely different set of risks from capital flows. However, the process of financial globalization is too far along for these economies and there is no turning back.

To analyze the evolution of this process, it is necessary to consider stocks of a country's foreign assets and liabilities, the net worth of a

FIGURE 4-1. International Capital Movements

Capital flows

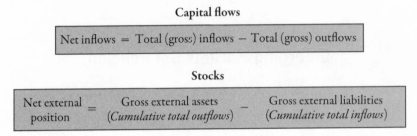

Net inflows = Total (gross) inflows − Total (gross) outflows

Stocks

$$\text{Net external position} = \underset{(\textit{Cumulative total outflows})}{\text{Gross external assets}} - \underset{(\textit{Cumulative total inflows})}{\text{Gross external liabilities}}$$

country as implied by the difference between those assets and liabilities, and also the flows of capital that add to assets or liabilities. Each of those concepts, summarized in Figure 4-1, matters in its own way in evaluating the cost-benefit trade-offs from financial globalization.

Country Balance Sheets Expand

Like corporations, national economies can also have balance sheets that capture their net worth. In the case of countries, we do not have a full accounting of domestic assets, which include a country's human and natural resources, and domestic liabilities. There do exist more limited balance sheets for each country vis-à-vis the rest of the world. Such a balance sheet, referred to as a country's international investment position (IIP), measures a country's gross external (foreign) assets and liabilities as well as the composition on each side of the balance sheet.

On this balance sheet, assets represent claims on other countries held by domestic residents, corporations, or even the government. Liabilities are obligations to the rest of the world, which could include a country's government debt and also corporate debt that is purchased by foreign investors. When Mary Smith of Toledo, Ohio, invests in a Vanguard emerging markets mutual fund that then takes her money and buys shares of an Indonesian firm or bonds issued by the Indonesian government, that investment represents an external asset of the U.S. and an external liability of Indonesia. When the Chinese central bank buys a billion dollars' worth of U.S. Treasury bonds, that amount becomes an external liability for the U.S. and an external asset for China. A country's net asset position—that is, assets minus liabilities—can be positive or negative. For the world as a whole, external positions must balance out, as one country's asset is another country's liability.

In principle, net positions alone should matter. If Mary Smith has more debt—car loans, student loans, credit card debt, and mortgages—than savings, then her net worth is negative. If she were to lose her job and the income that goes with it, she could be in trouble, as her debt exceeds her savings, and she may not have enough income to meet her debt payments. If she has more savings than all her debt, then her net worth is positive and she is in better financial shape to weather adverse financial circumstances, such as a spell of unemployment.

Gross and Net

An exclusive focus on net positions can be misleading, however. Larger gross positions make things riskier even for someone with a favorable net position. Even if her net worth was positive, Mary would be in trouble if she had a lot of debt, as her assets and income may not be as secure as she thinks. If an economic downturn led to a sharp fall in her equity portfolio at the same time she got laid off, she would be in a bad situation. Her debt level would not be affected by the downturn, nor would her required debt payments. With a weaker asset position and less income, she would have difficulty meeting her debt payments. Selling off some of her equities would be an option to stay afloat in the short term. But if a large number of other investors like her started selling their equities at the same time, then the value of those equities could fall, making things worse.

The importance of looking at gross rather than just net positions was illustrated dramatically during the financial crisis by the collapse of Lehman Brothers. Lehman, a Wall Street powerhouse with a storied past, was the fourth largest investment bank in the U.S. In early 2008, Lehman and its counterparties—other similar financial institutions that it did business with—had relatively small net open positions, with assets and liabilities being close to balanced. Of course, the structures of assets and liabilities were quite different and, more importantly, the gross outstanding positions on certain risky transactions were very large.

When stresses started building up in the financial system, banks curtailed lending to one another, and these gross positions turned out to be dangerous, especially when the counterparties on some of these transactions started facing liquidity problems. That is, the counterparties did not have enough cash (or assets that they could quickly convert into cash) to meet their short-term payment obligations. That gross positions appeared balanced meant little when one side of the deal was with a weak counterparty that was under financial pressure and could not honor its contractual obligations. This interlocking financial structure created cascading risks through the entire financial system when Lehman, which was the counterparty in a large number of financial transactions, failed.

What is true for individuals, companies, and financial institutions is relevant for countries as well. Rising gross external asset and liability positions have important implications for growth and financial stability. Large gross positions imply far greater risks than suggested just by looking at net positions, which could be much smaller or even be balanced. Larger gross positions could mean greater volatility of capital flows stemming from external shocks. Even modest moves by international investors to rebalance their portfolios could lead to large fluctuations in net flows to specific countries.

Maurice Obstfeld of the University of California, Berkeley, has emphasized the importance of monitoring gross external positions of country balance sheets. A great deal of research looking at different aspects of country balance sheet positions had preceded his analysis. Gian Maria Milesi-Ferretti at the International Monetary Fund (IMF) and Philip Lane at Trinity College, Dublin, have done pioneering work, using a variety of public and internal IMF sources, to build up a historical database on countries' external balance sheets. This research had seemed to be of interest mainly to wonky academics.

The global financial crisis—during which many financial firms with seemingly modest and manageable net positions got into trouble because of their large gross positions—began drawing broader attention to the importance of studying gross positions for countries as well. So when Obstfeld made his point about the dangers lurking in large gross positions on national balance sheets in a speech at the 2010 Jackson Hole conference, it resonated strongly with the central bankers present.

Rising gross positions are not necessarily a bad thing. If the composition of assets and liabilities is such that a country gets higher returns on its foreign assets and has to pay less on its foreign liabilities when its own economy is not doing well, then it promotes international risk sharing. This sort of "insurance" is one of the ostensible benefits of financial integration. By diversifying their portfolios through international investments, investors such as Mary Smith can reduce the riskiness of their portfolios. At times when investments in their home country are doing poorly, foreign investments may provide a cushion.

Gross assets and liabilities, all measured in dollars, have increased since 2000 for the three largest emerging market economies—Brazil, China, and India. The increases are greater for China and India, which started off at lower levels than Brazil did. Brazil and India have negative net asset positions—that is, their external liabilities exceed their external assets. China has a large net asset position that has been growing steadily since 2004.

The key point is that these economies' gross external asset and liability positions increased rapidly between 2000 and 2007 and then, after a brief pause at the initial stages of the crisis, have continued to increase. The same is true for most other emerging markets. In contrast, advanced economies' external balance sheets took a big hit during the financial crisis and have barely recovered, mainly because their banking sectors have sharply cut back on international exposure.

Flows Also Matter

Although stocks are important, flows also matter in the short run. If Mary Smith has taken on some debt, the required repayments on that debt and her other normal expenditures would constitute her financial outflows. What matters to her solvency in the short run is how her financial inflows stack up against her outflows. Her inflows include the flow of income from her employment and investments, and also any new loans she can get from her bank or other sources. Here again, the distinction between net and gross is significant. The level of net inflows may provide an incomplete picture of vulnerability to external shocks. Mary would be in big trouble if times were so tough in the economy that the bank called in her debt, she could not get any new loans, and she lost her job. Her outflows would have increased and her inflows would have shrunk simultaneously, a double blow.

Similarly, when an economy comes under pressure, gross inflows could stop, and gross outflows could surge simultaneously, leading to a double shock in terms of net flows. Kristin Forbes at the Massachusetts Institute of Technology and Francis Warnock at the University of Virginia have analyzed gross flows around crises and have tried to disentangle sudden stops or reversals of gross inflows (related to foreign investors) from surges of gross outflows (by residents). They find that gross inflows and outflows are driven by similar factors and that gross flows are more relevant than net flows for explaining currency crashes. Hence, rising gross flows may increase the risk of externally induced crises, even if a country's current account, which reflects net flows, looks reasonably balanced.

An additional complication in international finance is that changes in currency values need to be taken into account. As gross stocks of external assets and liabilities grow in size, currency volatility has a larger impact on fluctuations in external wealth and on current account balances. Assets and liabilities are typically denominated in different currencies, so a change in currency values can affect the two sides of the balance sheet differentially even if they were at similar levels to begin with. If a country faces a crisis, such as a financial meltdown or pressures on its sovereign debt, its currency would usually depreciate, thereby automatically transferring some of the adjustment costs onto foreign holders of its liabilities. But this is true only if a country's liabilities are denominated in the domestic currency. Liabilities denominated in foreign currencies, such as debt that has to be repaid in dollars, could worsen the impact of adverse shocks that lead to currency depreciation, as the value of such liabilities would then rise in domestic currency terms.

There is another wrinkle to this story—it makes a big difference which types of external assets and liabilities are on a country's balance sheet. Some liabilities, it turns out, are a lot safer than others.

Good and Bad Capital

There are three main types of capital, as summarized in Figure 4-2. These are foreign direct investment (FDI), portfolio equity, and debt. For the purposes of the analysis in this book, I include portfolio debt—foreign investment in a country's corporate or government bonds—as well as loans

FIGURE 4-2. Types of Capital

> **1. FDI: Foreign direct investment**
> An investor or corporation buys or sets up a firm in another country.
>
> **2. PE: Portfolio equity**
> An investor buys shares in a foreign company.
>
> **3. Debt: Portfolio debt + other investment**
>
> **3A. Portfolio debt**
> An investor buys bonds (debt) issued by a foreign corporation or government.
>
> **3B. Other investment**
> Typically, bank loans to a foreign corporation or government.

provided by foreign banks under the third category. There are marked differences in the relative costs and benefits of each type of capital.

A major reason many emerging markets faced crises in the 1980s and 1990s is that their external liabilities were mainly in the form of debt. At the 1999 Jackson Hole Symposium, the economists Barry Eichengreen of the University of California, Berkeley, and Ricardo Hausmann of Harvard University coined the term "original sin" to refer to the fact that, during the 1980s and 1990s, emerging markets seemed destined to be dealt an unfavorable hand by global investors. Their capital inflows were mostly in the form of loans from foreign banks and other types of debt that were short-term and denominated in foreign currencies.

This is not because emerging markets were blind to the dangers of debt, but because they were unable to get other types of finance. Foreign investors did not trust governments in developing countries (including emerging markets) that they lent to, worrying that in a pinch those governments would simply print more of their own currencies, eroding the value of the debt. To guard against this, they demanded repayment in hard currencies, such as the dollar. Besides, in their economies' go-go years, taking on debt and then rolling it over into new debt seemed like a cinch, so policymakers in developing countries were not too concerned about rising debt levels.

Many economies that built up large stocks of short-term foreign currency debt, especially those in Latin America, used much of those funds to expand government budget deficits and go on consumption binges rather than investing in productive capacity. This worsened the blow when hard times arrived; the debt had to be paid off, no new financing was available from international investors, and these countries had fewer products to sell abroad than if they had invested wisely.

What made it worse was that this debt was denominated in foreign currencies. When hit by crises, currencies of the borrowing countries plunged in value relative to hard currencies. This made the domestic currency value of the debt even higher. For instance, during the Asian financial crisis, Korean corporations borrowing in dollars were still earning Korean won on their domestic sales, but their debt burden had gone up, because the won was plunging in value against the dollar. Even well-managed companies with good prospects were ravaged by this "balance sheet" effect.

Compared to debt, FDI is more stable and has greater benefits. It involves a substantial investment in a firm, which could range from full ownership to a smaller stake but one with a controlling interest. Portfolio equity investment is similar but is done through buying shares in a company. Such investment can be large in absolute amounts but is typically small relative to the size of a particular company, so it does not involve enough of an ownership stake to provide significant corporate control. Because a small number of shares in a company can be sold more easily in equity markets than a large stake, or even the full firm, portfolio equity flows are easier to reverse and therefore tend to be more volatile than FDI. Dumping a few shares is a lot easier than selling off an entire company.

As a consequence, portfolio equity flows can be fickle and highly procyclical, increasing when an economy is doing well and falling when an economy is in the doldrums and could use more capital. Nevertheless, the threat posed by outflows of portfolio equity capital is far less devastating than the rollover risk on short-term foreign currency debt that used to plague emerging markets.

Sharing Rather Than Adding Risk

FDI and portfolio equity investment both have the right sorts of risk-sharing characteristics—foreign investors bear the risk related to their investments if a company does poorly and yields lower returns to its owners or shareholders. Of course, these investments also have upside benefits for foreign investors—if the companies they invest in generate higher profits than anticipated, these investors get their share. If a country's currency drops in value, foreign investors take their lumps, as their investments would then be worth less in terms of their domestic currency. The converse is true if the currency rises in value.

Thus, in the case of FDI and portfolio equity flows, foreign investors bear return risk as well as currency risk. In contrast, debt is doubly bad, because return and currency risks are both borne by the borrower. Of course, default risk is borne by domestic and foreign investors no matter the type of financing; when a firm goes bankrupt, all investors lose their shirts. Even in this case, debt investors get paid back from any residual assets of the bankrupt firm before other types of investors.

From the borrowing country's perspective, debt is clearly risky and ideally should be kept to low levels, especially if alternative sources of financing are available. That still leaves a more basic question unresolved. In light of the evidence discussed in Chapter 3, according to which developing countries that export capital grow faster than those that import it, why should a developing country even care about FDI inflows?

Collateral Benefits

Ayhan Kose, Kenneth Rogoff, Shang-Jin Wei, and I provided one answer to this question in research done in the early 2000s, when we were all working in the research department of the IMF. When it comes to foreign capital, emerging markets may be less interested in the money itself than in what comes with the money. We called these the "collateral benefits" of capital inflows. FDI investors have an incentive to increase the productivity of firms they are investing in by bringing in new technology, along with better managerial and corporate governance practices. Foreign portfolio investors provide more depth to equity markets and also give domestic firms an incentive to improve their accounting transparency and corporate governance to attract more of that investment.

The desire to attain some of these collateral benefits has led emerging markets to open up to foreign capital inflows even while they remain capital exporters in net terms (i.e., their outflows exceed their inflows). An interesting example is that of China, which has allowed foreign strategic investors—a small set of prominent banks from advanced economies—to take modest ownership stakes in large Chinese banks, which are all state-owned. This approach was ramped up in 2007 as part of a push to clean up the big banks' balance sheets and improve their performance prior to allowing those banks to undertake public stock offerings.

The Chinese government was not lacking in resources and certainly did not need foreign funds to build up the capital of these banks. But it hoped that foreign banks, enticed by the prospects of making a better return on their investments, would push to improve the corporate governance structures and risk-management capacity of their domestic banks. In retrospect, given what transpired during the financial crisis, perhaps relying on American and European banks to strengthen risk management in Chinese banks was not a stellar idea. Nevertheless, the concept of attaining collateral benefits from capital inflows was along the right lines and has been employed by other countries as well.

When one takes into account these benefits and the relative volatility of different types of capital, there seems to be a natural "pecking order" of external liabilities, with FDI being the best, portfolio equity flows following that, and debt being the least desirable. No doubt, the preponderance of debt on emerging markets' external balance sheets in the 1980s and 1990s was clearly a problem in that it exposed them to financial and balance of payments crises. A wave of academic literature following the Asian financial crisis and other crises of the 1990s settled on one variable as the primary risk factor in increasing vulnerability to crises—the level of short-term external debt denominated in foreign currencies.

Emerging market economies took these lessons to heart and received an assist from international investors during the period of the Great Moderation. This was the decade before the global financial crisis, when much of the world was experiencing stable growth and moderate inflation. Noting the strong growth prospects of emerging markets relative to their own economies, advanced economy investors began to pour money into emerging markets, but now in a more benign form of financial capital.

Emerging Markets Shed Risky Liabilities

During the 2000s, the composition of external liabilities of emerging market economies changed dramatically. Figure 4-3 shows a major shift in the external liability structure of emerging markets toward better and

FIGURE 4-3. Emerging Markets Shift Out of Debt into Safer External Liabilities

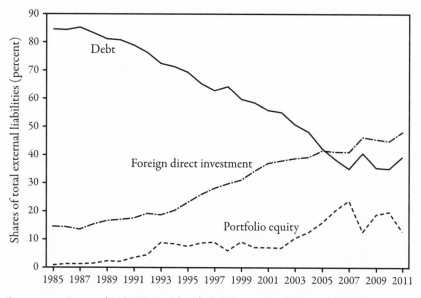

Data sources: Lane and Milesi-Ferretti (2011); IMF International Financial Statistics.

Notes: Stocks of different types of external liabilities—foreign direct investment, portfolio equity, and debt—are shown as ratios of total external liabilities. Each type is summed across all emerging market economies and then expressed as a ratio of total external liabilities for those economies.

less volatile forms of capital. In the past, these economies' external liabilities were dominated by debt, but now FDI has become predominant, and portfolio equity has also risen in importance. In the mid-1980s, debt liabilities accounted for about 85 percent of emerging markets' external liabilities. By 2007, this average share had fallen below 40 percent, and it has stayed at that level since.

FDI now accounts for the largest share—nearly half—of all external liabilities of the emerging markets. The share of portfolio equity liabilities, although lower, has also increased significantly relative to its level in 2000. Together, the average share of FDI and portfolio equity liabilities in total external liabilities climbed to about 60 percent in 2011 (the latest year for which data are available for all the countries in my analysis), compared to 42 percent in 2000. Table A-1 in the Appendix has more details for the emerging markets.

These averages conceal significant differences across countries. In 2012, FDI and portfolio equity together accounted for more than two-thirds of total external liabilities for Brazil and China, 49 percent for India, 58 percent for Russia, and 73 percent for South Africa. These numbers provide an interesting contrast with those for advanced economies. For most of those economies, FDI and portfolio equity liabilities account for less than one-third of total external liabilities. It turns out that, for all the major advanced economies—Germany, Japan, the U.K., and the U.S.—the category "other investment," which mainly covers debt obtained in the form of bank loans, is an important share of liabilities. When one adds in portfolio debt, comprising corporate as well as government debt securities, it is clear that debt accounts for the majority of external liabilities. For more details on the balance sheet positions of each of the major advanced and emerging market economies as of 2012, see Table A-2 in the Appendix.

For emerging markets, the shift in the structure of liabilities even as their balance sheets were expanding during 2000–2011 is striking. Over this period, changes in FDI liabilities alone account for nearly half of the increase in their overall liabilities. On average, FDI and portfolio equity liabilities together account for two-thirds of the increase in liabilities (data for individual countries is presented in Table A-3 in the Appendix).

These data reveal a marked shift in the composition of external liabilities of emerging markets. The shift toward FDI and portfolio equity is consistent with greater international risk sharing. Changes in the structure of liabilities have also reduced emerging markets' vulnerability to balance of payments and currency crises. This is not a uniformly true proposition, as emerging markets in Eastern Europe had become more reliant on foreign bank loans before the crisis. Western European banks established a dominant presence in many of these countries and financed the region's domestic demand boom before the global financial crisis. Those banks came under pressure during the crisis and stopped lending, making emerging markets in Eastern Europe more vulnerable to the global downturn than those in other regions. Aside from this region, however, the large majority of emerging markets have experienced positive shifts in the structure of their external liabilities.

Old Risks Fade, New Risks Emerge

Traditionally, emerging markets were exposed to risks through their dependence on capital inflows and the structure of their external liabilities. Few of the major emerging markets are now heavily dependent on foreign finance as measured by the scale of net inflows. Even those economies like Brazil and India that are running current account deficits have large stocks of foreign exchange reserves. There are of course exceptions. For instance, Turkey is in a vulnerable position, as it has a large current account deficit and relies mainly on volatile portfolio equity inflows to finance that deficit. Nevertheless, the broad picture is that the scourge of short-term foreign currency–denominated debt has diminished substantially.

Flexible exchange rate regimes adopted by many emerging markets have also made currency crashes less of a concern. Such crashes often followed a long period of forced disequilibrium in currency markets, a phenomenon that is less likely when exchange rates are flexible and market determined. There are still a few holdouts. China manages its exchange rate tightly relative to the U.S. dollar. India has adopted a policy of "leaning against the wind"—intervening in foreign exchange markets to prevent sharp fluctuations of its currency but otherwise not trying to target a specific level of its currency or preventing its movement in either direction. There are a few other cases of emerging markets trying to manage their currencies to some extent, but by and large, flexible exchange rate regimes are becoming common.

Emerging markets' external balance sheets certainly look more stable than in the past. Still, their high and increasing integration into global financial markets implies that they will be subject to greater spillovers from macroeconomic conditions in advanced economies. For instance, as their gross external positions become larger, emerging markets will face greater capital flow volatility on account of changes in interest rates and other market conditions in advanced economies. Even with no changes in economic conditions in capital flow recipient countries, these countries could face larger inflows or outflows simply because of portfolio rebalancing by advanced economy investors.

These traditional risks from financial openness have not been eliminated but have become less lethal relative to domestic risks.

Capital Flows and Domestic Risks

For emerging market economies, the main concern about financial openness now is that it heightens domestic risks. For instance, foreign capital inflows into countries that have shallow and weakly regulated financial markets may not be channeled into productive long-term investments. Rather, those funds might end up fueling asset market booms, often in equity and real estate markets. These booms generally end in crashes. Many studies have identified rapid expansion of domestic credit in the run-up to the recent crisis as a factor that led to worse outcomes for some emerging markets, particularly those in Eastern Europe.

Financial market development that fails to keep pace with increasing outward orientation of domestic firms also creates risks for emerging markets. Firms have an incentive to take on foreign currency–denominated debt as a way of getting cheaper funding than is available domestically and simultaneously hedging against (or even betting on) currency appreciation. For instance, in 2007, Indian firms were eager to issue foreign currency debt, because they viewed it as one way of betting on appreciation of the Indian rupee. If the rupee did appreciate, they would have to come up with fewer rupees to pay off the debt. Normally, such hedging can be done using currency derivatives markets. But the Indian central bank had been wary of authorizing the establishment of those markets in India because of concerns that they would become hives of speculative activity rather than just meeting the needs of companies to hedge their foreign currency export earnings or their payments for imports. As a result, shifting the structure of financing became a way for companies to hedge their currency risk while raising capital from abroad.

Capital flows also have distributional consequences, a matter of particular concern to emerging market economies that are nervous about social stability, as many of them have threadbare social safety nets. More open economies tend to be prone to greater inequality for a number of reasons. First, during the early stages of an economy's opening up, capital account openness tends to favor the rich and the elites. When there are still restrictions on foreign capital, large and politically well-connected firms obtain preferential access to foreign financing; these firms can thus become even larger relative to smaller domestic firms that are reliant on inefficient domestic financial institutions. This phenomenon of crony capitalism played a role in precipitating the Asian financial crisis. Larger firms in the manufacturing sector typically tend to be more capital intensive and generate less employment than smaller firms, further skewing the benefits from financial openness.

Second, foreign finance that pours into equity markets and raises valuations tends to have greater benefits for households that have more financial wealth in the form of equity investments. Third, capital account openness can create inequities in terms of diversification and risk sharing. Richer households are able to share risk through their international investments. Even in countries with open capital accounts, this is a problem for poorer households that do not have easy access to investment vehicles, such as mutual funds, to invest abroad.

Fourth, because poorer households have less access to foreign investment opportunities, they disproportionately bear the costs of domestic policies that keep interest rates on banking deposits low. For instance, in China, capital controls on outflows have been eased, allowing households to take out money for investments abroad. Richer households have connections and access to formal and informal channels that can help them transfer money out relatively easily. However, poorer households do not have access to similar opportunities to easily invest abroad. So the available choices are either the highly volatile Chinese stock market or safe bank deposits that, because of government caps on deposit interest rates, paid negative or low inflation-adjusted interest rates for much of the past decade.

Safer but Still Exposed

Two main themes come out of the analysis in this chapter and the preceding one. First, the period since 2000 has been characterized by massive uphill capital flows from emerging markets, especially China, to advanced economies, mainly the U.S. These flows have abated but not reversed course in the aftermath of the global financial crisis. Private capital flows have indeed been going downhill—from advanced to emerging market economies—but these have been swamped by official flows going in the other direction.

Second, emerging market economies have become more integrated into financial markets. As the magnitudes of their flows and stocks of foreign capital have increased, these economies are increasingly exposed to external risks. On the plus side, the structure of foreign liabilities of emerging markets has shifted from risky debt to more stable forms of capital, especially FDI. But even benign capital flows can heighten domestic risks, including inflation, asset booms, and social instability. Thus, for all the progress they have made on bulletproofing their external balance sheets, emerging markets remain vulnerable to the vagaries of international capital flows.

These themes are closely related. Scars from the many crises that befell emerging market economies during the past couple of decades are still raw in the minds of their politicians and bureaucrats. As we shall see in the next chapter, these economies' quest for safety is transforming the structure of global capital flows and ironically making the world less safe.

The Quest for Safety

He hoped and prayed that there wasn't an afterlife. Then he realized there was
a contradiction involved here and merely hoped that there wasn't an afterlife.
Life, the Universe and Everything, Douglas Adams

Six and a half trillion dollars. Even if one considers a trillion the new billion, that is still a lot of money. This is the amount of foreign exchange reserves that emerging market economies have accumulated in the decade and a half following the Asian financial crisis of 1997–98. Figure 5-1 shows the steady upward march of the stocks of foreign exchange reserves held by all emerging and developing economies, with the total stock topping \$7 trillion at the end of 2012. China accounts for about half of this accumulation, and other emerging markets and a few oil exporters account for virtually all of the remainder. There are many explanations for this massive reserve buildup, but it is helpful to first understand the mechanics of reserve accumulation.

Shunning Appreciation

During the 2000s, emerging markets received a large amount of private capital inflows, and many of them also ran trade surpluses. When money comes into an economy either because of export earnings or investment flows from abroad, there is greater demand for the domestic currency. Exporters have to pay their workers' wages and their suppliers' bills using the domestic currency. This is also the case for investment projects—building materials, labor, and land all have to be paid for in the domestic currency.

The laws of supply and demand apply to currencies as well. When the demand for a currency increases, its price goes up. In this case, the price is measured relative to other currencies. This price is the exchange rate—usually expressed as the number of units of a domestic currency needed to buy a unit of a foreign currency. So when the Chinese renminbi's exchange rate goes from 8 yuan per dollar to 7 yuan per dollar,

FIGURE 5-1. Rising Stocks of Foreign Exchange Reserves

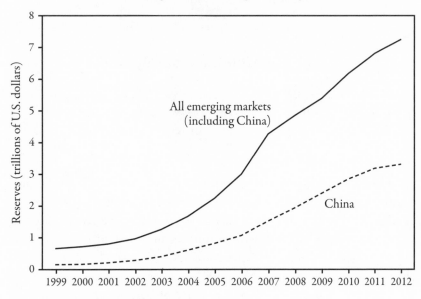

Data sources: IMF; People's Bank of China.

the renminbi has become more expensive relative to the dollar. The appreciation in the renminbi's value means that it takes fewer yuan to buy one dollar. Or, reciprocally, each yuan can now be exchanged for more dollars.

Appreciation in the value of the domestic currency—an increase in its value relative to other currencies—is good for consumers. It makes foreign goods cheaper, raising the overall purchasing power of household incomes. In the above example of renminbi appreciation, a Chinese tourist in New York City can now buy a (genuine) $600 Coach handbag for 4,200 yuan rather than 4,800 yuan—a nice discount.

There is a downside to currency appreciation, however. Cheap imports from abroad hurt domestic producers, as they have to cut their prices to stay competitive or end up losing market share. Exporters find their profit margins shrinking in terms of the domestic currency and face the risk of losing market share for their products. Take a Chinese shoe manufacturer who charges $50 for a pair of finely crafted leather boots exported to the U.S. (the boots may be priced at $500 in a Los Angeles boutique, but that is a different story altogether). If the yuan appreciates from 8 yuan per dollar to 7 yuan per dollar and the manufacturer keeps the price at $50, her revenue drops from 400 yuan to 350 yuan per pair. Because she cannot cut her workers' wages without drawing complaints and the interest she pays to the bank for her working capital remains the same, her profits shrink. She could raise her prices, but this would make her goods less competitive if there were alternatives from India or Vietnam that U.S. shoe retailers could turn to instead.

Building Up Reserves

To offset currency appreciation, emerging market central banks sometimes intervene in foreign exchange markets. This involves selling the domestic currency and buying hard currencies like U.S. dollars—currencies that are easily convertible and widely accepted around the world. Selling the domestic currency offsets the higher demand for it. Such intervention limits domestic currency appreciation and helps a country's trade balance by limiting imports and propping up exports. These purchases of hard currency assets are the reason that, despite large private capital inflows, many emerging markets have net capital *outflows*, as indicated by the earlier discussion on uphill capital flows.

Managing a currency's value is a tricky business. Take the case of China. Because the major currencies trade freely among themselves, the renminbi's value can be managed only against one of those currencies. China chooses to manage the renminbi's value against the dollar because the U.S. is one of China's largest trading partners and because of the dollar's importance in world financial markets. So the renminbi's value goes up and down relative to the euro, in tandem with the dollar's own market fluctuations against the euro. Most countries that manage their currencies, especially those in Asia, also tend to use their own currency's value relative to the dollar as the benchmark.

Following such foreign exchange market interventions, a country's central bank has to find safe and liquid investments where it can park its foreign currency purchases. Investments that satisfy these criteria are typically government bonds of major advanced economies, such as the U.S., the euro zone, Japan, U.K., and Switzerland. These investments constitute a country's foreign exchange reserves. A country's reserve assets can include other liquid assets, such as gold, but foreign exchange reserves now account for about 85 percent of global reserves.

Reserves as Insurance

Other than helping to boost exports and tamp down imports, the accumulation of hard currency reserves serves another useful purpose for emerging markets. It gives them a layer of insurance against crises, as reserve accumulation is in effect a way of putting money away for a rainy day. The prospect of a country having difficulty meeting its debt obligations to international investors or running out of hard currency to pay for its imports could turn into a self-fulfilling prophecy if foreign investors were to shun a country that looked vulnerable. This could lead to sudden stops of capital inflows, capital flow reversals, and even flight of domestic savings from the banking system. A sizable stock of hard currency reserves makes it less likely that investors will flee from a country at the first sign of trouble.

Even if an economy were to be enveloped by a crisis, reserves can provide a buffer to soften the destructive effects of volatile capital flows. Countries that had larger stocks of reserves relative to their economic size seem to have weathered the global financial crisis better than those with smaller stocks. The logic is simple and in some ways similar to that for an individual worker—the more money you have in the bank, the less likely a spell of unemployment will put you in deep financial distress.

One interpretation of the massive accumulation of reserves by emerging markets is that these economies are willing to do whatever it takes to insure themselves against the sorts of disasters they faced in the 1970s, 1980s, and 1990s, and the perils they continue to face today. The Asian financial crisis of 1997–98, for instance, decimated many Asian emerging markets, and it took some of them years to recover. More importantly, these countries had to go hat in hand to the IMF. In exchange for bailouts to keep their economies afloat, they had to accept strict conditions imposed by the IMF. They were forced to undertake strict belt tightening measures, such as cutting government expenditures, which created considerable social and political turmoil. One of the iconic images of the Asian crisis is that of a stern-looking Michel Camdessus, then the head of the IMF, with his hands folded and glaring in schoolmarm fashion at President Suharto of Indonesia signing an agreement with the IMF in January 1998. The Suharto regime collapsed soon thereafter.

There are precedents from even earlier times. The humiliation of going to the IMF when India's foreign currency reserves had run down to just $1 billion is seared in the minds of Indian officialdom to this day. In the middle of July 1991, the IMF forced India to devalue its currency sharply as a condition for financial assistance. The fact is that India was trying to prop up the value of its currency artificially, and the IMF recognized that this policy was not tenable, which some Indian officials could not bring themselves to admit. Whatever the merits of this adjustment, the fact that the IMF had India by the throat and could extract a steep price in exchange for a loan stuck in the craw of Indian officials and has influenced their behavior since then.

Policymakers in emerging markets have developed a strong aversion to relying on the IMF's largesse in their times of distress and have instead turned to self-insurance. This practice raises a number of operational questions.

The Big Bazooka Principle

How much insurance does a country need? Metaphors are not good guideposts for policy formulation, but they can influence the thinking of policymakers in important ways. To answer the question of what is an adequate level of reserves, one can look to a metaphor that was born in the nadir of the financial crisis.

A Bazooka Fails but Sets a Standard

In the summer of 2008, two institutions that were crucial to U.S. mortgage markets—Fannie Mae and Freddie Mac—had been under intense pressure in financial markets and barely managed to eke out enough borrowing to stay afloat. The Senate Committee on Banking, Housing, and Urban Affairs convened a hearing on the morning of July 15, 2008, to review the government's handling of the situation. Fed Chairman Ben Bernanke, U.S. Treasury Secretary Hank Paulson, and Securities and Exchange Commission Chairman Chris Cox took the stand in front of a combative group of senators, with both Democrats and Republicans concerned and angry about the way the government was handling problems in the mortgage giants. In response to a question from one of the senators, Hank Paulson uttered these memorable lines:

> if you've got a squirt-gun in your pocket you may have to take it out. If you've got a bazooka, and people know you've got it, you may not have to take it out. . . . By increasing confidence, it will greatly reduce the likelihood it will ever be used.

The bazooka was his new authority to take over the mortgage finance giants, if needed, to ensure their financial stability. Rather than restoring confidence, however, this hastened the end game for those two institutions. Once Paulson indicated that the implicit government guarantee the institutions enjoyed would be turned into an explicit government bailout if needed, Fannie and Freddie were no longer viable as independent institutions and were soon taken over by the government.

U.S. Treasury Secretary Henry (Hank) Paulson, Fed Chairman Ben Bernanke, and Securities and Exchange Commission Chairman Christopher Cox. Hearing of the Senate Committee on Banking, Housing, and Urban Affairs, July 15, 2008. (Bloomberg via Getty Images.)

Paulson's bazooka failed in its stated purpose, but the metaphor became a guiding principle for other central bank interventions and for reserve accumulation by emerging market central banks. The implicit principle is that a central bank needs enough reserves to be able to tell speculators: if you try to break our currency to make it crash in value, we will break you.

How Much Is Enough?

The criterion of reserve adequacy that was in vogue in the 1990s was that a country needed enough reserves to cover six months' worth of a country's imports. The financial crises of the 1990s led to a different benchmark, one related to the level of short-term external debt. The new criterion was suggested in 1999 by Pablo Guidotti, then the deputy finance minister of Argentina. It became popular after Fed Chairman Alan Greenspan cited it favorably in a speech later that year and came to be known as the Guidotti-Greenspan rule.

A simplified version of this rule is that at any point a country should have enough reserves to cover all of its short-term external debt (debt with an original maturity of one year or less). The relevance of this rule was corroborated by a large body of research around the same period indicating that the level of short-term foreign currency debt was the proximate determinant of many of the crises during the previous two decades. A variant of this rule is that a country needs enough reserves to repay all of its external debt maturing over a one-year horizon. Based on either of these criteria, most major emerging markets had accumulated more than sufficient reserves by the early 2000s.

Some researchers have tried to use a broader set of criteria to explain why emerging markets continue to accumulate reserves despite having already blown past these conventional criteria of reserve adequacy by the middle of the previous decade. Protecting a currency peg or even a tightly managed exchange rate is one reason countries like to hold reserves. In times of financial stress, a large stock of reserves can help maintain a currency's value and prevent it from depreciating. China continues to manage its exchange rate, but most other major emerging markets now let their currencies float relatively freely, except to "lean against the wind" to limit sharp short-term fluctuations. In general, given the move to more flexible exchange rates, the currency regime per se ought to have become a less important factor than in the past in driving reserve accumulation.

Researchers were also spurred to look at other criteria related to measures of the stability and openness of a country's financial markets. For instance, a country may be concerned about the stability of its banking sector and may want to have enough reserves to protect its banks in case a large fraction of deposits were to fly out of the country for any reason. Adding these criteria to existing statistical frameworks helps them do a better job of explaining the incentives behind the sharp run-up in reserves during the past decade. Even with this set of augmented criteria, it is difficult to rationalize the continued increase in reserves after the mid-2000s, especially among Asian economies.

Game Changer

The financial crisis and its painful aftershocks have shifted the debate on reserve adequacy. All previous notions of reserve adequacy took a beating when the crisis hit. There was a giant sucking sound as foreign capital retreated from emerging market economies (and many advanced economies as well) toward the U.S. and other safe havens. Many emerging markets spent large portions of their reserves protecting their currencies, which were in danger of collapsing.

India lost about $66 billion of its stock of $305 billion of foreign exchange reserves in a matter of six months. Russia's reserves fell by a third over an eight month period starting from July 2008. In a selected group of 13 countries that experienced significant reserve losses (a group in which I have included one advanced economy—Korea), on average 25 percent of peak reserve stocks were lost over an eight month period. Details for individual countries are shown in Table A-4 in the Appendix. Not all emerging markets lost much of their stock of reserves; China even continued to accumulate reserves during the crisis.

One perspective on these numbers is that, after all, reserves are there to be used, and a country losing a quarter of its reserves at a time when global financial meltdown was imminent certainly does not sound like reason for panic. Among central bankers, however, there is a saying that in bad times what matters is not just the level of reserves but, more importantly, the direction and rate of change of reserves. According to this logic, once reserves start falling, even a large cushion of protection can evaporate fairly quickly. When reserves fall sharply, nervous investors might start pulling more money out of the country, rapidly worsening the situation. The rate of decline in reserves that many emerging markets experienced during the crisis has led to concerns among many of them that they ought to have even more reserves.

With rising financial integration and ever larger positions of gross flows and stocks, emerging markets now face stronger incentives to obtain higher levels of insurance through the accumulation of massive stocks of reserves. Virtually all emerging markets have been rebuilding or continuing to increase their reserve stocks after 2009. By the end of 2012, most of the countries that experienced substantial reserve losses during the crisis had rebuilt their reserve positions and were approaching or had already exceeded their pre-crisis levels of reserves. For India and Russia, foreign exchange reserves still remain below their pre-crisis highs, suggesting that these economies may be looking to rebuild their stocks.

Chile has a floating exchange rate, so it does not typically intervene in foreign exchange markets. With its good macroeconomic policies since the early 2000s, the country had come to be seen as one of Latin America's success stories, with strong growth and moderate inflation. But even Chile proved vulnerable during the financial crisis, as the Chilean peso's value fell sharply in 2008 and GDP growth rate turned negative in 2009. Although the economy rebounded soon thereafter, the Chilean government was stung by this episode and decided that it needed to protect itself better.

In a speech delivered on January 17, 2011, the Chilean central bank governor José De Gregorio announced an explicit plan to hoard reserves for precautionary reasons. He first cited various risks in the external scenario —high commodity prices, low interest rates, a depreciating U.S. dollar, and financial tensions in Europe—and then made this declaration:

> Considering this [*sic*] risks and the fact that the real exchange
> rate had appreciated significantly, the Board of the Central Bank
> decided, on January 3rd, to start a program of foreign currency
> purchases aimed at strengthening its international liquidity
> position. Thus, the Central Bank will hoard additional interna-
> tional reserves amounting to US$12.0 billion over the year 2011,
> via periodic purchases of foreign currency. . . . This program will

take the Central Bank's international liquidity position to the equivalent of 17% of GDP, which is comparable with those of other economies similar to Chile.

Another reason that central bankers take steps to boost their reserve holdings is the view that a higher level of reserves provides better access to global financial markets and helps maintain such access in difficult times. The Central Bank of Nigeria notes the following as one of its rationales for accumulating reserves:

> To boost a country's credit worthiness[,] external reserves provide a cushion at a time when access to the international capital market is difficult or not possible. A respectable level of international reserves improves a country's credit worthiness and reputation by enabling a regular servicing of the external debt[,] thereby avoiding the payment of penalty and charges. Furthermore, a country's usable foreign exchange reserve is an important variable in the country risk models used by credit rating agencies and international financial institutions.

The South African Reserve Bank makes this point in more flowery language:

> It should be noted that an adequate level of reserves is required for almost every country that seeks to employ the savings of other nations to develop its own economy. It is ironic but true that a small country needs foreign reserves earned through its own productive efforts and accumulated through its own virtuous savings before it can gain access to the savings of other countries.

Colombia's central bank, the Banco de la República, explicitly states that its objectives for reserve accumulation are twofold—preventing excessive volatility in the exchange rate and preserving the government's and private sector's access to international capital markets:

> The level of international reserves is seen as an indicator of the domestic borrower's payment ability. Rating agencies and foreign

lenders believe that adequate reserve levels allow domestic residents to meet foreign currency obligations, such as import payments and servicing of foreign debt at a time when the country faces difficulties accessing external financing.

In June 2008, amid global financial turmoil, the bank's board adopted a policy of buying a minimum of $20 million in the open market each day to increase Colombia's pool of reserves. This policy was ended in late 2011 and then revived in 2012. Colombia is one of the few emerging markets that did not lose a significant amount of reserves during the crisis, and its stock of foreign exchange reserves has risen by about 65 percent, from $21 billion in May 2008 to $35 billion at the end of 2012.

Sky's the Limit?

The principle guiding central bankers' decisions on reserve accumulation seems to be that more is better, but clearly there are costs that have to be taken into account. Is there a limit to reserve accumulation—a point at which the costs clearly exceed the benefits? What is the threshold at which an emerging market central banker will feel comforted that she has enough of a stockpile to ward off the destructive effects of capital flow volatility?

Bulking Up the Bazooka

In many ways, reserve accumulation has become a welcome by-product of foreign exchange market intervention to hold back currency appreciation. So this makes it even less likely that emerging market countries in particular will hesitate to intervene in foreign exchange markets. As far as they are concerned, the policy has both short-term and long-term benefits.

Figure 5-2 shows the rising rate of reserve accumulation by emerging markets, which rose steadily each year through the early to mid-2000s. It hit its peak in 2007 when the major emerging markets built up nearly $1.3 trillion of additional reserves just in that one year, with China accounting for about a third of this build-up. With many emerging markets dipping into their reserve stocks in 2008 and 2009, the overall rate of reserve accumulation fell sharply; China was the one country still

FIGURE 5-2. Building Up Reserves

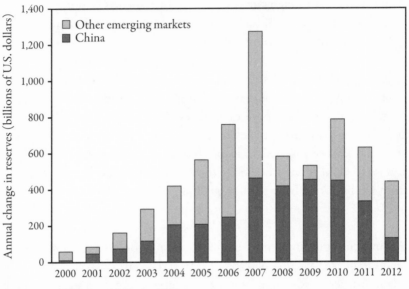

Data sources: IMF; People's Bank of China.

Note: Annual changes in stocks of foreign exchange reserves are shown.

building up (prodigious) amounts of reserves in those two years. In 2010, annual reserve accumulation by emerging markets went back up and has averaged over $600 billion per year during 2010–12. There is no doubt that China plays a significant role in the overall reserve accumulation by emerging market economies. But it is equally clear that explaining the emerging markets' reserve accumulation has to be about more than just China and its mercantilist policies.

Reserve accumulation has had an important effect on the structure of the external balance sheets of emerging market economies. Let us turn once again to their international investment positions. We examined changes in the structure of emerging markets' external liabilities in Chapter 4. Now consider the asset side. The major shift on the asset side of emerging markets' external balance sheets has been the increase in foreign exchange reserves as a share of total external assets. Looking across countries, the median share of foreign exchange reserves in total external assets rose from less than 25 percent in 1990 to 45 percent in 2011. Excluding China makes little difference to this median share. If one were to include China and examine the share of total foreign exchange reserves of all emerging markets combined relative to the total external assets of those countries (rather than the median based on data for each country), the average ratio would be much higher, close to 60 percent in 2011.

The changing structure of emerging market balance sheets is clearer when one looks at the change in external assets over 2000–2011 (details for individual countries are in the last column of Appendix Table A-3). During this period, accumulation of foreign exchange reserves accounts for about half of the overall increase in external assets. These results, again, are not just driven by China. Most emerging markets have experienced a significant increase in the share of foreign exchange reserves in total external assets. These changes reflect the continuation of a process that started in the late 1980s and was only temporarily halted by the global financial crisis.

Squirreling Away Nuts (or Bazooka Grenades) for the Winter

Emerging market central banks that are accumulating reserves have difficult and weighty decisions to make about where to park their reserves. These decisions become more complicated as their reserve stocks balloon. Whether reserve accumulation is driven primarily by mercantilist motives of promoting exports or by precautionary motives, management of those reserves is complicated, because it involves a variety of economic and political calculations. For obvious reasons, managers of these reserves are typically reluctant to take any gambles with their rainy day funds. They also need to make sure they can liquidate their investments quickly if the need should arise.

Safety First

A recurring theme in central banks' official guidelines for reserve management is that safety of the national wealth is paramount. Reserve managers therefore place priority on safety and liquidity, with returns being a tertiary consideration. China's reserves are managed by the State Administration of Foreign Exchange (SAFE), an arm of the People's Bank of China (PBC), which is China's central bank. The SAFE website lays out its principles of reserve management:

The nature of China's foreign exchange reserves requires that their operation and management adhere to the principles of security, liquidity, and increases in value, among which security is the primary principle. In addition, the foreign exchange reserves should maintain sufficient liquidity to satisfy the general demand for external payments, and also to play an effective role in safeguarding the stability and security of the national economy and finance. Under the precondition of guaranteeing overall security and liquidity, the operation of our foreign exchange reserves shall strive for higher investment returns in an effort to help attain the goal of maintaining and increasing their value.

This theme is echoed by other central banks. Banco Central do Brasil notes that its "reserves are managed to ensure safety, liquidity, and profitability." The National Bank of Hungary (NBH) has this investment policy for its reserves: "With respect to the classical investment triad (return-liquidity-safety), the investment philosophy of the NBH is to achieve maximum return on reserves while maintaining the highest attainable liquidity and safety." The Korean central bank has the following reserve management objectives: "Bank of Korea (BOK) holds foreign exchange reserves to maintain a capacity for intervention in the foreign exchange market, to cope with internal and external shocks, and to preserve the value of the national wealth. Therefore, the BOK puts the focus on safety and liquidity, while also endeavoring to generate high returns." All of these statements indicate that safety and liquidity generally take precedence over yield.

There is some evidence, based on a survey of selected central banks conducted by the Bank for International Settlements (BIS) at the end of 2006, that rising reserve stocks and concerns about low yields had led to slightly more aggressive management of reserves by some central banks. However, the financial crisis quickly restored the earlier ordering of criteria—with safety and liquidity taking precedence over returns—and refocused the attention of reserve managers on risk.

Risks Abound

Reserve managers have to contend with a variety of risks to their investments. One is credit risk, the possibility of default on debt or other investments that a central bank has made. Liquidity risk is the risk that a central bank may not be able to cash in its investments at short notice or, if it does so, that it will adversely affect the value of those investments as they are being sold. Then there is market risk, which includes currency and interest rate risks. Currency risk arises from exchange rate uncertainty, whereas interest rate risk (or, more broadly, return risk) is the risk that the value of investments will fall because of market conditions.

India's central bank, the Reserve Bank of India, summarizes its objectives for reserve management and the various kinds of risk it tries to cope with as follows:

> The guiding objectives of foreign exchange reserves management in India are similar to those of many central banks in the world.... While liquidity and safety constitute the twin objectives of reserves management in India, return optimisation becomes an embedded strategy within this framework.... The strategy for reserves management places emphasis on managing and controlling the exposure to financial and operational risks associated with deployment of reserves.... The Reserve Bank has been extremely sensitive to the credit risk it faces on the investment of foreign exchange reserves in the international markets.

Credit risk is clearly one of the biggest concerns. It would be difficult and politically damaging for a central bank to explain to its domestic audience that it invested the nation's wealth in assets that were subject to default. From the bazooka perspective, being able to liquidate a large volume of assets at short notice is crucial for reserves to be credible as a defensive mechanism to scare off currency speculators. Liquidity risk is particularly relevant in times of crises.

Typically, only government debt of the major advanced economies has these characteristics of safety and liquidity. Investors, including foreign central banks, are usually willing to pay a price for these characteristics —a price that is measured in terms of the additional returns they could have made on higher-yield investments, which would of course be riskier and may be harder to dispose of in times of financial distress. Low interest rates in the advanced economies, even on their long-term government bonds, and prospects that these rates are likely to remain low for a number of years have led central banks to reexamine their investment portfolios.

Taking Some Modest and Considered Risks

Given their enormous stocks of reserves and renewed concerns about low government bond yields in advanced economies, many emerging markets have taken to setting up sovereign wealth funds to manage their portfolios more aggressively and generate higher returns without entirely forsaking safety. These funds are less constrained in their investment strategies than central banks, as they are long-term investors with fewer concerns about the liquidity of their investments. Such funds are hardly a new phenomenon. Many countries that have large stocks of nonrenewable natural resources have set up these funds to invest their savings for the benefit of future generations of their citizens. Three of the world's largest sovereign wealth funds, each with over $600 billion in assets under management as of July 2013, are those of three oil-exporting countries: Norway, Saudi Arabia, and the United Arab Emirates (Abu Dhabi).

Sovereign wealth funds set up to manage foreign exchange reserves that are not built up primarily through commodity exports have become more important over time. Of the total assets of global sovereign wealth funds of about $5.9 trillion in July 2013, about $2.4 trillion was accounted for by funds of countries that are not major commodity exporters. China, Hong Kong, and Singapore account for the bulk of the assets of this latter group. Countries like Brazil, Korea, and Malaysia also have long-established funds, some of them with significant amounts of capital.

China has quickly made a big splash in this sphere of global finance. Its wealth fund, the China Investment Corporation (CIC), was launched in September 2007 with a capital of about $200 billion taken from China's foreign exchange reserves. CIC got off to a rocky start as its initial investments in Morgan Stanley and the private equity group Blackstone turned sour when the financial crisis hurt the value of those investments. This made CIC more conservative in its investment approach and also made the Chinese government somewhat wary of shifting more foreign exchange reserves to be managed by CIC. Nevertheless, the ballooning stock of reserves in 2009 and 2010 left China with little option but to seek more profitable investment opportunities. With additional capital injections and returns from its earlier investments, CIC had nearly

$600 billion in assets under management by the middle of 2013, including some domestic investments.

In a less transparent manner than CIC, the State Administration of Foreign Exchange (SAFE), which manages China's foreign exchange reserves, has been funneling money to its own investment arm. According to some reports, SAFE Investment Company, operating out of Hong Kong, had about $570 billion in assets under management in 2012. In January 2013, SAFE announced that its Co-Financing Office would be seeking "innovative" use of resources and "supporting financial institutions in serving China's economic growth and going-out strategy." This was a formal acknowledgement of an office whose existence seems to date back at least to 2011.

Because sovereign wealth funds are driven to seek sound long-term investments rather than those that might yield high short-term returns, they are sometimes seen as a stabilizing force in international finance, similar to other long-term institutional investors, such as pension funds. In view of their long horizons, these funds can also afford to take slightly more risks than central banks when designing their investment strategies. With issues of national patrimony involved, however, there is a limit to how much risk they can take on through investments in equities. Moreover, for most emerging markets, foreign exchange reserve management is still driven by the key principles of safety and liquidity. Although sovereign wealth funds are likely to gain in prominence as countries look for better returns from their stocks of reserves, they will at best temper rather than reduce the increasing demand for safe assets.

The Price of Safety Goes Up

Even while the demand for safe assets through reserve accumulation continues to rise, the aftermath of the financial crisis has driven up other sources of demand for these assets and, at the same time, reduced their supply.

Many private banks got into trouble during the crisis, because they did not have enough equity capital (or net worth, the difference between their assets and liabilities). Most of their financing had been in the form of short-term liabilities, including deposits and loans from other institutions, which made them vulnerable to a loss of depositor confidence during the crisis. Moreover, they did not have enough of a buffer of cash and liquid securities to deal with short-term cash flow needs.

Recent regulatory changes have raised capital requirements on banks and added a specific liquidity (cash) requirement. A new set of banking regulations with these and other elements, referred to as Basel III (named after the town in Switzerland where the Bank for International Settlements has its headquarters), has been agreed to by most countries. One of the key elements of Basel III is that all banks have to hold more capital relative to their deposits, which constitute their liabilities. Banks designated as systemically important (mostly very large banks) have to hold an even higher level of capital to offset the greater risk that their failure could have damaging effects on the financial system.

Each bank also has to satisfy a "liquidity coverage ratio." That is, it must hold enough high-quality liquid assets that can be converted into cash easily to meet its expected liquidity needs for a 30 day period if it were under financial stress. The types of securities that can be counted toward this liquidity buffer were initially restricted to cash, reserve holdings at national central banks, and government securities. In January 2013, the Basel Committee on Banking Supervision ruled that the liquidity ratio could be partially satisfied by other types of securities, including certain equities and residential mortgage-backed securities, giving banks at least a partial reprieve on the amount of government securities they will need to hold. Nevertheless, government securities are seen both by banks themselves and their regulators as the most desirable securities for meeting the liquidity coverage ratio.

Collateral requirements have also shifted the demand for safe assets. Many financial transactions need collateral. For instance, in derivatives markets where big players trade directly with each other, the two parties often require some collateral from each other. After the financial crisis, even major financial market players have turned to government securities as the only acceptable collateral.

It is obvious what all of this means—a greater demand for high-quality government debt.

Supply of Private Safe Assets Shrinks

Events since 2008 have affected not just the demand but also the supply of safe assets. One of the major innovations in the U.S. mortgage markets during the 2000s was the advent of securitization. Mortgages were spun off into securities with different risk ratings, allowing banks to take mortgages and any risk associated with them off their books, and providing attractive investment opportunities to investors hungry for yield at a time of low interest rates. These securities were set up in different tranches, with the riskier ones having the status of junk bonds but the safest of them getting the top AAA rating from credit rating agencies. The logic seemed sound—even if there were some defaults on mortgages, the top tranches would be safe, as there was, after all, little chance the housing market would entirely collapse.

The flaw in the logic was revealed when the U.S. housing market began to cool off in 2007. Investors and financial institutions that had used those highly rated securities to borrow and make speculative higher yield investments that were turning sour started trying to dump those securities simultaneously. This infected the entire mortgage-backed securities market, causing even the market for AAA-rated securities to freeze up during the crisis, as there were only sellers and virtually no buyers. The IMF puts it this way:

> AAA-rated securitizations were found to embed much higher
> default risks than warranted by their high ratings. For example, as
> of August 2009, 63 percent of AAA-rated straight private label
> mortgage-backed securities issued from 2005 to 2007 had been
> downgraded, and 52 percent were downgraded to BB or lower. . . .
> Haircuts on the highest rated securitized instruments in the U.S.
> private bilateral repo market increased sharply from near-zero
> precrisis levels to more than 30 percent for certain instruments.

Thus, many supposedly safe private securities turned out to be anything but. There are still some securities, corporate bonds, and other types of private debt instruments that continue to be regarded as safe assets, as they have AAA ratings. However, the numbers of some of these categories, especially AAA-rated corporate debt, have fallen sharply in the U.S.

In 1983, 32 nonfinancial companies in the U.S. had credit that was rated AAA. Today, just four nonfinancial corporations retain that coveted status—Automatic Data Processing, Exxon Mobil, Johnson & Johnson, and Microsoft. This low number is partly because many of the newer large and successful corporations in the U.S. have traditionally eschewed debt, preferring to raise capital through issuance of equity alone. For instance, it was only in late 2012 that Amazon entered the debt market after being out of it for about 15 years. Apple issued debt for the first time in April 2013. Interestingly, even cash-rich and profitable companies like Amazon and Apple could not secure AAA ratings for their corporate debt. Apple, for instance, is seen as a company with good but uncertain long-term prospects given the highly competitive nature of markets for its products.

The IMF estimates that the total issuance of private sector securities in the United States and Europe fell from $3 trillion in 2007 to less than $750 billion in 2010. Compounding this shrinkage in the supply of high-quality private debt is the fact that, in the aftermath of the crisis, the debt of government-sponsored enterprises (GSEs) in the U.S. is no longer regarded as equivalent to U.S. government debt in terms of safety.

GSEs such as Fannie Mae and Freddie Mac issued a large amount of debt before the crisis, amounting to about $3 trillion in 2007. The implicit assumption had been that GSE debt, although not technically guaranteed by the U.S. government, was effectively backed by such a guarantee. This assumption proved to be correct, as investors in the GSEs—including foreign central banks that had bought these securities for their reserve portfolios—were in fact bailed out by the U.S. government as part of its attempts to stanch the collapse of the housing market. Nevertheless, the riskiness of these securities has clearly increased, and they are no longer regarded as safe assets.

The temptation to create new safe assets to meet growing demand has certainly not gone away. In principle, it is not difficult. An investor can buy risky debt that pays a higher rate of return than safer debt and then buy a credit default swap that would pay out in case of default on that debt. What the financial crisis has shown, however, is that such actions may reduce the risk for an individual investor but can, in some circumstances, increase the risks for the financial system as a whole.

Indeed, one of the core insights of Raghuram Rajan's famous presentation at the 2005 Jackson Hole Symposium is that financial innovations may lead to a pooling of risk in vulnerable parts of the financial system rather than to a dispersal of risk. A vivid example is the near-collapse of the U.S. insurance giant American International Group, which was brought to its knees by its huge issuance of corporate credit default swaps that it had to make good on when the crisis hit and set off a wave of corporate bankruptcies. If American International Group had failed, it would have damaged a large number of firms that had bought insurance from it.

The implication of this discussion is that private securities are going to carry a taint, especially among managers of foreign exchange reserves, even if credit rating agencies give them their top rating. Will safe government securities make up for the gap, especially now that many advanced economies are racking up large amounts of public debt?

Public Debt Looks Less Safe

During the 1990s, most advanced economies had AAA-rated government debt. The worsening public deficit and debt situations of many of these economies meant that only two-thirds of these economies had AAA-rated government debt at the end of 2007. By early 2012, this fraction had dropped to about half, cutting into the supply of safe sovereign debt. One of the countries that lost its AAA rating is the U.S. As noted earlier, Standard and Poor's downgrade of U.S. sovereign debt from AAA to AA+ does not seem to have had much effect on the perception of its debt as a safe asset. For other countries, such a downgrade matters more and often takes their debt out of the safe asset category.

It is now abundantly clear, for instance, that not all euro zone bonds are equally safe. German government debt still counts as a safe asset, but the same cannot be said for sovereign debt of other large euro zone economies, such as Italy and Spain, let alone the smaller economies on the periphery of the zone. At the end of 2012, the core euro zone countries—Germany, France, the Netherlands, Austria, Finland, and Luxembourg (in order of absolute amounts of debt)—accounted for just over half of total gross government debt of euro zone countries. Roughly 40 percent of the total was accounted for by the troubled euro zone periphery—Italy, Spain, Greece, Portugal, and Ireland.

In 2010–11, foreign net purchases of government debt were positive only for France and Germany, among all the euro zone countries. Now that even the sovereign bonds of countries like Austria, France, and the U.K. have lost their AAA status, foreign investors are viewing those bonds more warily, although they are unlikely to dump them en masse, as alternatives are hard to come by. At any rate, the size of the "safe" part of the euro zone government debt market is clearly much smaller than the total size of this market. The ECB noted in a July 2013 report on the international role of the euro that

> in 2012 the euro area sovereign debt crisis continued to weigh on the international use of the euro, which declined moderately in some market segments. The persistent fragmentation of the euro area financial system is one of the main underlying causes of these developments, as it affects the depth and liquidity of euro area capital markets.

To sum up, risk was evidently underpriced in financial markets in the lead-up to the crisis, with the supply of ostensibly safe assets going up thanks to financial market alchemy. After the crisis, the price of safety has gone up in tandem with the higher demand and lower supply of safe assets. Government debt of a small set of major advanced economies —especially U.S. Treasuries, German bunds, and Japanese government bonds—now accounts for the preponderance of safe assets.

Bazookas Can Be Costly Even If They Are Not Used

Even setting aside various risks on government debt of the major advanced economies, which I will turn to in the next chapter, accumulating reserves is not a cost-free proposition. Emerging market economies presumably have productive uses for that money at home, but instead the reserves get invested in the government bonds of advanced economies, which pay low rates of return. Dani Rodrik estimates that developing economies pay a cost of about 1 percent of GDP annually when they invest in advanced economy government bonds and then borrow from abroad to finance domestic investment. His estimates are based on the stocks of foreign exchange reserves in 2004. With the substantial increase in reserve stocks and the decline in advanced economy government bond yields since then, these opportunity costs are no doubt higher now. Of course, some emerging market government bond yields have fallen as well, but the gap in productive investment opportunities between emerging markets and advanced economies has, if anything, risen further in favor of the former group since the mid-2000s.

Costly Sterilization

To intervene in foreign exchange markets and buy dollars (or other hard currencies), a central bank has to print more of its own money. The increase in money supply can fuel domestic inflation. To prevent inflation from rising, central banks resort to an operation called "sterilization"— selling government or central bank bonds to soak up the additional money they have injected into the economy. Putting more bonds in the hands of investors and households and taking a corresponding amount of money out of circulation reduces inflationary pressures.

Selling more of these bonds requires paying higher interest rates to convince investors to hold them. This ends up costing the government or central bank (and ultimately, the taxpayer) significant sums of money, as the interest payments on those sterilization bonds are typically higher than the rate of return on advanced economy government bonds that reserves are parked in.

As an example, the yield on Indian government securities ranging from 3-month to 10-year maturities, which provides a measure of sterilization costs, was about 8–9 percent for much of 2012. In contrast, the yield on U.S. government securities for most of this period was close to or below 2 percent, even for 10-year bonds. This yawning gap of more than 6 percent per year represents a direct cost to the Indian government in terms of what it pays out on its sterilization instrument relative to the returns on its foreign exchange reserves held in U.S. Treasury bonds. The yields on sovereign bonds of the euro zone and Japan are no better.

Part of this yield gap could be made up by a depreciation of the rupee relative to the dollar—as that would mean a gain on foreign bond holdings, when measured in terms of the domestic currency. But that is hardly a sure thing in the short term. In fact, the rupee appreciated by 13 percent relative to the dollar from the end of 2005 to the end of 2007, a period when the country's stock of foreign exchange reserves doubled from $131 billion to $267 billion. In 2012 and through the first quarter of 2013, the rupee was weak against the dollar, but not by enough to offset the huge interest differential, implying that sterilization costs remained high.

For many emerging markets whose currencies have been appreciating against the dollar, the situation is more complicated. In addition to the higher interest rates they have to pay on domestic bonds relative to earnings on foreign bonds, appreciation of the domestic currency implies a lower value of foreign bond holdings measured in that currency. For East Asian economies other than Indonesia, most of which have had low interest rates but appreciating currencies in recent years, the opportunity cost (yield gap) of investing in U.S. dollar reserves has been estimated at about 2 percent a year. With many of these economies building up reserves that are quite high relative to GDP, this implies a large fiscal cost.

Central bankers are acutely aware of the costs. In a paper published in August 2012, Governor José Darío Uribe of the Banco de la República, Colombia's central bank, made it clear that he was cognizant of the costs of sterilized foreign exchange intervention undertaken by his bank. He noted that the "accumulation of reserves always starts from a careful analysis of the costs and benefits, and of the opportunity costs, . . . and taking into account that sterilizing reserve accumulation costs about 9 billion pesos ($4.9 million) for every $100 million bought."

Other Costs

Some economies limit their sterilization costs through financial repression. In China, the government puts a cap on bank deposit rates, which reduces the cost of funds for banks. This encourages the state-owned banks to buy central bank bonds for relatively low yields while still making a profit. Thus, financial repression makes foreign exchange market intervention and sterilization less expensive in the short run, but it has other costs. The controlled interest rate structure in China reduces banking sector competition and impedes the efficient operation of financial markets. It also imposes direct costs on households, who have earned low or negative inflation-adjusted rates of return on their bank deposits for most of the past decade.

These costs are far from trivial. Nicholas Lardy of the Peterson Institute estimates that Chinese households face a cost of nearly 4 percent of GDP per year on account of this financial repression, which keeps the returns on their bank deposits lower than it would be in a more competitive banking system. Thus, households pay the costs of sterilization through low returns on deposits in the state-owned banking system rather than through higher taxes.

Self-insurance through reserve accumulation may also prove expensive in the long run if there is an eventual capital loss from the anticipated depreciation of advanced economy currencies relative to those of emerging markets or if advanced economy governments drive down the real value of their bonds through inflation. I explore these channels in more detail in the next chapter.

The main conclusion from this section is that the massive accumulation of reserves by emerging markets shows that they are willing to pay a high price for insurance against the sorts of disasters they faced in the past. It is of course difficult to conclusively disentangle purely mercantilist motives from precautionary motives for building up reserves. In addition to anecdotal evidence—such as the statements of central bankers cited earlier in this chapter—there is some empirical evidence favoring the precautionary view. In any case, the motives may be less important for the purposes of the analysis in this book than the outcome—rising stocks of reserves in search of a safe home.

Backfiring Bazookas: Could Safe Assets Turn Risky?

Lawrence Summers of Harvard University noted in a speech at the Reserve Bank of India in 2006, "it is an irony of our times that the majority of the world's poorest people now live in countries with vast international financial reserves."

Even with a more benign structure of foreign liabilities, emerging markets have not fully torn themselves away from the desire for insurance that would provide an infusion of liquidity at times of global crises. Given the devastating effects of crises, it seems like a fair bargain for these countries to purchase insurance against such catastrophic events. The reality, however, is that emerging markets ought to be concerned about buying increasing quantities of government bonds of advanced economies.

There is a possible collective action problem stemming from reserve accumulation by emerging markets, as it provides cheap financing for the fiscal profligacy of advanced economies while increasing the risks of future crises. During the financial crisis, there was a concern that if a number of emerging markets simultaneously tried to liquidate their holdings of U.S. government securities, financial markets could be further destabilized. Thus, in many ways, massive reserve accumulation might end up making those reserves less valuable at a time of global crisis and in fact reduces the value of insurance as it heightens global risks.

A remarkable paradox in international finance is that the emerging markets' appetite for self-insurance has, if anything, increased global risks and transferred the major risks on those countries' balance sheets from the liability side to the asset side. The shift in the structure of external liabilities away from debt and toward foreign direct investment and equity investments has resulted in better risk-sharing arrangements with international investors. In contrast, the large and rising share of advanced economy government bonds in emerging markets' external assets has increased risks on that side of their balance sheets. The notion that the flow of official capital from emerging markets represents a search for "safe" assets seems increasingly tenuous.

How can investments in ostensibly secure government debt turn risky? To answer that, it is necessary to turn to an examination of the public debt trajectories of the U.S. and other advanced economies, which present an increasingly unsettling picture.

6

A Trillion Dollar Con Game?

*As they say in poker, if you've been in the game 30 minutes
and you don't know who the patsy is, you're the patsy.*

Warren Buffett, Sage of Omaha

On June 1, 2009, Timothy Geithner entered a conference hall at Peking
University to give a speech on the U.S.-China economic relationship.
The event would kick off his first visit to China as U.S. Treasury secretary. The hall was packed with faculty, students, and a swarm of journalists. Geithner began by reminiscing about his first visit to China in the
summer of 1981 to study Mandarin at Peking University. He then spoke
about the U.S. economy and the scope for improved relations between
the two countries, throwing in a Mandarin phrase signifying cooperation for good measure.

The question and answer session following the speech got off to a
rocky start with a question about Taiwan. The nervous moderator, Professor Zhou Qiren, looked for someone to ask a friendlier question and
his eyes landed on Zhang Boyang, a boyish young student and one of the
brightest minds in his cohort. Boyang posed this question to Geithner:

> Professor Krugman visited Peking University in May and deliv-
> ered a speech. He argued that the crisis may be much longer than
> the general expectation and worried about a second round shock
> to the U.S. This argument makes us again worry about the safety
> of Chinese assets in U.S. How do you think of it?

Geithner's response was quick: "Chinese assets are *very* safe." The
ensuing guffaw of laughter from the students, who could sense Geithner's awkwardness in his body language and intonation, was reported
widely in Chinese and international media. Geithner would go on to
give a more detailed explanation, but the audience's reaction to his initial

U.S. Treasury Secretary Timothy Geithner with his former teacher Fu Min, just prior to his speech at Peking University, June 1, 2009. (Tiantian Wang, China Photo Press.)

response set the tone for his visit. The student, who asked the question that reverberated in headlines around the world, went on to graduate at the top of his class and is now a student of mine at Cornell.

China's concerns, encapsulated by the student's question, are shared by other countries as well. From 2000 to 2012, the rest of the world transferred about 7 trillion dollars to the U.S. This is the total current account deficit that the U.S. has run over this period and that has been financed by other countries. Over the same period, the total global accumulation of foreign exchange reserves was about $9 trillion, with $6.5 trillion accounted for by emerging and developing economies and the rest by advanced economies. Assuming that three-fifths of global foreign exchange reserve accumulation goes into U.S. dollar–denominated assets, about $5.5 trillion of net capital inflows into the U.S. are accounted for by reserve accumulation.

A large share of this money has come from emerging market economies as a consequence of their prodigious reserve accumulation. In other words, a set of countries with an average per capita income of roughly $8,000 a year has been financing an economy where the per capita income is about six times higher. Much of this money has gone into U.S. Treasury debt.

Have the emerging markets been set up, or set themselves up, as suckers in a giant global confidence game? The answer is a subtle one.

Safe Assets Balloon and Become More Fragile

To begin with, consider the largest category of safe assets—government bonds of advanced economies. It is important to keep some definitions in mind, as there are various concepts of public debt that tend to get conflated in popular discussions.

Gross debt, a broader concept than net debt, includes debt that is held by different arms of the government (see Figure 6-1). For instance, in the U.S., the social security trust funds have over the years accumulated sur-

FIGURE 6-1. Who Holds U.S. Federal Government Debt?

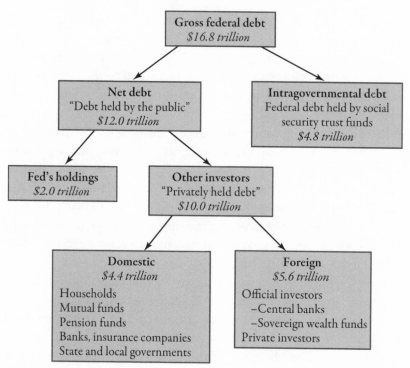

Data sources: U.S. Treasury Bulletin, June 2013: Tables FD-1, OFS-1, OFS-2, and U.S. Treasury International Capital System: Table on "Major Foreign Holders of Treasury Securities," September 2013. Note: Numbers shown in this figure are for June 2013.

pluses that, by law, have to be invested in "securities guaranteed as to both principal and interest by the Federal government." These special securities are available only to the trust funds and, unlike marketable securities available to the public, can be redeemed at any time at face value. Net debt in the U.S. is "debt held by the public," a broad definition that covers domestic and foreign investors, including foreign central banks and the holdings of the Federal Reserve. The Fed is technically "an independent entity within the government" rather than part of the U.S. government.

The magnitude of the difference between the two concepts of debt is far from trivial. In the U.S., net debt hit $12 trillion in June 2013, whereas gross debt was $16.8 trillion. The Fed holds about $2 trillion of net debt. The remainder—roughly $10 trillion—is classified as "privately held" and includes Treasury securities held by various domestic and foreign investors.

In Japan, net debt at the end of 2012 was $8.1 trillion, whereas gross debt amounted to about $14.2 trillion. The difference in Japan's case is attributable not just to the government bonds held by government agencies, such as the National Pension Fund, but also to the large stock of financial assets that the Japanese government owns, which reduces net debt.

There is an ongoing debate among economists about which definition should be used to evaluate whether a country's debt is in the danger zone. Even if part of gross debt is owed by one arm of the government to another part, the government as a whole eventually has to pay off that debt. When the U.S. social security trust funds start drawing down on their surplus as the population ages and the ratio of social security recipients to workers rises, the government will have to generate real resources to meet its social security obligations.

However, for analyzing the reliance of national governments on foreign financing of their debt, net debt is a more suitable concept, as it represents the portion of the debt that can be traded in financial markets. Most components in gross but not net debt are typically held domestically. A more comprehensive picture of a country's debt would also include private debt, but my interest here is more in assets that are relevant for reserve accumulation by emerging markets. As discussed in the previous chapter, the supply of AAA-rated corporate debt and asset-backed securities has shrunk. Moreover, the safety of even some of these highly rated securities is questionable at a time of financial meltdown.

Disturbing Debt Dynamics

The global financial crisis triggered a sharp increase in public debt levels, both in absolute terms and relative to GDP. The level of combined net government debt in the world—henceforth referred to as global public (or government) debt—rose from $23 trillion in 2007, just prior to the financial crisis, to $41 trillion in 2012 (see Figure 6-2). Nearly $16 trillion of this increase in net debt was accounted for by advanced economies, pushing their total stock of debt to $35 trillion by the end of 2012. For these economies, the coordinated fiscal stimulus that was launched at

FIGURE 6-2. Global Government Debt Levels

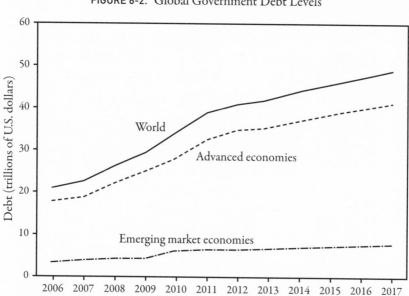

Data sources: IMF Fiscal Monitor; IMF International Financial Statistics.

Notes: The combined level of general government net debt for all advanced and emerging market economies is shown, with each economy's data converted to U.S. dollars at market exchange rates. The data for advanced and emerging market economies together add up to the world aggregates. Gross debt data are used for the following economies that do not report net debt: advanced economies—Czech Republic, Greece, Hong Kong, Singapore, Slovak Republic, and Slovenia; emerging market economies—Argentina, China, India, Indonesia, Malaysia, Philippines, Romania, Russia, and Thailand. Data for 2013–17 are based on IMF forecasts.

the time of the financial crisis and banking sector bailouts led to the massive increase in public debt.

The dynamics of public debt for advanced economies do not look promising over the next few years. Their combined public debt is expected to rise to $41 trillion by 2017, double the level in 2007. This will amount to about 81 percent of expected GDP in these economies in 2017, compared to a debt to GDP ratio of 48 percent in 2007 (see Figure 6-3).

Public debt dynamics in emerging markets look quite different. The average debt to GDP ratio of emerging market economies, which was 29 percent of GDP in 2007, is expected to *decline* to about 23 percent of GDP by 2017. In other words, the gap in average debt to GDP ratios between advanced and emerging market economies is expected to widen steadily in the coming years.

These developments are indicative of the transformative shift in the balance of economic power between these two groups of economies. As

FIGURE 6-3. Global Government Debt Relative to Output

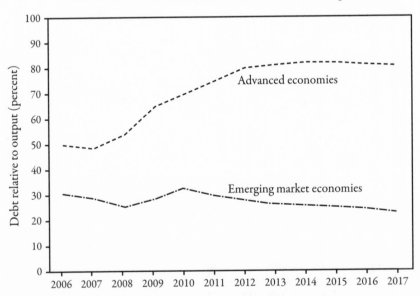

Data sources: IMF Fiscal Monitor; IMF International Financial Statistics.

Notes: For each group of economies, combined general government net debt is shown, expressed as a ratio of combined GDP for all economies in the group. Data for 2013–17 are based on IMF forecasts.

described in my 2010 book with Ayhan Kose, this phenomenon picked up pace at the turn of the millennium and was given a boost by the financial crisis. Changes in the global distribution of debt and GDP provide telling signs of this shift.

In 2007, emerging markets accounted for 25 percent of global GDP and 17 percent of global debt. By 2017, they are expected to produce 40 percent of global GDP and account for just 16 percent of global debt. These figures and a more detailed breakdown are shown in Appendix Figures A-1 and A-2.

There is an even starker contrast between the two groups of countries when one compares their contributions to growth in global debt versus growth in global GDP. Emerging markets contribute far more to growth in global GDP than to the growth in global public debt. These economies accounted for 14 percent of the increase in global debt levels from 2007 to 2012. In contrast, their contribution to the increase in global GDP over this period was 70 percent. The numbers are equally stark when one examines forecasts for the subsequent five years. From 2012 to 2017, emerging markets are expected to account for about three-fifths of global GDP growth but less than one-fifth of global public debt accumulation. In other words, emerging markets are adding substantially to global GDP, whereas advanced economies are mainly adding to global public debt (see Figure A-3 in the Appendix for details).

The U.S. and Japan are certainly heavy hitters when it comes to debt accumulation. These two economies are making a far greater contribution to the rise in global debt than to the rise in global GDP. The U.S. contributed 38 percent of the increase in global debt from 2007 to 2012 and is expected to account for nearly half of the anticipated increase from 2012 to 2017. Its contributions to the increases in global GDP over those two periods are 12 percent and 23 percent, respectively. Japan accounted for 25 percent of the increase in debt from 2007 to 2012 and is expected to add 9 percent from 2012 to 2017, whereas its contributions to the increase in global GDP are far more modest.

One can find reason to quibble with these numbers, which paint a relatively favorable picture of fiscal discipline in emerging markets. The reported debt levels of emerging markets should certainly be interpreted with caution. In China, for instance, financial liabilities of provincial governments as well as contingent liabilities, such as nonperforming assets held by the state-owned banking system, imply a much higher value of central government debt obligations than indicated by official statistics. The same is true of other emerging markets that have state-owned banking systems and underfunded public pension systems. Of course, as the recent crisis has shown, advanced economy governments arguably have similar implicit contingent liabilities if their big banks were to run aground or their public pension systems were to run out of money.

It is worth honing in on one set of numbers from this analysis that is of particular relevance for the structure of the international monetary system. In 2007, the four major reserve currency areas—the euro zone, Japan, the U.K., and the U.S.—together accounted for 64 percent of global GDP and 80 percent of global debt. It is expected that, by 2017, they will account for a similar share of global debt but only 50 percent of global GDP (see Figures A-1 and A-2 in the Appendix).

Digging a Deeper Hole

The bottom line is that advanced economies have dug themselves into a deep hole of debt from which they will find it difficult to extricate themselves. Their fiscal prospects look even gloomier once one looks beyond the next five years. First, most of these countries are experiencing little population growth, with fertility rates falling below the replacement rate needed to replenish the population. By 2030, most advanced economies will experience a shrinking labor force that, in turn, implies slower growth unless there is a compensating increase in investment or productivity growth. In advanced economies like Japan and Italy, the labor force is already declining.

Many emerging markets face similar problems but not to the same degree. A handful of emerging markets like India and Indonesia have young populations and could in fact reap a "demographic dividend" if they play their cards right. Interestingly, among the advanced economies, the U.S. is in a relatively favorable position, as it has a fertility rate that is close to replacement rate, and its labor force will continue to grow even two decades from now. Among the emerging markets, China is in a less favorable position, because the one-child policy instituted in 1979 has, by some measures, already led to a shrinking labor pool.

Most advanced economies are in a double bind, because, in addition to shrinking workforces, they face rapidly aging populations, which will increase health care and pension expenditures. By 2030, old-age dependency ratios—the ratio of the elderly population to the working-aged population—will be close to or above 50 percent in countries like Germany and Japan. The U.S. will have one of the lower dependency ratios among advanced economies, with a ratio of about 1 elderly person to 3 working-aged persons. But even this ratio will be higher than that of all the major emerging market economies. High and rising dependency ratios in the advanced economies will put further strain on public expenditures and divert money away from education, investment, and other productivity-enhancing expenditures.

Given their weak growth prospects and unfavorable demographic trends, one thing seems certain—the major reserve currency economies will be producing a large quantity of government-owned "safe assets" in the years ahead. With worsening public debt dynamics and a sharply rising debt burden, however, the safety of these assets is an increasingly dubious proposition. Ballooning public debt in these economies could itself become a threat to domestic and global financial stability.

This is only one of many worries for emerging markets that have invested their reserves in assets denominated in the currencies of the advanced economies, especially the dollar. These currencies themselves bear some risks.

Should Emerging Markets Fret over Their Foreign Bond Holdings?

The dollar must fall in value. That proposition seems self-evident to most macroeconomists, who view it as essential for the adjustment that must take place in the U.S. and in the world economy. A decline in the dollar's value against the currencies of the major trading partners of the U.S. would make exports more competitive and would also make imports more expensive for U.S. consumers. This would help bring down the U.S. trade deficit to a level that is sustainable over the long term. But betting on this self-evident proposition of a falling dollar has often proved to be a bad short-term bet, especially in times of global financial distress.

What can we say with any reasonable confidence about the dollar's value in the years ahead? Economists are not much better than others at predicting short-term movements in exchange rates. Over horizons of a week, a month, or even a year, exchange rates tend to be driven by a variety of factors. Random shifts in investor sentiment often drive currency values up or down in a manner that seems disconnected from economic fundamentals, such as growth and unemployment.

Short-term investors tend to focus on nominal exchange rates, but what really matters in terms of the purchasing power of one currency relative to another is the inflation-adjusted—or "real"—exchange rate. The nominal exchange rate is the market price of one currency relative to another. The real exchange rate adjusts for differences in price levels between countries and is a better measure of one currency's purchasing power relative to another. In other words, it measures the cost of the same basket of goods and services across countries. These two measures of the exchange rate generally move in the same direction, but the difference between them can be large. For instance, from January 2005 to March 2013, the nominal exchange rate of the renminbi relative to the dollar appreciated by 33 percent, while the renminbi's real exchange rate appreciated by 38 percent.

Although short-term currency movements are hard to predict, economists have a better understanding of what drives long-term changes in real exchange rates. The currency of a country that has higher productivity growth relative to its trading partners eventually tends to appreciate in value relative to those partners' currencies. As productivity increases, wages in a country will eventually increase, because higher productivity increases the demand for labor. Moreover, a faster-growing economy will also tend to attract capital inflows. Both these factors will eventually push up the price of the domestic currency, although existing statistical models do not tell us exactly when this is likely to happen. The relationship between productivity growth and exchange rate appreciation tends to hold better over longer horizons—not so well at a one-year horizon, somewhat better at a five-year horizon, and more so at horizons of ten years or longer.

Labor productivity growth has been higher in emerging markets than in the advanced economies, and this is likely to remain the case for some time. In the latter group, rising public debt levels imply significant crowding-out of government expenditure on items like education, infrastructure investment, and health; this in turn will hurt productivity growth. Balance sheets of households and the financial sector in these economies were severely damaged by the financial crisis and have still not fully recovered, putting a further crimp on these economies' growth prospects. All these factors imply a persistent productivity growth gap relative to emerging markets, whose currencies will therefore tend to appreciate in the long run relative to those of the major advanced economies.

There are some wildcards that, in principle, have the potential to alter the long-term productivity and currency trends discussed above. For instance, the prospect of an energy revolution in the U.S. has stirred up considerable excitement. Technologies that allow producers to tap the large reserves of oil and natural gas in U.S. shale formations are seen as a potential game changer in global energy markets. By reducing net energy imports, which account for nearly half of the U.S. trade deficit according to some estimates, output from this resource could result in a sizable reduction in U.S. trade and current account deficits. However, this revolution is in its early stages, and the promised benefits are far from certain.

The U.S. Department of Energy estimates that oil and gas production from shale formations was worth a quarter of a trillion dollars in 2012, roughly 1.5 percent of U.S. GDP, and is forecast to rise to about half a trillion dollars a year by 2035. Private sector analysts have a range of estimates about the potential impact on GDP, adding 0.1 to 0.3 percentage points to U.S. GDP growth each year, and on trade, reducing the trade deficit by an amount equal to about one tenth to one quarter of its level in 2012. These estimates suggest that a full-fledged energy revolution would have a significant impact on long-term prospects for the U.S. current account deficit and the dollar. Nevertheless, it is unlikely, even based on the more optimistic estimates, that this revolution will alter or overcome the other fundamental forces that point to a long-term depreciation of the dollar.

Uncomfortable Implications of Changing Currency Values

One implication of a depreciation of the reserve currencies relative to the emerging market currencies is that, through the stocks of foreign currency reserves, there would be an implicit transfer of wealth from poorer to richer economies. When the dollar depreciates in value relative to the renminbi, the value in renminbi of China's dollar reserve holdings will decline (of course, the dollar value of those reserves held in dollars will remain unchanged). These "currency valuation" effects can be quite large.

Some numbers for China and the U.S. provide an illustration. In China, labor productivity growth in the manufacturing sector is estimated to have been about 11 percent a year, compared to 3 percent a year in the U.S. during the 2000s. Assume (conservatively) that China will experience only half that rate of productivity growth over the next decade and (optimistically) that the U.S. can maintain its recent rate of productivity growth. Then the average annual productivity growth in China will be 2.5 percentage points higher than that in the U.S. The cumulative productivity differential between the two countries will amount to roughly 28 percent over ten years (the compounding effect implies that just multiplying 2.5 by 10 would not yield the right answer). Assuming full adjustment, the Chinese currency is thus likely to appreciate by 25–30 percent in inflation-adjusted terms relative to the U.S. dollar. Even if China does not allow the nominal value of the renminbi to appreciate to this extent, this adjustment could come through higher inflation in China relative to the U.S.

China does not report the currency composition of its foreign exchange reserves. Based on various snippets of evidence and anecdotal information, it is widely believed that at least 60 percent of China's foreign currency reserves, which stood at $3.5 trillion in June 2013, are held in U.S. dollars. That would amount to about $2 trillion. The official foreign exchange reserves do not fully account for dollar-denominated assets held by China. These assets include reserves that were transferred (on paper) to the state-owned commercial banks at various times to infuse additional capital onto their balance sheets, investments of the sovereign wealth fund (China Investment Corporation), and other investments by government-owned institutions and private investors. Assuming those investments add up to about $500 billion yields a total of $2.5 trillion worth of dollar-denominated assets. Thus, if China does not shift its investment patterns, it will in effect lose about $700 billion in terms of its domestic currency over the next decade simply because of currency valuation effects.

This is a concern not just for China but for other emerging markets as well. Indeed, the trend in the dollar's value over the past decade is clearly negative. Over longer periods, the dollar's value has of course swung sharply in both directions. However, as demonstrated in earlier chapters, rising global financial integration, large U.S. current account deficits, and massive official inflows from the rest of the world are relatively recent phenomena. Hence, for analyzing the dollar trap and its implications, I focus on the period since 2000.

Figure 6-4 shows that since 2000 the dollar has depreciated in both real and nominal terms relative to a broad basket of currencies of its trading partners by about 1 percent a year. Some of this depreciation has taken place against the currencies of other advanced economies, but the dollar has also depreciated significantly against some major emerging market economies, especially in inflation-adjusted terms. A continuation of this trend spells losses for China and other emerging markets on their dollar reserve holdings.

Diversification Does Not Help

Perhaps the answer for emerging markets is to shift away from the dollar to other hard currencies, such as euros or Japanese yen. This comes up

FIGURE 6-4. The Dollar Trends Down

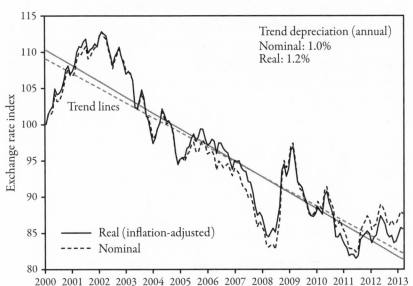

Data source: Bank for International Settlements.

Notes: Trade-weighted real and nominal effective exchange rate indices (base year 2000 = 100) are computed relative to a broad basket of 61 currencies. A decline in the effective exchange rate implies depreciation. The straight lines show linear time trends in the nominal (dashed line) and real (solid line) effective exchange rates.

against the reality that the renminbi and many other emerging market currencies have been appreciating against other major hard currencies as well. Based on the overall level of foreign exchange reserves and the fact that a vast majority of these reserves are held in U.S. dollars, euros, and yen, the implications in terms of a capital loss in domestic currency terms for emerging markets are quite substantial. For instance, assume that 40 percent of China's foreign exchange reserves are held in currencies other than the U.S. dollar. This would amount to about $1.4 trillion based on data for June 2013. A 10 percent exchange rate appreciation of the renminbi against those currencies would imply a capital loss of about $140 billion for China from currency valuation effects.

This issue raises an important point regarding reserve management. Diversification across different hard currencies does not protect emerging markets from adverse currency valuation effects on their foreign exchange reserves. None of the large advanced economies looks likely to come close to matching productivity growth in the major emerging markets. The Conference Board, a U.S. research organization, estimates that the average productivity differential between emerging markets and the major advanced economies will be about 3 percentage points per year in 2012–13. In their comprehensive study of global productivity, Dale Jorgensen of Harvard University and Khuong Vu of the National University of Singapore forecast that productivity growth over the next decade is likely to average 1.3 percent per year for the Group of Seven large advanced economies (Canada, France, Germany, Italy, Japan, U.K., and U.S.). For six major emerging markets and South Korea, average productivity growth is expected to be 4.8 percent. These numbers imply a productivity differential of 3.5 percentage points per year.

The implication is that currencies such as the euro and yen provide little recourse for countries that are trying to escape from the dollar's grasp by shifting out of dollar-denominated safe assets. Using more conservative estimates than those discussed above, productivity growth in the emerging markets will be on average about 2 percent higher than in the advanced economies. If this pattern holds up, one might expect to see that magnitude of an exchange rate appreciation of emerging market currencies relative to advanced economy currencies. In other words, the value of their foreign exchange reserve holdings, measured in domestic currency terms, will fall by about 20 percent over the next decade. This works out to an implicit transfer of about $1.4 trillion from the poorer to richer economies.

Just Bookkeeping?

One counterargument to this logic about implicit wealth transfers stemming from a depreciating dollar is that the currency value is of little consequence, as the dollar holdings represent claims on U.S. goods and services that are denominated in dollars. Marking reserve holdings up or down based on currency fluctuations is, in this view, purely a bookkeeping matter with no real consequences.

The following colorfully phrased question was posed to the administrators at the State Administration of Foreign Exchange, which manages China's foreign exchange reserves:

> some people still believe that an RMB [renminbi] appreciation will gradually dissipate our wealth [held as] foreign exchange reserves just like a cooked duck flying away. So, will an appreciation of the RMB really lead to actual losses of foreign exchange reserves and even social welfare?

SAFE's official response was as follows (both the question and response appear on its website):

> An appreciation of the RMB will not directly causes [*sic*] losses of Chinas [*sic*] foreign exchange reserves. . . . Variations in the RMB/ USD exchange rate will result in a change in the book value of the RMB . . . which is not the actually realized gains or losses . . . and thus will not have a direct impact on the effective purchasing power of the foreign exchange reserves. Changes in foreign exchange will only occur when the foreign exchange reserves are repatriated from overseas countries (regions) and converted into RMB. At present, China has no need to repatriate its foreign exchange reserves on a large scale.

The reality is not quite so simple. When intervening in foreign exchange markets and accumulating reserves, the People's Bank of China (PBC) sells renminbi and buys dollars. To offset this increase in the domestic money supply that could fuel inflation, the PBC issues central bank bonds that are effectively liabilities denominated in renminbi. These renminbi liabilities are roughly matched by corresponding dollar assets on the balance sheet of the PBC. If the renminbi value of the reserves portfolio falls because of dollar depreciation versus the renminbi, the PBC has to book a loss on its balance sheet. This loss may well be manageable in purely economic terms, but it could be politically embarrassing. The PBC bonds are mainly sold to state-owned banks, so this all stays within the government. But eventually the government must cover these losses.

In some cases, foreign exchange reserves are seen as insurance not just against capital flow volatility but also against domestic financial instability. The Chinese government has used its reserves to cover bad loans and rebuild the capital base of the major state-owned banks. For instance, in January 2004, the government injected a total of $45 billion of foreign exchange reserves into the Bank of China and China Construction Bank, two of the four major state-owned banks, through the government-run Central Huijin Investment Company. In this case, because all items on the banks' balance sheets are in renminbi, the reserves were in effect brought back home for domestic objectives. In practice, the banks could continue to hold the capital in the same investments as reserves, but those assets would have to be valued in renminbi on the banks' balance sheets. Thus, a bank recapitalization using foreign exchange reserves forces the government to recognize the currency valuation losses on the relevant portion of its foreign exchange reserves.

These issues raise disquieting questions about what it means for emerging markets to hold government bonds of advanced economies as safe assets when even the principal value of those assets is subject to risk.

Taking Creditors to the Cleaners

The levels of debt in many major advanced economies have generated serious concerns about how these economies will meet their debt repayment obligations. Debt can of course be rolled over indefinitely, so long as it stays within bounds. But the reality is that debt levels in these economies are already high, rising steadily, and could get worse as population aging leads to greater burdens on public pension systems and the health care systems.

One easy way for a government to pay off debt denominated in its own currency is to print money. An increase in the money supply will raise the level of domestic inflation and reduce the real value of government debt. The ownership of debt then becomes a key issue in determining the winners and losers from such an action. If debt is owned domestically, then inflation in effect represents a transfer between different groups in a country. For instance, retirees who have a large portion of their savings in safe government bonds would suffer as their interest payments shrink in inflation-adjusted terms. Borrowers with fixed-rate loans would benefit, as the real value of their loan payments would fall, effectively reducing their debt burden. Although the winners would be happy, the losers would certainly create political problems for the government.

There is a bigger problem with inflation as a strategy for paying down a country's debt. Inflation is difficult to control once it gets out of hand. It is driven not just by what is happening today but also by expectations about the economy's conditions and government policies in the future. Just peoples' belief that the government may resort to monetary financing of public debt in the future can drive up inflation expectations and lead to a spike in current inflation, even if there are absolutely no changes in policies today. This is where the central bank's credibility in fighting inflation, irrespective of the economic and political consequences of the policies needed to do that, becomes crucial. If a central bank is seen as being the lackey of the government, willing to print money to finance government debts, then inflation expectations can become "unanchored," a relatively innocuous-sounding expression that belies the damaging consequences of high and spiraling inflation.

Another concern is that once a government defaults on some of its real obligations by engineering an inflation spike or by getting investors to accept a loss on their bond holdings, then savers and investors are going to be less willing to lend to that government. This reluctance will drive up interest rates and the costs to the government of issuing debt in the future. Of course, such defaults have happened in the past. For instance, the U.S. government partially defaulted on the war bonds it issued during World War I. Clearly, financial markets' memory does not go back too far, and U.S. government bonds are now considered among the safest investments.

Sharing the Pain with Foreign Investors

Politically, it would be far easier for a government to rely on inflation to reduce its debt obligations if the debt were owned by foreigners. In that case, a spike in inflation would hurt all holders of government bonds, but the pain would be assuaged, as some of it would be shared with foreign investors.

Not many countries are in the fortunate position of being able to shift the cost of default on sovereign debt to investors from abroad. Here again, the U.S. is special. Figure 6-5 shows how much government net debt of the major reserve currency economies is owned by foreign investors. In this part of the analysis, I focus only on central government debt, as local and state government debt is usually not favored by foreign official investors. In the case of the U.S., foreign investors—both official and private—hold about $5.6 trillion of public debt (as of December 2012),

FIGURE 6-5. Ownership of Net Government Debt: Japan, U.K., and U.S.

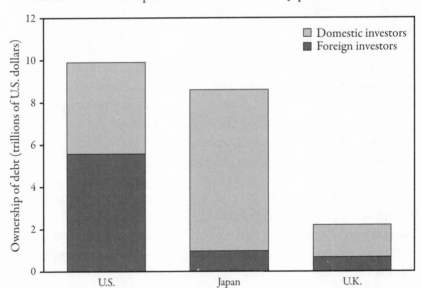

Data sources: U.S. Treasury Department; Bank of Japan; U.K. Office of Debt Management.
Notes: Data shown are for December 2012. For the U.S., the net debt concept used here is "privately held debt," which excludes intragovernmental debt holdings as well as the Fed's holdings of Treasury securities. See the Notes section (page 336) for more details on the data.

amounting to 56 percent of the outstanding stock of net public debt, excluding the holdings of the Federal Reserve. Foreign official investors account for $4 trillion, roughly three-quarters of those holdings.

The share of foreign ownership is lower for the U.K.—about one-third of its net debt is held by foreign investors—and even lower—just 11 percent —for Japan, which has a high domestic savings rate. About one-third of Switzerland's debt is held by foreign investors (not shown in this figure, as the size of its debt stock is quite small).

Foreign ownership of euro zone debt is harder to estimate because of extensive cross-national holdings within the euro zone itself. IMF data indicate that about half of the gross debt of euro zone countries is held by foreigners, with France and Germany having foreign ownership ratios of their debt of nearly 60 percent. However, the IMF estimates that about one-quarter of the outstanding debt of all euro zone countries together is held by other euro zone residents outside the issuing country. Only the remaining quarter is held by residents outside the euro zone. The ECB estimates an even lower figure for foreign ownership of euro zone debt, just 17 percent.

The conclusion is that, in terms of both absolute magnitudes and relative shares, the U.S. relies more on foreign financing of its debt than other major reserve currency economies.

The implication of the high share of foreign ownership of U.S. Treasury debt is that, if the U.S. were to inflate away some of the real value of its debt obligations, foreign investors would share about half of the burden along with domestic investors. This leaves foreign investors, including foreign central banks, considerably exposed to U.S. inflation and other risks related to the buildup of debt in the U.S. And yet, no doubt fully aware of the risks they are taking, these investors continue to buy Treasury debt.

Figure 6-6 shows the extent to which investors from outside the U.S. finance its debt accumulation. The figure shows annual increases in the stock of net debt that is privately held and corresponding increases in the amount of this debt held by such investors. Foreign investors have clearly played an important role in the financing of U.S. debt, especially in the huge buildup of U.S. public debt starting in 2008. From the end of 2007 through the end of 2012, privately held U.S. Treasury debt rose by $5.5 trillion. Foreign investors financed $3.3 trillion, or three-fifths, of this increase.

FIGURE 6-6. Foreign Financing of Privately Held U.S. Federal Government Debt

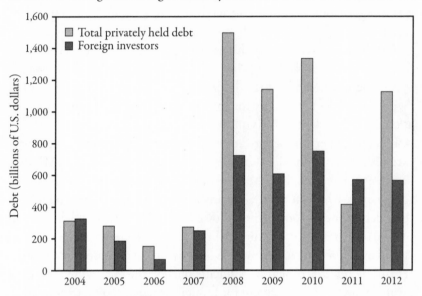

Data source: U.S. Treasury Bulletin, September 2013.

Notes: Each bar denotes changes in privately held debt—the total level and the level accounted for by foreign investors—calculated as the change in end-of-year debt stocks (as reported in columns (3) and (11) in Table OFS-2 of data source). Privately held debt excludes Treasury securities held by government agencies and the Fed. Foreign financing in a given year can exceed total annual debt financing (as in 2011) if domestic investors reduce their holdings of Treasury securities in that year.

A Calculated Risk: Domestic Investors Share in the Pain

Are foreign investors letting themselves be willingly duped? They might in fact be taking a calculated risk rather than a foolish one. The political economy implications of the ownership structure of the U.S. public debt are interesting. That more than half of net privately held debt is owned by foreigners certainly makes it a lot less painful for the U.S. to inflate away the value of its debt. At the same time, the remaining portion that is held by domestic investors is a sizable amount of over $4 trillion. Figure 6-7 provides a breakdown of the domestic holdings of net privately held debt in the U.S. The main domestic investors include pension funds (who hold 20 percent), mutual funds (20 percent), financial institutions (14 percent), state and local governments (11 percent), and households and other investors (35 percent).

FIGURE 6-7. Domestic Ownership of Privately Held
U.S. Federal Government Debt, 2012

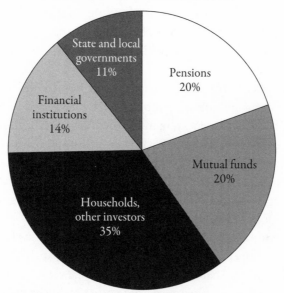

Data source: Table OFS-2 (Ownership of Federal Securities), U.S. Treasury Bulletin, June 2013.
Notes: Data shown are for December 2012. The category "Pensions" covers private pension funds as well as state and local government pensions. Private pensions include U.S. Treasury securities held by the Federal Employees Retirement System Thrift Savings Plan G Fund. The category "Mutual funds" covers money market mutual funds, mutual funds, and closed-end investment companies. The category "Financial institutions" covers insurance companies and depository institutions, which include U.S. chartered depository institutions, foreign banking offices in the U.S., banks in U.S.-affiliated areas, credit unions, and bank holding companies. The category "Households, other investors" covers individuals, government-sponsored enterprises, brokers and dealers, bank personal trusts and estates, corporate and noncorporate businesses, and other investors. U.S. savings bonds are also included in this category.

Treasury securities constitute an important part of individual investment portfolios, either directly or through mutual funds and pension funds. They are also disproportionately represented in the portfolios of investors who have a low tolerance for risk. Retirees and those approaching retirement tend to be more conservative in their investment choices, preferring safety and a low return rather than risky investments. For instance, consider the popular life cycle funds offered by companies, such as Fidelity and Vanguard. These funds automatically adjust investors' portfolios over time until a target date that is usually set to match retirement age. These funds change the balance of investments over time from more risky ones like equities to less risky ones like government debt and high-grade corporate debt issued by corporations that are perceived to be rock-solid and unlikely to default. Such funds usually have 40–50 percent of their investments in these highly rated fixed-income investments by the target date.

These numbers suggest that the domestic holders of Treasury debt are potent voting and lobbying blocs. Older voters tend to have a high propensity to vote. Moreover, many of them live in crucial swing states like Florida that have a disproportionate bearing on the outcomes of U.S. presidential elections. Insurance companies as well as state and local governments would clearly be unhappy about an erosion of the value of their holdings of Treasury securities. These groups have a lot of political clout in Washington.

This situation creates an interesting balance of interests from a political economy perspective. Foreign investors know that they would be on the hook for a major share of the losses in the real value of Treasury debt if the U.S. decided to inflate away some of its real debt obligations. Of course, they would suffer even more than domestic investors from a burst of inflation—through a drop in bond prices (as nominal interest rates are likely to rise if inflation spikes) and a decline in the value of the dollar. Nevertheless, the degree of pain that would also be suffered by domestic holders of Treasury debt, who have considerable political influence, makes it less likely that inflation would be seen as a viable way to reduce public debt.

In short, the profile of domestic holders of U.S. Treasury debt renders it politically difficult to use inflation to pay down the debt. High inflation would not be politically acceptable in the U.S., and it could be difficult to put the inflation genie back in the bottle once it is unleashed.

Even setting aside these political considerations, the economic calculus of inflation as a way to pay down government debt is complicated. An increase in current or expected inflation would raise interest rates, driving up the government's borrowing costs. In June 2013, Treasury bills, which have a maturity of one year or less, amounted to $1.6 trillion. This debt, along with the maturing portion of longer-term Treasury notes and bonds, would have to be refinanced at higher rates. Treasury securities that are directly indexed to inflation (Treasury Inflation-Protected Securities, or TIPS) amounted to $900 billion in June 2013, roughly 9 percent of privately held Treasury debt. Social Security benefits and some other government expenditure programs are also indexed to Consumer Price Index (CPI) inflation. Major parts of the budget, such as Medicare and Medicaid expenditures, are implicitly indexed, as the cost of those services will rise with inflation. All these elements would offset part of the benefit of reducing the inflation-adjusted value of the outstanding debt stock.

These considerations imply that foreign investors are less likely to shy away from turning to U.S. Treasury debt as a safe haven in troubled times.

No Fear of Selective Default

The structure of the U.S. Treasury debt market and the country's legal framework are important to foreign investors as they contemplate this landscape and consider the risks of a default that would be aimed squarely and exclusively at them. Concerns about such a selective default turn out to be unfounded.

Given the size of the Treasury debt market and the volume of trading in that market, it would be enormously challenging to sort out bonds owned by different types of investors. As indicated by the analysis earlier in this chapter, the government does of course report prodigious amounts of information on what types of investors hold Treasury debt. But that information is based on surveys and other reporting tools, rather than on registration of ownership or other direct tracking of bonds' final ownership. The lack of definitive information about the ultimate ownership of Treasury securities makes it technically very difficult for the U.S. government to selectively default on just that portion of debt owned by foreign investors.

Even if these technical constraints could be overcome, the legal framework would come into play. The U.S. government is not legally permitted to discriminate among different types of investors. This is a point of contention among legal scholars, though it appears that legislative action by the U.S. Congress would be needed to permit selective default, and even that might not pass Constitutional muster. Both domestic and foreign investors could take the U.S. government to court in the event of a default. The window of time needed for Congressional actions could make the legal points moot, as foreign investors could quickly unload their holdings, although this could be difficult for major official holders like China and Japan that hold more than a trillion dollars each of Treasury debt.

It is conceivable that the U.S. could directly negotiate with a major official holder of Treasury debt to repudiate some debt obligations to that country. Of course, there is little reason for a foreign country to agree to write off some of its Treasury debt unless it was in its own interest to do so. The U.S. does not have many credible economic levers to pursue such a negotiation. Perhaps there are other levers.

In a November 2011 *New York Times* op-ed titled "To Save Our Economy, Ditch Taiwan," an independent commentator argued that President Obama should negotiate with Chinese leaders to write off the American debt held by China in return for a promise to end American military assistance and arms sales to Taiwan. The commentator perceptively noted that his proposal would be dismissed as being absurd; at least that part of the op-ed was correct, although perhaps not by intention. If the U.S. were to start negotiating over repayment of its debt, investors' confidence in that debt would be shaken.

The conclusion from this analysis is that foreign investors have many layers of protection to prevent them from being singled out for default on their holdings of Treasury debt. In light of the factors discussed earlier, this protection gives them powerful economic incentives to continue financing U.S. debt accumulation.

Must It End?

Individuals have to pay off their college loans, home mortgage, and other loans sooner or later—unless they declare bankruptcy. The reason individuals cannot roll over debt indefinitely is that they will die sooner or later, and there is no easy legal recourse for a creditor to go after the borrower's heirs (except if the deceased has left an estate or if the debt is jointly held with survivors). In contrast, countries do not usually die off, and their debts can last into perpetuity. There is a set of circumstances in which the rest of the world can continue financing U.S. debt accumulation forever.

The rate at which a country's debt level changes depends on four factors —the existing level of debt, the inflation-adjusted (real) interest rate, the growth rate of the economy, and the primary budget balance (which is the difference between government revenues and expenditures excluding interest payments on the debt). The debt stock rises when the interest rate is higher than the growth rate; that is, the economy is not growing and generating resources at the same rate at which interest payments are accumulating on the debt. When the primary budget balance is positive, so the government is raising more revenues than it spends, the debt stock declines, as the extra revenues can be used to pay down debt.

This simple formula has powerful implications. If the U.S. government can borrow cheaply—at near zero rates in inflation-adjusted terms—while its economy grows at 2–3 percent per year, then the U.S. can actually run a persistent primary budget deficit without increasing its debt to GDP ratio. To finance this deficit, the U.S. may owe increasing amounts of debt to the rest of the world, and other countries could well be loath to finance U.S. deficits forever. But technically, there is no reason the U.S. has to actually pay off its debt obligations.

For a country like Greece, this formula delivers a triple whammy. As the debt crisis unfolded, Greece faced high borrowing costs, and its growth rate turned negative. In addition, Greece was running a primary budget deficit. Small wonder that the Greek debt situation looked unsustainable and will clearly be difficult to pull out from, as every element of the formula needs to be fixed to put debt on a sustainable path.

Of course, the implications of continually rising debt levels and their sustainability depend to a large extent on whether these debts are financed from domestic savings or by foreign investors. That the private savings rate in Japan is high and savers seem willing to invest in Japanese government bonds has made it easier for that country to finance large budget deficits and build up an enormous level of debt without concerns about debt vulnerability. In contrast, the U.S. is more exposed to the whims of foreign investors, as its domestic savings rate is rather low.

Uncle Sam Is Very Special

The U.S., it turns out, is even more special than the data have suggested so far. To a large extent, its foreign liabilities are in the form of fixed-income investments. Portfolio debt and bank loans, which involve fixed interest payments irrespective of the state of the debtor country's economy, account for 55 percent of its external liabilities and only 31 percent of its external assets. The composition of U.S. investments abroad is quite different from that of foreign investments in the U.S. FDI and portfolio equity, which tend to be riskier but allow an investor to share in the upside potential if things should pan out well, account for half of U.S. external assets. Such investments typically have higher expected returns on average, given that they are riskier. Thus, on average, the U.S. should be earning higher returns on its foreign investments than it has had to pay to foreigners for their investments in the U.S.

However, the evidence supporting this hypothesis is not clear cut. Pierre-Olivier Gourinchas of the University of California, Berkeley, and Hélène Rey of the London Business School found evidence in favor of this hypothesis. They also argued that the reason for higher returns earned by U.S. investors relative to foreign investors was only partially due to the different composition of U.S. foreign assets and liabilities. Strikingly, they found that U.S. investors were earning better returns on every category of investments—bonds, stocks, and loans—than investors from abroad were making on their U.S. investments. Francis Warnock of the University of Virginia and his various co-authors have contested those results, arguing that they are based on a misinterpretation of the data. Warnock's research concludes that U.S. investors typically do not earn much higher returns than do foreign investors in specific investment categories.

Even setting aside the distribution of its external assets and liabilities among different classes of investments, the U.S. is in a favorable position in terms of the currency composition of its assets and liabilities. Its liabilities are all denominated in dollars, which is certainly convenient for the country that prints dollars. U.S. external assets are mostly denominated in those of foreign currencies, which means that U.S. investors are exposed to the risk of a decline in the value of their investments if other currencies were to depreciate against the dollar.

But what would happen if foreign investors were to pull their money out of the U.S., leading to a sharp *fall* in the exchange rate of the dollar relative to other currencies? The value of U.S. liabilities would not fall. But the value of its assets would go up in dollar terms. Thus, the U.S. would make a one-time windfall gain from the fall in its currency's value. Such is the benefit of the exorbitant privilege enjoyed by the world's dominant reserve currency.

Creditor Pays Up, Debtor Rakes It In

The irony of the situation is highlighted by looking at patterns of net investment income. This is the difference between a country's earnings on its investments abroad and foreigners' earnings on their investments in that country. Given China's status as a net creditor to the world, with its foreign assets exceeding its foreign liabilities by $1.7 trillion, these earnings should be significant. Instead, in 2012, China had a net investment income of *minus* $57 billion. In other words, it paid out far more to foreign investors than it earned on its investments abroad. In contrast, the U.S., a net debtor to the tune of $4.4 trillion, had a *positive* net investment income of $206 billion.

The year 2012 was hardly special. For most of the past decade, China has had a negative or barely positive net investment income, while the U.S. has had a large positive income flow. Germany and Japan have positive net investment income flows as well, but that is as it should be, because both countries are net creditors.

China's overseas investments have generated puny returns partly because foreign exchange reserves held in low-yielding advanced economy bonds constitute a large share of its foreign assets. These returns have also been hurt by the appreciation of the renminbi relative to the U.S. dollar and other advanced economy currencies. This is a discomfiting situation for China, as its investment income position looks feeble by any measure, even as it builds up an increasingly large foreign asset position.

Some authors contend that the positive U.S. income flows indicate that its investments abroad are undercounted—perhaps such investments should take into account not just exports of financial capital but also technology. Additionally, when such investors as emerging market central banks invest in U.S. Treasuries, they are willing to accept a low rate of return because of the liquidity and insurance value of those investments. The ability to provide those services to foreign investors is an intangible asset of the U.S. and highlights the privileged position of its currency.

Some (Temporary) Compensation from the U.S.

The U.S. does not just extract an exorbitant privilege. It actually does provide a buffer to the rest of the world in bad times, partly because the

U.S. has made more risky investments in which it has an equity share. Because its portfolio of external assets is riskier, while its external liabilities are dominated by fixed-income investments, the U.S. bears a greater burden of the loss when a global crisis hits all economies and their stock markets. During the recent financial crisis, the structure of U.S. external assets and liabilities, as well as the dollar's strength, led to a huge "wealth transfer" from the U.S. to the rest of the world. Pierre-Olivier Gourinchas and Hélène Rey, along with Kai Truempler of the London Business School, estimate that, between the last quarter of 2007 and the first quarter of 2009, the U.S. transferred about $2.2 trillion to the rest of the world.

How did this transfer happen? First of all, as noted earlier, panicky investors in search of a sanctuary poured money into U.S. government bonds. These massive capital inflows led to a sharp appreciation of the dollar against virtually every other currency. Following the logic laid out earlier in the chapter, the dollar value of U.S. liabilities remained the same while the dollar value of its external assets plummeted due to the depreciation of foreign currencies. Moreover, as interest rates in the U.S. fell sharply because of the surge in demand for Treasury bonds, thereby driving up their price, the value of foreign investors' holdings of those bonds increased. Meanwhile, with equity markets tumbling worldwide, the value of U.S. investments abroad fell sharply, a decline that was accentuated by the depreciation of foreign currencies.

Oddly enough, there were no celebrations on the streets of Beijing or São Paulo for having finally stuck it to the Yankees. The reason of course is that this massive "transfer" was on paper only, and the lucky winners were in no position to cash out. All they could do was hold on to their U.S. investments until global financial markets stabilized, which then also led to the U.S. dollar once again falling in value and reversing much of this short-term transfer.

We Hate You Guys

Luo Ping, a senior official at the China Banking Regulatory Commission, is a rarity among Chinese officials—a jovial character who speaks his mind freely and in plain colloquial English. At a global risk management convention in New York in February 2009, he was asked whether China would continue buying U.S. Treasuries and whether Beijing was concerned about the U.S. debt situation. His response was sharp and forth-right as always: "We hate you guys. Once you start issuing $1 trillion–$2 trillion . . . we know the dollar is going to depreciate, so we hate you guys but there is nothing much we can do." He added that China had lit-tle choice but to continue buying Treasuries despite misgivings about the state of U.S. public finances. "Except for U.S. Treasuries, what can you hold? Gold? You do not hold Japanese government bonds or UK bonds. U.S. Treasuries are the safe haven. For everyone, including China, it is the only option." Luo was articulating the pain of Chinese officials ensnared in the dollar trap, with no easy way out.

As the financial crisis intensified, China's holdings of U.S. govern-ment debt, particularly debt in the financially troubled government-sponsored enterprises (GSEs), such as Fannie Mae and Freddie Mac, were a source of consternation and worry among officials and the pub-lic in China. Various Chinese commentators and academics proposed schemes for the U.S. government to provide guarantees to the Chinese government that there would be no losses on its investments in Treasury or GSE securities. At a press conference held on March 13, 2009, at the end of the National People's Congress, Premier Wen Jiabao specifically addressed this issue. He was quoted as saying "we are certainly con-cerned about the security of our assets" and later added "I am a little concerned."

A confidential communication from the U.S. embassy in Beijing noted that such comments were not new but that they had not previ-ously been expressed so directly and at such a senior level. But the embas-sy's view was that Beijing would not, or could not, act on its concerns in any meaningful way:

> China's leaders are aware that, while they can purchase more or fewer USD-denominated assets at their margin, their holdings are so enormous that they cannot reallocate the currency compo-sition of their portfolio to any meaningful extent without leading to large capital losses and thus further public—and internal—criticism.

The report also went on to note that the U.S. government's intervention in Fannie Mae and Freddie Mac effectively guaranteed the claims of senior creditors, "the largest of which is most likely SAFE" (the State Administration for Foreign Exchange).

The following extract, taken from an unclassified U.S. embassy summary of a meeting between two senior U.S. Congressmen and the Chinese Minister of Commerce Chen Deming on May 31, 2009, clearly and succinctly sums up China's quandary as seen from the American perspective:

> Chen offered his views on China's purchase of U.S. Treasury bills as a means to invest its U.S. trade surplus. Chen said China "must" buy U.S. Treasuries because insufficient depth exists in Japanese yen- and Euro-denominated debt. If China were to make larger purchases in these markets, it might raise their prices dramatically. In addition, as total worldwide gold production is only 2400 tons per year, it would be impossible for China to purchase sufficient gold reserves. "So the only way for China is to continue to buy T-bills," he concluded.

The U.S. embassy staff's sanguine view that China was locked into its U.S. dollar investments would be put to the test soon thereafter, as trade tensions between the two countries were about to flare up anew.

A Rhetorical Threat

On September 11, 2009, the U.S. announced that it would impose tariffs on Chinese tire imports. The public reaction from Chinese officials was strident, but through back channels they indicated a willingness to sort out trade-related issues away from the media glare. In contrast to this restraint, there was an outpouring of visceral anti-American sentiment among China's netizens, with many press articles and commentators whipping up this sentiment further by calling on their government to retaliate by selling U.S. Treasury bonds.

As word of this threat reached Washington, where concerns about the ballooning U.S. public debt were at a fever pitch, the U.S. embassy in Beijing sought to reassure Washington that it was an empty threat. They sent a confidential assessment of the situation that included a sardonic reference to China being mired in a trap:

> Many bloggers and commentators have suggested that China sell U.S. treasury bonds to protest the 421 tire decision. . . . We have

absolutely no indication that either the Chinese government or large investors are considering this option; not only would it be extremely difficult for reserve managers to find alternative investments, but a large sell-off of treasuries would cause a dramatic drop in the value of the Chinese government's holdings. At most, this incident has again highlighted China's continued uncomfortable (an [*sic*] unavoidable) reliance on U.S. Treasuries to absorb its massive foreign exchange reserves; it remains to be seen whether this will help spur real rebalancing with a goal of reducing reserve accumulation, or just additional inadequate schemes to try to "diversify" China's investments.

The issue of potential losses on holdings of U.S. Treasuries remains an acutely delicate problem for the Chinese government. There is a palpable sense among many Chinese citizens that reserves are accumulated by the toil of Chinese workers and that these resources are then used to finance the profligate spending of U.S. consumers rather than for domestic development. To address rising anger voiced in internet comments that China is being taken for a ride by the U.S., SAFE posted an extensive Q&A on its website in July 2011. Here is a sample:

Q: According to a report by the U.S. Department of the Treasury, China is the largest holder of U.S. Treasury bonds. Lately, credit rating agencies, including Standard & Poor's, Moody's, and Fitch, have repeatedly issued warnings about the U.S. debt problem. In the case of a USD depreciation and a future rise in inflation in the U.S., is it a growing risk to hold such a large sum of U.S. Treasury bonds? Will this sum be reduced in the future?

A: U.S. Treasury bonds are both a reflection of the credibility of the U.S. government and a critical variety of investment for U.S. and international institutional investors.... We have noted the latest views expressed by Standard & Poor's and other rating companies regarding the credit rating of the U.S. sovereign debt, and we expect that the U.S. government will take responsible policy measures to boost the confidence of

the international financial market and respect and guarantee
the interests of its investors.

Diversification of foreign exchange reserves through sovereign wealth
funds is also a challenging proposition when large amounts of money are
involved. Consider China's sovereign wealth fund—the CIC. At the end
of 2011, it had $482 billion in assets. About 15 percent of its assets was in
government bonds and government agency bonds, presumably mostly in
U.S. securities. In early 2013, CIC Chairman Lou Jiwei was quoted as
saying that although U.S. Treasuries were "still a safe asset at the moment,"
he was trying to reduce his fund's "over-reliance" on U.S. debt. However,
he noted that it would hurt the fund's ability to manage risk if it stopped
buying U.S. Treasuries altogether and added "If we buy it, over the long
term, it's not a good asset. So our approach is limited buying." CIC is
probably equally caught in the dollar's web on its other investments. For
instance, its public equities portfolio accounted for about 25 percent of
its total assets, and a large share of that portfolio, more than 40 percent,
was invested in North America.

A French Connection

There is a historical precedent to the bind that China finds itself in on
account of its massive foreign exchange reserves. Olivier Accominotti of
the London School of Economics has argued that, in the interwar period
from 1928 to 1936, the Banque de France was caught in a "sterling trap." In
1926, the French government attempted to fix the value of its currency,
the French franc, relative to sterling and the dollar. From 1926 to 1928,
France accumulated a large stock of foreign exchange reserves as it sought
to keep the franc from appreciating because of trade surpluses and repa-
triation of capital that had flown out of the country in prior years when
the franc was beset by crises. By 1928, the British pound sterling was the
dominant currency in France's reserve portfolio, which in turn accounted
for more than half of the world's foreign exchange reserves.

In his memoirs, Émile Moreau, Governor of the Banque de France
from 1926 to 1930, characterized the dilemma he faced on account of the
franc's strength relative to the sterling. Recounting the difficulty he faced
during his time in office, he wrote: "we are obliged to use purely techni-

cal means to fight speculation on the rise of the franc. The Bank of France will attempt to restrict the credits put at the disposal of speculators on foreign markets." In other words, the Banque de France would fight back against attempts to push up the value of the franc and try to cut off funding to speculators who were considered responsible.

Moreau then honed in on the problem he faced—the currency on the other side was weak and could not hold its own against the franc:

> Here, unfortunately, the problem of sterling crops up. The English monetary system is so fragile and the stability of the pound so tenuous that the British currency is in danger of being shaken by the display of strength our enormous sterling credits in London allow us. This is what Mr. Montagu Norman, governor of the Bank of England, came to explain to me.

Between June 1928 and September 1931, the Banque de France sold nearly two-thirds of its sterling portfolio and moved into dollars. Over the next two years, it liquidated its foreign exchange reserves portfolio and switched almost entirely to holdings of gold. This process was not smooth. The Banque de France started reducing its holdings of sterling as that currency came under pressure to depreciate, but those very actions worsened the pressures on the sterling.

In late 1930 and early 1931, the French in fact briefly intervened to support the sterling, as they wanted to keep that currency from falling further, in the hope of stabilizing its value and reducing the losses from their sales of sterling securities. Given the sterling's poor credibility and the sheer volume of sterling reserves it held, the Banque de France could not maintain this risky and expensive strategy for long. Eventually, it stopped supporting the sterling and liquidated its entire position in a short period. This happened as the value of the sterling was collapsing, resulting in large losses that put the Banque de France into technical bankruptcy and required a government rescue.

This historical episode is sobering for China to consider as it contemplates the trap it has ensnared itself in. The PBC faces the prospect of significant losses on its reserve portfolio if it were to try to disentangle itself from the trap through any precipitous actions to shift out of the dollar. The PBC is a part of China's government, and any such losses would be absorbed by the government. Thus, the PBC's balance sheet position and the implications of such losses for its net worth are not in themselves the major concern. Nevertheless, the political fallout could be ugly if the Chinese public learned of the magnitude of these losses, which would be seen as a transfer of wealth to the U.S. China now has a strong incentive to support the dollar's value, limiting its losses for the time being but at the cost of getting even more entangled in the dollar's sticky web.

The Web Tightens

China is hardly an exception. The U.S. has drawn foreign investors, especially emerging market central banks, into the web of its Treasury debt. And now they cannot easily escape. The U.S. Federal Reserve has tightened this web further. Given its status as the home of the principal global reserve currency, the U.S. has also been able to hold foreign countries captive through its monetary policy actions. When the U.S. floods the global financial system with money, other countries face two unappealing choices. They can either let their currencies appreciate relative to the dollar, or they can buy U.S. debt to tamp down this appreciation. If they allow their currencies to appreciate, their exports become less competitive, and they take a loss on the value of the dollar-denominated debt that they already hold. If they buy dollars to limit appreciation, they would have to further increase their holdings of U.S. Treasury securities and take a loss on those when the dollar eventually depreciates.

So the choice the U.S. offers to the rest of the world is simple: you get to choose when to take a loss on your holdings of our debt—now or later. Faced with this stark choice between two evils, many emerging markets end up being boxed in to maintain export growth by accepting the unpleasant trade-off of a loss on their reserve holdings in the future. The choices they have made—intervening in foreign exchange markets and accumulating reserves as a self-insurance mechanism—have only fueled U.S. fiscal profligacy and strengthened the dollar's leading role in the global monetary system.

Small wonder that policymakers in emerging markets are frustrated and want to fight back with any measures they can muster. And fight back they have, with an open declaration of currency wars.

PART THREE

Inadequate Institutions

Currency Wars

That men would die was a matter of necessity; which men would die, though, was a matter of circumstance, and Yossarian was willing to be the victim of anything but circumstance. But that was war. Just about all he could find in its favor was that it paid well and liberated children from the pernicious influence of their parents.

Catch-22, Joseph Heller

In the fall of 2010, Brazil was reeling from a sharp currency appreciation and was caught in a pincer-like grip between two big economic powers. On one side, the Chinese were not permitting their currency to appreciate and were trying to deflect capital inflows. Because Brazil's exports of commodities such as iron ore and soybeans are largely tied to China's growth performance, the Brazilian currency, the real, had become a "proxy play" on the renminbi. Investors were in effect betting that strong growth in China would boost growth in Brazil as well, lifting the value of the real. On the other side were the Americans, whose central bank was pumping money into the economy, keeping interest rates low, and setting off expectations of dollar depreciation. The Fed's actions were making it easier for investors to get cheap financing that they could use to make bets on currencies that they expected would appreciate in value, including the real.

From the beginning of that year through the early fall, the Brazilian real had risen in value by about 25 percent relative to the U.S. dollar, making the real one of the strongest performing currencies in the world. A strong currency is a mixed blessing. It makes imports cheaper and raises the purchasing power of residents. In contrast, manufacturers and exporters were howling at the huge hit to the competitiveness of their products in markets around the world, including in Brazil itself. They faced two unwelcome choices. They could raise the foreign prices of their products to meet their labor, material, and other costs, all of which still had to be paid in reais, while their revenues were falling in terms of reais (reais is the plural form of the real; an appreciation means fewer reais per unit of foreign currency). This action would mean a loss in market share to producers from other countries, especially China, whose products would be cheaper. The other equally unpleasant alternative was to change foreign prices only moderately and, instead, take a hit on their profit margins.

On September 27, 2010, Brazil's finance minister Guido Mantega took the stage at an event in São Paulo, where he spoke to the country's industrial leaders ahead of presidential elections that weekend. Frustrated by the complications caused for Brazil by the policies of other countries, he used these words to characterize the situation as he saw it: "We are in the midst of an international currency war, a general weakening of currency. This threatens us because it takes away our competitiveness."

The martial allegory struck a chord, perfectly capturing the sense that currency management had become a tool of international economic warfare rather than just a matter of domestic policy. Headlines in all the major newspapers followed and crystallized anger about U.S. monetary policy, as the Fed was seen as impervious to the fallout of its actions on the rest of the world. Mantega had neatly summarized the sense of conflict, but the issue had been brewing for a while. It would dominate the discussions in the weeks leading up to the next meeting of world leaders at the Summit of the Group of 20 (G-20), a forum for the major advanced and emerging market economies.

Timing Is Everything

The Korean government was proud to host the November 2010 G-20 Summit, the first country outside the major advanced economies to host this august gathering of world leaders. The government had made extensive preparations and, with the help of many committees and high-caliber academic advisors, had come up with a plan to put its stamp on the world of global finance. The hosts were eager to do this by steering the G-20 away from short-term crisis management, now that the worst of the financial crisis was over, and bringing long-term issues to the fore. The theme of the summit would be the development of "global safety nets." These were to include a set of mechanisms to reduce emerging markets' need to self-insure by building up foreign exchange reserves and improved programs at the global financial institutions to assist countries in need of assistance, without a raft of intrusive conditions attached to the loans.

A couple of months before the summit, which was set for November 11–12 in Seoul, these grand plans started to fall apart.

The U.S. Federal Reserve had been worried about the anemic pace of growth in the U.S. economy and, with unemployment stubbornly stuck in the range of 9.5–10 percent, felt that it was not delivering on its dual mandate—maximum employment consistent with price stability. Fed Chairman Ben Bernanke indicated in his speech at the Jackson Hole conference on August 27, 2010, that the Fed was ready to consider additional monetary stimulus measures if the economy stayed weak.

Then, with spectacularly bad timing from the point of view of international diplomacy, Quantitative Easing Round 2—or QE2—was announced on November 3, about a week before the Seoul summit. QE2 involved printing money to buy $600 billion worth of long-term Treasury bonds with the intention of driving up their prices and, consequently, driving down long-term interest rates. This followed on the heels of QE1, which lasted from November 2008 through March 2010 and during which the Fed purchased a total of $1.25 trillion of mortgage-backed securities and $175 billion of the debt of government-sponsored enterprises, such as Fannie Mae and Freddie Mac.

Bernanke's speech was carefully parsed in the U.S. and abroad. He had noted that net exports were not likely to add much to U.S. economic growth in the short term. The words "currency" and "depreciation" were hardly mentioned in the speech. This was to make the point that the objective of QE2 was not to boost exports by driving down the value of the dollar but rather to stoke domestic consumption and investment by holding down borrowing costs for households and businesses.

The rest of the world saw things differently. The reaction to the speech was swift and furious. China issued the call to arms right away, claiming the U.S. was causing problems for the rest of the world by recklessly printing money. Chinese Vice Finance Minister Zhu Guangyao was quoted as saying that the U.S. Federal Reserve's decision to pump $600 billion into the economy might "shock" emerging markets by flooding them with capital. He added that the U.S. "has not fully taken into consideration the shock of excessive capital flows to the financial stability of emerging markets." Many other emerging markets lined up on China's side as they were experiencing a tidal wave of inflows. These inflows were adding to the domestic money supply in these countries and complicating their own fight against inflation. In the lead-up to the Seoul G-20 summit, all talk of safety nets was cast aside, and the subject of currency wars began to shape up as the main issue for discussion.

Shifting Alliances

The situation became even more peculiar when Germany and China struck up an alliance on this issue. Why did Germany line up with China? After all, since June 2005, when the renminbi was depegged from the dollar, the renminbi had appreciated by only 7 percent relative to the euro, a lot less than the renminbi's appreciation of nearly 20 percent versus the dollar. So Europe ought to have been even more forceful than the U.S. in its complaints about Chinese currency policy. Germany, it turns out, was largely protecting its interests rather than those of the euro zone.

The German economy is heavily reliant on exports, which amount to 58 percent of GDP (net exports, or exports minus imports, account for about 6 percent of GDP). Outside Europe, China has now become the biggest market for German products, including machinery and equipment, where German industry has been highly competitive relative to other exporters. German export competitiveness has certainly been helped by the euro's weakness but is largely the product of labor market and other reforms undertaken in the past decade that boosted manufacturing sector productivity. Access to China's markets is therefore more important for Germany than what China does with its currency.

Another factor was that in late October 2010—just a few weeks prior to the Seoul summit—the U.S. Treasury had proposed a set of "indicative guidelines" to help the IMF in its task of monitoring and evaluating global current account imbalances. The idea was that a country running a current account balance—either a surplus or deficit—above 4 percent of GDP should have its policies scrutinized carefully, as it was likely to be contributing to global imbalances and could need some policy adjustments. The number seemed to have been chosen carefully to target China —the U.S. and the U.K. were expected to have current account deficits of about 3 percent in 2010, whereas China's current account surplus was forecast to be about 5 percent. In targeting China, however, the

U.S. ensnared Germany as well. Germany had a current account surplus of 6 percent of GDP in 2008 and 2009, with a similar level expected for 2010. Germany has been rather sensitive about its current account surplus, a good part of which is accounted for by exports to the rest of Europe.

Rankled by U.S. actions to set a quantitative monitoring indicator for current account balances and feeling blindsided because the Germans had not been adequately consulted on the matter, German finance minister Wolfgang Schäuble entered headlong into the fray. He went on the offensive against the U.S., referring to the Fed's action as "clueless" and comparing the Fed's policies to China's currency policy, arguing that both would worsen imbalances. His subsequent remarks to *Der Spiegel* magazine were quoted widely. Referring to the Fed, he said:

> They make a reasonable balance between industrial and developing countries more difficult and they undermine the credibility of the US in finance policymaking. . . . It is not consistent when the Americans accuse the Chinese of exchange rate manipulation and then steer the dollar exchange rate artificially lower with the help of their [central bank's] printing press.

This was not the sort of reaction the U.S. had anticipated, especially from a country it considered an ally in economic matters.

Kick in the Backside Rather Than a Pat on the Back

One could fault Bernanke for bad timing and a tin ear, but he was doing what every central banker is hired to do, which is to adopt policies meant to deliver on his institution's domestic mandate. The negative reaction from other countries came as a surprise to the Fed, which perhaps expected a small pat on the back rather than recriminations for doing everything in its power to spur growth in the U.S. economy. What was good for the U.S. was surely good for the world, as it would do no one any favors if the world's largest economy remained in deep-seated malaise. The U.S. Treasury took a similar view and was no doubt glad the Fed had acted, particularly since fiscal policy was severely constrained by the already-enormous deficit and political pushback from the Republican-controlled Congress.

The U.S. delegation faced an added awkwardness at the Seoul summit as it was being berated by other delegations for the Fed's actions that were seen as irresponsible and willfully damaging to other countries' growth prospects. President Barack Obama and Treasury Secretary Timothy Geithner were in the uncomfortable position of taking the heat but were unable to forcefully defend the Fed's actions. In the U.S., there is a long and honorable tradition of the White House and especially the Treasury not commenting on or openly seeking to influence the Fed's policymaking. This is not just for appearances but is viewed as crucial for the Fed's credibility as an independent institution that is not subject to short-term political pressures. The reticence on the part of the U.S. delegation only emboldened China to rally other emerging markets around its position and push even harder against the U.S.

The currency war had taken over the Seoul G-20 summit and, to the intense frustration of the hosts, discussion of global safety nets and other longer-term issues receded into the background. The public war of words led to the usual drama about the wording of the communiqué—an official statement to be issued at the end of the summit—which would summarize the leaders' views on various matters. Some emerging markets wanted strong language about the risks being caused by the expansionary policies of the Fed, whereas many advanced economies, especially Canada and the U.S., were pushing for China and other emerging markets to be berated for not permitting their currencies to appreciate.

On currency issues, the final G-20 communiqué split the difference between advanced and emerging market economies. The relevant part of the communiqué pinned the blame roughly equally on both groups of countries, although in language that was couched in terms of both groups committing to better policies in the future:

> We will move toward more market-determined exchange rate systems and enhance exchange rate flexibility to reflect underlying economic fundamentals and refrain from competitive devaluation of currencies. Advanced economies, including those with reserve currencies, will be vigilant against excess volatility and disorderly movements in exchange rates. Together these actions will help mitigate the risk of excessive volatility in capital flows facing some emerging market economies.

As for the much-hyped issue of global safety nets, the conciliatory words inserted into the communiqué could barely disguise the lack of progress or even a strong desire to push forward with the agenda:

> Building on the achievements made to date on strengthening global financial safety nets, we need to do further work to improve our capacity to cope with future crises. . . . We agreed to explore ways to further improve the international monetary system. . . . We asked the IMF to deepen its work on all aspects of the international monetary system, including capital flow volatility. We look forward to reviewing further analysis and proposals over the next year.

In the world of international economic policy, asking the IMF to "deepen its work" on something indicates that there is some disagreement on the problem and considerable disagreement on possible solutions. Nevertheless, even asking the IMF to look into capital flow volatility was a signal that the emerging markets were beginning to shift the terrain of the debate to address their concerns about the dangers of unfettered capital flows.

Fighting Back with Rhetoric

Backed into a corner and under considerable international pressure, the U.S. felt it had to fight back. With the U.S. Treasury constrained in how aggressively it could wade into monetary policy matters, it would be up to the Federal Reserve to lead the charge. The task fell to the mild-mannered but battle-hardened Ben Bernanke, fresh from his duels with the U.S. Congress over steps taken to manage the financial crisis at home.

One week after the Seoul summit, Bernanke fired back at international critics of the Fed's quantitative easing policies. On November 18, 2010, he delivered a speech on "Rebalancing the Global Recovery" at a central banking conference in Frankfurt. He acknowledged that the Fed's actions might have increased capital flows to emerging markets, complicating their domestic policy management. But he argued that the Fed's actions were at most one contributing factor among many:

To a large degree, these capital flows have been driven by perceived return differentials that favor emerging markets, resulting
from factors such as stronger expected growth—both in the short
term and in the longer run—and higher interest rates, which
reflect differences in policy settings as well as other forces. . . .
[E]ven before the crisis, fast-growing emerging market economies
were attractive destinations for cross-border investment.

He then took direct aim at emerging markets, arguing that they had
only themselves to blame for the surges in capital inflows they were
experiencing:

beyond these fundamental factors, an important driver of the
rapid capital inflows to some emerging markets is incomplete
adjustment of exchange rates in those economies, which leads
investors to anticipate additional returns arising from expected
exchange rate appreciation.

The exchange rate adjustment is incomplete, in part, because
the authorities in some emerging market economies have intervened in foreign exchange markets to prevent or slow the appreciation of their currencies. . . . It is striking that, amid all the
concerns about renewed private capital inflows to the emerging
market economies, total capital, on net, is still flowing from
relatively labor-abundant emerging market economies to capital-
abundant advanced economies.

In the same speech, Bernanke then laid out clearly and succinctly the
U.S. view of how the world ought to work and what was the main obstacle
to smooth adjustment in international financial markets. He first set out
his analysis of what would happen if all countries' exchange rates were
fully flexible. In that case, advanced economies would loosen monetary
policy to support growth and fight deflation, whereas emerging markets
would tighten monetary policy to prevent overheating and inflation.
Higher interest rates in emerging markets would pull in more capital
inflows, leading to appreciation of their currencies. Bernanke argued this
was a good thing, even for the emerging markets themselves:

This currency appreciation would in turn tend to reduce net exports and current account surpluses in the emerging markets, thus helping cool these rapidly growing economies while adding to demand in the advanced economies. Moreover, currency appreciation would help shift a greater proportion of domestic output toward satisfying domestic needs in emerging markets. The net result would be more balanced and sustainable global economic growth.

Given these advantages of a system of market-determined exchange rates, why have officials in many emerging markets leaned against appreciation of their currencies toward levels more consistent with market fundamentals? The principal answer is that currency undervaluation on the part of some countries has been part of a long-term export-led strategy for growth and development.

These paragraphs succinctly articulate the view that most advanced economies hold to this day—that more flexible exchange rates in the emerging markets would fix a host of domestic as well as international problems. Managed exchange rates are seen as a contravention of the normal functioning of markets and the operation of adjustment mechanisms that would automatically fix any imbalances.

Finally, to those arguing that the crucial flaw in the global monetary system was the dominant role of the U.S. dollar that had let the U.S. get away with reckless policies, such as large budget and current account deficits, Bernanke had a sharp and pointed rejoinder:

As currently constituted, the international monetary system has a structural flaw: It lacks a mechanism, market based or otherwise, to induce needed adjustments by surplus countries, which can result in persistent imbalances.

In other words, the real problem in the monetary system was that there was no way to discipline countries maintaining undervalued exchange rates and running current account surpluses. If only those countries would fix their policies to generate more domestic demand, all would be well.

If there was any doubt remaining, currency wars had now broken out into the open.

A Condensed History of Currency Wars

Is currency really an instrument of war? Or is all the talk about currency wars just overheated rhetoric that distracts attention from what countries really need to do to set their economies back on track? Currencies are inherently an international matter, as they represent the price of one country's currency relative to that of another country. So when one currency's value goes down, some other currency's value must go up by a corresponding amount. And that is the unavoidable basis for conflict.

The notion of currency values being an economic tool goes back a long way and is linked to mercantilism, a concept that has its origins in the sixteenth century and took hold in the seventeenth and eighteenth centuries. Many European powers, including England and France, viewed a policy of accumulating gold and other precious metals through trade surpluses as a means to acquiring greater national wealth and power. Proponents of mercantilism viewed international trade and wealth accumulation as zero sum games across countries, with one country benefiting only at the expense of others.

David Hume and Adam Smith, among others, refuted the main tenets of mercantilism. They advocated for the benefits of free trade and argued that world wealth was not static.

John Maynard Keynes took a more nuanced view, arguing that under certain conditions

> it will be essential for the maintenance of prosperity that the
> authorities should pay close attention to the state of the balance
> of trade. For a favourable balance, provided it is not too large, will
> prove extremely stimulating; whilst an unfavourable balance may
> soon produce a state of persistent depression.

He noted that trying to promote the maximum favorable balance of trade could be counterproductive and argued that there was a better alternative:

It is the policy of an autonomous rate of interest, unimpeded by international preoccupations, and of a national investment programme directed to an optimum level of domestic employment which is twice blessed in the sense that it helps ourselves and our neighbours at the same time. And it is the simultaneous pursuit of these policies by all countries together which is capable of restoring economic health and strength internationally, whether we measure it by the level of domestic employment or by the volume of international trade.

Despite their acceptance of the broad benefits of free trade, however, governments find it difficult to resist the temptation to take measures intended to boost exports as a means to promote growth when domestic demand is weak. In the aftermath of the Great Depression, many countries tried to devalue their currencies and also imposed various sorts of trade restrictions to boost their exports and reduce imports as a way to stimulate growth. Instead, all these measures simply served to stifle the growth in trade, prolonging the depression. The post–World War II Bretton Woods system was in fact an attempt to bring order to international trade and finance by limiting national governments' use of competitive devaluations as a tool to promote domestic growth.

In more recent decades, many developing countries—including China —have used a strategy of devaluation to maintain external price competitiveness. Some economists, such as Surjit Bhalla of Oxus Investments and Dani Rodrik of Princeton, have resurrected the argument that currency undervaluation is helpful in the early stages of a country's economic development. The basic idea is that poor countries need to generate a manufacturing sector–led take-off to a high growth path. The problem is that when a relatively poor country starts experiencing high growth rates, it can get a flood of capital inflows from foreign investors, driving up the value of its currency. This currency appreciation chokes off manufacturing growth, as it reduces the competitiveness of a country's exports. A policy of undervaluation, it is argued, can counter this destructive effect of currency appreciation and boost the competitiveness of manufactured products in international markets.

This problem of currency appreciation is a different manifestation of the "Dutch Disease" effect that has bedeviled many resource-rich but otherwise poor economies. Many countries in Africa, for instance, have abundant natural resources but lack the financial capacity to undertake the massive investments needed to exploit those resources. Governments in the region welcomed with open arms foreign investors who had the technical expertise and financial heft needed to unlock those resources. The lure of big profits has led many large multinational companies to pour in large amounts of investment, despite all the risks of investing in economies with weak and unstable governments.

Those inflows of capital have the unfortunate side effect of currency appreciation, hurting whatever domestic industry there is to speak of in such countries. With the benefits of natural resource extraction flowing mainly to foreign investors and to the political and economic elites, these countries are then beset by the "natural resource curse." Exploiting the natural resources leaves a large part of the population no better off and often worse off, as manufacturing jobs disappear and corruption leads to a very uneven distribution of the benefits from natural resources.

The strategy of long-term undervaluation to counter the possible problems caused by currency appreciation sounds appealing but has serious negative consequences for domestic policies. It acts as an implicit transfer to firms in the exporting sector while hurting importers and consumers at large. Furthermore, in middle-income economies, it requires other policy contortions, such as forcing banks to buy sterilization bonds cheaply to conduct a policy of systematic undervaluation without setting off inflation. These costs are typically ignored in the calculations done by authors who praise the benefits of devaluation as a strategy for boosting competitiveness.

Nevertheless, it is a seductive argument for central bankers in emerging markets. The reality is that exporters generate more jobs than importers do. Moreover, the benefits of cheaper imports are usually spread out broadly among the population. These benefits often don't seem large enough to create a viable political constituency to support lower import costs. In contrast, exporters are a powerful political block, and the costs of currency appreciation hit them directly in the gut. Their complaints tend to resonate much more with politicians because jobs are involved, and politicians want to be seen as doing everything they can to protect domestic jobs, especially from what is seen as unfair foreign competition.

Although even the rapidly growing emerging markets are keen to protect their exports, middle-income countries like China surely are not concerned about a growth take-off or a natural resource curse. Why then are they beating the drums of war with such vigor, and is all the heated rhetoric justified? To put it more simply, are currency wars merely a matter of rhetoric or do they have substantive implications? One possibility is that disputes about currencies serve as a smokescreen that conveniently diverts attention from more difficult domestic economic reforms.

Are Currency Wars Overblown?

There are two aspects to the question about whether currency wars and the tools used to engage in them constitute a diversion from more fundamental policy changes that are needed. The first issue is whether advanced economies such as the U.S. that are pursuing expansionary monetary policies are covertly pursuing a strategy of devaluing their currencies to generate domestic growth. The second is whether emerging market economies have a legitimate grievance that they are on the receiving end of problems and risks generated by this loose monetary policy. Let us examine these issues in turn.

Unconventional Approach to Devaluation?

To the rest of the world, the Fed's unconventional monetary policy actions seemed designed to help the U.S. economy mainly by driving down the value of the dollar, a natural consequence of printing dollars indiscriminately. The Fed's views on the consequences of its actions were quite different. Although acknowledging that the dollar would probably fall in value relative to other major currencies as a result of quantitative easing, the Fed seemed to view exports as at best a marginal contributor to growth. Moreover, in line with Bernanke's earlier views about global imbalances, dollar depreciation was seen as a necessary component of a longer-term adjustment of these imbalances.

The Fed's guarded views about the contribution that export growth could make to a U.S. economic recovery were eclipsed by a pledge made by President Obama that continued to resonate when the Fed undertook QE2. By the end of 2009, job growth in the U.S. was still lackluster, and the unemployment rate hovered stubbornly at about 10 percent. With no realistic prospects of pushing any further fiscal stimulus through an uncooperative Congress, the president needed a strategy to show that he was still doing all he could to get the labor market back on its feet.

In his State of the Union address on January 27, 2010, President Obama pledged to double exports over the next five years, linking it to two million new jobs. This would imply an increase from $1.6 trillion in exports in 2009 to $3.2 trillion in 2015 and was to be achieved through various domestic policies, trade agreements, and by making sure that trading partners played by the rules:

> we need to export more of our goods. Because the more products we make and sell to other countries, the more jobs we support right here in America. So tonight, we set a new goal: We will double our exports over the next five years, an increase that will support two million jobs in America. To help meet this goal, we're launching a National Export Initiative that will help farmers and small businesses increase their exports, and reform export controls consistent with national security.
>
> We have to seek new markets aggressively, just as our competitors are. If America sits on the sidelines while other nations sign trade deals, we will lose the chance to create jobs on our shores. But realizing those benefits also means enforcing those agreements so our trading partners play by the rules. And that's why we'll continue to shape a Doha trade agreement that opens global markets, and why we will strengthen our trade relations in Asia and with key partners like South Korea and Panama and Colombia.

In his speech, the president did not say anything about currency values. Nor did he say anything about net exports, which is the same thing as the trade balance. U.S. imports tend to move closely with the business cycle, rising during recoveries and falling during downturns. So the president's pledge to double exports within five years could be perfectly consistent with no improvement or possibly even a worsening of the U.S. trade deficit over that period. But this subtlety was lost in public discussions abroad, where Bernanke's actions were seen as very much consistent with his president's goal of using exports as an engine for job growth.

Even if it wanted to, could the Fed engineer a depreciation of the dollar as its international critics were suggesting? There is no doubt that currencies are subject to the laws of supply and demand; increasing the supply of dollars should reduce its value relative to other currencies. That is not the end of the story, however. In principle, loose monetary policy in the form of large monetary injections should lead to higher inflationary expectations. This in turn might prop up inflation-adjusted (or real) exchange rates, even if the nominal exchange rate were to depreciate. Inflation-adjusted exchange rates are ultimately the main determinants of competitiveness in foreign markets.

In practice, things are even less clear-cut. If financial market participants viewed the Fed's quantitative easing measures as reflecting concerns about future economic weakness, then inflation could fall despite more money being pumped into the economy. In fact, inflationary expectations in the U.S. held steady at about 2 percent for an extended period after the financial crisis, despite rock-bottom interest rates and multiple rounds of quantitative easing. So if the nominal exchange rate falls as the supply of dollars increases and inflation stays unchanged, the Fed's actions would indeed lead to a depreciation of the dollar in inflation-adjusted terms.

There is yet another angle to this story. International investors could also be spooked by the Fed's actions, if they viewed such actions as signaling more rough economic times ahead. This could lead them to pour even more money into the safe haven of U.S. Treasury bonds. Such inflows prop up the dollar, which is exactly what has happened on many occasions recently. The special status of the U.S. dollar as the principal global reserve currency would of course be a key factor behind such an outcome.

Given all these twists and turns, as well as the Fed's stated views on the matter, it is hard to argue that the Fed's actions are aimed at driving down the dollar's value. It is also worth keeping in mind that total U.S. exports of goods and services in 2012 accounted for about 14 percent of GDP. So it would take a huge depreciation of the dollar to generate enough new export growth to give a significant boost to either GDP or employment growth.

Bernanke's views on the matter are summarized in remarks he made back in November 2002, a few months after he became a member of the

Federal Reserve Board of Governors and when the U.S. was facing the specter of deflation. In a speech in which he argued for aggressive monetary policy actions and listed various options for how the Fed could inject money into the economy, he made the following observation:

> since the United States is a large, relatively closed economy, manipulating the exchange value of the dollar would not be a particularly desirable way to fight domestic deflation, particularly given the range of other options available. Thus, I want to be absolutely clear that I am today neither forecasting nor recommending any attempt by U.S. policymakers to target the international value of the dollar.

Bernanke's statements notwithstanding, the rest of the world saw the Fed's actions as a thinly veiled attempt to drive down the value of the dollar.

Much Ado about Nothing?

Do emerging markets have a valid case that loose U.S. monetary policy hurts them? Again, the answer is a complex and subtle one. The first issue that needs to be addressed is whether quantitative easing has in fact led to capital flowing out of the U.S. and into emerging markets. There is certainly a lot of evidence from the past that low interest rates in the U.S. and other advanced economies push capital out to emerging markets in more normal times.

Although evidence from the recent bouts of monetary easing is less clear, it is plausible that the Fed's unconventional monetary policies are getting only limited traction in boosting aggregate demand in the U.S. Large corporations are accumulating sizable cash reserves in the face of uncertain economic prospects as the recovery continues to be weak. Financial institutions are not increasing lending to consumers and small firms, because the risks of default have risen after the crisis. Additionally, there are still some uncertainties about changes in banking regulation, both at home and abroad, so banks are saving up capital in the event they need more of it to satisfy regulatory requirements. In contrast, emerging markets are facing good growth prospects, so it is likely that private capital will continue flowing their way, especially as unconventional monetary policies make cheap money freely and easily available to large investors.

One of the key concerns for emerging markets is that capital inflows lead to currency appreciation. Exports are clearly important for growth, but their importance sometimes tends to be overstated. For example, Brazil, despite leading the charge on one side of the currency wars, has exports amounting to just 11 percent of its GDP. So a currency appreciation would hardly have a devastating effect on the economy if export growth were to slow down. Even China, often seen as an export-oriented economy, has continued growing strongly during and after the financial crisis, even though its export growth has slowed markedly and its trade surplus has shrunk from 7.6 percent of GDP in 2007 to 2.8 percent of GDP in 2012. But exporters get hit directly and hard when there is a currency appreciation, causing them to complain loudly. Their voices tend to echo even more loudly than usual in the corridors of power at times of low growth in output and employment.

The other big concern for emerging market central bankers is that capital inflows tend to worsen domestic inflation and fuel bubbles in asset markets. The inflation problem is actually worse for countries that have organized their monetary policy frameworks according to the textbook prescription—inflation targeting with flexible exchange rates.

Consider Thailand. With the Thai economy in tatters after the financial crisis in 1997, the nation's central bank dropped its long-standing pegged exchange rate regime and instead adopted monetary targeting that year. Then, to rebuild confidence and fix inflationary expectations, it moved to an inflation targeting regime in May 2000.

The Bank of Thailand's new framework worked well in its first few years, delivering low and stable inflation. In early 2008, with food prices rising and feeding through into overall consumer price inflation, the Thai central bank started raising interest rates gradually. This action brought in more capital inflows and drove up the value of the currency. Thus, in the context of the inflation targeting framework, the obvious policy response—higher interest rates to bring down domestic inflation—was only making things worse. In the latter half of 2008, of course, the crisis hit and the problem went away. But the dilemma has regularly resurfaced since the beginning of 2010, with the central bank struggling to manage domestic inflation without stoking more capital inflows and making the problem worse.

In addition to price inflation, emerging market policymakers are also concerned that these inflows lead to problems in their asset markets. Given that a lot of the flows to emerging markets are in the form of FDI and portfolio equity, these flows have the right sort of risk sharing characteristics, with foreign investors sharing both currency and return risk on their investments. Hence, these flows should be of less concern to policymakers in emerging markets than is debt, which has burned them in the past.

Here it is important to remember that currency wars are being fought against the background of not just higher private capital flows to the emerging markets but also greater capital flow volatility. Even though portfolio equity flows provide more effective risk sharing for emerging markets, these inflows can lead to asset market bubbles when domestic financial systems are not working well and then cause painful effects when those bubbles burst. Outflows of capital that tend to increase just when things are not going well domestically only make things worse. For instance, foreign inflows helped power India's equity market boom in 2011 that subsequently turned into a mini-bust as foreign capital retreated. In some economies, foreign money also tends to inflate real estate values, adding to asset bubbles.

Commodity Prices

A related concern that some emerging market policymakers have is that easy money in the advanced economies fuels worldwide commodity price surges, which selectively hurts emerging markets more than their advanced counterparts. India's Finance Minister P. Chidambaram raised the issue at a meeting with U.S. Treasury Secretary Timothy Geithner in October 2012. At a subsequent press conference, Chidambaram indicated he had discussed U.S. quantitative easing operations with Geithner and "raised the concern that it may impact commodity prices and commodity prices may rise." He noted that Geithner had dismissed those concerns but Chidambaram concluded "that is a matter we'll have to wait and see."

The logic behind this concern is that inflationary fears lead to more interest in commodities as an "asset class," as they are likely to retain value when a general increase in inflation occurs. There have also been concerns, which are difficult to substantiate, that the availability of easy money in the form of cheap loans has increased speculative activity in commodity markets, driving up the price of food and other commodities. Of course, higher commodity prices are not a uniform concern for emerging markets. Some commodity exporters benefit from high prices for their exports, but the increase in food prices does tend to hurt all these countries, especially because the share of food in average household expenditures tends to be much higher than in the richer advanced economies.

Currency Valuation and Volatility

The divergent perceptions about policy intentions do not run in just one direction, as advanced economies have their own specific complaints. Currency wars are often interpreted by officials in these economies as attempts by emerging markets to resist appreciation that would move currencies toward their equilibrium values. That opens up a new can of worms, starting with the difficulty of even defining the concept of an equilibrium exchange rate. In principle, this is the exchange rate consistent with a country having no domestic or external imbalances, such as large budget or current account deficits. Some economists have constructed estimates of equilibrium exchange rates based on various statistical models, but these estimates are subject to wide margins of error and inspire little confidence. Furthermore, a country's exchange rate can sometimes drift far off from its estimated equilibrium level for a variety of reasons, even if the exchange rate is freely determined by the market. It is usually not obvious why any such discrepancy should be fixed through an adjustment of domestic policies.

Besides, it is difficult to make unconditional statements about a currency's suitable value. Take China. The massive amount of exchange market intervention symbolized by the rapid buildup of foreign exchange reserves suggests that, in the absence of such intervention, the market-determined level of the currency would be higher. But this conclusion is conditional on the limited openness of the capital account. If controls on capital flows were relaxed further, leading to large outflows, the currency could well depreciate in the short run, despite all the rhetoric that the currency is undervalued and ought to appreciate.

Capital flow volatility also creates concerns about currency volatility. Currency markets are subject to overshooting, a common phenomenon, according to which currencies appreciate or depreciate by a large amount before settling down to smaller changes in either direction. In principle, short-term currency appreciations should not have large or persistent effects on exports. But many emerging markets specialize in low-technology products with razor-thin profit margins. Even a temporary loss of competitiveness because of a short-lived surge in the domestic currency's value can lead to many exporting firms going under as they lose market share to lower-wage competitors.

In short, framing currency wars through the prism of equilibrium currency values or specific currency regimes misses the point. Emerging market countries that have floating exchange rates as well as those with tightly managed exchange rates are on the same side on this issue. They have a long litany of woes, whether justified or not, about how the unconventional monetary policies of the advanced economy central banks are complicating their domestic macroeconomic management.

Squaring Up Opposing Views: Scale Matters

The Fed's view is that, for all their potential risks, the likely benefits of unconventional policies such as quantitative easing still make them worth a try. The rest of the world should, if anything, be thankful for the Fed's taking every conceivable measure to boost U.S. economic growth.

How can one reconcile the Fed's perspective with that of the emerging markets? One answer comes down to the issues of size and scale. Even if the capital flow implications of quantitative easing are modest from the perspective of global capital movements, the flows can be large from the point of view of host economies. Thailand has a GDP of $350 billion. For an economy of this size, coping with an inflow of $5–10 billion in a month, an amount that is a rounding error in global capital flows, creates enormous complications. Even for larger economies like Brazil or India, volumes of flows that seem small from an advanced economy perspective can cause risks of financial market instability, because their financial markets are not deep enough to absorb such inflows without setting off boom-bust cycles.

Another part of the answer, as noted above, is that emerging markets are concerned not just about the level of inflows but also about capital flow volatility. Low interest rates and cheap money in the U.S. will probably give way sooner or later to higher interest rates and tighter availability of credit. If all this happens in tandem with a U.S. recovery, money might flow out of emerging markets just as rapidly as it came in, triggering equity market and other asset market collapses. In fact, by August 2013, this scenario was becoming a reality, with many emerging market currencies and equity markets plunging in value.

The real concern for emerging markets boils down to this: The benefits of unconventional monetary policy through their effects on growth in advanced economies are uncertain and at best modest. Monetary policy can limit downside risks in advanced economies but cannot by itself revive and sustain growth. In contrast, the costs of such policies are immediate and often quite large in terms of the domestic policy complications that the spillovers of those actions cause for emerging markets.

The new generation of emerging market central bankers is an astute and pragmatic set. They do not want to put on a futile King Canute act, for they recognize all too well that they have little chance of stopping waves of capital inflows and currency appreciation driven by the right reasons—the fast productivity growth in their economies.* Their concern is that policies of the advanced economies are causing this to happen before the emerging markets are ready to deal with surges of inflows and rapid currency appreciation. So the emerging markets' strategy in the currency wars is not so much to reverse appreciation as it is to stave off excessive or too rapid appreciation. As Edwin Truman, a former senior official at the Fed, has put it elegantly, the strategy is one of "competitive non-appreciation" rather than competitive devaluation!

---

* Legend has it that King Canute, a king of England (of Danish origin) in the eleventh century, had his chair set on the seashore and commanded the waves to stop advancing. When the tide did come in and "disrespectfully drenched the king's feet and shins," he is said to have remarked, "Let all the world know that the power of kings is empty and worthless and there is no King worthy of the name save Him by whose will heaven, earth and sea obey eternal laws." This exercise was meant to convey a message to his sycophantic courtiers—that even a king has limits to his powers.

Collateral Damage and More Irony

Wars create collateral damage, and currency wars are no exception. Every central bank has domestic objectives, and only domestic objectives, in its mandate. But when large central banks act, the effects of their actions resonate throughout the world.

With the Fed flooding U.S. financial markets with money, investors have been turning some of their attention to other safe havens, including countries like Japan and Switzerland. Given the torpid state of the Japanese economy, which has been flirting with deflation for the past couple of decades, and the enormous scale of the country's debt, Japan would hardly seem to have the characteristics of an economy whose government debt or corporate securities one would turn to for safety. Yet, international investors eager to look to markets other than the U.S. for safety often turn to Japan, driving up the value of the yen to a level that worsens Japan's prospects of exporting its way out of a deep economic malaise. This behavior contributed to a sharp appreciation in the Japanese yen, which traded in a range of about 80 yen to the dollar for much of 2012, about 30 percent stronger than its level in the summer of 2008. The measures taken by the Bank of Japan (BoJ) in 2012 and 2013 to aggressively loosen monetary policy are in some ways a reaction to the Fed's actions and are directly tied to keeping down the value of the yen.

Another innocent bystander is Switzerland, a small economy with sound economic policies and a robust financial sector, which is widely regarded as a safe haven. In the aftermath of the financial crisis, a modest sliver of the global capital in search of a safe sanctuary headed toward the Swiss franc, enough to drive a surge in its external value. The Swiss franc appreciated from 1.52 per euro in July 2009 to 1.18 per euro by July 2011, an appreciation of 23 percent in just two years.

The extent of foreign exchange intervention by the BoJ and the Swiss National Bank (SNB) to prevent their currencies from appreciating even faster has been enormous. It has also created big risks for their central banks' balance sheets. In 2011, Japan's foreign exchange reserves went up by $185 billion dollars—an 18 percent jump in just one year. The SNB has been equally aggressive in buying up foreign currencies to keep its currency from appreciating against the euro. Between January 2009 and July 2011, Swiss foreign exchange reserves rose from $44 billion to $234 billion. Then, in August 2011 alone, reserves skyrocketed by another $83 billion.

With the country's manufacturing sector in pain as the Swiss franc continued to appreciate despite these measures, the SNB took more dramatic action. It first loosened monetary policy by cutting interest rates, temporarily knocking down the Swiss franc's value and providing a brief respite from its appreciation.

Then, on September 26, 2011, the SNB fired another of its own cannons in the currency wars. It stunned markets by putting a cap on the Swiss franc's appreciation, saying it would not let the currency trade at a level stronger than 1.20 francs per euro. The SNB declared that it would "enforce this minimum rate with the utmost determination and is prepared to buy foreign currency in unlimited quantities." In other words, it would intervene as much as needed in foreign exchange markets to prevent the franc from strengthening beyond the line it had drawn in the sand. This action caught markets by surprise, because Switzerland had long been committed to the free flow of capital and to fully flexible exchange rates. The move also signaled that currency wars were beginning to engulf smaller advanced economies and that more hostilities were in the offing.

Appreciation pressures on the Swiss franc then eased off but returned with force in the summer of 2012, when the euro zone crisis hit another critical stage. With another spike of $69 billion in June 2012 and further increases in the months that followed, the SNB had built up its stock of foreign exchange reserves to nearly $470 billion at the end of 2012, a tenfold increase in four years. To prevent a surge in domestic inflation (as it has been printing Swiss francs to purchase euros), the SNB has been sterilizing its intervention operations by selling liabilities denominated in its own currency. If the euro were to depreciate against the Swiss franc in the future, the SNB would take a big capital loss in domestic currency terms on its reserve portfolio. The SNB has made it clear that it fully recognizes the risk of a big loss but felt it had no option but to act forcefully to protect the Swiss economy.

Guns and Roses

The collateral damage from currency wars has been spreading quickly. Many countries, including some emerging markets, are trapped in the middle of the battles between China and the U.S., the two titans in the world economy. For instance, countries like India, which are sometimes equally frustrated by U.S. monetary policy and Chinese currency policy, were being furiously lobbied by both sides in the run-up to the Seoul G-20 summit. Caught in the middle and unwilling to make enemies on either side, Indian officials simultaneously lauded the benefits of exchange rate flexibility, warned about the dangers of protectionist policies, and appealed for more tempered monetary policy actions by advanced economy central banks. Indian Prime Minister Manmohan Singh made these remarks in his speech at the Seoul summit:

> we must at all costs avoid competitive devaluation and resist any resurgence of protectionism . . . exchange rates flexibility is an important instrument for achieving a sustainable current account position and our policies must reflect this consideration. At the same time, reserve currency countries have a special responsibility to ensure that their monetary policies do not lead to destabilizing capital flows, which can put pressure on emerging markets.

There is another wrinkle to the currency wars. When emerging markets intervene in foreign exchange markets as a defensive maneuver to tamp down appreciation of their currencies, they build up foreign exchange reserves. Where can they park those reserves? The euro is none too secure an investment, and Switzerland is too small. Then there is Japan, but Japan is itself intervening in foreign exchange markets and recycling safe haven inflows. So where does this money end up? No prizes for guessing—the U.S.!

So the cannonballs fired by the rest of the world turn into flowers by the time they reach enemy shores on the U.S. side. To heighten the irony, emerging markets now have an even stronger incentive to keep their currencies from appreciating against the dollar: to avoid taking a capital loss in domestic currency terms on their reserve portfolios.

Competitive nonappreciations through intervention in foreign exchange markets now take on a more complex function. They not only involve the maintenance of price competitiveness in external trade but also serve to limit a country's implicit wealth transfers to the rest of the world. Thus, among emerging markets, the fear of currency appreciation now has two underlying causes rather than just the implications for trade.

Other countries may win some of the skirmishes and battles, but, in some respects, the U.S. is going to achieve an even more favorable position as the currency wars wear on.

Strong Dollar Rhetoric

There is more irony to come. For in the midst of its criticisms of certain emerging markets' currency policies and emerging markets' protests about its monetary policy actions, the U.S. has over the past two decades consistently maintained the rhetoric of a strong dollar. This rhetoric was elevated to the status of policy by Robert Rubin, who was Treasury secretary from 1995 to 1999. In an interview in 1997, he said, "I believe a strong dollar is in our nation's interest." In fairness, Rubin apparently did note that it was pointless to try to artificially influence currency values, because they reflect economic fundamentals.

Nevertheless, subsequent Treasury secretaries have found it difficult to stray from this line, for fear that it would signal weakness. The next secretary, Lawrence Summers, affirmed that "The United States is unwavering in its strong dollar policy." Those who followed in this position reiterated this line in one context or another, always linking it to the national interest. Henry Paulson, Treasury secretary from 2006 to 2009, used this rhetoric with regularity and on one occasion went so far as to say, "In my heart and soul, I just know and believe that a strong dollar is in our nation's interest."

This rhetoric seems driven more by political than economic compulsions. The apparent logic is that a strong currency represents the strength of the country and its economy. Although a country's high productivity growth relative to those of its trading partners would indeed help its currency strengthen, the reverse proposition—that a stronger currency would help growth and competitiveness—has become part of the lore. In his Senate confirmation hearing in February 2013 prior to taking office, Treasury Secretary Jacob Lew made this statement:

Treasury has had a longstanding position through administrations of both parties over many years that a strong dollar is in the best interests of promoting U.S. growth, productivity and competitiveness. If confirmed, I would not change that policy.

Although they have become locked into this policy for domestic political reasons, U.S. policymakers no doubt understand the shaky economic foundations of this line of logic. Paul O'Neill, who was Treasury secretary from 2001 to 2002 and came to be seen as a maverick in the George W. Bush administration, was candid in an interview he gave after his resignation. He observed that "When I was Secretary of the Treasury I was not supposed to say anything but 'strong dollar, strong dollar.' I argued then and would argue now that the idea of a strong dollar policy is a vacuous notion."

Perhaps the rhetoric was really just a diversionary tactic. Fed Chairman Alan Greenspan told his colleagues in 2001 that he had cringed every time Robert Rubin repeated his mantra during the Clinton administration that the White House supported a strong dollar. Eventually, however, Greenspan became a fan of the slogan because, as he put it, "It was boring, it was dull, it was repetitive, it was nonintellectual and it worked like a charm."

The other oddity in the U.S., which is also true of many other advanced economies, is that management of the currency's value is under the purview of the U.S. Treasury and not the Fed. One would think that monetary policy is a key determinant of the exchange rate, but, in principle, Treasury has final authority over management of the dollar's value. At a press conference in 2011, Fed Chairman Ben Bernanke had this to say:

> First, I should start by saying that the Secretary of the Treasury,
> of course, is the spokesperson for U.S. policy on the dollar and
> Secretary Geithner had some words yesterday. Let me add to what
> he said first by saying that the Federal Reserve believes that a
> strong and stable dollar is both in the American interest and in
> the interest of the global economy.

So, while the world fears the consequences of a weaker dollar, the U.S. apparently fears it as well, notwithstanding its actions to the contrary and its stated objective of raising exports.

More Battles to Come?

On September 13, 2012, the U.S. Federal Reserve Open Market Committee launched a third round of quantitative easing, announcing an open-ended commitment to buying an additional $40 billion of agency mortgage-backed securities per month. The Committee also indicated it would continue with Operation Twist, selling short-term Treasury bonds and buying longer-term Treasury securities. The idea behind this operation was to keep long-term interest rates low to help the housing sector and boost investment and consumer demand. Finally, the Committee indicated it expected to keep short-term policy rates at or close to zero percent until mid-2015. This battery of aggressive measures was meant to "put downward pressure on longer-term interest rates, support mortgage markets, and help to make broader financial conditions more accommodative."

On the heels of the Fed's action, the BoJ followed with its own measures. Japan had been in the throes of deflation for most of 2009–11, and the picture did not look much brighter for 2012. With policy interest rates already at zero for a long period, higher inflation was the only hope for the BoJ to drive down inflation-adjusted interest rates and stoke economic activity. In February 2012, the BoJ had announced an inflation target of 1 percent. The target, although a low one, was meant as an important signal to the market of the BoJ's determination to support aggregate demand. After a brief spike in the first half of the year, consumer prices again began to fall in the summer of 2012. With a strengthening yen hurting exports, the economy was sputtering once again.

On September 19, less than a week after the Fed announcement of QE3 and to the dismay of emerging markets, the BoJ announced the next phase of its own quantitative easing. The BoJ expanded the bond-buying program it had put in place in October 2010 from 70 trillion yen to 80 trillion yen, an increase of roughly $125 billion. The BoJ expanded the program further in October and December, by about 10 trillion yen each time, taking the total to 101 trillion yen (nearly $1.2 trillion).

Interestingly, the announcement of its own unconventional monetary policy actions by the European Central Bank (ECB) in August 2012 did not trigger a negative reaction from emerging markets. The ECB's Outright Monetary Transactions program was in effect a commitment to buy the sovereign bonds of countries in the euro zone that were facing difficulties in financing their debt at reasonable interest rates—once those countries agreed to a program of budgetary, labor market, product market, and other reforms. The program was intended solely to boost confidence in bonds issued by any euro zone country, so that none of them would face punitive borrowing costs.

The ECB made it clear that its bond-buying operations would be sterilized, so that any money pumped into the system would be absorbed back through other means. This promise of sterilization was partly to placate the Germans, who were already unhappy with the ECB's actions, by reassuring them that at least these operations would not increase inflation. From the emerging markets' perspective, this move was welcome—stability in the euro zone was to everyone's benefit, and the ECB's promise to soak up most of its monetary injections meant that there was no additional money that could wend its way to other countries.

Renewed Tensions

The amounts involved in the U.S. and Japanese central banks' actions were not small potatoes even for those economies. Outflows of even a fraction of these amounts would be difficult for most emerging markets to cope with. Indeed, soon after the major central banks announced their policies, emerging markets started experiencing capital inflows and renewed currency appreciation. This trend may have been partly tied to a firming-up of the U.S. recovery and reduced prospects of a meltdown in Europe, but emerging markets saw the expansionary policies of the advanced economy central banks as the main factor behind capital and currency movements.

Reacting to these actions, Guido Mantega of Brazil was blunt as always, warning that quantitative easing by the major advanced economies would revive currency wars by forcing other countries to act to protect their own economies. He made it clear that Brazil would continue intervening heavily in foreign exchange markets to prevent the real from appreciating further. He was quoted as saying:

> [The United States and Japan] will be stimulating the currency wars as [they] will lead all countries also to pursue these wars. It's natural other countries will defend themselves. The [Brazilian] central bank will buy more reserves, we already have a very high

level of reserves and we will purchase more if there is a strong offer of dollars in the Brazilian economy . . . we won't allow our economy to become uncompetitive.

Meanwhile, the perspective on the other side of the battlefield also remains largely unchanged. Although global trade imbalances have shrunk, a sense of aggrievement still exists among policymakers in countries like the U.S. and the U.K., who contend that the fundamental obstacle to further adjustment of these imbalances is the lack of flexible exchange rates among the major emerging market economies.

On December 10, 2012, Sir Mervyn King, then governor of the Bank of England, delivered a speech to the Economic Club of New York. After speaking of the many domestic challenges his institution faced, he turned to problems of global economic coordination. He emphasized the importance of rebalancing trade, noting that consumer-driven economies like the U.K. and the U.S. continued to run large trade deficits, while countries like China continued to run large surpluses. His view was that currency wars were here to stay for a while:

> The pressures on deficit countries are inexorable because those are the countries that have built up debt and those are the countries that are having to adjust. The surplus countries are under no such pressure to do so and many of them show great reluctance to expand domestic spending to allow the deficit countries to re-balance. . . . [T]here has been no agreement on the need for working together to achieve some element of re-balancing the world economy. . . . [W]e will see . . . the growth of actively managed exchange rates as an alternative to the use of domestic monetary policy. . . . [Y]ou can see month by month the addition of the number of countries who feel that active exchange rate management, always of course to push their exchange rate down, is growing.

This narrative follows a familiar train of thought, that the advanced economies that are running current account deficits need to adjust their policies to bring down those deficits, but this adjustment is being stymied by the activist exchange rate policies of the surplus countries that are not doing what is needed to boost their own domestic demand.

Fred Bergsten of the Peterson Institute has referred to the U.S. as the "most injured party" in the currency wars and called for the U.S. to take actions, both unilateral and through international financial institutions, against countries like China that he classifies as currency manipulators.

Each Country for Itself

The specter of currency wars signifies more than just a tussle between advanced and emerging market economies. Soon after the BoJ announced a new round of monetary easing measures in January 2013 in response to strong and overt political pressure from the new Japanese government, Jens Weidmann, president of the Deutsche Bundesbank (Germany's formidable central bank), stepped in to the debate. He warned Japan not to "politicize" its exchange rate by trying to engineer a depreciation through even looser monetary policy. Weidmann was quoted as saying:

> A consequence, whether intended or not, could lead to an increasingly politicized exchange rate. Until now, the international monetary system has come through the crisis without a race to devaluation, and I really hope it stays that way.

This statement came just before the euro zone was dragged directly into the rhetoric of currency wars by Weidmann's European colleague, French President François Hollande. Echoing the sentiments of other European leaders, Hollande called for the euro zone to directly engage in the currency wars and prevent the euro from appreciating. In February 2013, he blamed the euro's appreciation for the zone's loss of competitiveness:

> The euro should not fluctuate according to the mood of the markets. A monetary zone must have an exchange rate policy. If not it will be subjected to an exchange rate that does not reflect the real state of the economy.

He went on to issue this explicit call to arms:

> The eurozone must, through its heads of state and government, decide on a medium-term exchange rate. We need to act at an international level to protect our own interests.

This call for the ECB to step in to prevent the euro from appreciating was anathema to the Germans, already concerned about the ECB getting diverted from its main mandate of price stability. German economy minister Philipp Rösler retorted strongly that the euro zone's top priority ought to be "strengthening competitiveness, rather than weakening the currency."

Meanwhile, the newly elected prime minister of Japan, Shinzo Abe, appointed Haruhiko Kuroda as the governor of the BoJ in March 2013. The clear objective of the appointment was to get monetary policy to fire on all cylinders to support the economy, including whatever degree of monetary expansion—and resulting currency depreciation—was necessary to pull the economy out of its deflationary spiral. With goods exports amounting to only 14 percent of GDP, it would take a large depreciation for exports to significantly boost GDP growth.

In April 2013, the BoJ came out with its guns blazing. It announced a new inflation target of 2 percent and a range of measures to attain that objective. The yen promptly started depreciating, especially against the U.S. dollar. This put the U.S. in an awkward position, glad that Japan was taking strong actions to revive its economy but unhappy that those actions were leading to a falling yen and pushing up the dollar's value. In its semi-annual currency report to the U.S. Congress in April 2013, the Treasury Department lobbed a direct warning at Japan:

> We will continue to press Japan to adhere to the commitments agreed to in the G-7 and G-20, to remain oriented towards meeting respective domestic objectives using domestic instruments and to refrain from competitive devaluation and targeting its exchange rate for competitive purposes.

Even as they welcomed Japan's attempts to revive its economy, the monetary policy actions also prompted sharp reactions from its Asian neighbors. South Korean Finance Minister Hyun Oh Seok said that Japan's weakening yen was hurting his country's economy more than any threats from North Korea.

In short, the world is happy to see the advanced economies taking measures to boost their economic growth, but not when there is a perception that this growth will come at the expense of other countries.

A Grim Reality

These developments and differing perspectives underlie big and, in some respects, unavoidable tensions in countries' use of macroeconomic policies to deal with their weak economies. With their high levels of public debt, advanced economies are boxed in when it comes to their ability to use fiscal policy to support economic growth. In most emerging market economies, fiscal policy is less constrained by high debt levels but runs up against constraints, such as inadequate social transfer mechanisms, that make it difficult to deploy fiscal policy effectively at short notice. In many economies, both advanced and emerging, deep reforms to labor and product markets and financial systems are necessary to improve competitiveness and growth. But those reforms are difficult, as they often involve wrenching changes and are politically very costly.

History is littered with examples of politicians who forced their countries to confront tough choices and paid a heavy political price for doing so, even if their economies eventually benefited. Even the self-professedly austere Germans resisted such reforms. They turned their leader, Chancellor Gerhard Schröder, out of office for taking tough measures that have helped Germany become the competitive export machine it is today.

In 2003, German unemployment had risen to nearly 10 percent, and the economy had stopped growing. Schröder unveiled the Agenda 2010 program of reforms in March 2003. The reforms streamlined labor laws, cut unemployment benefits, reduced taxes, and revamped a slew of welfare programs. The reforms came at a heavy political price for Schröder, who faced street demonstrations, rising opposition in his own party and, finally, an electoral defeat when he called early national parliamentary elections in 2005. The economic reforms started to turn the economy around by 2006, which was too late for Schröder.

Politicians find it difficult to do the right thing in the short run, leaving monetary policy to do the heavy lifting. Consequently, around the world monetary policy has become the first—and often the only—line of defense against macroeconomic shocks, both domestic and external. Even advanced economies face a delicate balance between the benefits and costs of quantitative easing and other unconventional monetary policy actions. There is no easy way to bridge the fundamental disconnect in the way this balance is perceived by policymakers in advanced economies and emerging markets. The rising global integration of financial markets is inevitably going to lead to increasing currency competition. The grim reality is that monetary policy is the only game in town, and it is going to remain a zero sum game through its effects on currencies.

This portends a bleak situation for emerging market economies. José De Gregorio, former governor of the Banco Central de Chile, has argued that it is futile for emerging markets to employ foreign exchange intervention or capital controls to keep capital inflows out and maintain undervalued currencies. He notes that adopting these strategies as a response to currency wars leads emerging markets to institute a range of policies that hurt the domestic economy by creating various distortions, especially in financial markets. Or, as he put it more eloquently at a public event in Washington, DC, some countries engaging in currency wars are ultimately setting themselves up for "currency suicide."

Even if currency wars are seen just as short-term frictions that will fade away, they could well take on lives of their own. The threat of trade protectionism is on the rise and has compromised momentum toward more liberal trade regimes around the world. Given the lasting damage that could be wrought by currency wars if they lead to the erection of barriers to the free flow of trade and capital, peacekeepers have tried to step in and seek an end to the conflict. Could they succeed in getting countries to consider the common good and replace conflict with cooperation?

To answer this question, it is worth examining an episode that preceded the global financial crisis, when tensions about currency policies were rising and a mediator stepped in to try to resolve the problem. How that episode played out, as described in the next chapter, is instructive. It illustrates the difficulties of translating high-minded rhetoric about policy coordination into actions.

Seeking a Truce on Currency Wars

MR. FRANCE: *Men gamble everywhere, sir. The weakness is universal.*

MATT DILLON (Marshal of Dodge City, Kansas): *You can gamble here all you like, as long as you don't run a crooked game.*

MR. FRANCE: *That's precisely what I wanted to see you about, Marshal. It's not that I'm dishonest, but I've often been accused of being so. Sometimes makes for unpleasantness.*

MATT DILLON: *Around here it usually leads to gunplay. . . . That's why I don't tolerate anything but an honest game in Dodge.*

Gunsmoke, Episode 95: "The Gentleman"

Currency wars are a concern particularly at a time of weak global growth, as they could easily morph into outright trade wars. If countries find that their trading partners are manipulating their currencies, the natural response is often to erect trade barriers to keep out imports and also to help domestic exporters through subsidies and other schemes that make their goods more competitive in international markets. Given the extent of global trade flows, a disruption of trade could easily escalate and hurt world growth. This generates a tension—free trade can make everyone better off, but if countries see management of currency valuations as a key tool to promote their own exports, then trade itself becomes a subject of conflict rather than cooperation.

The challenge regarding currencies is how to manage what is essentially a zero sum game, which intrinsically makes it difficult to achieve a cooperative solution. There is a glimmer of hope—everyone recognizes that this game has the potential to turn uglier. If many countries try to skirt the (unwritten) rules at the same time, it can turn into a negative sum game, in which everyone is worse off. Therein ought to lie the basis for a coordinated solution.

However, coordination is easier in principle than in practice, especially at a time when economies around the world are hurting, beset by weak domestic demand and anemic employment growth. Putting aside short-term considerations for the longer-term good of everyone requires more political will and leadership than it is reasonable to ask politicians to muster. Politicians tend to have short horizons, often tied to election cycles, and are responsible only to their domestic constituencies.

There is no good substitute for a tough independent marshal who can keep the game honest. But it is not easy to keep things peaceful when the marshal has limited firepower and has to resort to cajoling. What is required to keep currency wars from flaring up is an institution, or a set of institutions working together, with the credibility to set up and enforce a set of ground rules—both in terms of macroeconomic policies that affect currency values and the mechanics of international trade. The two areas have been separated and delegated to different institutions—the IMF and the World Trade Organization, respectively—perhaps rightly so, as they require different sorts of expertise. The results in the first area have not been encouraging.

Is Peer Pressure the Right Prod for Better Policies?

The IMF was set up by the advanced industrial economies in 1945 to promote the stability of the international financial system. Its role has evolved with changing times. In the aftermath of the Great Depression and World War II, there was a concern that attempts at currency devaluation were hurting global trade and world economic growth; a system of fixed exchange rates among the currencies of the major economies was seen as one way around this problem. Hence, the IMF's main role in the first couple of decades of its existence was to manage the Bretton Woods system of fixed exchange rates. This involved monitoring countries' policies and providing financing to countries that had short-term balance of payments deficits.

The Bretton Woods system broke down in the early 1970s, and the IMF's role then changed—it started promoting the free flow of capital, flexible market-determined exchange rates, and liberalization of financial and goods markets. Over time, the IMF has increasingly turned into an arbiter of individual countries' macroeconomic policies and has sought to become the lender of last resort to countries in dire macroeconomic distress. It now has a membership that encompasses 188 countries.

The World Trade Organization is responsible for monitoring overt and covert trade restrictions used by countries to block trade and for intermediating trade disputes among countries. Currency and other macroeconomic policies are not under its purview, although in principle, some of these policies can give countries an unfair advantage in international trade. For instance, an undervalued currency is effectively a subsidy provided to a country's exporters. The reality, however, is that the World Trade Organization has a more limited charter and little expertise on macroeconomic issues. Logically, the IMF is the only international financial institution capable of arbitrating a global truce on currency wars.

Events in the early 2000s gave the IMF an opening to intervene in currency disputes. There was a growing concern among policymakers and academics that large current account surpluses in China and other emerging markets, which were financing rising current account deficits in the U.S. and many other advanced economies, were creating unsustainable imbalances in global demand. In 2005, Ben Bernanke gave his speech about the global savings glut, which crystallized these concerns from the advanced economy perspective. Bernanke's phrase subtly but clearly encapsulated the view that global imbalances were to a large extent the fault of countries that were running surpluses. Officials in China and other emerging markets, particularly those in Asia running current account surpluses, lashed back at what they viewed as a blatant case of the pot calling the kettle black.

As this war of words was heating up, current account imbalances were growing steadily. With oil prices high, economies in the Middle East were also racking up current account surpluses, on top of the growing surpluses of China and many other emerging market economies. Although other advanced economies like Australia, Spain, and the United Kingdom were also running current account deficits, the U.S. deficit was expanding and accounting for most of the other side of global imbalances.

Trying to Make Peace

There were increasing concerns that the imbalances could end badly, perhaps with a fiery crash in the dollar's value. With recriminations flying all around about who was to blame for the rising imbalances, the senior management of the IMF, egged on by the staff of the institution, decided to get the IMF involved as a neutral arbitrator. The management team wanted to take a stab at addressing the problem of global imbalances, but in a constructive way that would try to get all relevant parties involved rather than just point fingers at one or two countries.

In June 2006, with a flourish, the IMF announced its first multilateral consultation. Unlike its typical bilateral consultations conducted with one country at a time to assess that country's policies, the goal of this new initiative was to evaluate the consistency of policies among a group of major economies. The chosen ones, who all agreed to the process, were China, the euro zone, Japan, Saudi Arabia, and the United States. According to the IMF, the criteria for choosing them were that "The five economies are relevant to global imbalances in different ways: either because of their current account deficits or surpluses, or because they represent a very large share of world output."

The goals of the process were noble ones, intended to herald a new era of cooperation under the auspices of the IMF:

> The multilateral consultation approach is an example of the IMF's role as a vehicle for international cooperation. It provides a channel for analysis and consensus-building and a framework that helps our members overcome hurdles to individual action by emphasizing the benefits of collaborative actions.

As it turned out, each participant expected that the blame would be directed elsewhere, and that they themselves would get off lightly.

After technical meetings with officials of the relevant countries in the summer and fall of 2006, the time came for final high-level meetings between the head of the IMF and senior economic officials of each of those countries, typically the finance minister and central bank governor. These concluding meetings had been conducted with the other participating economies, and finally it was the turn of the U.S. All of a sudden, the U.S. lost all interest in the process, and its senior officials became unavailable for meetings to wrap up the report. Even though the IMF team was unlikely to learn anything new and surprising from such meetings, the fact was that the multilateral consultations could not be concluded without a formal high-level meeting with the senior officials of the world's largest economy. So the process dragged on for a number of months, and the report was finally published only in April 2007 after the meeting with U.S. officials was eventually completed.

Why did the U.S. back off? For one simple reason—the U.S. Treasury had presumed that the IMF would be critical of China's currency policies above all else, but it became clear that the report would in fact be more balanced, with equally forceful language about the risks posed by U.S. fiscal and current account deficits. Once China saw the game that was being played by the U.S., its officials became more reserved about the report and basically gave it a cold shoulder from that point on.

The report did not just stop with a diagnosis of the sources of global imbalances and other problems in the world economy. Each country purportedly agreed to undertake a set of reforms and policy changes, and the presumption was that those commitments could then be enforced through peer pressure. The IMF could claim victory for having generated such a broad range of commitments, conveniently ignoring the fact that the IMF and the international community had no leverage to get these large economies to stick to their pledges. For instance, for all the talk of reducing external imbalances, China's current account surplus hit a staggeringly high ratio of 10.7 percent of GDP by the end of 2007.

Moreover, much of the text in the document about promised reforms was in the vague parlance already in use by these governments. The ostensible Chinese commitment to improve the flexibility of the currency regime was based on this promise: "The exchange rate formation mechanism will be improved in a gradual and controllable manner." This formulaic language had been used by China's government for many years and means little of substance. Even the IMF acknowledged its executive board's assessment that the policy measures promised by each country did not amount to much: "While these policies are generally not as ambitious as the IMF has recommended in individual Article IV consultations or the WEO [World Economic Outlook], they nonetheless constitute significant steps forward."

Although it continued to pay lip service to supporting the multilateral consultations, Hank Paulson's U.S. Treasury Department decided that a more forceful approach was needed to deal with China and that the IMF would have to be the instrument. Facing increasing pressure from the U.S. to get tough on China's currency policies, the IMF managing director, a Spaniard named Rodrigo de Rato, then took a precipitous step that would bring improvements in the IMF's relationship with China to a grinding halt.

The IMF Attacks China, Then Retreats

The history of the rocky relationship between China and the IMF goes back more than a decade. China's currency policy has been a long-standing point of contention between its government and the IMF. There was a well-orchestrated routine for how the two sides handled this topic. I beheld this first-hand when I was appointed head of the IMF's China division in 2002. The China team would send out in advance an extensive list of questions for each meeting that we would have in Beijing and other cities. We would get written answers, and the meeting would then largely involve a recitation of many of those answers when we attempted to ask follow-up questions. The response to the question about China's exchange rate regime had been standard and unwavering: "China's exchange rate is determined by market forces and the authorities endeavor to promote the formation of the exchange rate in a stable manner."

Getting ready for our first trip to Beijing, my team added a follow-up written question asking about the workings of the market mechanism for the exchange rate. The response was one that nicely summed up the Chinese approach to market forces: "The exchange rate is fully determined by market supply and demand. The authorities endeavor to manage both supply and demand in a manner that promotes the stable formation of the exchange rate mechanism." In other words, they controlled both supply and demand to get the desired "market-determined" renminbi exchange rate. The Chinese government clearly had a unique perspective on the operation of market forces! By the time I left the China division and returned to the IMF's Research Department at the end of 2004, little progress had been made on the currency issue.

The next summer, China made a modest but dramatic move. On July 21, 2005, the government adjusted up the value of the currency by 1.8 percent relative to the dollar and announced that it would allow the currency to move a little each day relative to its level the previous day. The amount of volatility within each day would be limited to a narrow range of plus or minus 0.3 percent relative to the midpoint set by the People's

Bank of China (PBC). In principle, the currency could thus appreciate by 0.3 percent a day, which could add up to a lot over the course of even one month.

The news was greeted with much excitement, as it was widely taken to be a first step in making the currency regime more flexible. The reality did not quite live up to the high expectations. In practice, the renminbi's appreciation was slow, adding up to barely 5 percent relative to the U.S. dollar one year later. This change was viewed as being too slow to affect global imbalances, because China's trade surplus was continuing to expand and its stock of foreign exchange reserves was growing by leaps and bounds—it had crossed $800 billion by the end of 2005.

By 2006, the IMF was being pushed by many advanced economies, particularly the U.S., to strengthen its criticism of China's currency policies. The IMF needed a better tool to be able to do this, and of course it would not be tenable to single out China. In the middle of 2006, just as the multilateral consultation was getting under way, the IMF also decided to start a review of its procedures for monitoring countries' macroeconomic policies. The procedures were still governed by a document referred to as the "1977 Decision on Surveillance Over Exchange Rates," which clearly needed some updating, as it was toothless on the subject of currency-related policies. It was a reasonable argument that, with rising global financial integration, any country's tampering with exchange rates could affect other countries as well and that the IMF therefore needed to beef up its reviews of currency policies.

The process of revamping the monitoring procedure was resisted by many emerging markets that saw it as simply another tool for the IMF to criticize their policies at the behest of the advanced economies. That the multilateral consultation had fizzled to a damp squib by early 2007 made this issue highly charged, as it had become clear to the emerging markets that the deck was stacked against them as the advanced economies would always have their way. Nevertheless, the understanding was that the revamp would go forward, be debated by the IMF's executive board toward the end of 2007, and become operational soon thereafter.

During the IMF team's visit to Beijing in May 2007, the Chinese expressed displeasure with the process, but they were clearly pulling their punches until that year's report on China was out of the way. The IMF's board was to discuss that report in early July, and the expectation was that the recommendations would go into effect soon thereafter.

Then, in the first week of June 2007, IMF Managing Director Rodrigo de Rato dropped a bombshell.

A Blow to the Chin

De Rato called for an urgent meeting of the IMF's executive board and, with a shorter advance notice period than usual, rammed through the new policies. On June 15, the IMF adopted a new set of procedures for monitoring each country's exchange rate policies, replacing the procedures that had been in place since 1977. The way this change was railroaded through the IMF's executive board was clearly not standard, and the strong feeling in the building was that de Rato had caved in to intense pressure from the U.S.

The document summarizing the new procedures contained strong language on currency manipulation, making it clear that the IMF was arming itself with tools to take on countries that were manipulating their currencies for their own advantage. Despite all the careful language, it was clear that this was to be a cannon squarely aimed at one country—China. The language echoed what the U.S. had been saying all along about China's currency policies—that they were designed to give an unfair competitive edge to China's exports and were the key contributors to global financial instability:

> The new Decision provides more complete guidance to members for the conduct of their exchange rate policies, so as to cover all major causes of external instability rooted in these policies. The 1977 Decision enjoined members to avoid exchange rate manipulation for specific purposes, in particular to gain an unfair competitive advantage over other Fund members. The new Decision adds a principle recommending that members avoid exchange rate policies that *result* [emphasis in original] in external instability, regardless of their purpose, thereby capturing exchange rate policies that have proven to be a major source of instability over the past decades.

Governor Zhou Xiaochuan of the PBC and his colleagues were apoplectic. They knew that this move by the IMF would be seen as a slap in China's face. The PBC had used up significant political capital to get the top leadership of the Chinese Communist Party to agree to a delinking of the renminbi from the dollar in June 2005. Despite strong opposition from the Ministry of Commerce, which saw itself as the defender of the interests of exporters, the PBC had convinced top political leaders that a modest shift in currency policies would help China earn a lot of brownie points in global economic discussions. And now, two years after that move, the IMF was instead going to take China to the woodshed.

Rumors began circulating in Beijing that Governor Zhou had overplayed his hand and would be shunted aside after this fiasco. It was hard to believe that anything to do with the IMF could reverberate among high-level political circles in Beijing. However, the Governor was constantly under attack from traditionalists in the Party, who saw him as much too aligned with the West and willing to undertake reforms that may not necessarily be good for China. The imbroglio with the IMF provided an opportunity for reactionaries in the Party to argue that the West—especially the U.S. and its lackey, the IMF—would never be satisfied with anything China did and would always ask for more.

The reaction was swift and sharp. China quickly shut down the process of its bilateral consultation with the IMF. That year's report had already been circulated to the IMF's executive board, something normally done two weeks before the meeting. But the report was put on hold as the Chinese rejected even the notion of holding a board meeting to discuss that year's report. Instead, they asked for a new team to come to Beijing in the fall of 2007 and explain to them how exchange rates would be assessed under the new methodology—which the Chinese already knew perfectly well—and then come back again to explain how the new methodology would be applied to China. The IMF obliged, then kept updating and rewriting its report every couple of months. But the hope that the Chinese would come around and approve the report—a necessary step before it could be discussed by the IMF's executive board—proved futile.

Now the IMF had a problem on its hands. It could not claim to be doing effective surveillance of the global economy when it could not report on meetings with the government of the second-largest economy in the world. In August 2008, the IMF tried to mollify China by setting up an "ad hoc consultation" to discuss exchange rate policies on a separate track. The Chinese refused to play ball and, as the financial crisis started to hammer the world, the stalemate continued.

Beating a Retreat

Two years later, on June 22, 2009, the IMF mounted a full-scale retreat. Now that the U.S. had its hands full coping with the financial crisis, the IMF could go back to tending to its other large members without fear of recriminations from its largest shareholder. It felt compelled to do this, as it could hardly claim to be an objective referee of global economic policies if it could not publish a report evaluating the policies of the economy making the biggest contribution to world growth.

The document announcing the retreat was put out quietly and with minimum fuss. It was titled "The 2007 Surveillance Decision: Revised Operational Guidance." It started with a remarkably blunt preamble, acknowledging that the new approach had blown up in the IMF's face:

> Implementation of the Decision appears to be broadly achieving
> its objectives, but suffered one major setback. The 2008 Triennial
> Surveillance Review (TSR) found that the focus of surveillance
> has sharpened significantly and that the coverage and quality of
> analysis of exchange rate issues has improved. However, the
> attempt to apply exchange rate-related "labels"—for instance, the
> use of specific terminology such as "fundamental misalignment" . . .
> has proved [*sic*] an impediment to effective implementation of the
> Decision. The TSR noted widespread concerns about cross-country
> consistency in exchange rate analysis, and that undue importance
> should not be attached to precise calculations, given the inherent
> methodological and data limitations.

At the IMF, one quickly learns what certain phrases mean. To say that a policy "appears to be broadly achieving its objectives" implies that it is not working too well.

The next paragraph of the report was remarkable for an IMF document. Without any further attempt to gloss things over or suggest that they were "broadly" going according to plan, the report made it clear that the 2007 decision had damaged the IMF's ability to monitor and evaluate currency policies. Although not explicitly naming China, the report also acknowledged that that decision was directly responsible for the hold-up in consultations with "a few members":

> In addition, there were indications that the attempt to apply labels may even have *weakened* [emphasis in original] the candor of some assessments. Moreover, difficulties in implementing this aspect of the Decision have been the main reason why Article IV consultations with a few members have fallen far behind schedule. These extensive delays have resulted in *less* [emphasis in original] focus by the IMF on members' exchange rate policies in key cases. In those cases, and in putting together a multilateral picture of the world economy, this has undermined IMF surveillance, running counter to the objectives of the 2007 Decision and damaging the IMF's credibility.

The IMF is not often given to such searing indictments of its own policies. What made it easier in this case is that the previous policy was tied to Rodrigo de Rato, the managing director who had pushed it through. De Rato left the IMF in October 2007, so the new managing director, Dominique Strauss-Kahn, was free to blame it all on his predecessor and go back to a clean slate.

After having declared the new approach a failure, the institution then announced its retreat. Country reports would no longer have to make explicit calls about a currency's undervaluation and would have to acknowledge that it was difficult to tell whether a currency's value was at a suitable level or not:

> the guidance would be revised to eliminate the requirement to use specific terms such as "fundamental misalignment" and to make a number of other changes that will acknowledge the large degree of judgment required in the analysis and, in practice, reserve findings on the nonobservance of a Principle for the most egregious cases. Consequently, management also intends to withdraw its statement of August 4, 2008 on the use of ad hoc consultations, which, contrary to expectations, did not help bring to conclusion long-

delayed consultations. These changes will facilitate more effective surveillance.

China graciously accepted the IMF's surrender. On July 8, 2009, after a three-year hiatus, the IMF's executive board finally discussed the China report. Nevertheless, the report was not published that year, as the language about China's currency was still too strong for the government's comfort.

By 2010, the Chinese indicated that they had no objections to the IMF publishing the report from that year's consultation—so long as their disagreement with the IMF's views was highlighted in the report. So that year's published report contained this convoluted boilerplate statement about the currency: "Staff believe that the renminbi remains substantially below the level that is consistent with medium-term fundamentals" and included a strong denial from the authorities that this assessment was based on an analytically sound argument. The report danced around the word "undervaluation," and it included laudatory remarks about what China had done with its currency regime while guardedly describing what it needed to do in the future:

> The central bank's recent decision to return to the managed floating regime that was in place prior to the global financial crisis is extremely welcome. This decision affords the central bank considerable flexibility to tighten monetary conditions through an appreciation of the exchange rate. Going forward, the central bank will need to avoid having movements in the real effective exchange rate determined by the relative strength or weakness of the U.S. dollar, particularly given the very different cyclical conditions in the two economies.

The outcome of these episodes was clear. The IMF had been defanged and would no longer publicly take on China or any of the major advanced economies on this issue. Each country was now on its own in the currency wars.

The developments described in this chapter span the period leading up to and covering the initial phase of the global financial crisis. When the crisis hit, however, leaders of the world's major economies closed ranks, and the spirit of cooperation was revived. Would the collaborative approach built in the darkest days the world economy has experienced in a long time prove enduring or not? While this chapter has established that the answer is negative in the context of currency wars, the next chapter investigates the broader aspects of international policy coordination and how those fared.

It Takes Twenty to Tango

ANDREA (Galileo's student): *Unhappy is the land that breeds no hero.*
GALILEO: *No, Andrea. Unhappy is the land that needs a hero.*

Life of Galileo, Bertolt Brecht

April 2, 2009 dawned as a cloudy and cool day in London, typical spring weather for one of the world's leading international financial centers. The mood was equally gloomy, with a sense of foreboding, in the realm of global finance. That day marked the culmination of a tense two-day summit at which the city hosted the leaders of the world's most powerful economies—the Group of 20 (G-20). There had been a great deal of drama overnight as the leaders, along with teams of aides, sought to fine-tune their communiqué—the official statement that would summarize their discussions and commitments. This was to be a declaration of a grand plan to stem the crisis and get the world economy back on its feet. There was eager anticipation that the leaders would announce major new policy measures.

Gordon Brown, the British prime minister, would have his moment before the cameras later that day. Striding boldly to the podium and standing before an audience that included many journalists from around the world hanging onto his every word, he made a dramatic statement about how the G-20 had decided to act together to shore up world financial markets and get started on reforming the international monetary system. He also announced that the countries had agreed to add $1 trillion to the pool of resources of the major international financial institutions, mostly the IMF. These institutions could use the money to protect poorer countries from the fallout of the crisis. The rhetoric was soaring, befitting the occasion:

> The old Washington consensus is over. Today we have reached a
> new consensus—that we take global action together to deal with

the problems we face. . . . A new world order is emerging and with it the foundations of a new and progressive era of international cooperation.

This was the finest moment of the G-20 when, in the crucible of the crisis, the leaders of a band of disparate countries came together on one stage and announced to the world that they would work together to deal with the short-term crisis and take measures to ensure that it would never happen again. As President Obama put it, "By any measure, the London summit was historic. It was historic because of the size and scope of the challenge we face and because of the timeliness and magnitude of our response."

The feel-good *kumbaya* moment turned out to be a little less perfect as the leaders returned to their national capitals and time wore on. Once the choir had stopped singing hosannas to global cooperation, there was a scramble for details to fill in the blanks left unfilled in Brown's statement. The grand announcement of the G-20 having come up with $1 trillion in new resources, including $750 billion for the IMF, turned out to be premature. For instance, the Chinese government provided no confirmation of the $40 billion that Gordon Brown claimed China had committed to this resource boost. It turned out that only a "generalized pledge" was obtained from countries like China to contribute to the IMF's resources rather than a hard, unconditional commitment.

All this confusion notwithstanding, Gordon Brown had his moment of glory just as he had hoped for. Unfortunately, this might well have been the pinnacle of his political glory. Brown's political fortunes soon began to unravel and ended up with his being booted out of office by the British electorate in May 2010. The trajectory of Brown's political fortunes serves as an apt metaphor for how the much-vaunted unity of the G-20 also began to slowly come apart after this summit. The ennobling prospect of world leaders working together for the common good faltered as it came head to head with the ground realities of domestic politics.

Global coordination of macroeconomic and regulatory policies seems like a desirable objective. The G-20 summit perhaps did have a subtle but positive reinforcing effect on business and consumer confidence, giving a small added boost to the effects of individual countries' fiscal policy

G-20 leaders at London Summit. U.K. Prime Minister Gordon Brown, the host, is in the center of the front row. April 2, 2009. (Photo Presidencia del Gobierno de España.)

measures during the worst of the global financial crisis. The notion was that, even though countries were being driven largely by domestic imperatives, having G-20 leaders stand together and announce the measures they were taking would inspire confidence that these measures would generate even more bang for the buck.

There was a related economic angle as well. Economic theory predicts that a country undertaking fiscal expansion—through some combination of cutting taxes and increasing government expenditures—would see its currency appreciate. This currency appreciation would result in a "leakage" of some of the stimulative effects of those policies, as it would pull in more imports, make the country's exports more expensive abroad, and cause the trade balance to fall. But if all the major economies undertook simultaneous fiscal expansion, conceivably this leakage would be reduced and make fiscal policy more potent within each country, encouraging policymakers to use that policy tool more aggressively.

By the fall of 2009, the worst seemed to be over. In September, G-20 leaders met in Pittsburgh and declared victory: "It worked." The statement they released at the end of their summit went on from that declaration:

Our forceful response helped stop the dangerous, sharp decline in global activity and stabilize financial markets. Industrial output is now rising in nearly all our economies. International trade is starting to recover. . . . Our national commitments to restore growth resulted in the largest and most coordinated fiscal and monetary stimulus ever undertaken.

This declaration of victory proved premature, and the paeans to coopera- tion would soon give way to recriminations, as typified by the currency wars described in Chapter 7.

Global Policy Coordination in Good and Bad Times

Coordination of policies sounds good in theory but is complicated in practice. First of all, difficult issues of national governance must be con- tended with. National legislatures and policymakers are elected to put their own country's interests first. When national and international interests coincide, as happened in the midst of the financial crisis, coor- dination works well. There are other precedents as well, such as the 1985 Plaza Accord, when there was a happy coincidence of domestic and global interests, although such an alignment of interests seems to happen only under otherwise very unhappy circumstances.

Meeting of Minds at the Plaza

In 1985, a persistently strong dollar and high U.S. current account deficits were giving rise to protectionist pressures and fears of turmoil in global financial markets. Top finance officials of the five major economic pow- ers at the time—France, Germany, Japan, the U.K., and the U.S.—met at the Plaza Hotel in New York in September and signed an agreement to take steps that would guide down the value of the dollar. Each signatory committed not just to intervention in foreign exchange markets but also to a set of domestic policies that would help reduce trade imbalances. Germany and Japan agreed to take steps aimed at boosting domestic demand, while the U.S. agreed to cut its budget deficit.

Efforts to drive down the dollar's value were so successful that the five countries, joined by Canada, signed another agreement in 1987—the Louvre accord—that signaled a commitment to stop the dollar from falling further. Although these accords were successful in influencing currency values, the agreements in fact had little effect on the domestic policies of these countries. Even though most of the agreed-on policy commitments were in each nation's own long-term interests, currency intervention proved easier than shifting domestic policies. Policy quick-fixes indeed seem to be easier to implement than more basic reforms that trade off some short-run pain for longer-term benefits.

Barriers to Coordination

Putting aside national interests for the common good becomes especially difficult when there is an apparent conflict between national and global interests in the short term. It is difficult for politicians to sell to their domestic constituencies disciplined policies that might slow growth in the short run but benefit both domestic and global growth and stability over longer periods. This has been a problem even in the context of the euro zone, whose members were not able to stick to their commitments to fiscal discipline despite having signed agreements to keep their deficits and debt levels in check and to monitor one another's public finances.

Furthermore, institutions such as central banks do not have any global considerations as part of their mandate, and they are answerable to their national authorities, so each central bank must do what is right for its country, even if those interests diverge from the broader global interest. Central banks are already getting broader and more diffuse mandates, which could affect their efficiency and independence. In the aftermath of the crisis, they are being asked to take on bigger roles in ensuring not just low inflation and unemployment but also financial stability. They may have little choice but to take on those mandates to maintain their political legitimacy. Adding broader cross-national considerations could complicate those mandates.

Perhaps this view is too pessimistic. Coordination of financial sector regulatory policies could promote global financial stability, which is a desirable objective for any central bank. There are of course powerful vested interests in each country that try to block any reforms, and coordination could be one way to overcome those obstacles to reform. For instance, agreement on a common set of banking regulations could help each country push back against attempts by big and politically well-connected banks to scuttle reforms that would reduce their profitability. One problem is that no obvious commitment mechanism exists to make sure all countries stick to their parts of the bargain through an enforceable international agreement. But this problem may not be insurmountable, so long as domestic and global interests are roughly congruent.

When it comes to monetary policy, however, the situation is inherently set up for conflict. The element of competitiveness enters through the effects of monetary policy on exchange rates. Because an exchange rate is the price of one currency relative to another, monetary policy in one country by construction affects the exchange rate of that country and, therefore, the exchange rates and trade competitiveness of its trading partners.

For economies that trade a lot, the exchange rate is a crucial price, as it determines the competitiveness of exports. For emerging market economies, the stakes are even higher. Their traders are less able to cope with currency volatility, given the low level of development of currency derivatives markets that help to hedge currency risk. Moreover, some smaller emerging market economies are specialized and rely on exports of commodities for a large portion of their GDP. Many emerging markets also tend to rely on exports of relatively low-tech goods, where the margins are low, so even short-run currency appreciations can have devastating consequences for exporters.

As things stand, it would be heresy for a central banker to say that she was factoring into her decisions the effects of her institution's policies on other countries, except insofar as they could have second-round effects on her own country. It was up to fearless academics to propose a framework for confronting those issues.

An Attempt at Herding Cats

In 2011, I was a member of a committee of academics and former central bankers that wrote a report on "Rethinking Central Banking." This self-constituted committee had assigned to itself the task of thinking about reforms to global institutional structures without being too constrained by the status quo and the practical challenges of effecting any big changes. So we could afford to think big instead of just tinkering at the margins.

In one part of the report that received a lot of attention, we discussed the tensions that arise because central banks of large economies do not take into account the effects that their policies have on other economies. We argued that the major central banks, in both advanced economies and emerging markets, should not limit their coordination to periods of extreme global financial stress. Rather, those central banks ought to pay more attention to their collective policy stance and its global implications even in normal times. Of course, this would require that domestic political authorities be persuaded to allow broader considerations to play a role in their central banks' monetary policy frameworks. To make the idea work, an institutional mechanism was needed. So we had this to say:

> We ... propose that a small group of systemically significant central banks, perhaps called the International Monetary Policy Committee, should meet regularly under the auspices of the Committee on the Global Financial System of the BIS [Bank for International Settlements]. This group would discuss and assess the implications of their policies for global liquidity, leverage, and exposures, and the appropriateness of their joint money and credit policies from the point of view of global price, output, and financial stability.

Our recommendation received two types of equally dismissive responses. One was that it would never work. Asking central bankers to reconcile their domestic objectives with considerations of the foreign spillover effects of their policies was a nonstarter. The second was that it was already happening anyway. The latter response was based on the meetings that central bank governors regularly hold at the BIS. But our point was that those informal and closed-door discussions were no substitute for a forum where global spillovers and coordination could be discussed explicitly. We also argued that the discipline of writing a short report assessing and justifying their policies from this global perspective and pointing out areas of dissent or inconsistency would help central bankers in balancing their political pressures at home and abroad.

Such a report would fit in with the goal of increasing central bank transparency. Most major central banks, both in advanced economies and emerging markets, are trying to become more transparent and open, although there is enormous variation in how much progress each one has made. In April 2011, Ben Bernanke started holding press conferences following the release of the Federal Open Market Committee statement. For an even longer period, the BoJ and the ECB have been holding press conferences to explain their monetary policy decisions. Other central banks have started releasing many of their documents and summaries of their policy deliberations online.

Our view was that communication of central bank actions is equally important at the global level as it is for a domestic audience. The hope was that the need to issue periodic public reports could help central bankers identify instances where individual central banks' policies were at cross-purposes with those of other central banks. With time, this practice could nudge them, however modestly, to start taking into account some of the external consequences of their policies. This recommendation was not made lightly, for it would add to the already complicated mix of domestic mandates that today's central bankers have to cope with. Nevertheless, we felt it was important to place the issue squarely on the table, as it needed to be addressed in some form or another as the world became more financially connected and central banks' actions affected one another more and more.

Lars Svensson, a deputy governor at the Swedish central bank (and a former professor at Princeton University), took us on directly in a paper delivered at a Federal Reserve Bank of San Francisco conference in November 2011. Referring to our recommendation that central banks should pay more attention to their collective policy stance and its global implications, he wrote:

> I do not agree with that conclusion. The Federal Reserve's mandate concerns U.S. inflation and employment, and the Federal Reserve is not responsible for inflation, real developments, and monetary policy in other countries except as they feed back into the United States. That responsibility should rest with the policy authorities in those countries. Countries that choose to stabilize their dollar exchange rate or even peg to the dollar will tend to import U.S. expansionary monetary policy into their own country.... A flexible exchange rate would give the countries the option of conducting an independent monetary policy appropriate for the country in

question. . . . If countries nevertheless choose a peg to the dollar, with capital inflows, bubbles, and other negative effects, they are themselves responsible for those effects.

Svensson had concisely captured the prevailing view among advanced economy central bankers: they had neither the responsibility nor the mandate to think about the spillover effects of their policies on other countries. If only emerging markets would adopt flexible exchange rates and stop intervening in foreign exchange markets, there would be no problem, as currency movements would act as a natural adjustment mechanism.

With radical solutions off the table, it was back to tinkering with existing institutions to make progress on the issue of global spillovers.

The IMF Tries to Regain Its Mojo

With recriminations flying and global coordination falling victim to narrow country interests, it is clear that a referee of some sort will be needed to prevent adverse outcomes such as trade protectionism or barriers to the flow of capital that could hurt everyone. Some international financial institutions were set up in the postwar period to play precisely this role. The role of such institutions has returned to the forefront now that the internal tensions in the G-20 are being clearly exposed. Perhaps we should turn to one of these institutions, which was discussed in the previous chapter, to solve this conundrum and get countries pulling in the same direction.

In the mid-1990s, the IMF was angling for jurisdiction over countries' capital accounts and making a big push for capital account liberalization around the world. The 1997–98 Asian financial crisis put an end to that. That crisis was widely seen as being precipitated by capital account opening that exposed economies in the region to the volatility of foreign capital flows. The global financial crisis has brought things full circle, with the IMF trying to make a back door play for jurisdiction over international capital movements, although with a great deal more circumspection in its endorsement of capital account opening.

Under the "Articles of Agreement" that govern the operation of the institution, the IMF has the responsibility to monitor capital flows related to current account transactions. Countries would be in violation of IMF rules if they tried to restrict capital flows associated with trade transactions (payments related to the import and export of goods and services) or remittances being sent home by workers with jobs outside their home countries.

However, most global capital flows these days have less to do with trade transactions and are more about cross-border investment flows—these would be classified as capital account transactions. Other than collecting and publishing data, the IMF has no say over how these flows are enabled, regulated, or restricted by different countries. The IMF has made a bid to exercise control over capital account transactions as well, arguing that this control is essential for its goal of promoting global financial stability. This has proven contentious, as there is little consensus about how to define guidelines for whether current account or capital account balances are at the right level for a country at a particular time. The bid also got a strong pushback from emerging markets, who were suspicious of the IMF's intentions.

A different tack has been pushed by emerging markets, which have been frustrated at being beset by problems caused by the fiscal profligacy and other undisciplined policies of the advanced economies. Many emerging market policymakers have argued that, instead of preaching to the emerging markets, institutions such as the IMF ought to focus more on global instability caused by the suppliers of private capital—who are of course largely from richer and more advanced economies. Emerging markets were in effect telling the IMF to act as traffic police, getting the SUV-driving maniacs to stop speeding rather than blaming the smaller cars puttering along on the capital flow highway that sometimes end up as road kill, even if they themselves do everything right and play by the rules.

A Rulebook for Capital Flows

The IMF, recognizing that it needed to be more sensitive to the needs of emerging markets and trying to assuage these increasingly influential members, undertook an ambitious project to define a set of guidelines for global capital flows. At the November 2010 summit in Seoul, the G-20 leaders directed the IMF to conduct more analysis along these lines. This was a convenient sop for all countries, which could redirect any blame from themselves to a "system," exemplified by volatile and unpredictable capital flows, that was not working well and needed to be fixed.

The IMF's managing director at the time, Dominique Strauss-Kahn, never one to let an opportunity pass, recognized that this directive was enough of an opening for the IMF to get more directly involved in the functioning of global capital markets. He received support from French President Nicolas Sarkozy, who was next in line to hold the presidency of the G-20. Strauss-Kahn quickly transformed the goal of harnessing undisciplined capital flows into one of bringing countries' capital account policies under IMF surveillance. This was to be accomplished by developing a set of principles for capital account management.

French President Nicolas Sarkozy and IMF Managing Director Dominique Strauss-Kahn. July 9, 2009. (Michael Gottschalk, AFP / Getty Images.)

The project, enthusiastically championed by Sarkozy, was in some respects a noble one. The stated objective was to codify "rules of the road" to protect countries that have the right policies but get caught up in spillovers of global turmoil or the knock-on effects of policies undertaken by large economies. Capital flow guidelines would give the IMF a tool to evaluate the cross-border effects of advanced economies' policies.

The idea was initially an appealing one for emerging markets, whose officials felt that for far too long, institutions like the IMF have tended to lay the blame for capital flow volatility on the policies and institutions of the host countries. Officials in these economies think that whether or not their behavior is virtuous is irrelevant when the consequences of advanced economies' economic mismanagement wash on to their shores. Furthermore, financial institutions from advanced economies are capable of wreaking considerable damage, but many of them, such as hedge funds, fly under the radar of their home country financial regulators.

The Rules Hit a Roadblock

For all the nobility of the IMF's intentions—and to the surprise of the economists working on the project—the response to the report proposing a framework for rules of the road for capital flows was uniformly and resoundingly negative. Advanced economies dismissed any notion of the IMF playing a role in evaluating whether capital flows into or out of their economies were reasonable relative to economic fundamentals. Emerging markets realized that the IMF was never going to have much leverage over the advanced economies and might use any new framework simply to expand its jurisdiction over emerging markets' policies. Countries like Brazil certainly did not want the IMF to be in the position of evaluating whether their capital account policies were reasonable, reflecting the suspicion of emerging markets that the institution would always put the interests and agenda of advanced economies first.

The discussion of the report at the IMF executive board on December 17, 2010, was a heated and rancorous one that laid bare the opposition from all sides to what was seen as either an unnecessary intrusion or a power grab. The official summary of the meeting tried to put the best possible spin on a bad outcome:

Directors expressed a wide range of views regarding amendment of the Articles of Agreement to provide a more complete and consistent legal framework for addressing issues related to capital flows. While a number of Directors were open to considering an amendment of the Articles in the future, most felt that it would be premature to initiate a discussion on this step without further analysis and practical experience.

For those in the international policy community, the code words were unambiguous. "A wide range of views" implies disagreement. "While a number of Directors were open . . . , most felt that it would be premature" meant that the project had been declared dead on arrival.

Never one to be deterred from his grand visions, Sarkozy made a fresh appeal in January 2011 for a code of conduct to regulate international capital flows. He signaled that he wanted to make it a major achievement of the G-20 summit to be held in Cannes that fall. Strauss-Kahn picked up on this signal, seeing another opportunity for the IMF to put this issue back on the table. But the Cannes summit, like the previous year's Seoul summit, would be taken over by more pressing matters, such as the euro zone debt crisis and ongoing currency wars. So, as with many other grand proposals, plans to construct rules of the road fell by the wayside.

Setting Standards

Politics aside, thorny analytical issues are always involved in designing a framework setting out reasonable guidelines for capital flows. To make progress on this requires clear standards against which to assess current account balances and capital flows. Economic theory does not provide good benchmarks for evaluating the direction and patterns of capital flows, especially given various frictions that prevent markets from working smoothly—including information barriers, weak financial regulation, and perverse incentives for investment managers that lead to their focusing on short-term profits. As discussed earlier, the standard neoclassical theory does not seem to work too well—capital is flowing uphill rather than downhill as predicted by the theory. Also contrary to the theory, developing countries with small current account deficits or larger surpluses seem to have done better in terms of growth outcomes.

Other attempts to create measures of "equilibrium" or desirable current account positions have floundered, not for want of effort, but because it is a complex issue. Even broad notions of equilibrium current accounts are useful only as long-run constructs, and the mapping from the long run to the present is more complicated. One would have to take into account business cycle conditions and other special factors in a particular country, which tilt the process more toward judgment (and therefore make it subject to manipulation) rather than toward a straightforward application of a general formula.

Another issue is the need to assess whether current account balances are being driven by transitory or permanent shocks, which makes it difficult to arrive at sound judgments about the desirable levels of those balances. Determining the right level of current account balances will become even more complicated as currency valuation effects and earnings on foreign investments increasingly drive movements in current accounts. These complexities will make it difficult to construct useful guidelines for capital flows that have broad applicability and immediate relevance.

Getting Markets to Work Better

Rather than focus on evaluating the appropriateness and sustainability of current account balances and exchange rates, a more productive analytical approach is to start with some basic questions about why global capital markets are not working as they should. For all its warts, the benchmark theoretical model of unrestricted financial flows, with capital markets efficiently allocating funds to their most productive uses around the world, can serve as a useful frame of reference for such an analysis. In generic terms, it is possible to construct a list of elements for an ideal world from the perspective of emerging markets:

- Stable long-term capital flows that have significant direct and indirect (collateral) benefits.
- Flows driven by macroeconomic fundamentals, such as growth, productivity, and business cycle conditions, and not subject to sharp, random stops or reversals.
- Flows that cushion domestic business cycle fluctuations.

- Good policies—fiscal and monetary discipline—in advanced economies.
- Well-regulated financial markets.

The reality is a little different:

- Foreign direct investment (FDI) now constitutes a large portion of net flows to emerging markets, which is good. But bank flows that are often volatile and destabilizing still play a large role in global finance, especially in terms of flows among advanced economies.
- Capital flows are prone to herding behavior, mass euphoria, and panics that may have little to do with economic fundamentals.
- Flows are procyclical—creating problems with demand management on both the upswings (inflationary pressures, asset bubbles, etc.) and downswings of domestic business cycles.
- Monetary policy in advanced economies may itself be contributing to capital flow volatility and financial risks. Fiscal policy in these economies is also adding to global financial and macroeconomic stresses.
- There has been limited progress in bringing financial markets under a tighter regulatory rein. Meanwhile, the shadow banking system—comprising hedge funds, private equity, and other types of firms that are lightly regulated—remains large and is likely to grow further.

The gulf between the ideal version and the reality of global finance is wide and will not be easy to bridge. Large reserve currency economies are not subject to market discipline, as they can finance large amounts of foreign borrowing at low cost. Capital markets are not doing their job well, either within or across countries, and many obvious distortions affect financial market outcomes. Weak financial market regulation gives financial institutions free rein to make highly leveraged bets that often translate into large and volatile cross-border capital flows. Perverse incentives for asset managers lead them to focus on short-term profits. Moral hazard is another usual suspect—there are institutions (as well as countries) that may be seen as systemically important and too big to fail, allowing them to wreak even more havoc.

Sensible and practical answers exist for some of these problems. Unconstrained leverage is a problem that can be handled through regulatory tools. Increased capital requirements and other constraints on big financial institutions, along with frameworks that allow for orderly resolution of failing institutions, reduce the damage they can cause if they falter. Global coordination of regulatory policies would clearly be helpful to tackle some of these issues and to prevent regulatory arbitrage (movement of financial institutions' operational bases to jurisdictions where regulation is weakest).

Some of these steps are gradually being implemented under Basel III, a new international regulatory framework for banks. However, this framework is voluntary, and countries can choose if and when they adopt it. Certain key advanced economies, such as the U.S. and the U.K., have signed on to the framework but have been accused of dragging their feet on implementing the reforms. Even in the best of circumstances, some unevenness in the implementation and follow-through on these reforms is inevitable, given the large differences in financial market and regulatory structures across countries.

In short, it is going to be a steep, uphill, and probably futile climb to try to fully discipline international capital flows.

Virtuous Policies Are Not Enough

Many problems that come under the rubric of harmful policy spillovers can be traced to weak macroeconomic and financial regulatory policies among both the suppliers and recipients of capital. Nevertheless, it is difficult to explain short-run movements in either prices or quantities related to international finance—exchange rates and capital flows—using just macroeconomic fundamentals. Fluctuations in currency values and capital flows sometimes seem detached from fundamentals and can be driven purely by sharp swings in investor sentiment triggered by perceptions rather than reality. So, getting domestic policies right may not be sufficient to fix short-term volatility, which might well be an intrinsic feature of private capital markets.

If capital flows were responding purely to economic fundamentals, then it would be conceptually easier to focus on domestic policies in both host and recipient countries for capital flows and to try to get them in order. But differences in policies could generate tensions simply because countries are at different phases of the business cycle. Policies that are right for one country could lead to flows that are undesirable from the perspective of other countries, causing problems for the latter. Loose monetary policy may be right for advanced economies that are stuck in recession and fear deflation but could be bad for emerging markets experiencing much better growth and inflationary pressures. No rulebook for capital flows can deal with this basic tension. It is also not straightforward to disentangle temporary flows from more persistent ones, adding yet another layer of complication to any conceptual framework.

Apart from all these roadblocks, one core question is whether the IMF can help solve specific market failures through coordination. Other than for financial regulation, a compelling case has yet to be made that multilateral coordination, either through the IMF or some other channel, would be the right solution to the problem of volatile capital flows that breed financial and macroeconomic instabilities.

This leaves policymakers in emerging market economies in a tight corner. For all their allure, policy coordination and the establishment of rules for the orderly flow of capital may not be realistic solutions, especially where sovereign nations are involved. With coordination off the table, countries have been driven to look for self-defense strategies.

The Siren Song of Capital Controls

MAJOR EVANS: *Just what do you have in mind, Marshal?*

MATT DILLON (Marshal of Dodge City, Kansas): *I'll have to tell you later—if it works. . . .*

MAJOR EVANS: *I just hope you know what you're doing.*

MATT DILLON: *Major, does a man ever know?*

Gunsmoke, Episode 89: "The Gun Smuggler"

With coordination clearly not working and policymakers in emerging market economies feeling under siege, they have returned to an old tool that had been discredited as being ineffective at best and harmful at worst—capital controls. After all, who could blame them for turning to desperate measures in desperate times? With emerging markets having increasing economic influence in the global arena, these countries have also begun to shift the terms of the debate, arguing that capital controls are a legitimate defensive tool to deal with surges of inflows. Such inflows can leave long-lasting scars on a country's manufacturing sector and export market shares if they result in sharp currency appreciations. Although capital controls have their dark side, do they have a legitimate role if used judiciously and as a last resort?

Capital Controls Make a Comeback

Capital controls have a long and undistinguished history in international finance, but they are coming back into vogue. In the past, many emerging markets have tried using these controls to prevent capital flight by domestic and foreign investors when bad macroeconomic policies spell trouble. Others have been reluctant to drop controls at all, based on the legitimate fear that their financial markets could be overwhelmed by capital inflows and that opening up channels for outflows could cause their weak banking systems to collapse. Unrestricted capital flows could spell disaster for an economy that has dysfunctional financial markets, high levels of corruption, and weak monetary and fiscal policies.

Facing sharp currency appreciation and fearing asset price booms fueled by hot money, some emerging markets have taken to re-imposing narrow capital controls to limit inflows. When dealing with pressures from exporters hurt by rising exchange rates, nervous officials in many other emerging markets have contemplated broader controls on capital inflows.

Mixed Evidence on Effectiveness

The evidence on the effectiveness of capital controls is far from conclusive. Selective capital controls have been touted as a solution to the problem that broad capital controls can have undesirable side effects, scaring off international investors entirely. This approach involves developing a hierarchy of good and bad flows and then trying to keep out just the latter. As discussed in Chapter 4, long-term investments, especially FDI, are seen as more favorable and stable than short-term ones. When they make these investments, foreign investors are not just looking to make a quick buck and then make a dash for the exits when circumstances turn rough. In contrast, short-term debt, which turns into a burden in bad times, is seen as especially pernicious. Inflows into equity markets have some benefits but can also be flighty, fueling stock market booms and then exacerbating market downturns.

Many countries have tried to limit the latter two types of flows. The problem is that money tends to be fungible—one form of capital can easily be transformed into another—making such fine distinctions hard to enforce. For instance, in certain periods, India's restrictions on debt inflows have led to money coming into the stock market, which is quite open to inflows, and apparently then being swapped for debt domestically through debt-equity swaps. In countries with relatively well-developed financial markets that facilitate complex financial transactions, such fungibility is an even bigger issue, and it proves difficult to keep money from coming in (or leaving) through multiple channels.

Still, there is some evidence that carefully targeted controls, if backed up by other policies, can affect the composition and maturity structure of inflows. The canonical example is that of Chile, which in 1991 imposed an unremunerated reserve requirement on short-term inflows. This requirement was effectively a tax, as it required foreign investors to put part of their investments into a reserve account that paid no interest for a year before they could use that money. This control was regularly modified and updated but stayed on the books until 1998. Over that period, it did have the positive effect of tilting the balance toward longer-term inflows, which were not subject to the tax.

Controls are much less effective at influencing the total volume of inflows, which is what matters for currency appreciation. This was true in the Chilean case as well. When there are strong incentives for money to flow across borders, it will find a way. Irrespective of legal restrictions on flows, the capital account becomes more porous as trade expands, financial markets develop and become more sophisticated, and corporations and financial institutions increase their cross-border operations. These channels make it easier to circumvent capital controls. This is especially true in circumstances where the incentives, such as cross-border interest differentials, are strong enough.

Even in a tightly managed economy like China's, massive inflows have been able to find their way around capital controls over the past decade. One way to evade capital controls, for instance, is through misinvoicing of trade transactions, which is difficult to trace and serves as an easy conduit for money to flow into or out of an economy. There is a suspicion that Chinese exports are often invoiced at a higher value than their actual price. This allows the circumvention of controls on capital inflows, as all of the money coming in as export receipts is in principle based on legitimate trade transactions and therefore not subject to restrictions.

Worth a Try?

Even if they might prove ineffective, are capital controls worth a try as they are costless? Capital controls have real costs even if they succeed only modestly in stanching inflows. Such controls can sometimes turn out to be attempts by well-connected business elites and politicians to enrich themselves. The controls tend to shift inflows toward firms that have better political connections, breeding corruption. Capital controls also create a layer of protection from competition for those firms that are better connected, politically or economically, or have the sheer heft to get around the restrictions. Large firms tend to have better access to financial markets abroad, so controls on inflows tend to hurt smaller firms disproportionately.

Imposing controls also spawns uncertainty about a country's policies. Cat-and-mouse games ensue as the authorities try to stay one step ahead of investors, who quickly find ways to evade controls. This dynamic creates further policy uncertainty, which is not good for growth or stability. In the Chilean case, the government had to frequently rework its capital controls to try to stymie investors who had found ways around the existing sets of controls. The controls on short-term inflows were circumvented by labeling those inflows as long-term inflows, which were not subject to controls, and using domestic financial transactions to swap inflows of different maturities. In a country like Brazil that has sophisticated financial markets, instruments such as derivatives and the ability to devise financial transactions that swap one type of inflow for another make it even easier to circumvent capital controls.

It gets worse if investors, either domestic or foreign, interpret the imposition of even modest controls as a sign of unstable policies.

A Central Bank's Reputation Takes a Baht

In December 2006, Thailand's central bank was facing intense pressure to act. With short-term capital flooding in, the Thai baht was at a nine-year high against the dollar after a 12 percent appreciation during the year, raising the hackles of Thai exporters, whose competitiveness was being battered in international markets. Although currency appreciation made imports cheaper, the inflows of foreign capital were pushing domestic inflation to uncomfortably high levels. The central bank was constrained in acting to control inflation, knowing that raising interest rates sharply to tamp down inflation could in fact attract more capital and make the inflation problem worse. The stock market was booming, leading to worries that a bubble was forming, which could eventually collapse and cause pain to domestic investors.

On December 18, 2006, the governor of the Bank of Thailand, Tarisa Watanagase, announced the imposition of capital controls on portfolio inflows—30 percent of such investments would have to be deposited in a reserve account, where they would earn no interest, for one year. Such funds would also be subjected to a 33 percent tax if withdrawn in less than a year. Other countries have imposed such unremunerated reserve requirements, and surely, thought central bank officials, markets would understand the logic and necessity of such a move. That evening, the governor left Bangkok, reportedly on a trip to Chiang Mai that had been planned earlier.

When Thai stock markets opened the next morning, the reaction to the previous day's action was swift and brutal. Foreign investors, fearing that the move signaled further controls to come, began to liquidate their stock positions, and domestic investors followed suit. In less than two hours, the main market index fell by nearly 15 percent. Trading was shut down. That evening, the Thai finance minister, Pridiyathorn Devakula, announced that the capital control measure had been pulled back significantly and would not apply to stock market investors.

This was a double embarrassment for the Thai central bank—not only had it come across as clumsy and unprepared for market reaction, but it looked like it had been overridden by the finance minister, a blow to the bank's credibility and independence. Governor Tarisa subsequently defended the central bank's actions in imposing the controls, noting that huge imbalances in global trade and savings were sending large amounts of money sloshing into and out of economies like hers. She cautioned that "if this sort of problem is not cured in a cooperative manner, we could see similar measures elsewhere. Each country will have to find a way to take matters into its own hands."

Emerging Markets Act and the IMF Follows

Countries under siege have not been shy about imposing controls on specific types of flows that they view as damaging, even while recognizing that such controls are a last resort and provide at best limited and temporary protection. Since 2009, when advanced economy central banks started resorting to unconventional monetary policies and massive quantitative easing, some countries—including Brazil, Indonesia, Korea, Peru, and Thailand—have imposed controls designed to limit inflows. Interestingly, only a handful of countries have put controls on outflows recently—notably Argentina, Cyprus, Iceland, and Ukraine.

Argentina is, as always, a special case. Since the re-election of President Cristina Kirchner in October 2011, her government has imposed a series of controls to stem outflows and shore up central bank reserves. Argentina's government has been at loggerheads with the international community on account of its erratic policies, including nationalization of industries owned by foreigners and concerns about manipulated economic data. Hence, Argentina has struck out on its own in implementing such controls, paying little heed to the views of foreign investors or international financial institutions.

Other countries imposing controls on outflows under dire economic circumstances have not had such a free hand. Facing a meltdown of its banking system, which had accumulated massive foreign liabilities, Iceland shut off outflows completely in 2008 by eliminating the convertibility of domestic currency accounts for capital account transactions. In 2008, Ukraine was hit by a sharp fall in prices for its exports (metals), a collapse in export demand, and a reversal of capital flows. Facing a banking and currency crisis, the government put in place many regulatory measures on banks and other institutions to reduce capital outflows and defend the exchange rate. Cyprus imposed stringent controls on outflows in March 2013 to forestall a banking collapse.

All three of these European countries needed IMF financial support to get through their respective crises, so they had to be cautious when seeking IMF approval for capital controls. They did so by making the case that the controls were warranted by extreme circumstances and that they would be temporary.

In contrast, countries putting controls on inflows have not bothered much one way or the other about the IMF's views on the matter. Sensing a loss of influence as it had little leverage over countries imposing controls, the IMF started to come around to the view that controls were okay so long as they were put in place for the right reasons and under the right circumstances. The intellectual machinery of the IMF started grinding its wheels in the direction of building a framework for what was already happening in practice, in the hope that this would then allow the institution to start exerting more influence over the process.

Labels Matter

In international economic policy, as in most other areas, labeling is important. To cleanse capital controls of their stigma, the first order of business was to rename them in a way that clarified the objective as managing rather than blocking flows. So the IMF renamed capital controls as Capital Flow Management measures (CFMs). Then, on December 3, 2012, the IMF released a paper laying out its institutional view on the liberalization and management of capital flows. In typically grandiose language that tries to cover all bases, the announcement went as follows: "The IMF has developed a comprehensive, flexible, and balanced view on the management of global capital flows to help give countries clear and consistent policy advice." The report was clear that the IMF was not providing a blanket endorsement of capital controls and that their legitimacy would be determined by circumstances specific to each country and for a particular period:

> In certain circumstances, introducing CFMs can be useful, particularly when underlying macroeconomic conditions are highly uncertain, the room for macroeconomic policy adjustment is limited, or appropriate policies take undue time to be effective. CFMs could also be appropriate to safeguard financial stability when inflow surges contribute to systemic risks in the financial sector.

Such well-intentioned statements with multiple qualifications and caveats hardly provide concrete guidance. The IMF added another qualification, making it clear that capital controls should not be thought of as a substitute for other policies: "CFMs should be targeted, transparent and generally temporary—being lifted once the surge abates, in light of their costs."

The IMF's openness to capital controls, with a neatly alliterative qualification about when and how they should be used (targeted, transparent, temporary), did not entirely endear it to emerging markets, who remain deeply suspicious of its intentions. The feisty Paulo Nogueira Batista, the representative for Brazil and a group of other Latin American economies on the IMF's executive board, had this to say in response to the report:

> The IMF is eager to adopt a prescriptive approach and to advise countries on how to liberalize and manage capital flows. However, the institution's track record in this area is far from stellar. The ongoing crisis has yet to have a full impact on the way the IMF considers capital flows. The extent of the damage that large and volatile flows can cause to recipient countries has not been sufficiently recognized. The Fund has barely explored the effects

of advanced countries' monetary, financial and other policies on capital flows—the so-called push factors. There is a lack of evenhandedness.

These remarks echoed his earlier statements that the IMF was absolving the advanced economies of blame in creating destabilizing capital flows. The news service Reuters quoted an Indian finance ministry official as endorsing this sentiment, saying that each country knew best how to control its inflows and outflows and that these policies should not be based on recommendations from the IMF:

> This talk of capital controls came about because of loose monetary policies by Europe and the U.S. When they set about bringing in those monetary policies, they did not care about the spillover effects it would have on the rest of the global [economy]. And now the IMF wants us, in a way, to clean up.

The reality on the ground is that emerging markets are going to take matters into their own hands. It does not matter whether the IMF approves or not. Still, the framework is important. And the IMF has made a useful conceptual distinction between controls that are aimed at preventing financial instability and those that are meant to prevent currency appreciation. So long as controls can be justified on financial stability grounds and are applied in a nondiscriminatory manner to both domestic and foreign investors (or domestic and foreign institutions), they have the IMF's blessing. This distinction gets a lot blurrier in practice, and the so-called macro-prudential measures may be hard to tell apart from more blatantly protectionist policies. Moreover, evaluating when capital controls are legitimate requires fine judgments about the temporary versus persistent nature of flows, which is difficult to do in real time.

The Bottom Line on Controls

Capital controls may no longer be a bad idea. But they are still not a great idea and are far more attractive in theory than in practice. The dangerous seduction of quick-fixes like capital controls is that they provide a false sense of security and delay needed adjustments in an economy. Dealing with the effects of one set of distortions by adding more distortions in the form of capital controls and other ad hoc measures may ultimately prove counterproductive by worsening policy instability.

Mantras about good fiscal and monetary policies may give little solace to a central banker or finance minister desperate to stave off surging inflows and placate domestic clamor for blocking currency appreciation. But knee-jerk reactions to stifle the exchange rate appreciation that should follow from strong productivity growth eventually only stoke more inflows.

None of this is to say that the risks of foreign capital flows have evaporated and that emerging markets should throw open their capital accounts at one shot. There are still huge inefficiencies in international financial markets, which remain beset by herd behavior and other pathologies. The harsh reality is that emerging market policymakers have little choice but to actively manage the process of capital account opening to improve the benefit-cost trade-off, rather than try to resist it by imposing controls. Otherwise, they may end up with the worst of all worlds—the costs of capital controls, domestic policy complications from volatile capital flows, and few of the potential benefits of foreign capital.

A Better Approach but Not a Panacea

There is a better and more realistic approach for emerging markets to deal with capital flows, one that is more under their own control. This strategy centers on getting the basics right, from financial development and banking regulation to fiscal and monetary policies, so that capital flows in a more stable and efficient manner.

Certain concrete actions can help. Many Asian economies, including large ones like China and India, lack well-developed corporate bond markets. This is a result of regulatory impediments as well as a host of other factors, including the absence of clear legal frameworks. Corporate bonds can attract longer-term investors, letting them benefit from the relatively strong growth prospects of these economies, and can help channel those funds into investments that have a longer-term payoff. Improving corporate governance and promoting rigorous and transparent accounting procedures would also encourage growth of bond markets. Moreover, these steps would help direct foreign capital to better managed and more productive companies. In short, broader and better regulated financial markets can help emerging markets to absorb inflows and effectively channel them into productive rather than speculative activities.

Financial market development would help reduce the burden on central banks to recycle capital inflows through foreign exchange market intervention. Households in these economies have a strong incentive to invest abroad—at least for diversification purposes, if nothing else. To do this, they need instruments other than just banking deposits. Basic securities and mutual funds, rather than any exotic financial products, are necessary and sufficient to help retail investors achieve better diversification of their portfolios through international investment. It is also in the self-interest of emerging markets as a group to foster financial market development. It will allow them to invest more among themselves instead of financing fiscal profligacy in advanced economies.

Macroeconomic policies also play a useful role in reducing exposure to risks from capital flow volatility. Countries with weak economic policies that result in high levels of public debt or volatile inflation not only get less favorable—that is, less stable—types of inflows but are also likely to be hurt more by capital flow volatility. India, for instance, has a high level of public debt (67 percent of GDP in 2012) and a large current account deficit (5 percent of GDP in 2012), meaning that its public finances and external finances are both points of vulnerability. India has a high private saving rate—and needs a high investment rate to grow—but undisciplined government spending has created large budget deficits that in turn contribute to large current account deficits. Thus, when capital inflows dry up, India either has to cut its consumption and investment or must eat into its international reserves. Neither of these is an attractive option. Turkey is another country with a large current account deficit and therefore is heavily reliant on foreign finance. Bringing down government deficits and debt to manageable levels and tackling other problems that breed large current account deficits can help make emerging markets more resilient to the volatility of capital flows.

Reality Not Quite As Neat

As usual, the reality is more complex than is suggested by the above orthodox prescriptions. One paradox is that in the short run, emerging markets with better financial markets and good growth prospects may end up having to deal with a larger volume of inflows than those with underdeveloped financial markets that intrinsically limit foreign investment.

Take a country like Malaysia. It has reasonably well-developed financial markets and is seen as less plagued by corruption compared to some of its close neighbors. When Asian economies are doing well, Malaysia feels that it receives disproportionate attention from foreign investors, simply because they have better access to investment opportunities there relative to a country like the Philippines, which is less financially developed.

Sukhdave Singh, deputy governor of Bank Negara Malaysia (Malaysia's central bank), has succinctly summed up this dilemma:

Some would argue that having deeper financial markets would allow EMEs [emerging market economies] to better absorb these capital inflows. This may or may not be the case. It is not easy for EMEs to develop such deep markets and, even if they do, deeper financial markets are a double-edged sword. While the availability of more instruments and participants may mitigate the extreme volatility seen in shallow markets, it may also be the case that the availability of deep and liquid markets may end up attracting more capital inflows. In that case, the job of the central bank may be no easier. In fact, with the larger flows, it may be that the central bank would have to hold a higher volume of reserves in order to mitigate the impact of these flows on the domestic financial system.

Another case from Asia highlights the complex cost-benefit calculus of opening up financial markets to foreign capital. India has benefited greatly from the ease with which foreign investors can invest in its stock markets. This presents a stark contrast with China, where equity investment by investors from other countries is heavily restricted. Foreign inflows have helped deepen and increase liquidity in India's stock markets. Inflows have provided a useful source of financing for Indian corporations that no longer have to rely just on the domestic banking system, which has limited capacity to fund the country's megacorporations. For all their benefits, however, foreign equity inflows have also added to the volatility of India's stock markets and to currency volatility. The saving grace is that foreign investors bear both the currency and return risks on their stock investments, so the burden of this volatility does not fall solely on Indian residents.

No Place to Hide

The discomforting conclusion from the analysis in this chapter is that there are no easy answers. Sound fiscal and monetary policies, along with better financial markets, can help manage capital flows but might also lead to perverse outcomes by bringing in more capital when it is least needed. So, as their capital accounts become more open by choice or otherwise, all the forces that impel emerging markets to accumulate more foreign exchange reserves to protect themselves from volatile capital flows are stronger than before.

Those countries with weak financial markets and institutions are subject to inflation and asset market booms, because they cannot absorb inflows effectively, making them susceptible to domestic crashes and large capital outflows. Those with better financial markets get more than their fair share of inflows in good times and therefore feel an equal need to build up large stocks of reserves to protect themselves from capital flow volatility.

This dilemma was summed up by Marion Williams, then governor of the Central Bank of Barbados, in a speech he delivered in 2005:

> Perversely, because Caribbean capital markets are not yet very deep, capital flows tend to be less volatile, so for the time being, there is no evidence of excessive volatility in the capital markets of most of the English-speaking Caribbean. . . . as the Caribbean deepens its capital market—which it is making every effort to do—Central Banks in the region may need to hold higher levels of foreign exchange reserves in order to deal with the volatility which can result unless they are willing to let the exchange rate depreciate.

In short, with financial market development and greater integration into global financial markets, emerging markets of all stripes now have even greater demand for safe assets, which leads them to—you guessed it— accumulating even more dollar-denominated assets.

Global coordination and self-defense through capital controls both seem like logical, but ultimately unviable, strategies for countries caught up in the maelstrom of capital flows, who would like to stay safe but without slipping deeper into the dollar's clutches. Perhaps the answer lies somewhere in the middle, between full-fledged coordination and solitary self defense. In the next chapter, I turn to a few middle-of-the-road solutions—various manifestations of global financial safety nets that have been proposed or are already in operation—to see whether they constitute viable alternatives that could ease the iron grip of the dollar.

Safety Nets with Gaping Holes

No man is an island,
Entire of itself.
Each is a piece of the continent,
A part of the main.
If a clod be washed away by the sea,
Europe is the less.
As well as if a promontory were.

As well as if a manor of thine own
Or of thine friend's were.
Each man's death diminishes me,
For I am involved in mankind.
Therefore, send not to know
For whom the bell tolls,
It tolls for thee.

John Donne

Replace "man" with "country" and you get a sense of how John Donne's words must resonate with besieged policymakers in emerging markets. When they hear a bell tolling in the form of a financial crisis in any part of the world, they are well aware that it could be tolling for them, too.

With global coordination off the table and self-defense ineffectual, they have tried to find other ways to circle the wagons and fend off the marauding hordes of currency speculators. They have also reached for other lifelines. Each of these approaches has its flaws and limitations. Once the issue is clearly framed—that countries want insurance against crises—there is a simpler and more obvious solution. Before getting to that, however, it is instructive to examine why the existing alternatives, which I review below, do not provide a resolution and, in some ways, only reinforce the status quo.

Swap Lines

Every central bank has one powerful armament in its arsenal—the ability to print money. Monetary economists have taken one important lesson from the U.S. Great Depression in the 1930s and Japan's Long Recession in the 1990s—a central bank can make a bad economic situation worse if it declines to use this armament or even if it holds its powder dry for too long.

In 2000, while still a Princeton University professor, Ben Bernanke wrote an essay titled "Japanese Monetary Policy: A Case of Self-Induced Paralysis?" As is evident from the title, he excoriated Japanese monetary policy, arguing that to a large extent Japan's dismal economic performance was the result of passive monetary policy. In biting language, he noted "I agree with the conventional wisdom that attributes much of Japan's current dilemma to exceptionally poor monetary policymaking over the past 15 years." He argued that the Bank of Japan (BoJ) ought to consider printing money and either handing it over to households or buying financial assets to reverse the deflationary spiral and drive down real interest rates.

This prescription highlights a big advantage of fiat money, a term that refers to legal tender that is issued by central banks and that has no intrinsic value. Unlike some alternatives, such as a gold standard, where expansion of the money supply would be tightly constrained in the short run by the availability of gold, fiat money has the virtue of being easily expandable in supply.

For most central banks, especially those with a history of not keeping inflation under control and having little choice but to run the printing presses to finance government deficits, this strategy has to be used with great caution, as it can set off inflationary spirals and currency declines. The major central banks, such as the European Central Bank (ECB) and the BoJ, can use this weapon with fewer fears of negative repercussions. Still, there is only one central bank in the world that can do this on a scale massive enough to provide liquidity not just to its own financial institutions but also to other central banks around the world—the Federal Reserve.

Swapping for Dollars

In December 2007, as financial market stresses were building up in the U.S., the Fed set up a program, the Term Auction Facility, to provide funding to U.S. banks in its role as lender of last resort. As financial markets in the other countries were unraveling in the fall of 2008, there was an acute shortage of dollars around the world. Before the crisis, many multinational banks based in other advanced economies, especially European ones, had come to rely on cheap wholesale dollar funding available in the U.S. These banks faced a severe capital shortage as the crisis un-folded, because they did not have the same access to dollar deposits as U.S. banks. The ECB and other central banks in Europe needed to have access to dollars to meet the liquidity shortages that some of the banks in their countries were facing.

With interbank funding frozen, the Fed realized that it needed a mechanism to reduce dollar funding pressures among overseas banks, mostly based in advanced economies, including many that had extensive operations in the U.S. Meanwhile, some emerging market central banks were concerned that, despite their large stocks of foreign exchange reserves, they would face liquidity problems if they started experiencing capital outflows and began to run down their reserves. These develop-ments could fuel further nervousness and feed into even more outflows. The Fed was also cognizant that a mass liquidation of Treasury bonds would add to the havoc in financial markets.

To meet the surging demand for dollars, the Fed threw lifelines to a number of central banks around the world. The lifeline, technically called a liquidity swap arrangement, is in effect a currency swap agree-ment under which the Fed agrees to accept another country's currency in return for a loan in dollars. The central bank initiating the swap transac-tion makes a promise to return the dollars in a specified period of time and to buy back its own currency that it had posted as collateral. The cen-tral bank borrowing the reserves takes on the exchange rate risk involved in the transaction. The initial transaction takes place at the prevailing market exchange rate, and the borrowing central bank eventually swaps back the dollars for its own currency at the same exchange rate. Usually, the borrowing central bank also pays interest on its loan of dollars that is equal to the amount it earns on its dollar lending operations to private banks in its own country.

The Federal Open Market Committee (FOMC) authorized tempo-rary dollar liquidity swap arrangements with 14 foreign central banks between December 12, 2007, and October 29, 2008. The arrangements were set to expire on February 1, 2010. The FOMC publicly announces the list of foreign central banks with which it signs swap arrangements. Information about countries that sought but were *not* granted swap ar-rangements is not public. Therein lies a tale of intrigue.

The Chosen Ones

Five of the central banks that the Federal Reserve established temporary swap arrangements with during 2007–08 were the major ones—the Bank of Canada, the Bank of England, the BoJ, the ECB, and the Swiss National Bank. One glaring omission is China's central bank, the People's Bank of China. The PBC did not ask for a swap line, as it had access to enough dollar reserves, and Chinese banks did not need hard currency liquidity—they have limited operations abroad and their major funding source is domestic deposits. Moreover, since the PBC manages a nonconvertible currency whose use in international transactions is limited, it would not have been seen by the Fed as a suitable partner for these swap arrangements.

Following the collapse of Lehman Brothers on September 15, 2008, the Fed ramped up these swap lines. On September 24, new swap lines were set up with the Reserve Bank of Australia, Danmarks Nationalbank (Denmark), Norges Bank (Norway), and Sveriges Riksbank (Sweden). On September 29, the swap lines with these and the previous five central banks were expanded by raising the ceilings on the amounts of dollars they could borrow from the Fed. Then, on October 13–14, as market pressures intensified, the Fed made a dramatic move. It removed the caps on swap lines with the Bank of England, the BoJ, the ECB, and the Swiss National Bank, giving them access to unlimited amounts of short-term dollar financing.

As the financial crisis reverberated around the world, the Fed set up temporary swap arrangements in late October with four central banks in Asia and Latin America—the Bank of Korea, Banco do Brasil, Banco de México, and the Monetary Authority of Singapore. Each of these was for a relatively modest amount of $30 billion. The Reserve Bank of New Zealand also got a swap arrangement around the same time.

Overall use of the swap lines increased sharply in October 2008 and peaked at nearly $600 billion in mid-December 2008. The biggest users of the swap lines were the ECB, the BoJ, and the Bank of England. Their peak balances in late November/early December amounted to $291 billion, $122 billion, and $45 billion, respectively. The four central banks that did not use their swap lines at all were the Reserve Bank of New Zealand, Bank of Canada, Banco do Brasil, and the Monetary Authority of Singapore. It is interesting to note that the major central banks actually used their access to dollars far more than the smaller advanced economy and emerging market central banks did.

Even for those emerging market central banks that did not draw on their swap lines, the vote of confidence implicit in the Fed's agreements was important during a stressful period. For the Brazilian central bank, the $30 billion swap line was relatively small compared to the $206 billion of foreign exchange reserves it held in September 2008. Nevertheless, Brazil clearly appreciated the backstop to its reserves provided by the swap line.

The swap lines were not always just a one-way trade by the Fed. Temporary foreign currency liquidity swap arrangements were authorized with four foreign central banks—the Bank of England, the ECB, the BoJ, and the Swiss National Bank—on April 6, 2009. These swaps would give the Fed access to the foreign currencies issued by these central banks if U.S. financial institutions needed them to sustain their operations abroad. The Fed never drew on those swap lines.

All these swap lines offered to and by the Fed expired in February 2010, as planned. In May 2010, when new strains emerged in short-term dollar funding markets abroad, the FOMC re-authorized dollar liquidity swap lines with the five major foreign central banks through January 2011. In the fall of 2011, a worsening of the euro zone debt crisis was again roiling financial markets. On November 30, 2011, the FOMC authorized another round of currency swap arrangements between the Federal Reserve and the five major central banks involved in the earlier operations. In addition, these foreign central banks also established bilateral swap arrangements with one another. These swap lines were authorized as a contingency measure, so that central banks could offer liquidity in foreign currencies if market conditions warranted such actions. In December 2012, the central banks re-authorized these bilateral arrangements through February 2014.

Self-Serving Charity Pays Off

The Fed's actions in this matter during and after the financial crisis came under severe criticism at home, especially because there was little transparency about what financial institutions in which countries were getting the money. There was also more pointed criticism that the Fed was going beyond its national mandate and acting as the lender of last resort in other countries as well. In December 2011, Gerald P. O'Driscoll Jr., a former vice president of the Federal Reserve Bank of Dallas, wrote a scathing op-ed in the Wall Street Journal accusing the Fed of covertly bailing out European banks and putting U.S. taxpayers' money at risk. William Dudley, president of the Federal Reserve Bank of New York, responded in the same newspaper:

> I would like to clarify the purpose of the dollar-swap program recently undertaken by the Federal Reserve, which is to help insulate U.S. markets from the pressures in Europe and support the availability of credit to U.S. households and businesses.

The response went on to explain that it was important to provide dollar liquidity to central banks of countries with financial institutions head-quartered outside the U.S., so that those banks could continue to provide credit and other financial services in the U.S. Of course, the Fed could not dictate which financial institutions those central banks were going to support and also whether those institutions would use that money to finance their operations in the U.S. or elsewhere. But the response did have this reassurance:

> The swaps further this interest while fully protecting the U.S. taxpayer. The Federal Reserve temporarily provides a central bank with dollars in exchange for its currency at a fixed exchange rate and receives a fee. That central bank in turn lends those dollars to private institutions on a collateralized basis and assumes any credit risk.

The foreign central banks borrowing dollars from the Fed and lending to private banks in their countries would take on any risks of those banks going under. These loans did not pose any risks to the Fed, as it was deemed a near certainty that the foreign central banks would repay the Fed in full. The note ended with this statement:

> The swaps, which have been used as a policy tool dating back to 1962, are fully disclosed to the public and their usage updated

weekly on the Federal Reserve's website. Their current use is consistent with the Federal Reserve's mandated responsibility to provide liquidity to the financial system in times of stress in order to shield the U.S. economy, to the extent possible, from the severe effects of financial instability, regardless of its source.

In other words, the Fed saw the swap arrangements not as a generous gesture to a world reeling from the U.S. financial meltdown but as a policy that was mainly in the interests of the U.S. It was an effective way of providing liquidity to foreign banks, especially those operating in the U.S., while transferring to other central banks the job of assessing the creditworthiness of foreign financial institutions as well as the risks of lending to them.

At a Congressional committee hearing on March 27, 2012, Dudley was asked directly whether the swap arrangements would enhance the dollar's reserve currency status. His response:

> I don't think it is a major factor, but I think at the margin it probably enhances the dollar as a reserve currency. . . . the fact that the Federal Reserve is willing to engage in dollar swaps probably makes people more comfortable to use the dollars to finance international transactions around the world.

He added that this was not a motivation for the U.S. to undertake those arrangements. During that testimony, Dudley also noted that the Fed had earned a profit of $4 billion through the swaps. Not a bad deal for the U.S. to make money helping other countries cope with problems that in many cases directly or indirectly had their origins in the U.S.!

The Spurned

The list of fourteen central banks that received swap lines from the Fed during the worst of the crisis is an intriguing one. Consistent with Dudley's statement, the set seems to reflect considerations about countries with which the U.S. shares strong common economic and political interests, especially those in Europe. Although it is interesting to see which countries made it on to the list, a more important question is whether there were countries that would have liked to be on the list but did not make the cut. Many countries did seem to be mainly seeking the Fed's benediction, with the swap lines seen as vital signals of approval that would provide another layer of protection from wolves in the market, even if the amounts involved were small. Of course, the Fed could not identify countries whose entreaties it had rejected, and few countries would admit in public that they had sought support from the Fed and been rebuffed, as this could immediately bring the wolves to the door.

Some documentation has recently surfaced that sheds new light on this issue. In addition to the firestorm they created in the world of international security, Wikileaks cables turn out to contain considerable information on such sensitive economic issues. A set of these cables tells a fascinating story—I have used only those whose substance could be independently verified through other channels.

In October 2008, Chilean central bank Governor José De Gregorio met with the U.S. ambassador to Chile, Paul Simons, in Santiago, Chile. While noting that Chile had adequate reserves and had no immediate financial requirement for a swap line with the U.S. Federal Reserve, De Gregorio argued that Chile had performed in an exemplary fashion and its record should be recognized in some way. A U.S. embassy report on the meeting noted that "De Gregorio specifically requested some public statement from a senior Treasury or Federal Reserve official, which would recognize Chile's positive handling of the global financial crisis and its clear eligibility (if not need) for a swap line similar to those provided to Brazil and Mexico." No such statement was forthcoming.

In January 2009, Peruvian Finance Minister Luis Valdivieso requested a currency swap from the Fed. He could point to Peru's excellent track record in terms of inflation, deficits, and debt. Moreover, it had accumulated $32 billion in reserves, which was enough to pay off all its public debt, both domestic and external. Still, the government wanted an additional line of insurance in case the global economy deteriorated that year.

The U.S. Treasury and Federal Reserve rebuffed Valdivieso (he noted in public that he also expected to be rebuffed by China's central bank, which he was approaching as well). He said that a deal with the U.S. was unlikely, notwithstanding his country's disciplined macroeconomic policies, because "we are small countries." The President of the Dominican Republic made a similar request on February 2, 2009, citing the close ties between his country and the U.S., while acknowledging that his was a small country and that the Fed seemed to have set up arrangements only with larger economies. He did not receive a positive response.

In February 2009, U.S. Secretary of State Hillary Clinton was in Jakarta, Indonesia, as part of an Asian tour. In a meeting with her, President Susilo Bambang Yudhoyono sought access to a Federal Reserve currency swap line. At a different meeting on February 18, Indonesian Foreign Minister Hassan Wirajuda reiterated this request, even if the swap line was only for half the amount that Brazil, Mexico, and Singapore had received. With a long agenda of her own and unwilling to deal with issues outside the State Department's mandate, Secretary Clinton ignored this request. On March 10, 2009, the U.S. embassy in Jakarta conveyed to State Department headquarters and the White House a request from a number of senior Indonesian officials for a response to their request for a swap line. Indonesia's request was politely but firmly declined.

The Spurned Seek Other Suitors

Central banks that did not receive the Fed's benediction began to look elsewhere for support. On March 25, 2009, the U.S. embassy in Jakarta sent a confidential memo to State Department headquarters in Washington, DC. The memo, titled "Indonesia-China Currency Swap Viewed as Sign of Positive Chinese Engagement," reported that Indonesia and China had signed a bilateral local currency swap arrangement worth $15 billion. Although it noted that the swap would have limited value for Indonesia because the yuan was not convertible, the memo indicated that the arrangement was getting good press reviews.

The memo pointed to a *Jakarta Globe* article that characterized the agreement as "crucial for Indonesia's efforts to diversify away from reliance on the United States and Western-based multilateral institutions, and represents further sign [*sic*] of China's growing economic clout." The embassy report somewhat petulantly summarized the bottom line for the U.S.: "The Indonesian government will, however unfairly, contrast China,s [*sic*] engagement with the absence of a Federal Reserve currency swap line for Indonesia."

In October 2009, the U.S. embassy in Jakarta reiterated the implications of the Fed's denial of a currency swap to Indonesia in a separate cable:

While the deal [with China] offered limited utility to Bank Indonesia, it sent a signal to Indonesia that China is a friend. The absence of a Federal Reserve currency swap was interpreted by the Indonesians as carrying the opposite message from the U.S.

In November 2012, Duvvuri Subbarao, the governor of India's central bank, told a gathering of Indian businessmen that his request for a dollar-rupee swap facility had been turned down by U.S. officials. The request had been made a month earlier, when Treasury Secretary Timothy Geithner and Fed Chairman Ben Bernanke visited India. Subbarao was quoted as saying, "They didn't say yes or no but the reservation they have against giving us a facility is that the rupee is not a fully convertible currency." Failing at its preferred option of an arrangement with the Fed, in December 2012, India signed a three-year $15 billion bilateral swap arrangement with the BoJ. This agreement contained a proviso that it would be activated only if India had already secured an IMF loan or was close to doing so. In effect, India remains on its own and has every incentive to expand its self-insurance by accumulating more reserves to reduce its exposure to crises.

The Fed was not the only major central bank supporting other central banks. In the early days of the financial crisis, the ECB and the BoJ also set up new bilateral swap lines or expanded existing ones with some countries that did not have access to swap lines from the Fed. For instance, in the fall of 2008, the ECB signed euro liquidity arrangements for up to 5 billion euros with Hungary and up to 10 billion euros with Poland. These arrangements were all typically for modest amounts, and it is not obvious that the signaling effects were as powerful as those provided by the Fed's swap lines. Moreover, the arrangements were clearly made available only to a selective group of central banks.

This selectivity is the core problem with the swap lines provided by the Fed or other major central banks, even though there is no doubt that they helped many central banks get through the crisis without using up too much of their own reserves. The determination of who gets these swap lines is clearly a political matter. Because there is uncertainty about which countries will receive the Fed's benediction, emerging markets cannot count on being protected by the major central banks. So they will continue to accumulate reserves in the interests of self-preservation, even if the costs of doing so are high.

All hope is not yet lost—perhaps the answer is for emerging markets, at times of need, to lean more on one another rather than on the big economic powers. Some moves in this direction were afoot even before the financial crisis.

Pooling Up to a Bigger Bazooka

On May 6, 2000, finance ministers of the Association of Southeast Asian Nations (ASEAN) and three other major Asian economies—China, Korea, and Japan—met in the picturesque city of Chiang Mai in northern Thailand. The ministers and other officials from these countries had convened for the annual meeting of the Asian Development Bank. Some of these countries had still not fully recovered from the Asian financial crisis of 1997–98 and were seething at what they viewed as harsh and unfair treatment by the IMF, which they felt had made things worse by forcing them to undertake strict fiscal austerity measures. The finance ministers signed an agreement that would come to be known as the Chiang Mai Initiative (CMI), formalizing a set of bilateral swap agreements among the countries in the region.

The CMI stands as one of the leading examples of how emerging markets have taken to boosting the firewalls around their economies by pooling their reserves through currency swaps and other arrangements. Such regional insurance mechanisms, whereby the other members of the pool agree to use their reserves to bail out one of their members that may need protection, are seen as logical add-ons to regional trade and financial agreements that bind countries in a region more closely. The CMI was seen by some Asian leaders as a building block for an Asian Monetary Fund, which would one day supplant the IMF's influence in the region.

The CMI faced its first big test during the global financial crisis. The complicated bilateral arrangements were clearly inadequate: the amounts involved were small, and the setup did not work well when most countries in the region came under pressure simultaneously. The ten members of ASEAN collectively lost $53 billion of foreign exchange reserves, 10 percent of their total stock, between April and October 2008.

In December 2009, the countries involved in the CMI upgraded it through the Chiang Mai Initiative Multilateralization (CMIM), cutting through the complex thicket of bilateral arrangements and replacing them with a streamlined facility for pooling reserves. The new initiative involves an expanded swap arrangement among the ASEAN countries complemented by a network of bilateral agreements among ASEAN countries, China, Japan, and Korea. The overall size of the pool was $120 billion, with 80 percent of this coming from China, Japan, and Korea. In May 2012, the size of the new arrangement was raised to $240 billion.

The CMIM is not a simple insurance pool and has some interesting twists. One is that the disbursement of any funds has to be approved by a majority vote, with countries' voting shares being tied to their contributions to the pool of funds. The second is that the CMIM still relies on the IMF's expertise for monitoring a country's policies and for determining what measures it needs to put into place if it is experiencing a crisis. A country in crisis can draw on 30 percent of its CMIM line of credit with no questions asked and without recourse to an IMF program. The rest of the credit line is available to the country only after it has secured an IMF lending program or at least entered into negotiations for one.

In principle, the CMIM has access to a deep pool of resources. At the end of 2012, the ten ASEAN economies together had about $780 billion in foreign exchange reserves. Adding in the massive reserve stockpiles of China and Japan as well as Korea's more modest stock, reserves of the ASEAN+3 amount to a total of $5.5 trillion. For all the talk of Asian harmony, however, there is a great deal of mistrust among the countries involved, fueled by geopolitical rivalries and a long history of conflict in some cases. China and Japan are still locked in a struggle to assert their dominance in Asia. Many ASEAN members are deeply suspicious of China's territorial ambitions in the region.

Given this configuration of conflicting political interests, the ASEAN economies are unlikely to be comfortable seeing the CMIM as anything more than a supplement to a strategy of self-insurance by building up their own stocks of foreign currency reserves. The amounts involved in the CMIM are still small and inadequate for providing much protection, especially for the larger economies in the region. In principle, each original ASEAN member can draw up to about $23 billion, at best a modest amount for a large country such as Indonesia. Moreover, only $7 billion can be drawn without getting approval from the IMF, further reducing the value of this insurance pool relative to self-insurance.

Regional insurance mechanisms all suffer from a more basic problem. Typically, crises tend to simultaneously hit many countries in a region, especially as the export and financial interdependence among countries in the region tends to be quite strong. In Asia, for instance, growing trade integration has led to increasing specialization, with different countries specializing in different parts of the supply chain for specific products. A vivid example of this interdependence is how the floods in Thailand during its monsoon season in 2011 affected other countries in Asia. Shipments of automobile components and computer hard drives from Thailand were affected by the floods, causing ripple effects throughout the region, including in Japan. Similarly, many foreign investors view Asian emerging markets as a common asset class, implying that trouble in one country in the region may lead to a pullout of funds from the entire region.

In periods of financial stress, the entire region may need its stock of reserves simultaneously, reducing the ability of any country to provide insurance to others in the region. This brings up an additional twist to the CMIM—it does not actually have money to disburse and is, instead, a set of commitments by the members of the pool to provide those funds in case they are needed. The reliability of those commitments may be tested sorely in the event of a regional crisis.

Firewall Made of BRICS

Regional pooling arrangements like the CMIM are hardly the only game in town. The five major emerging markets, known as the BRICS (Brazil, Russia, India, China, and South Africa), among them have about $4.6 trillion in foreign exchange reserves (as of June 2013). Frustrated by the lack of progress on reforms of the global monetary system and their continued dependence on the dollar, they have decided to take matters into their own hands. At their summit in Durban, South Africa, in March 2013, leaders of these five countries agreed to set up a New Development Bank to finance infrastructure and sustainable development projects in their countries. They also agreed to set up a Contingent Reserve Arrangement—a pool of reserves—to provide mutual support to one another in times of crises.

Indian Prime Minister Manmohan Singh, Chinese President Xi Jinping, South African President Jacob Zuma, Brazilian President Dilma Roussef, and Russian President Vladimir Putin. BRICS Summit in Durban, South Africa. March 27, 2013. (Alexander Joe, AFP / Getty Images.)

The size of the BRICS' individual reserve holdings could make a pool of their reserves—even one that includes only part of their individual reserve holdings—into a big enough bazooka to scare off speculators trying to drive down a particular currency's value. However, countries in the group do not necessarily have common economic and political interests. For instance, India and China have a long history of border disputes. India would be loath to depend on Chinese largesse in the event it needed a huge infusion of reserves for fear that China would use it as leverage in their territorial disputes. Although China and Russia have been on the same side on many international disputes concerning developments in places like Iran and Syria, their contiguous border and disagreements on issues related to energy extraction have created bouts of tension.

These tensions among the BRICS are likely to intensify as China attempts to shift the balance of regional political power in its favor using its growing economic influence. Contractual arrangements among these countries would not have the force of law and could not be enforced in an international court. Thus, the contract would have to be based on trust, which may falter in the midst of a global crisis.

Indeed, these concerns proved to be stumbling blocks, making the outcome of the Durban summit less impressive than initial reports had suggested. Expectations that details about the financing and governance structure of the New Development Bank would be announced at that summit proved premature, as the leaders failed to reach agreement on either of those issues. Likewise, the leaders could only agree that the Contingent Reserve Arrangement was in principle a good idea. Specifics, including the amount of the pool—which had been scaled down to $100 billion from higher numbers suggested by some of the countries in the group during earlier discussions—were left to be resolved later. The expectation at the time was that both the New Development Bank and the Contingent Reserve Arrangement would be in place, although with only modest levels of capital, in the next one to two years.

Such initiatives as swap lines and currency reserve pools are reasonable and add useful layers of protection for reducing a country's vulnerability to crises, but they are unlikely to replace a country's own foreign exchange reserves as the desirable first line of defense. Perhaps only a truly global institution can step in to solve the problems of commitment and trust.

The IMF Gets Flexible

The IMF has traditionally provided loans to countries that are hit by or are at the edge of slipping into crises. The lending programs come with large doses of "conditionality," a set of conditions that a country's government has to accept and then deliver on. These conditions are the bitter medicine that many countries need—more fiscal and monetary discipline, cuts in bloated government budgets, labor market reforms, bank restructuring, and so on. And that is exactly why government officials prefer to avoid the IMF.

To its credit, the IMF has tried to be responsive to the needs of its potential clients, especially those that could be regarded as innocent bystanders—countries with good policies that simply get caught up in a global or regional crisis through no fault of their own. In 2009, the IMF instituted a new lending program called the Flexible Credit Line (FCL). The idea was that a country could qualify in advance for this lending so long as it met certain criteria. If hit by a crisis, the country would then get financial assistance up to a predetermined amount with no conditions attached to that money. To qualify, the IMF would assess if a country "(a) has very strong economic fundamentals and institutional policy frameworks; (b) is implementing—and has a sustained track record of implementing—very strong policies; and (c) remains committed to maintaining such policies in the future."

To counter concerns that these conditions were rather vague, the IMF developed a more precise set of criteria. To be eligible, a country would need to have sound public finances, low and stable inflation, a sustainable current account position, an adequate level of foreign reserves, a healthy banking system, and effective financial regulation. This was clearly a high bar for qualification, for even most advanced economies would not be able to clear it. A country that qualified for this program would be getting the IMF's good housekeeping seal of approval. The attractiveness of the program was obvious—not only would a country that signed up to the program have easy access to money to fend off speculators, but also the very fact of its qualification would make a country less likely to be subject to speculative attacks.

The program was rolled out with much fanfare on March 24, 2009, and the IMF readied itself for the rush of applications. The rush did not materialize, to put it mildly. Deflated by the outcome but unwilling to give up, the IMF's management decided that the problem was that the first country to move would consider itself exposed to predators. Market participants might ask why the country needed to protect itself and wonder if it had hidden problems. Maybe that is why there were no takers. Once one country had signed up, no doubt others would quickly see the benefits and line up.

Mexico became the first country to sign up, about a month later, for this insurance program. Thanks to Mexican Finance Minister Agustín Carstens, who had been one of the deputy managing directors at the IMF from 2004 to 2008, the FCL had its first client. Poland and then Colombia also signed up in May 2009. But that was it. To date, those are the three countries that have signed up for the FCL. Each of them is an important country, though none is especially large, and even these countries continue to self-insure by building up reserves. From May 2009 to the end of 2012, the total foreign exchange reserves of these three countries rose from $168 billion to nearly $300 billion.

Could the FCL have been designed better? Interestingly, there is some evidence that signing up for the FCL reduced borrowing costs for the three countries that qualified for the program, although that evidence is by no means conclusive, given the small number of countries involved. In any case, it has apparently not been sufficient to overcome the stigma effect and other problems, as there have been no additional takers for the FCL.

Perhaps it should not have been a big surprise that the program was not wildly popular. Many countries worry that, rather than signaling strength, the very fact of signing up for an IMF credit line could imply that they anticipate trouble. This might spook foreign investors, exactly the outcome the insurance is meant to avoid. The other concern is that a country could be eligible for the program and qualify for it but not get a renewal if its policies were to slip. The IMF, doing its job right, would then refuse to renew the credit line just when a country needed it. This denial would be a signal to markets of the IMF's concerns about a country's policies and would draw unwanted attention to brewing problems.

The IMF does not give up easily on potential business opportunities. Deciding that the problem may have been too strict a set of criteria but not wanting to water down the FCL program, the IMF created a new program—the Precautionary Credit Line (PCL). It was announced on August 30, 2010, with a little less fanfare than the FCL but with expectations still high about the participation level.

For Those Good but Not Good Enough

A poor cousin of the FCL, the PCL was designed to "meet the needs of countries that, despite having sound policies and fundamentals, have some remaining vulnerabilities that preclude them from using the Flexible Credit Line." In other words, this scheme was for countries whose policies the IMF could not fully endorse and was reluctant to give an open-ended credit line to. Shockingly, only one country—Macedonia—volunteered to have its policies rated as being good enough for the PCL but not quite good enough for the FCL. The reason is obvious—in a world where there is the AAA rating and then everything else, getting an AA or A rating might sound good but in fact would simply draw attention to a country's policy weaknesses.

In November 2011, the PCL was modified and became the Precautionary and Liquidity Line. Burying one acronym and creating another did not change the result—the modified credit line has no new takers to date. Even Macedonia dropped out of the program in January 2013, two years after it signed up. As the IMF put it delicately in a review of these lending programs that it conducted in 2011: "The relatively limited interest likely reflects ongoing concerns regarding stigma, a preference for self insurance through reserves, as well as some other issues (e.g., qualification, access, flexibility, and subjectivity)."

The IMF has also proposed a global stabilization mechanism that pulls together all these programs. The idea is that, if there were to be a systemic crisis, the IMF would parachute in and quickly evaluate which program a country could be eligible for, so that it would have ready access to funds as soon as trouble lapped up on its shores. This approach has its own risks. To have the IMF act as a credit rating agency and start making its pronouncements about which country qualifies for which program right as the crisis is unfolding could backfire. This would immediately set off panic about weak countries and make things worse.

Trying to Do Too Much

For all its efforts, the question of how the IMF can lessen the demand for safe assets and bring more stability to the global monetary system remains unresolved. A fundamental problem is that the institution has two key roles in the international monetary system: surveillance—monitoring of countries' economic policies and performance—and crisis lending.

Why cannot the IMF provide insurance and at the same time be an independent and objective arbiter of good policies, a role it plays well? There would be logic to such an arrangement—if a credit rating agency such as Moody's had to stand behind its ratings by being on the hook for bailing out companies whose finances it had rated as being rock solid, that would certainly make a difference to the quality of its ratings. As things stand, Moody's rating of a company (or a country) is considered free speech, with no consequences other than the hit to its reputation if the rating proves wildly off base.

However, things are more complicated in the international dimension. These two roles—surveillance and lending—might prove fundamentally incompatible if the objectives are to provide global insurance through the IMF and to reduce incentives for the systemically important emerging market economies to self-insure by building up huge war chests of reserves.

In playing this dual role, the IMF faces three obstacles, in addition to the stigma effect discussed above. First, the (much-needed) austerity policies that it foists on countries have made any involvement with the IMF damaging for politicians in emerging markets, especially in Asia (hence the urge for countries to self-insure by accumulating reserves, even if that is costly).

Second, IMF resources are simply not enough—even a trillion dollars is not what it used to be, especially in the context of a global crisis. The value of an IMF loan used to be that the seal of approval for a country's policy commitments accompanying that loan would induce private capital to flow in. As the events during the financial crisis have shown, that multiplier effect of IMF lending cannot be counted on during a global crisis. Countries that accepted IMF conditions and signed loan programs did not attract much private capital.

Third, the IMF cannot credibly commit to maintaining an open credit line and not attaching ex post conditions to its loans if a country that qualifies for a program like the FCL starts running bad policies. Besides, what the IMF giveth, the IMF can taketh away. Experience shows that the rules of the game can be changed quickly in the midst of a crisis.

The approaches discussed above are attempts to modify existing institutional setups to find a way to provide insurance. Perhaps the answer is simpler and staring us in the face. First it is essential to cut away the institutional chaff and focus on the crucial element—insurance.

A Simple Proposal to Fix a Big Problem

Because reserve accumulation by some countries perpetuates global current account imbalances, a key issue is how to align countries' incentives so that they take into account the effects of their policies on global financial stability—a classic collective action problem. The problem is a global one, and there might be a global solution: an insurance pool that reduces incentives for reserve buildups and helps focus attention on international spillovers of individual countries' macroeconomic policies.

A Proposal for Global Liquidity Insurance

The preceding discussion suggests that an obvious answer is an insurance pool for the world's major economies—mainly but not necessarily just for the emerging markets. Here is how it would work. Each country would pay a modest entry fee, between $1 billion and $10 billion, depending on its size as measured by GDP, to provide an initial capital base for the pool. It would then pay an annual premium for buying insurance that it could call on in the event of a crisis.

The premium would depend on the level of insurance desired and on average could be about 5 percent of the face value of the insurance policy ($5 billion in annual premiums for $100 billion of insurance). This premium level would be of roughly the same order of magnitude as the fiscal cost of reserve accumulation through sterilized intervention and the implied cost of a 2–3 percent annual depreciation of the reserve currencies' values against emerging market currencies over the long term, based on productivity growth differentials.

The level of the premium in a particular year would depend not only on the level of insurance desired but also on the quality of a country's policies. A country that chose to run large budget deficits or that accumulated large amounts of debt, thereby increasing its exposure to crises, would be required to pay higher premiums for a given level of insurance. The principle is analogous to car insurance, where owners of more expensive cars and riskier drivers (based on verifiable characteristics like age and gender) face higher premiums. There would be discounts from the base level for countries that have demonstrated policy discipline.

Premiums would have to be based on simple and transparent rules. For instance, one rule could be that a current account deficit larger than 3 percent of a country's GDP triggers a higher premium. Other criteria that affect premiums could be based on such variables as budget deficits, public debt, and external debt (all relative to GDP). To keep things simple, there would be no country-specific adjustments—such as adjusting the budget deficit for business cycle conditions—as that would be contentious and also difficult to deal with in real time.

The premiums would increase in a nonlinear (more than proportional) fashion with the persistence and levels of policies that contributed to an economy's vulnerability. A country running large budget deficits or continuing to accumulate large stocks of external debt in successive years would face higher premiums over time. In this way, the country's contributions to rising global risks would be accounted for. Likewise, there would be a nonlinear premium schedule for countries requiring larger levels of insurance relative to their economic size. That is, premiums would increase more than proportionally if a small country wanted a lot of insurance. As the premiums and the size of the insurance pool increased, the premiums could gradually be scaled down for all countries.

This is a transparent rules-based mechanism that strengthens the power of moral suasion to induce a country to at least partially internalize the effects of its own policies on global risks. There is no stigma or signaling effect associated with the premium levels, as they are based on country variables that are all public knowledge. Some commentators on earlier versions of this proposal have even suggested that these premiums could be linked to market-based measures of country risk as captured by debt or spreads on credit default swaps on government bonds. However, policymakers will be reluctant to participate in an insurance scheme where premiums are subject to shifts in market sentiments that may or may not be based on economic fundamentals. After all, markets are not always right.

Operation of the Insurance System

The premiums would be invested in a portfolio consisting of government bonds of the U.S., euro zone, and Japan. In return for getting this financing for some of their debt, the Federal Reserve, ECB, and BoJ would be obliged to backstop the pool's lines of credit in the event of a global crisis. This agreement would simply institutionalize ex ante swap arrangements of the sort that these three central banks opened up ex post during the crisis to provide liquidity to other central banks.

The insurance payout would be in the form of a credit line open for a year rather than an outright grant. The interest rate would be nonpunitive and based on the yields on short-term government securities in the countries backing up the insurance pool. The country drawing on this insurance would be required to pay back the borrowed amount within the one-year period in the same hard currency that it gets for the loan, much like the currency swap lines discussed earlier in this chapter. So if a country's currency depreciated in the ensuing year, it would have a higher debt burden in domestic currency terms. To some extent, this feature would be an incentive for the country not to persist with bad policies under the protection provided by the credit line.

The country would not be able to buy additional insurance until there was a full repayment of the initial draw from the insurance pool. Premiums would be raised substantially if a country wished to renew its insurance in the next period after drawing on the credit line without any measurable improvements in its policies.

Thus, the insurance would be suitable only for liquidity crises—an extreme but temporary cash flow crunch. For an economy facing a solvency crisis, a chronic inability to meet its financial obligations, the insurance payout would at best buy a limited amount of breathing space. One could think of IMF aid programs as being relevant for solvency risk and this insurance mechanism as being relevant for liquidity risk. Once the credit line lapses and if the country turns out to have a solvency rather than liquidity problem (which may be difficult to determine ex ante), then the premiums would rise to punitive levels. In that case, the country would have to go to the IMF for traditional borrowing with the usual set of tough conditions.

Greece is an example of a country for which this liquidity insurance program would not be relevant. Even before the crisis, based on its high budget deficits and debt levels (which were already high before it became apparent that its fiscal books had been doctored), it would have had to pay extremely high premiums to get any insurance at all. Even if the Greek government could afford those premiums, the modest line of credit it would have access to through such an insurance scheme would not be of much use (the line of credit would be modest because, given Greece's macroeconomic situation, the premiums would be prohibitively high to get sizable insurance beyond a modest level). The country clearly has a fiscal solvency problem, as its debt level is rising and unsustainable, rather than a temporary liquidity problem.

The mechanism described here is different from traditional insurance, where the idea is to pool risks. For instance, by adding a large number of people to an automobile insurance pool, the premium each person pays can be kept at a modest level, as only a small fraction of the people in the group will actually experience an accident. In the case of the country insurance proposal, such pooling is harder, as the main risk may be global and may affect all countries, as was the case during the financial crisis. Such risk also makes it hard to price the premiums in an actuarially "fair" way, with total premiums roughly equal to the expected payout in any given period. The difficulty in doing this is that the major risks are by definition correlated across countries if the underlying shock is global.

The scheme is simple enough that it could easily be managed by an institution such as the Bank for International Settlements. The mission of the BIS is "to serve central banks in their pursuit of monetary and financial stability, to foster international cooperation in those areas and to act as a bank for central banks." This mission fits in perfectly with the objectives and structure of the insurance scheme. Because the BIS itself does not monitor countries' policies, it could run the scheme as a neutral party.

The crux of the proposal is that it depoliticizes access to liquidity, either from the major advanced economy central banks or the IMF, in the event of a major global shock. It would free up the IMF to do what it does best—monitoring countries' macroeconomic policies and fixing the policies of countries that have brought on themselves solvency problems in terms of domestic or external debt.

Some Questions

Is it politically feasible for a national government to pay premiums for such insurance? Given that this option would be cheaper (or at least not more expensive) than the fiscal costs of sterilizing reserves that are built up for insurance purposes, would not involve currency risk, and would involve a relatively modest premium, it should not be difficult for a government to make a strong case to its citizens for participation in such a scheme. For some emerging markets, it would be seen as a small price to pay for staying out of the clutches of the IMF.

What about the problem of moral hazard—politicians undertaking reckless policies because their country is protected by insurance? The notion of moral hazard arises in the context of many insurance schemes—the idea is that insurance causes people to let down their guard, as they feel protected in the event of a loss. For instance, a car owner may tend to be less concerned about making sure his car is locked and parked in a secure location if the car is fully insured against theft.

Moral hazard is less of a problem in the case of countries, because national policies and their outcomes are publicly observable. A related problem is that investors might be more willing to lend money to countries with access to such insurance, because their debts are seen as repayable. This could also encourage fiscal profligacy. Rising insurance premiums as debt levels increase would help offset this problem.

Participation

Would the large economies, especially the major emerging markets, want to sign on to this program? Broad participation by the large economies—say, those in the G-20—would be essential for obviating the stigma effect (that the very act of seeking insurance might signal a country's weakness). Unlike for health insurance, where broadening the pool by mandating universal participation reduces premiums and adverse selection, the necessity for a broad mandate here would mainly be to deal with the stigma effect.

The solution is simple—make participation in this pool a condition for continued membership in a body, such as the Financial Stability Board (participation in the insurance pool would, however, not be a guarantee of membership in the Board). All countries would like to have a seat at the Financial Stability Board, which was set up in 2009, as it has a key role in developing principles for international financial regulation. This condition would remove the stigma effect and also have the virtue of tying together financial and macroeconomic policies, as their interaction is clearly crucial for global economic outcomes. Of course, no country would be forced to buy insurance but would have to pay the basic membership fee to be part of the pool.

Low-income countries might not be able to afford such insurance. But they need developmental assistance, not protection from currency crises. So this insurance pool would initially be meant primarily for major emerging market countries or even a broader range of middle-income economies, although others would be welcome to join.

Broader Benefits

If the insurance-related motive for reserve accumulation were attenuated by this explicit insurance scheme, it could help discipline advanced economies' fiscal policies by raising their borrowing costs, as foreign central banks would buy fewer of their bonds. Even though the insurance premiums would be invested in advanced economy bonds, the amounts would be far less than the amounts that emerging markets may otherwise accumulate for self-insurance through reserve accumulation. By pushing up interest rates in advanced economies, this scheme would also tamp down private capital flows that would otherwise be "pushed" to emerging markets by low interest rates in the advanced economies. This is an added benefit for emerging market economies concerned that cheap money in the U.S. and other advanced economies flows disproportionately in their direction, causing complications in their domestic macroeconomic management.

The existence of such an insurance scheme would also help separate out the motives—mercantilist versus precautionary—behind foreign exchange intervention and related reserve accumulation. The costs of reserve accumulation are seen by some emerging market policymakers as being balanced by the joint benefits of insurance and maintaining trade competitiveness. By providing an alternative (and cheaper) option for insurance, the mechanism proposed here would force emerging market economies to more directly take into account the costs of protecting trade competitiveness through intervention in currency markets.

Global financial stability is in everyone's interest, but it involves solving a collective action problem. This scheme would help get the incentives right. First, it reduces the incentives for emerging market economies to self-insure; in the event of a liquidity crisis, they would have access to a large insurance pool with no conditions attached. This access would allow them to conduct better macroeconomic policies rather than focus on accumulating reserves. Second, it mitigates the risk of spiraling global macroeconomic imbalances and the attendant risks of crises and their spillover effects. Third, it creates a transparent mechanism by which the global costs of a country's policies would be internalized to some extent or, at a minimum, made more visible.

Change Will Not Be Easy

Existing institutional arrangements—central bank swap lines, regional pools of reserves, flexible IMF programs—are all reasonable but indirect and ultimately inadequate approaches to providing country insurance. None of them is likely to result in a significant moderation of the demand for safe assets.

The proposal set out in this chapter for a simple form of country insurance is conceptually a lot cleaner but remains an idea for now. Unfortunately, there is little hope that the global monetary system will tear itself away anytime soon from the structure it now has. Existing international financial institutions are hardly eager to create competition for themselves, and the major advanced economies have little incentive to rock the boat.

If anything, the analysis in the last two chapters suggests that the dollar's dominance is becoming more firmly anchored by the continued quest for safe assets and their limited supply. But there are competitors to the dollar waiting in the wings, and some of them are now beginning to make a move to center stage. Let us now turn to some of these alternatives to the dollar, starting with the most intriguing and widely hyped of them all.

PART FOUR

Currency Competition

Is the Renminbi Ready for Prime Time?

Between the idea and the reality . . .
Between the conception and the creation . . .
Falls the shadow
"The Hollow Men," T. S. Eliot

Virtually nothing in human civilization lasts forever, and in all likelihood that will also be true of the dollar's dominance. For shifts in the balance of power among currencies, the relevant horizon is probably one or two generations. But generational shifts can sometimes occur at a rapid pace, even if the gestation period for such changes is long.

The right question to ask is not whether the U.S. dollar will remain the world's leading reserve currency forever but, rather, how much longer it can retain its leading role. A second fundamental question is whether the dollar will cede the throne to another currency or if the entire system of reserve currencies will be replaced by a different arrangement. This chapter and the next one tackle the first question. Following that, I will address the second, bigger question.

Rising Competition for the Dollar

Financial markets around the world are becoming more developed, so the U.S. cannot count on keeping its massive lead for more than a few years. Even relatively small financial centers, such as Hong Kong and Singapore, have caught up to the U.S. or are close to doing so, especially in the breadth and sophistication of the financial products and services they offer. Moreover, with financial transactions being conducted largely through electronic platforms, physical distance and even time zones may become less important than they are now. These changes will give countries with new and edgier financial markets a fighting chance of punching above their weight in global finance, so long as those markets are seen as being well regulated and backed up by trustworthy public institutions.

What, then, are the prospects of other currencies displacing the dollar from the center of the global monetary system? Or, somewhat more realistically, will there be viable alternatives that erode the dollar's prominence and make it just one player among many?

To a large extent, the answers depend on which alternatives to the dollar are ready to take on more prominent roles. Many advanced economy currencies are looking rather feeble, as their economies face prospects of weak growth at best. It seems unlikely that any of them can mount a strong challenge to the dollar. A smaller but stronger euro zone could put the euro back in contention, but that is a story for another day. That leaves the currencies of emerging markets. These countries are growing fast and playing an increasingly prominent role in the world economy.

In terms of size and dynamism, China stands out. It is now the world's second-largest economy and the largest contributor to global growth. It may soon overtake the U.S. as the world's largest economy. Thus, it seems only a matter of time before the renminbi develops into a major international currency. Talk of the renminbi's ascendance might seem premature, because China has neither a flexible exchange rate nor an open capital account. These are considered essential prerequisites for a currency to have a major role in global financial markets. Still, the Chinese government has recently taken a number of steps to increase the international use of the renminbi. Given China's sheer size and its rising shares of global GDP and trade, these steps are gaining traction and portend a prominent international role for the renminbi.

In this chapter, I discuss the prospects for the renminbi. The next chapter analyzes a broader range of alternatives—currencies as well as other reserve assets.

Going Global—Cautiously

A great deal of hyperbole surrounds the renminbi, with some commentators going so far as to argue that its displacement of the dollar as the leading reserve currency is imminent. Such hyperbole feeds into the fascination and fear that Americans, in particular, have about China. The reality, for better or worse, is less exciting.

It is important to first get some concepts straight. Popular discussions about the renminbi tend to conflate three related but distinct aspects of a currency's role in international finance:

- *Capital account convertibility:* the level of restrictions on a country's inflows and outflows of financial capital. An open capital account has minimal restrictions on cross-border capital flows, implying that the domestic currency can be freely converted into foreign currencies (or vice versa) at market exchange rates.

- *Internationalization:* a currency's use in denominating and settling cross-border trade and financial transactions, that is, its use as an international unit of account and medium of exchange.

- *Reserve currency:* whether assets denominated in the currency are held by foreign central banks as protection against balance of payments crises.

A currency's convertibility and its international usage are different concepts, and neither one is a necessary or sufficient condition for the other. The renminbi, as we will see, is a prime example of a currency that is increasingly being used in international transactions, even though China maintains restrictions on capital flows. And of course there are many countries that have fully open capital accounts but whose currencies do not have broad acceptance in global markets.

An additional wrinkle is that a fully open capital account does not necessarily imply a floating, fully market-determined exchange rate. For instance, Hong Kong has an open capital account but, through a currency board arrangement, its currency is in effect pegged to the U.S. dollar.

It turns out that all these conditions—capital account convertibility, internationalization, and floating exchange rate—are necessary for a currency to become a reserve currency. I begin by considering how much progress China has made in each of these dimensions.

Opening Up the Capital Account

On paper, China still has a large number of restrictions on the free flow of capital across its borders. Many restrictions on both inflows and outflows have been loosened over time, partly to encourage the renminbi's use as an international currency. In most cases, these restrictions have been made less stringent rather than being eliminated entirely.

In recent years, the government has encouraged outflows by corporations and institutional investors, including pension funds and insurance companies, to offset some of the pressures for currency appreciation arising from trade surpluses and capital inflows. Controls on inflows are also being gradually eased, albeit with many restrictions still in place. The government has always welcomed foreign direct investment (FDI). Now the government has started allowing selected foreign investors to invest more broadly in Chinese stock and bond markets through the Qualified Foreign Institutional Investors (QFII) program.

Other than capital account restrictions, an alternative approach to evaluate an economy's financial openness is to examine the total amount of foreign assets and liabilities. The level of China's gross external position has grown rapidly, roughly tripling in size in just five years, to more than $8.5 trillion in 2012. This figure exceeds the gross external positions of other key emerging markets and also that of Switzerland, but it is less than that of other major reserve currency economies. The ratio of China's gross external assets plus liabilities to GDP, a more relevant measure of financial openness relative to the size of the economy, is now above 100 percent. Measured by this ratio, China's de facto financial openness lags behind those of all the reserve currency economies, although it exceeds those of most other emerging markets.

In short, China has an extensive capital control regime in place, but it is selectively and cautiously dismantling these controls. Partly as a result of this dismantling, the country's capital account is becoming increasingly open in de facto terms, but the government is far from allowing the extent of free flow of capital that is typical of reserve currencies.

The Exchange Rate Regime

The renminbi exchange rate was pegged to the dollar from 1997 to 2005. The currency was allowed to appreciate gradually against the dollar starting in July 2005. With the onset of the global financial crisis, the dollar peg was reinstituted in July 2008 before being relaxed again in June 2010. Despite various moves to make the renminbi's exchange rate more flexible, including a widening of the daily fluctuation band around the previous day's midpoint to plus or minus 1 percent, the renminbi continues to be tightly managed against the U.S. dollar.

By limiting the flow of money in either direction, the capital account restrictions help control the value of the renminbi, which now trades on both onshore and offshore markets. The exchange rates on these two markets are denoted by the symbols CNY (onshore) and CNH (offshore). Onshore trade takes place through the China Foreign Exchange Trade System, which is managed by the PBC. The offshore trades mostly take place on the Hong Kong Interbank Market. Mainland government regulations mandate these separate markets for the trading of renminbi. The onshore market is subject to the Mainland's capital account restrictions, and the renminbi's value on that market is therefore more under the PBC's control. In contrast to the CNY market, the CNH market is not subject to direct official control or intervention.

Exchange rates on the two markets have generally moved in lockstep since the end of 2010, reflecting the rising integration of China's onshore and offshore financial markets. However, the flow of money between the CNH and CNY markets is still restricted by capital controls and other regulations, so their integration is far from complete and the two exchange rates occasionally diverge from each other.

Putting the Cart before the Horse

Is China putting the cart before the horse by pushing forward with capital account opening before freeing up its exchange rate? This strategy is usually risky. A fixed or tightly managed nominal exchange rate makes it harder to cope with capital flow volatility, because the exchange rate cannot act as a shock absorber. For instance, when net capital inflows increase as a result of an increase in the domestic interest rate, the exchange rate usually appreciates, which limits further inflows due to the rise in the price of the currency. A fixed exchange rate subverts this adjustment mechanism, pulling in more inflows and spawning more volatility.

Another source of risk is that an open capital account often encourages an accumulation of external debt. China's external debt is below 10 percent of GDP, and its external balance sheet is well insulated from external shocks, as net foreign assets amounted to $1.7 trillion at the end of 2012. In other words, China has enough foreign assets not just to meet its external debt obligations but also to cover all its foreign liabilities. Thus, the structure and size of China's external liabilities pose few risks.

The bigger risks, as discussed in Chapter 4, may be domestic ones. The combination of a tightly managed exchange rate and an increasingly open capital account restricts a central bank's ability to use such monetary policy instruments as interest rates to manage domestic growth and inflation. This constraint applies to China as well. Despite a broad set of capital controls, China's capital account is in fact rather porous, especially when interest differentials with the rest of the world increase and the incentives to evade controls become larger. Consider a situation in which the U.S. has low rates to prop up its growth, whereas China ought to have significantly higher interest rates to manage inflation. In such a situation, the Chinese central bank would be constrained in raising rates, as that may attract more inflows, in turn putting more pressure on the currency to appreciate. Indeed, simply the expectations of renminbi appreciation that resulted from the tight management of the renminbi's value may have fueled more speculative inflows in previous years.

Moreover, lifting restrictions on capital flows could be risky for the financial system. The Chinese government had until recently kept a floor on the rates banks charge on their loans, and the interest rate they can pay on deposits is still capped. The net interest margin, the difference between minimum lending rates and maximum deposit rates, could not be reduced by competition among banks, helping the banks make tidy profits. This has been at the expense of depositors. The cap on deposit rates has meant that bank deposits have yielded low or even negative inflation-adjusted interest rates for most of the past decade. Freeing up outflows further while maintaining the cap on deposit interest rates could cause households and corporations to shift deposits out of the banking system and take the money offshore. Massive deposit withdrawals can damage banks and strain the entire domestic financial system.

How worried should China be about these risks? The government has enough control of its financial markets and enough resources to back up its banks, so that these risks are probably not likely to morph into a full-blown banking or broader financial crisis. Besides, so long as inflation-adjusted interest rates in advanced economies remain low and bank deposits in China continue to be implicitly insured by the government, the incentives to move money offshore are weak.

Even if it is not easy to lay out a full-blown financial crisis scenario for China, there are many fragilities in the banking system and in the unregulated part of the financial system that are still cause for serious concern. Many of the loans made by state-owned banks, including those made to unprofitable state-owned enterprises and some shell corporations set up by provincial governments to fund their pet projects, are unlikely to be paid back in full. Savers and borrowers are increasingly turning to informal financial institutions and products that are not regulated or covered by implicit government guarantees.

An increasingly open capital account could bring some of these tensions to a simmer and perhaps even cause them to boil over. So how is China managing the difficult act of getting the sequence of its reforms right?

Could Stepping Stones Turn Slippery?

Every discussion of China's approach to reforms is obliged to reference the aphorism attributed to Deng Xiaoping that "one must cross the river by feeling the stones." Deng was a reformist leader credited with moving the country toward a market economy. In the shadow of Mao Zedong's disastrous Great Leap Forward, Deng's approach was seen as a pragmatic one and the preferred alternative to rushing ahead amidst treacherous and murky waters.

Since Deng's time, the Chinese have taken a cautious approach to some reforms, such as changes to tax policies. They have been effective at undertaking such reforms in a piecemeal manner—test out a reform in a province, see what works and what does not, and then roll out the program nationwide. The Chinese government was among the few to systematically adopt this "learning by doing" approach to the process of economic reforms, always starting with modest steps and absorbing practical lessons from actual outcomes before scaling up those reforms to the national level.

In 2006, Raghuram Rajan and I published an essay on China's reforms. The essay had two main points. First, we made the case that China had reached a stage in its reform process where incremental steps would no longer be sufficient. We argued—quite persuasively in our view and in those of some influential commentators—that learning by doing has its limits. An incremental approach to reforms may no longer be tenable for China, we said, especially when it comes to issues such as exchange rate flexibility and capital account liberalization. The logic was simple— if you try to make the currency more flexible gradually, a wave of capital would flood the economy, notwithstanding capital controls, as there would be a tempting opportunity for a one-way bet on the currency's appreciation.

Second, building on some research done in 2005 with Thomas Rumbaugh and Qing Wang, then my colleagues at the IMF, Rajan and I also argued that it was important to get the sequence right. There were good reasons for China to move ahead with exchange rate flexibility before opening up the capital account.

Capital Account Liberalization with Chinese Characteristics

The Chinese proved us partially wrong on the first count and are taking the opposite approach on the second. Not only did they manage to maintain a glacial pace when it came to making the exchange rate regime more flexible, but they also undertook capital account opening in small but rapid steps even while keeping the exchange rate tightly managed. The Chinese government likes to stay in control and does not take any major risks. And it was clear that they wanted to take a similar approach even to large-scale macroeconomic reforms. So how could they implement a gradual opening without losing control of the capital account?

By 2007, the renminbi was under enormous pressure to appreciate, as China was piling up ever-larger trade surpluses and capital flows were pouring in due to the strong desire of foreign investors to participate in and benefit from China's growth. The government was eager to encourage some private capital outflows to offset the capital inflows.

In August 2007, the government unveiled the "through-train," a channel that made it easier for Mainland retail investors to directly buy equities traded in Hong Kong. Anticipation of large sums of money gushing in to Hong Kong pushed its stock market index, the Hang Seng, to a record high in October. Just the prospect that the program might end up being not just a success but a wild success that could result in their losing control of the channel prompted Chinese regulators to have second thoughts. The regulators were particularly concerned that Chinese households could lose money if they took the opportunity to invest in Hong Kong just when that market looked like it was in the midst of an unhealthy boom. Later that year, the through-train ran out of track and came to a halt as the government scrapped the plan even before it actually came into full-fledged operation.

The Chinese government's next step to liberalize outflows was a safer approach, in line with a proposal that Rajan and I had published in a different article in 2008. We argued that it was inefficient for the government to recycle foreign currency inflows through official channels in the form of reserve accumulation. Rather, we suggested that allowing for private capital outflows using a controlled approach—through licensed mutual funds with specific investment quotas—would be better in many ways. It would reduce the need for foreign exchange market intervention, give private investors a chance to diversify their portfolios by increasing foreign investments, and also prod Chinese banks to improve their performance by increasing competition in the financial system.

In effect, this was what the government chose to do by expanding the Qualified Domestic Institutional Investor (QDII) scheme, a controlled channel allowing for more outflows of capital, in 2010. QDIIs include securities firms; asset management companies; and some large institutional investors, such as insurance companies. QDIIs could gather funds from retail investors, pool those funds, and then invest abroad. Of course, some risk is involved, but the fact that the QDIIs would presumably have better information and invest more wisely than the average retail investor improved the risk-benefit trade-off. More importantly, the QDII approach gave the government more control about when and how much money could be taken offshore, as the QDIIs were given specific investment quotas each year.

Although the QDII approach was working well, the experience with the through-train made the Chinese government reluctant to create more channels that could spin out of control. So how could they move forward on gradually easing controls to allow the renminbi to play a bigger role in international financial markets? And how could they promote the denomination of trade and financial transactions in renminbi without opening the capital account and allowing renminbi to flow more freely into and out of China? Once again, China would turn to Hong Kong.

Promoting International Use of the Currency

With its sophisticated financial markets, strong supervisory and other institutions, and a compliant local government beholden to Beijing, Hong Kong provides a perfect testing ground for policy reforms. It allows the

Chinese government to experimentally promote the renminbi's international use without losing control. Not only could the authorities keep the Mainland financial markets insulated from what was happening in Hong Kong, but they also knew that they could shut things down easily if the reforms created conditions that were causing a loss of control. Meanwhile, its status as an international financial center meant that Hong Kong could actively help build up the renminbi's role, at least in Asia.

China had begun tapping Hong Kong's potential as a center for promoting the renminbi's international role many years before. As early as 2004, residents in Hong Kong had been allowed to open deposit accounts denominated in renminbi. In 2007, China began to take additional steps to promote the international use of its currency, in most cases using Hong Kong as the platform.

Given China's rapidly expanding trade volumes, encouraging greater use of the renminbi in trade settlement was a logical step in the currency's internationalization process. In the relatively short period since its inception in 2009, cross-border trade settlement in the Chinese currency has expanded rapidly. In 2012, trade settlements in renminbi amounted to $465 billion, roughly 11 percent of China's total trade in goods and services.

As with most other data for China, a story hides behind the numbers. Data for these settlement transactions can be analyzed separately for imports and exports. Those data show that, in the first couple of years, most renminbi trade settlement was for transactions that represented imports by China. Payments by Chinese importers in renminbi allow foreign traders to acquire renminbi that are difficult to acquire offshore through other channels. In contrast, there was little settlement in renminbi of China's exports, suggesting that recipients of exports from China either had limited amounts of the currency or were disinclined to reduce their holdings.

One interpretation of this one-sided pattern of trade settlements is that it reflects the desire of foreign traders to bet on the renminbi's appreciation by acquiring as much of the currency as possible. This is another indication of how China's rising trade and financial integration with global markets will make it increasingly difficult to tightly manage the currency's external value. By the latter half of 2012, when appreciation pressures on the renminbi began to ease up, trade settlement in renminbi became more balanced between import and export transactions.

Settling trade transactions in renminbi requires access to that currency. To support these transactions, the Hong Kong Interbank Market initiated a renminbi settlement system in March 2006. This system provides services, such as check clearing, remittance processing, and bankcard payment mechanisms. Another major development is the rising issuance of renminbi-denominated bonds, known as dim sum bonds, in Hong Kong. These steps are all gaining traction, although they remain modest in scale. Still, the initiation and rapid expansion of different elements of the offshore renminbi market signal that the currency has gained a foothold in trade and financial transactions in Asia.

Settling Accounts Directly

China is also taking steps to promote the use of its currency through bilateral agreements with its other major trading partners. In December 2010, the Moscow Interbank Currency Exchange initiated direct trading between the renminbi and the Russian ruble. An exchange for rubles and renminbi was opened in Shanghai at about the same time. In June 2011, the central banks of the two countries signed a formal agreement to promote bilateral local currency settlement. These steps have facilitated settlement of trade transactions between the two countries in their own currencies rather than in dollars. The amounts involved are small so far, but that could change soon. China's voracious appetite for energy and Russia's rising energy exports could lead to a rapid expansion of trade and local currency trade settlement between the two countries, bypassing the dollar as the settlement currency. In December 2012, China and South Korea agreed to increase the use of renminbi and Korean won in their bilateral trade. In April 2013, China signed a direct currency agreement with Australia, a major source of its commodity imports.

One of these bilateral arrangements that is likely to shape finance in Asia is the pact that China and Japan signed in December 2011 to promote the use of their currencies for bilateral trade and investment flows. Trade between the two economies amounted to about $330 billion in 2012, whereas bilateral financial flows are estimated to be less than $150 billion. Assuming that all these transactions are currently settled in dollars and will eventually be settled in the two countries' currencies, the effect of switching from dollar-intermediated transactions would still be relatively modest at the global level. Over time, the effects could be larger, as the decline in currency transaction costs and exchange rate uncertainty could boost trade and financial flows between the two countries.

Financial Markets—A Weak Link in the Renminbi as Reserve Currency Project

With the capital account becoming more open and the currency gaining acceptance in international financial markets, is the renminbi's future as a reserve currency assured? Some economists have argued that China's sheer size and dynamism will propel the renminbi to become a global reserve currency. Although China's growth over the past three decades is awe inspiring, one must keep in mind that China has become big and influential before it has become rich and, more importantly, before it has well-developed financial markets or broadly trusted public institutions. After all, if size were the main criterion, it is unlikely that a small country like Switzerland, which has a GDP less than one-tenth that of China, would have one of the significant reserve currencies in the world.

Financial market development in the home country turns out to be one of the key determinants of a currency's international status. Historically, each reserve currency has risen on the international stage under unique circumstances and has been spurred by different motivations. However, one common factor is that this rise has always required financial markets that can cope with the varied and voluminous demands of private and official foreign investors. There are three relevant aspects of financial market development:

- *Breadth:* the availability of a broad range of financial instruments, including markets for hedging risk;
- *Depth:* a large volume of financial instruments in specific markets; and
- *Liquidity:* a high level of turnover (trading volume).

By these measures, China still has a long way to go.

Banks and Equity Markets

China's financial system remains dominated by banks, with the government directly controlling most of the banking system. Regulatory constraints on other financial markets and policies that favor the banking sector relative to the rest of the financial system—including an interest rate structure that inhibits competition and boosts banks' profits—have hindered broader financial development.

Admittedly, China has made progress in the development of its equity markets. In 2005, reforms were introduced to allow previously non-tradable shares in Chinese companies to float freely. Until then, a large block of shares in these companies had been kept off the market, and only a small proportion of shares in each company was actively traded. These reforms had a dramatic effect. Market capitalization and turnover surged immediately thereafter and have grown sixfold since then. Trading volume has climbed more than tenfold.

Capitalization and turnover in Chinese equity markets now exceed those of most other economies, with the notable exception of the U.S. Equity markets do in principle provide renminbi-denominated instruments that can be held by both domestic and foreign investors, but significant restrictions still apply to foreign investors' participation in these markets. Moreover, Chinese stock markets are volatile and prone to concerns about weak corporate governance and shoddy accounting practices. So the country's deep equity markets may be of limited help in making the renminbi an international currency in the near future.

More Debt Needed

China's aspirations to make the renminbi a global reserve currency hinge in large part on the pace of development of the government debt market. Reserve currency economies are expected to issue high-quality and credit-worthy government debt or government-backed debt instruments that can serve as safe and liquid assets. The current level of government debt in China is low compared to that of most advanced economies. In a more normal world, this ought to be an advantage for China, given that it provides more credibility about the government's fiscal and inflation policies. But in the mixed-up monetary system we now have, the limited supply of safe and liquid renminbi-denominated assets works against the renminbi's ascendance to reserve currency status.

Without a sufficiently large and liquid debt market, the renminbi cannot be used widely as a reserve currency. To make the currency attractive to foreign central banks and large institutional investors, they will need access to renminbi-denominated government and corporate debt as safe assets for their portfolios.

By most measures, the size and liquidity of China's debt market lag far behind those of the major reserve currency economies. The stock of domestic debt securities has risen sharply during the past few years but from a low base. Corporate debt issued by nonfinancial corporations was practically nonexistent until 2005. By 2012, debt securities issued by financial and nonfinancial corporations had risen to $2.5 trillion. The size of China's government bond markets, measured by the market value of the stock of outstanding debt securities issued by all levels of government, was roughly $1.3 trillion in 2012.

Thus, China's overall domestic debt market was valued at $3.8 trillion in 2012, significantly lower than that of the top three reserve currency areas—the U.S., the euro zone, and Japan (see Figure 12-1). The U.S. domestic debt securities market, including marketable bonds issued by private firms and different levels of government, had a capital value of nearly $33 trillion. Interestingly, the quantity of China's outstanding domestic debt securities is greater than that of the U.K. and Switzerland, two reserve currency economies. This suggests that the size of the domestic debt market per se may not prevent the Chinese currency from going global, although foreign investors' restricted access to this market remains an issue.

The status of China's currency depends on its use in international financial transactions as well. Foreign exchange market turnover is a good indicator of a currency's potential for developing into a vehicle currency, one that is used for denomination and settlement of trade transactions. The renminbi accounts for 2 percent of all turnover in foreign exchange markets (this is out of 200 percent, as each transaction involves two currencies). In terms of the geographic distribution of foreign exchange turnover, however, China has the advantage of having Hong Kong as an important financial center for settling foreign exchange transactions. Hong Kong accounts for nearly 5 percent of global foreign exchange market turnover, compared to 41 percent for the U.K. and 19 percent for the U.S., which could eventually put the renminbi on a competitive footing in attaining the role of an international currency.

The main conclusion from this section is that, notwithstanding recent progress, China falls short on many dimensions of financial market de-

FIGURE 12-1. Domestic Debt Securities Markets in Selected Economies

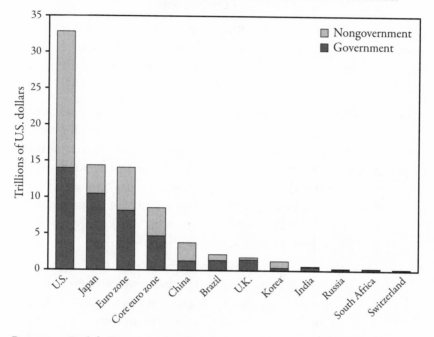

Data source: Bank for International Settlements.

Notes: Data are shown for 2012. Nongovernment debt includes domestic debt issued by financial and nonfinancial corporations. Government debt includes debt securities issued by national, state, and local governments. For this figure, the core euro zone is defined as including Austria, Finland, France, Germany, and the Netherlands. Because of lack of data, the following countries are excluded from all calculations for the euro zone: Cyprus, Estonia, Greece, Luxembourg, Malta, Portugal, Slovakia, and Slovenia. For Austria, Finland, India, and the U.K., Bank for International Settlements data for December 2011 are used, as consistent data were not available for 2012. For the Netherlands, total nongovernment debt is used in lieu of domestic nongovernment debt due to inconsistencies in domestic debt data.

velopment. Based on this key criterion, achieving reserve currency status for the renminbi is probably a long way off. China's steps to aggressively promote its currency's international role are likely to be impeded over the medium term by the weaknesses of its financial system. And China cannot escape all the laws of economics, as some reforms cannot be disentangled from one another. For instance, it will be difficult to fully develop China's foreign exchange and derivatives markets in the absence of substantial capital account liberalization.

The Reserve Currency Scorecard

There is no clear template specifying what it takes for a currency to become a reserve currency but, based on historical evidence, a few criteria matter. In light of the preceding discussion, let us consider how the renminbi stacks up against the main criteria:

- *Economic size:* A country's size and its shares of global trade and finance are important, but not crucial, determinants of the status of its currency as a reserve currency. China now accounts for 10 percent of world GDP (15 percent if measured by purchasing power parity rather than market exchange rates) and 9 percent of world trade. In 2011–12, it is estimated to have accounted for about one-quarter of world GDP growth. Size is clearly the ace up China's sleeve in the reserve currency sweepstakes.

- *Open capital account:* Reserves must be acceptable as payments to a country's trade and financial partners, which requires that the currency be easily tradable in global financial markets. This condition is difficult to meet if a country imposes restrictions on capital flows and if its foreign exchange markets are thin and subject to direct control by the government. China is gradually and selectively easing restrictions on both inflows and outflows. The capital account has become increasingly open in de facto terms, but extensive capital controls are still in place.

- *Flexible exchange rate:* Reserve currencies are typically traded freely, and their external value is market determined, although this does not preclude occasional bouts of intervention in foreign exchange markets by the country's central bank. China still has a tightly managed exchange rate, which will become increasingly hard to manage as the capital account becomes more open.

- *Macroeconomic policies:* Investors in a country's sovereign assets must have faith in its commitment to low inflation and sustainable levels of public debt, so the value of the currency is not in danger of being eroded. China has a lower ratio of explicit public debt to GDP than most major reserve currency economies and has maintained moderate inflation in recent years.

- *Financial market development:* A country must have broad, deep, and liquid financial markets, so that international investors will have access to a wide array of financial assets denominated in its currency. China's financial markets remain limited and under-developed, and they continue to be dominated by a banking system that is hobbled by a number of constraints and inefficiencies.

Although China measures up favorably on the first criterion and is making progress on the next three, the last one—financial market development—will ultimately determine winners and losers in the global reserve currency contest. This is the area in which China falls short and is unlikely to catch up to the U.S. and other reserve currency economies in the next few years. Financial development is closely tied to the quality of a country's public institutions and legal framework, topics that I investigate further in Chapter 15.

Notwithstanding its underdeveloped financial markets, China is trying to create a new playbook for its currency. Remarkably, it is making progress in elevating the renminbi to the status of a major player in international finance, despite the lagging economic infrastructure needed to support it in that role.

The Renminbi Takes Off

The renminbi is already making its presence felt in the intricate dance among reserve currencies, in part as the result of policy actions by the Chinese government. China's rising economic prowess, especially in international trade, has played a key role.

Currency Swaps with China Proliferate

Since 2009, the PBC has moved aggressively to establish bilateral swap lines with other central banks to facilitate and expand the use of the renminbi in international trade and financial transactions. In fact, China had established swap lines with many Asian central banks even before it started to actively promote the international use of its currency. Most of these were dollar-renminbi swaps under which China would provide U.S. dollars in exchange for the local currency of the counter-party economy. In other words, the foreign exchange reserves of economies like China would often serve as an additional credit line facility if the counterparty economy were to face a liquidity crunch stemming from a balance of payments or financial crisis.

There is one noteworthy difference between the earlier swap agreements and those the PBC has signed since 2009. Every single one of the swaps now in place is in terms of local currencies—that is, the PBC commits to exchange other central banks' currencies for renminbi. By June 2013, 20 central banks had signed such local currency swap agreements with the PBC. The combined commitment the PBC has made under these 20 agreements is about renminbi (RMB) 2.2 trillion (roughly $360 billion). The list of central banks and the maximum amount of each agreement are listed in Appendix Table A-5. Some of these countries, such as Australia, Brazil, Korea, and Malaysia, have significant trade deficits with China. For these and other countries that import large quantities of goods from China, renminbi swap lines may help conserve dollars at times of crises, as they would provide access to renminbi that could be used to pay for those imports. Although the amounts are modest, the PBC is clearly making an active effort to make the central banks of a broad group of economies comfortable and familiar with renminbi-denominated instruments and financial facilities.

It is not just emerging market and smaller advanced economies that are hopping onto the renminbi currency swap train as it gathers momentum. Eager to expand its renminbi business and with the goal of making London a major center for renminbi-denominated transactions, by early 2013 even the Bank of England was contemplating such a swap line. Chris Salmon, a senior official at the Bank of England, put it this way:

there is a perception that market confidence would be boosted if the Bank and the PBOC [PBC] agreed [on] a swap line. The rationale for a swap would be to reduce the tail risk of lost market liquidity, which is basically the same rationale underpinning the swaps agreed [on] between the network of G-7 central banks and Switzerland. It may therefore be helpful to remove any residual uncertainty about our attitude: the Bank is ready in principle to agree [on] a swap line with the PBOC, assuming a mutually agreeable format can be identified.

In many ways this statement was remarkable—elevating a swap agreement with the PBC to the same status as one among major advanced economy central banks. In June 2013, the Bank of England signed a swap agreement with a maximum value of about $33 billion, making it the first G-7 central bank to sign one with the PBC. Not to be left out, Christian Noyer, the governor of the Banque de France, expressed similar intentions about setting up a currency swap agreement between his institution and the PBC.

Proliferating currency swaps are hardly the only way in which the renminbi is becoming a global currency.

A Red-Tinged Bazooka

In principle, only liquid financial assets denominated in convertible currencies can be counted as part of a country's foreign exchange reserves. Yet, despite its lack of convertibility, the renminbi is already beginning to appear in a few central banks' reserve portfolios. Malaysia pioneered this trend in 2010, although the central bank, Bank Negara Malaysia, has never formally declared that it is buying renminbi assets. Other Asian central banks are also looking to renminbi assets as an avenue for diversifying their foreign exchange reserves. In 2012, Bank Indonesia announced that it had started buying bonds on China's interbank market to help diversify its reserves. The Bank of Korea and Bank of Thailand have also declared their intentions to buy renminbi securities for their reserve portfolios.

A few central banks outside Asia are also acquiring renminbi reserves. In November 2011, Austria's central bank, the Oesterreichische Nationalbank (OeNB), trumpeted its agreement with the PBC that "enables the OeNB to invest via the PBC in Renminbi-denominated assets." The press release noted proudly that "This is the first agreement of this kind signed by the PBC with a non-Asia central bank, and can be seen as an important step in the good relationship between the PBC and the OeNB." However, the Austrian central bank had already been beaten to the punch when it came to acquiring renminbi-denominated reserves.

The Central Bank of Nigeria issued a statement on September 5, 2011, announcing that it "has finalized arrangements to diversify its external reserves holdings by including the Chinese renminbi (RMB) to [*sic*] the existing currency mix of United States dollars (USD), the euro (EUR) and the British pound sterling (GBP)." That year, renminbi bonds accounted for about 0.3 percent of its foreign exchange reserve portfolio; U.S. dollar assets accounted for 90 percent of the portfolio. Governor Sanusi Lamido Sanusi said in reference to buying more renminbi assets that "We are looking at anything to start with from 5 to 10 percent of our reserves."

Chile's central bank had started investing in renminbi assets even earlier, with renminbi assets accounting for about 0.3 percent of its reserves by mid-2011. By the middle of 2012, Banco Central de Chile had decided to invest 2 percent of its investment portfolio in renminbi-denominated instruments.

Official statements and news reports suggest that other central banks are also considering adding renminbi assets to their reserve portfolios. An interesting point is that these holdings cannot in principle be regarded as reserves by the IMF, as the renminbi is not a convertible currency. But this does not seem to matter for these central banks, because they view renminbi-denominated assets, just as they do other reserve currency-denominated assets, as providing insurance against balance of payments pressures.

Going back to the bazooka principle, the point of reserves is that they should frighten off speculators who want to attack a country's currency. If part of the bazooka is red-tinged rather than just built of greenbacks, the question is not whether the IMF considers it a legitimate part of the bazooka but what market participants think about it. With China growing and becoming more influential, renminbi reserves may be worth as much as hard currency reserves issued by advanced economies that are in weaker economic shape.

Building Bridges to a Rising Power

Why are so many countries eager to sign currency swap lines with China and even hold its currency in their reserve portfolios? My contention is that this trend is less a sign of the renminbi's inevitable march to global dominance than it is a low-cost bet on a likely outcome of a convertible and more widely accepted global currency. Equally important is the desire on the part of many economies to maintain a good economic relationship with China in anticipation of its rising economic power.

The amounts of the swap lines that many central banks have signed with the PBC are small and by themselves would not provide much protection from a crisis. Initially, these amounts would be helpful only for settling trade transactions. But with an agreement already in place, it would be easier for a central bank to negotiate larger agreements with the PBC and eventually create an additional layer of insurance when the amount grows sufficiently large and the renminbi becomes a reserve currency. Holding even a modest amount of renminbi reserves is a way of buying protection from China, which in turn may be better motivated to provide help to a central bank that has helped the renminbi in its early stages of ascendance.

These moves to build bridges to the PBC are all modest in size but symbolically important in signaling the shift in perception about the renminbi's stability and its future role in the international monetary system. The clamor on the part of so many countries—small and large, within and outside Asia—to develop bilateral financial arrangements with China is striking. Central banks around the world are preparing for a future in which the renminbi will play an increasingly prominent role in international finance.

Matchmaking for the Renminbi and Special Drawing Rights

On March 23, 2009, Zhou Xiaochuan, the cerebral and understated governor of the PBC, stirred up a hornet's nest. Frustrated by the lack of progress on monetary reforms despite grand statements by G-20 leaders, he issued a paper on the PBC's website that would reverberate around the world. The paper was simply entitled "Reform the International Monetary System." It laid out the case for Special Drawing Rights (SDRs) to play a more prominent role in global finance and coyly hinted that the composition of the SDR needed to keep up with changing times by incorporating the currencies of the major emerging market economies.

What is an SDR and what was the fuss about? SDRs constitute an international reserve asset created by the IMF. The SDR exists only on the books of the IMF, and its value is based on a basket of four reserve currencies—the U.S. dollar, the euro, the Japanese yen, and the pound sterling. SDRs are distributed among IMF members on the basis of their

Yi Gang, Deputy Governor of People's Bank of China (PBC) and Administrator of State Administration of Foreign Exchange, and Zhou Xiaochuan, Governor of PBC. March 13, 2013. (Feng Li, Getty Images.)

voting shares at the institution. These allocations get added to a country's international reserves, as they can be exchanged for any of those hard currencies through the IMF, with no questions asked or conditions attached. Note that the four currencies are all freely convertible, which the renminbi is not, and are widely traded.

The proposal to give SDRs more prominence was seen as a direct shot across the bow at the U.S. dollar. It was also widely interpreted as staking a claim for the Chinese currency's global importance to be recognized by its inclusion in the exclusive group of currencies in the SDR basket, which does not even include some smaller reserve currencies, such as the Swiss franc.

Sarkozy Cozies Up to Beijing

There was a great deal of discussion in 2011 about a proposal to include the renminbi in the SDR basket. The French government, during its presidency of the G-20 that year, promoted this proposal at different venues, viewing it as a critical component of the reform of the international monetary system. Convinced that the best approach to promote this idea would be to have an "academic" discussion of currency issues in the lead-up to the summit, the French government persuaded their Chinese counterparts to host a conference in the spring of 2011. The setting chosen for the event in March was the Purple Palace hotel in Nanjing, the former Southern Capital of China.

The conference managed to rope in senior financial officials from most G-20 countries and a sprinkling of academics. With no communiqué to be drafted, the closed-door discussions were remarkably frank, and an academic atmosphere certainly pervaded the proceedings. But there was enough drama for the press to feast on. The opening session alone was open to the press. In his speech to inaugurate the conference, French President Nicolas Sarkozy put the issue of the renminbi's inclusion in the SDR basket squarely on the table, starting with a gentle dig at Timothy Geithner:

> We must accompany the inevitable internationalization of the major global currencies. This does not of course mean, cher Tim, challenging the important role of the dollar, nobody would think of doing that, and the euro, which must be stable currencies. But the internationalization of some other currencies is already a reality. . . . I am thinking of course of the yuan and I welcome the ambition of the Chinese authorities in this respect.
>
> But isn't it the time today to reach agreement on the timetable for enlarging the basket of SDRs to include new emerging currencies, such as the yuan? Who could deny the major role the yuan plays in the international monetary system? Tribute is thus paid to the economic power and the political power of China, a major monetary power.

A few minutes into Sarkozy's speech, which got under way about half an hour late, many of the assembled journalists' Blackberries started buzzing with a high-priority message. It was the text of Geithner's prepared remarks, which he would deliver at the next session. Whether by design or not, the remarks provided a sharp counterpoint to Sarkozy's speech even as that speech was being delivered.

Geithner was blunt, noting that "weaknesses and inconsistencies" in the exchange rate policies of some emerging market countries should be the main focus of the G-20:

The major currencies are all flexible, with essentially full capital mobility. . . . Some emerging markets run tightly managed exchange rate regimes with very extensive capital controls, though this is starting to change. This asymmetry in exchange rate policies creates a lot of tension. . . . This is the most important problem to solve in the international monetary system today.

He then responded directly to the issue of including the renminbi in the SDR, laying down clear markers for the conditions that an economy had to meet for its currency to be considered for inclusion in the SDR basket:

we would support reforms to change the composition of the SDR. Over time, we believe that currencies of large economies heavily used in international trade and financial transactions should become part of the SDR basket, and that to achieve this objective, the concerned countries should have flexible exchange rate systems, independent central banks, and permit the free movement of capital flows.

The set of three conditions laid out at the end of this statement would clearly preclude the renminbi's inclusion in the SDR basket for a number of years.

A few Chinese officials felt compelled to mount a counter-offensive. Xia Bin, then a member of the PBC's Monetary Policy Committee, said that he would be happy to see the yuan eventually included in the SDR basket but added, "We cannot accept such bargaining" over prerequisites, such as full convertibility of the renminbi. Li Daokui, then another member of the PBC's Monetary Policy Committee, was even more strident, stating that "there is no doubt that the RMB should be included in the SDR; otherwise, the SDR will lose its meaning and authority."

After the conference, a small group of advanced economies led by the U.S. pushed back against what they viewed as a premature elevation of the renminbi's status. The communiqué issued at the conclusion of the November 2011 G-20 Summit in Cannes contained this language:

We agree that the SDR basket composition should continue to reflect the role of currencies in the global trading and financial system. The SDR composition assessment should be based on existing criteria, and we ask the IMF to further clarify them. . . . To adjust to currencies' changing role and characteristics over time, the composition of the SDR basket will be reviewed in 2015, or earlier, as currencies meet the existing criteria to enter the basket.

Interestingly, the French hosts were unable to retain in the final version of the communiqué some language they had inserted in earlier drafts that survived until almost the last iteration. At that stage, the U.S. and a couple of other countries indicated their strong reservations about the notion that a broader basket of currencies would enhance the SDR's credibility as a reserve asset. The excised sentences read as follows: "A broader SDR basket will be an important determinant of its attractiveness, and in turn influence its role as a global reserve asset. This will serve as a reference for appropriate reforms." During his final press conference at the conclusion of that summit, Sarkozy was more explicit about the French government's views on the matter: "The yuan is a clear candidate [for inclusion in the SDR basket], given China's commitment—which I noted with satisfaction—to gradual convertibility."

Beijing Cool, IMF Warm to Sarkozy's Overtures

Senior Chinese officials have themselves been more circumspect about the prospects of expanding the SDR basket. Yi Gang, the deputy governor of the PBC and also head of the State Administration of Foreign Exchange (SAFE), urged the IMF to conduct more research into a shadow SDR. He argued that

> the IMF should consider including currencies of the BRICS countries and other emerging economies when it next reviews its Special Drawing Right (SDR) system by 2015.

But Yi was also quoted as saying that "China is in no hurry as the SDR has so far been only a symbolic currency basket." In other words, China wanted to stake its claim to have the renminbi included in the SDR basket, but on its own terms and at its own pace.

SDRs currently account for about 3 percent of world official reserve asset holdings, so the direct effect of including the renminbi in the SDR basket would not be substantial. But the symbolic effect would be profound, as even the prospect of the renminbi becoming a part of the SDR basket would encourage central banks around the world to add renminbi assets to their reserve portfolios.

Technically, the renminbi cannot become a part of the SDR basket, because it is not a convertible currency. Still, the concept that a freely usable currency ought to qualify for the SDR basket has been thrust into the debate. The argument is that the renminbi already meets the criteria for a freely usable currency, as it is increasingly being used in trade settlement transactions and in the denomination of deposit accounts offshore.

The IMF's position in 2010 was clear and was summarized as follows in a report on its executive board's discussion of the matter:

> Directors noted that although China has become the third-largest
> exporter of goods and services on a five-year average basis and
> has taken steps to facilitate international use of its currency, the
> Chinese renminbi does not currently meet the criteria to be a
> freely usable currency and it would therefore not be included in
> the SDR basket at this time.

Thus, it appeared that the IMF intended to apply the convertibility criterion strictly, which would be logical, because any currency in the SDR basket would presumably automatically be counted as an official reserve currency.

With Sarkozy's encouragement, his compatriot, IMF Managing Director Dominique Strauss-Kahn, used a loophole to change the IMF's tune. Technically, the SDR basket consists of the four currencies that are issued by IMF members (or monetary unions that include IMF members) that are the largest exporters and that have been determined by the IMF to be freely usable. The latter condition was added as a formal criterion only in 2000 and is clearly open to interpretation. The IMF's operational definition of a freely usable currency requires that the currency be widely used to make payments for international transactions and widely traded in the principal exchange markets. Thus, the criterion of convertibility is not strictly essential for a currency's inclusion in the SDR basket.

In November 2011, the IMF proposed the following indicators for evaluating a currency's potential for inclusion in the SDR basket:

- volume of transactions in foreign exchange spot markets;

- volume of transactions in foreign exchange derivatives markets and over-the-counter derivatives;

- existence of an appropriate market-based interest rate instrument; and

- currency composition of official reserve holdings.

No clear benchmarks exist for any of these criteria, suggesting that in the end—as long as some minimal thresholds are met on each of them—whether to include a currency in the SDR basket is a political decision. China probably already meets the first criterion and is making progress on the second one. Freeing up the structure of bank deposit rates is necessary to satisfy the third one, while the fourth criterion has already been met.

The IMF has left itself considerable room to maneuver in response to shifting political winds. For instance, when reviewing the currency composition of the SDR basket, the IMF coyly suggests that an ancillary indicator could be the number of countries holding a currency in their international reserve portfolios. This indicator would no doubt suit China well—as noted earlier in this chapter, some countries have already begun to hold renminbi assets in their reserve portfolios, even if the actual—or proposed—amounts are small as of now.

Whatever the outcome of this debate about whether the renminbi should be part of the SDR basket, its mere existence is a powerful signal of China's ascendance in the world economy.

Not Quite a Safe Haven

Even as China continued to post relatively good growth rates in the aftermath of the financial crisis and became the main driver of world growth, political uncertainty related to the leadership transition during the summer and fall of 2012 led to concerns about capital flight from China. On October 15, 2012, the *Wall Street Journal* ran an article titled "In Reversal, Cash Leaks out of China." The article began as follows:

China, once a catch basin for the world's money, is now watching cash stream out. Wealthy Chinese citizens are buying beachfront condos in Cyprus, paying big U.S. tuition bills for their children and stocking up on luxury goods in Singapore, frequently moving cash secretly through a flourishing network of money-transfer agents. Chinese companies, for their part, are making big-ticket foreign acquisitions, buying up natural resources and letting foreign profits accumulate overseas.

The article received a lot of attention, as it fed into the broader narrative of money fleeing China despite various restrictions on capital outflows. The article quoted my remark that "The wealthy in China have always had an open capital account." The point I was trying to make was that capital flight by the wealthy was nothing new, as they feared that political turmoil could lead to expropriation of their wealth, irrespective of whether it was legitimate or ill-gotten.

What was certainly true in 2012 was that weaker inflows and stronger outflows—including an increase in foreign currency deposits, as exporters held more of their earnings abroad in foreign currencies—led to a more balanced position of capital outflows and inflows. These swings seemed to be similar to those experienced by many other emerging markets.

In the first half of 2012, with the euro zone debt crisis worsening, investors worldwide seemed to be more concerned about safety than high returns. Consequently, capital flowed out of China and other emerging markets around the world to safe havens, especially to the U.S. but also to Japan and Switzerland. On July 26, 2012, Mario Draghi, president of the ECB, delivered his memorable "whatever it takes" speech. He said: "Within our mandate, the ECB is ready to do whatever it takes to preserve the euro. And believe me, it will be enough." On August 2, the ECB announced its Outright Monetary Transactions backstop for sovereign debt of the euro zone periphery economies. That eased concerns about global spillovers from euro zone problems, and capital started flowing back to emerging markets, including China.

These changes in the patterns and timing of flows illustrate one important point—that China is looking like other emerging markets in terms of the domestic and global factors that lead to capital flowing in or out.

When global financial conditions shift capital away from emerging markets, there is little basis for alarm about China if it, too, stops receiving waves of inflows. The period before 2012 may in fact have been the aberration. Indeed, for most of the previous decade, foreign investors—drawn in by the seductiveness of its growth story—steadily poured money into China, seemingly independent of factors such as world interest rates and worldwide financial market conditions.

Although gross capital outflows from China have increased significantly, they are consistent with the government's steps to liberalize outflows. Nongovernment outflows are likely to increase further as Chinese corporations look for investment opportunities abroad and as financial market development allows households to take advantage of avenues to diversify their savings into foreign investments. There is little reason (so far) to panic about China's rising capital outflows—they may be a sign of a maturing economy rather than a troubled one.

The End Game

Promoting the currency's international role is tied up with many complex domestic and geopolitical considerations. As with all of its policies, China is working toward multiple objectives. Although there may not be a grand strategic plan guiding specific actions taken by the government to promote the renminbi's prominence, remarkably, the component parts all point to a slow but consistent degree of progress on each of those objectives.

What's in It for China's Own Economic Development?

Chinese government officials have been far less prone to unbridled enthusiasm about the renminbi's prospects than are many commentators outside China. These officials recognize that the currency's increasingly prominent role is a mixed blessing. In the short run, it could increase the demand for the renminbi and intensify appreciation pressures on the currency. Although these pressures would be unwelcome, I have argued that there is a broader but subtler motivation behind the concept of making the renminbi a global reserve currency. In an article published in the *Wall Street Journal* in February 2012, I wrote:

An intriguing possibility is that we are seeing a Trojan horse strategy in play—reform-minded policy makers using the goal of making the yuan a global currency to promote much-needed domestic reforms to improve the balance and sustainability of China's growth. Uniting the country's citizens behind this nationalistic objective would build popular support for reforms needed to make it a reality—a better banking system, broader financial markets, a more flexible currency and other reforms.

The idea that a great economic power should have a currency to match its clout in other economic dimensions is certainly an appealing one. A convergence of popular sentiment within China around this idea could have beneficial effects for the broader agenda that reform-minded officials have sought to push forward. Conversations with reformers in the Chinese government indicate that they clearly understand the domestic dynamics at play but are careful not to overexpose or overplay their hand, preferring to nudge rather than aggressively push forward the renminbi's internationalization.

The renminbi's prospects as a global currency will ultimately be shaped by broader domestic policies, especially those related to financial market development, exchange rate flexibility, and capital account liberalization. Capital account liberalization could have broader benefits. For instance, an open capital account would catalyze progress toward China's objective of making Shanghai an international financial center. The various policy reforms that are needed to support the international role of the renminbi could thus create significant changes in China's economy and the patterns of its capital inflows and outflows.

Widening the Field of Play

To promote its broader international ambitions without waiting for its domestic policy reforms to catch up, China will continue promoting the international use of the renminbi using Hong Kong as a platform. Hong Kong's fear is that its fate may be that of a discarded lover when Beijing determines that its own financial markets are finally strong enough to allow for a more open capital account. Promotion of Shanghai as an international financial center would then take precedence and could hurt Hong Kong, especially if the territory has become highly dependent on renminbi business by then.

While using Hong Kong as the main staging ground for the internationalization of the renminbi, the Chinese government is also working to promote competition among financial centers eager to do renminbi business. Regional and international financial centers from Bangkok to Singapore and London to Tokyo are all being baited with small doses of opportunities to engage in renminbi transactions. This competition is useful for Beijing to be able to continue its program of internationalizing the renminbi without the usual prerequisite of opening its capital account and providing more renminbi liquidity. What keeps the various financial centers in Beijing's thrall is of course the possibility that renminbi business will expand sharply one day when China finally opens its capital account. Every one of these financial centers wants to be well positioned when that day comes.

The approach Beijing has taken toward capital account liberalization fits in with the government's broader objectives. Rather than ceding too much ground to the private sector, the government continues to play an important role in capital outflows, through its sovereign wealth fund, state-owned banks, and state enterprises. Their investments are consistent with China's broader economic and geopolitical goals, including acquiring advanced technology and increasing the country's sphere of influence around the world, especially in developing economies.

A Slow Move toward the End Game

Given its size and economic clout, China is adopting a unique approach to the renminbi's role in the global monetary system. As with virtually all other major reforms, China is striking out on its own path to a more open capital account. This strategy is likely to involve removing explicit controls while retaining "soft" control over inflows and outflows through administrative measures, such as registration and reporting requirements. Over the next few years, China will have a far more open capital account than it does today but with numerous administrative controls and regulations still in place. This approach will allow the renminbi to play an increasingly significant role in global trade and finance, but in a manner that allows the government to retain some control over capital flows.

An interesting issue is whether there is a policy goal short of full capital account convertibility that provides a better benefit/risk trade-off. The former head of the Hong Kong Monetary Authority, Joseph Yam, has been actively engaged in advising the Chinese government on these issues. In an influential paper, Yam has argued that the long-term objective for China ought to be full capital account convertibility, which he defines as relaxation of capital controls but with some administrative controls for regulatory purposes. He draws a careful distinction between this regime and one with entirely unfettered capital flows, referred to as free capital account convertibility. This is a subtle but important distinction that has resonated well with the Chinese leadership, given that full convertibility by this definition provides a path to an open capital account without entirely ceding control to market forces.

The Impact on the World

Yi Gang, the PBC deputy governor, has clearly articulated how China sees the renminbi internationalization project as a gradual process that is tied to other aspects of China's own development:

> Whether the pace of the internationalization is a little bit quicker or slower, it is always and completely the choice of the market. I would be actually pleased to see people have more confidence in the renminbi and choose it over other currencies thanks to a more sophisticated market, better implementation of China's monetary policy, China's macroeconomic stability and social stability, and stronger rule of law.

In other words, China is in no hurry and will make progress on the internationalization of the renminbi at a pace and manner of its choosing. Yi's carefully chosen words also signal a clear understanding that internationalization is not an end in itself and must proceed in tandem with other aspects of domestic financial and institutional development.

Even with only gradual financial market development, my prediction is that the renminbi will be included in the basket of currencies that constitute the IMF's SDR basket within the next three to five years. The IMF needs China a lot more than China needs the IMF, and the prospect of the renminbi's inclusion in the SDR basket could be seen as a way for the IMF—and the international community that it represents—to exercise leverage over China in internalizing the global repercussions of its domestic policies. The idea is that this leverage would come from a sense of moral obligation among China's leadership to pay more heed to the interests of the rest of the world if the elevation of the renminbi to the SDR basket signified the acceptance of China as a great economic power. Perhaps fear of this leverage is why, after putting the subject on the table, Chinese officials have been rather more circumspect in pushing for an expansion of the SDR basket and have tried to bring other emerging market currencies into the discussion as well.

Although China's rapidly growing economy and its dynamism are enormous advantages that will help promote the international use of its currency, its low level of financial market development is a major constraint on the likelihood of the renminbi attaining reserve currency status. Moreover, in the absence of an open capital account and convertibility of the currency, it is unlikely that the renminbi will become a prominent reserve currency, let alone challenge the dollar's status as the leading one. A huge gulf still exists between China and the U.S. in the availability of safe and liquid assets, such as government bonds. The depth, breadth, and liquidity of U.S. financial markets will serve as a potent buffer against threats to the dollar's preeminent status. I anticipate that the renminbi will become a competitive reserve currency within the next decade, eroding but not displacing the dollar's dominance.

Does this mean the dollar's position as the king of the hill is secure for now? In fact, many other alternatives are nipping at the dollar's heels. In the next chapter, I turn to some of the contenders for the status of global reserve assets.

Other Contenders
Nipping at the Dollar's Heels

MAJOR STRASSER: *By the way, the murder of the couriers, what has been done?*
CAPTAIN RENAULT: *Realizing the importance of the case, my men are rounding up twice the usual number of suspects.*

Casablanca

While the renminbi waits in the wings, there are other potential alternatives to the dollar that are worth contemplating. After all, many other emerging market economies are growing fast, and some of them have more open and better-developed financial markets than China has. There are now three emerging markets other than China among the ten largest economies in the world—Brazil, India, and Russia. Are any of their currencies viable reserve assets? What about other alternatives that seem to serve as a hedge against inflation, such as gold? Perhaps electronic currencies like bitcoins that are not issued by a government are the wave of the future and could displace the dollar as the medium of exchange even in the United States?

Before delving into these questions, it is important to address a more fundamental issue. The world now has multiple reserve currencies but is experiencing various tensions because of the dominance of one of those currencies, whose home country is seen by some as abusing its position of privilege and contributing to financial instability. While contemplating a future where other currencies and reserve assets rise to challenge the dollar, it is worth considering the implications of such a shift. A basic question is whether the alternatives are necessarily better, or would more fragmentation leave the world economy adrift without an anchor at times of crises.

Is a System with More Reserve Currencies Better?

An economist's instinct is to view competition as improving efficiency and leading to better economic outcomes. It ought to be no different when it comes to currencies. If countries benefit from having their currency become a reserve asset, competition should lead to better outcomes as countries strive to make their currencies safer and more stable.

Benefits of Being a Reserve Currency

In the competition among reserve currencies, prestige looms large. When a country's domestic currency has the status of a reserve currency, it means that the country has "arrived" on the international stage and earned the confidence of international investors. Reserve currency status also has other tangible benefits. It means, for instance, that a country's importers and exporters can settle international trade transactions in the domestic currency, reducing their exposure to currency risk.

Another benefit is that of seigniorage revenue, the difference between the purchasing power of money and the cost of producing it. This source of revenue is available to any central bank that issues its own currency. A related but subtly different concept is that of revenue accruing from the "inflation tax." An increase in the money supply tends to drive up inflation and reduce the inflation-adjusted value of the debt a government incurs when it finances its purchases of goods and services by issuing debt rather than using current tax revenues. In other words, the government can pay for goods and services now or in the future simply by printing money to pay down its debts.

However, relying heavily on seigniorage revenues to finance government expenditures can be counterproductive, as that would just fuel high inflation. In some extreme cases, inflation can spiral out of control and render money worthless as people try to spend it as soon as the government prints and distributes it. During the German hyperinflation in the early 1920s, peak monthly inflation hit about 29,000 percent, meaning that prices were doubling about once every four days. In the fall of 2008, Zimbabwe had a daily inflation rate of about 100 percent, implying that prices were doubling once a day. A loaf of bread cost about 300 billion Zimbabwean dollars in early January 2009. The Reserve Bank of Zimbabwe printed notes for up to one hundred trillion Zimbabwean dollars—worth about $300 in mid-January 2009—before eventually abandoning the currency altogether and allowing foreign currencies to be used for domestic transactions.

These extreme examples illustrate the point that seigniorage revenue has to be treated cautiously. Similarly, reliance on the inflation tax can be dangerous, as it could set off an inflationary spiral.

In the case of a reserve currency, there is an added twist to consider in regard to these two sources of revenue from the creation of money. Consider the inflation tax. Most of the currency issued by a country's central bank usually tends to circulate domestically, so the inflation tax is borne by residents. In the case of a reserve currency, however, the inflation tax is partly borne by foreign residents.

The U.S. had about $1.18 trillion of currency in circulation as of March 2013—about $1.13 trillion in banknotes and the rest in coins. It is estimated that about two-thirds of dollar banknotes, worth about $750 billion, are held outside the U.S. With inflation at 2 percent, that implies an inflation tax of about $15 billion per year paid by the rest of the world to the U.S. The value of euros in circulation at the end of 2012 was about $1.24 trillion, with about 20–25 percent of euro banknotes estimated to be held outside the euro zone. So 2 percent inflation implies inflation tax revenues of about $6 billion from foreign residents. Hardly staggering sums, but seigniorage and the inflation tax can clearly be tidy sources of revenue, ones that are especially attractive for a reserve currency, as some of the revenue is gathered from foreign residents.

Given all these benefits, there are—in principle—strong incentives for a country that issues a reserve currency to ensure its safety and reliability through prudent monetary and fiscal policies, so investors can have faith that the value of the currency will not be eroded by high inflation or other bad economic outcomes. The reality has been quite different, with the dollar giving the U.S. cover to be less cautious with its private and government spending than other countries that are typically constrained by rising interest rates as their borrowing increases.

Although it does face competition from currencies such as the euro and yen, the dollar's dominance allows it to borrow cheaply from the rest of the world to finance its prolonged consumption binge. These economic "rents" earned by the dollar stemming from its status in the marketplace of currencies seem large enough that there is a strong incentive for competitors to enter the marketplace of currencies and try to get a portion of these rents for themselves.

However, the persistence of economic rents usually signals that there are hindrances to easy entry into the market by putative competitors. There are obviously barriers to entry, as indicated by the list of prerequisites for a country's currency to become a reserve currency, so the dollar's rents cannot be easily taken over by competitors. An interesting analogy can be made to the situation where a large and well-entrenched incumbent dumps its product onto the market cheaply to drive out new entrants who may lack the financial wherewithal to compete at low prices.

This is one way to interpret the Fed's strategy since the financial crisis—that it is dumping dollars into world financial markets to keep competitors at bay. In principle, the rapid expansion of a currency's supply should debase its value, but currency markets seem to operate under different rules, at least when it comes to the dollar. The easy availability of dollars, backed by trust in the Fed, has allowed the currency to keep its market share intact. Nevertheless, the enormous changes under way in the global landscape could lead to more competitors for the dollar.

Haunted by Triffin

Are there any downsides to a country's currency being a reserve currency? One problem is that it increases the demand for financial assets denominated in that currency, generating pressures for its appreciation. As discussed in Chapter 7, Japan and Switzerland faced an acute version of this problem as the search for safety led many foreign investors to their currencies in 2012.

During the 1970s, as the deutsche mark was increasingly being used as a reserve currency, the Germans took steps, through capital controls, to discourage the international use of the currency. Otmar Emminger, the Deutsche Bundesbank president from 1977 to 1979, publicly expressed the concern that, if the deutsche mark gained in prominence as a reserve currency, there could be speculative inflows into the mark. This concern also holds for China. As the renminbi becomes an increasingly prominent currency, demand for the currency will rise as it comes to be used more widely in international transactions. Rising demand will make it harder to tamp down the renminbi's value relative to other currencies.

Another downside that is often cited is that a reserve currency economy has an obligation to provide the world with liquidity. The logic is captured in the notion of the Triffin dilemma: to produce the net liquid-ity that the world needs, the country at the center of the global monetary system must run current account deficits. According to this view, the U.S. is running current account deficits out of a sense of noblesse oblige rather than because of its spendthrift ways. This was certainly true in the 1960s, when the economist Robert Triffin articulated the proposition that bears his name. Global capital flows were limited at the time and, under the gold standard, the U.S. needed to supply net reserves to the world to meet the demand for reserves.

Times have changed, but the Triffin dilemma is still sometimes mis-takenly invoked in discussions of reserve currencies. To be clear—it is not necessary for a country to run a current account deficit to have its currency attain reserve currency status. The Triffin view is manifestly not true in the cases of currencies like the Japanese yen and the Swiss franc. Both countries have run current account surpluses over the past decade and a half while retaining their position as major reserve currencies. Similarly, even while its currency's importance in the global portfolio of reserve currencies was rising, the euro was running a roughly balanced current account position with the rest of the world.

Perhaps the Triffin dilemma is still relevant, but only for the country that is the major provider of global liquidity (i.e., the U.S.). Even this proposition is questionable, given the high level of integration of global financial markets through cross-border capital flows.

Conceptually, in a world with large capital flows, a country can pro-vide a range of safe assets to foreign investors and still run a balanced current account if it matches the inflows with a similar amount of invest-ments abroad. What is far more important for reserve currency status than the home country's current account position is the availability of high-quality safe assets, typically government bonds and top-grade cor-porate bonds, denominated in that currency.

The implication of this logic is that a larger set of viable reserve cur-rencies could take the pressure off one dominant currency, such as the dollar, to provide liquidity to the global financial system. Financial mar-ket development could increase the number of currencies that can stake a legitimate claim to being reserve currencies, a prospect that becomes more palatable if there is no attendant obligation for the relevant coun-tries to run current account deficits.

However, developing deep and well-regulated financial markets takes considerable time, so the emergence of viable new reserve currencies is at best a long-term proposition. There are other radical solutions that have therefore been proposed to prevent currency fluctuations, which are seen as an inevitable and undesirable side-effect of the current configuration of reserve currencies.

Is a Single Currency or World Currency the Solution?

Some have argued that the world ought to have a single global currency, so that currency volatility is no longer a problem. Having one currency would also have additional benefits—including reducing transaction costs on cross-border dealings, thereby promoting the freer flow of goods, services, and money. This concept raises a whole host of thorny operational questions—among them: Who would be in charge of issuing the currency? And who would get the benefits of seigniorage revenues from currency issuance?

Robert Mundell of Columbia University has made a case for a world currency that all other currencies in the world would be pegged to. In this scenario, there would be multiple currencies but no volatility of exchange rates. This situation harkens back to the Bretton Woods period, although under that regime, all other major currencies were pegged to a national currency—the dollar (which, in turn, was convertible to gold at a fixed price).

Both these constructs—a single global currency or a world currency—would deprive countries of independent monetary policy, taking away one of the most potent tools to deal with adverse shocks that hurt growth. The reality is that countries are exposed to different types of economic disturbances, as each country has a different economic structure. The exchange rate between national currencies acts as a shock absorber in times of distress and can also help in dampening bouts of excessive growth. In good times, rising capital inflows tend to generate currency appreciation, which reduces export growth and then eventually brings down inflows as growth slows. In bad times, currency depreciation can boost a country's exports and at least partially offset a decline in domestic demand.

Of course, exchange rate volatility can sometimes make things a lot worse. As discussed earlier, during the Asian financial crisis of 2007–08, countries such as Korea and Thailand experienced enormous difficulties as they had borrowed from foreign investors through loans denominated in dollars. As money flowed out from these countries, their currencies depreciated, making the debt burden even higher in terms of the domestic currencies. The revenues and assets of corporations in these countries were in domestic currencies, but their liabilities were in dollars. This currency mismatch had a devastating effect on firms, many of which may in fact have been solvent, as liquidity dried up and they were unable to service their debt obligations. The underlying problem was not that of volatile currencies, but rather the policies that made these economies vulnerable to sharp shifts in investor sentiment.

A single currency might not be the right answer, but that still leaves open the question of how many reserve currencies would be ideal for promoting global financial stability.

How Many Currencies Would Be Best?

There is no clear guidance from economic theory about how many currencies would be best for a world economy that is becoming increasingly tightly integrated. Having multiple currencies but just one principal reserve currency has fueled a number of complications. In particular, this situation has allowed global current account imbalances to persist, suggesting that it may not be the optimal answer from the perspective of promoting stability of the global financial system.

The case for a system with multiple reserve currencies coexisting in a stable competitive equilibrium might be convincing if the world economy were starting with a clean slate. But the argument in favor of such a system is now far from clear-cut, given the present state of financial markets and the level of international financial integration.

Events during the financial crisis present a counterargument to the notion that having more reserve currencies is better. The dollar's dominance allowed the Fed to act as a credible global lender of last resort—providing liquidity to foreign central banks and, through them, to financial institutions worldwide—a role that few other central banks are capable of playing. In the absence of an entity that could provide the world with the type of liquidity that it needed, the crisis could have been much worse. It is difficult to envision any other economy capable of matching the U.S. when it comes to the size of its financial markets and level of institutional development, both of which a competitor would need in order to rival the U.S. in its prodigious production of safe assets.

However, there is a risk of confusing cause and effect here. One of the reasons the world was in search of dollar liquidity during the crisis is that many global banks had sought large amounts of cheap dollar funding to finance their worldwide operations. Low U.S. interest rates, which led to an aggressive search for yield through financial innovations, and the fertile ground provided by U.S. financial markets for such sophistry led many global banks to become dependent on dollar liquidity.

For now, the reality is that the U.S. remains the only credible provider of unlimited amounts of liquidity that can execute such actions, which involve massive money creation to finance purchases of various securities, without those actions themselves creating immediate financial turmoil. In other words, a sharp turn away from the dollar could make the world economy more vulnerable to a financial meltdown if that meant the dollar no longer had its leading role, which in turn has anchored the Fed's powers as global lender of last resort.

Although there might be no viable alternative to the dollar in the short run, a world with multiple robust reserve currencies seems like a desirable outcome in the long run to reduce the dependence on dollar financing. While the renminbi gradually makes its move toward center stage, what are the prospects of other currencies that have hitherto been in the background of global finance rising to compete with the dollar?

Do Emerging Market Currencies Have a Place in Global Finance?

If alliteration were destiny, then the following would be the currencies of the future—real, ruble, rupee, renminbi, and rand. These are the currencies of five of the most prominent emerging market economies—the BRICS. Because size—as measured by shares of world GDP and trade as well as contributions to world GDP growth—seems to be an important determinant of the renminbi's rising prominence, it is worth considering how the other currencies stack up relative to one another and the dollar.

The combined size and firepower of the BRICS is quantitatively impressive, coming close to challenging the position of the U.S. in some dimensions and even exceeding it in others. The overall GDP of this group rivals that of the U.S., and together they have contributed far more to global growth than the U.S. has since the financial crisis. In fact, they accounted for about half of global growth in 2011–12. They also account for about 16 percent of world trade compared to the U.S. share of 11 percent. Table 13-1 shows that even this small group of major emerging markets represents a diverse set of economies. Brazil and Russia, with per capita incomes of over $12,000, are richer than the others. India is at the other extreme with a per capita income of about $1,500 at market exchange rates and about $3,800 when measured at purchasing power parity exchange rates. There is still a large gap in per capita incomes between the richest of these economies and the U.S. Still, this is a group of economically powerful countries, even if their per capita incomes belie their overall strength.

In terms of GDP levels, China is clearly the behemoth in this group, although most of the others are no slouches, with Brazil, India, and Russia accounting for between 3 and 6 percent of global GDP each, depending on whether national GDP is evaluated using market exchange rates or purchasing power parity exchange rates. South Africa has become an honorary member of this group but is a relatively small economy compared to the rest, accounting for less than 1 percent of world GDP.

Brazil and India have a lot more gross public debt than do the other countries in this group. However, factors that are virtues for countries that have already attained reserve currency status—sizable government budget deficits and current account deficits—are seen as signs of weakness in an emerging market economy. India has high levels of both deficits, putting its growth prospects under a cloud. Besides, there are significant restrictions on foreign investors wishing to invest in its government and corporate bond markets, a situation that is also true of China and some other emerging markets. Brazil's history of hyperinflation is now a distant memory since the Banco do Brasil adopted inflation targeting in 1999, but the country is still seen as somewhat unstable politically and economically.

One of the de jure measures of financial openness (based on legal impediments to the free movement of capital) suggests that Brazil and Russia have equally open capital accounts. However, in de facto terms (based on the size of external assets and liabilities relative to GDP), Brazil is more open. China, India, and South Africa have many more restrictions on capital flows.

TABLE 13-1. How Do Emerging Markets Measure Up against the U.S.?

2012	Brazil	China	India	Russia	South Africa	BRICS total	U.S.
Share of world GDP (percent)							
Market exchange rate	3.3	11.5	2.5	2.8	0.5	20.7	21.9
PPP exchange rate	2.8	14.9	5.6	3.0	0.7	27.1	18.9
Contribution to global real GDP growth (percentage points)							
Market exchange rate[a]	0.03	0.81	0.08	0.09	0.01	1.03	0.47
PPP exchange rate[b]	0.03	1.11	0.18	0.10	0.02	1.44	0.42
Per capita income (U.S. dollars)							
Market exchange rate	12,079	6,076	1,492	14,247	7,507	4,963	49,922
PPP exchange rate	11,875	9,162	3,830	17,709	11,375	7,531	49,922
Share of world trade (percent)							
Goods and services[c]	1.4	9.7	2.3	2.2	0.5	16.2	10.8
Goods	1.3	10.6	2.2	2.3	0.6	17.0	10.7
Public debt to GDP (percent)							
Net debt	35.2	—	—	—	35.6	—	71.6
Gross debt	68.5	22.8	66.8	10.9	42.3	34.5	101.2
Capital account openness							
Chinn-Ito Index[d]	0.2	−1.2	−1.2	0.4	−1.2	—	2.4
Modified Schindler Index[e]	0.8	0.0	0.0	0.0	0.4	—	0.8

Data sources: IMF World Economic Outlook; U.S. Treasury; IMF Direction of Trade Statistics; World Bank World Development Indicators; Chinn and Ito (2008); Schindler (2009).

Notes: "GDP" is gross domestic product. Purchasing power parity (PPP) exchange rates adjust for differences in the domestic purchasing power of national currencies. "BRICS" stands for Brazil, Russia, India, China, and South Africa.

[a] Global real GDP growth (measured at market exchange rates) in 2012 = 2.48 percent.

[b] Global real GDP growth (measured at PPP exchange rates) in 2012 = 2.94 percent.

[c] Data are for 2011.

[d] Values are for the average for 2009–11. The index ranges from −2.5 (closed) to 2.5 (fully open).

[e] Values are for 2005. This index is expressed as 1 minus the value of the original Schindler Index, so that 0 represents a closed capital account, and 1 represents a fully open capital account.

Other than Brazil, the remaining economies have limited financial market development. Although the financial markets of all these economies have become more developed in recent years, they remain largely bank dominated. Firms receive most of their financing from banks rather than equity or corporate debt markets. Equity markets in some of these countries have become deeper and more liquid in recent years, providing an alternative to bank finance for firms (and also an alternative to bank deposits for savers). In contrast, in all these countries the availability of government debt and high-quality corporate debt remains quite limited for investors from abroad. The U.S. alone has outstanding domestic debt securities valued at nearly five times that of all five of these economies combined ($33 trillion versus $7 trillion in 2012, according to BIS statistics). Their smaller debt markets, in addition to political uncertainties and weak legal frameworks, make it likely that emerging market economies will be seen mainly as high risk–high reward investment destinations rather than as safe havens.

Building on the discussion in Chapter 12, among the major emerging markets, China seems to be best positioned to elevate its currency to prominence in international finance. Viewing other leading emerging markets through the prism of the criteria discussed in that chapter, it appears unlikely that any other of their currencies is likely to be ready over the next decade to play a prominent role in international finance.

Could the main emerging markets band together to create an alternative reserve asset backed jointly by their governments? There are many practical impediments to creating a new reserve asset, and it would require considerable coordination of policies—the euro zone has shown how difficult it is to accomplish this across a group of politically independent countries.

It is highly unlikely that this group of emerging market economies can go beyond opportunistic joint initiatives on certain matters and move toward closer economic ties and coordination of policies, given that they have different and often conflicting strategic interests. Other than their size and dynamism, the threads that connect their interests are fragile and could easily unravel in a crisis. The plans of the BRICS to jointly set up a New Development Bank and a Contingent Reserve Arrangement are significant steps, but it is unlikely that these institutions will attain enough mass to shake up existing international monetary arrangements. BRICS summits are likely to remain a forum for symbolically important but substantively modest steps taken by these countries to free themselves from the shackles of the present structure of global finance.

Other Faith-Based Alternatives

Given the high stakes involved, it is not just traditional national currencies that are in the game. In this section, I examine one popular reserve asset that has gained importance as a safe asset but does not work so well as a medium of exchange, and two types of "currencies" that could in principle erode the medium of exchange function of existing fiat monies, such as the dollar. Fiat monies, legal tender issued by national central banks, have the advantage of being used as units of account and mediums of exchange as well as stores of value. In principle, these functions do not necessarily have to be tied together. The store of value attribute is more important for a reserve asset, but its role in financial markets becomes limited in the absence of the other attributes. Similarly, it turns out to be difficult for a medium of exchange to gain traction if it is not also a reliable store of value.

Gold

Troubles in world financial markets invariably bring out the gold bugs—investors who view gold as the only truly safe asset and others who believe that money should be backed by gold to discipline monetary policy. The notion is that the limited supply of gold—which is a non-renewable resource—would eliminate the temptation to inflate its supply, thereby preserving its value as well as that of any currency that is backed by it.

Gold does have a history of serving in this role. It was a major reserve asset in the years leading up to the Great Depression, which preceded World War II. Economic historians, such as Barry Eichengreen, have made the case that the gold standard prolonged the Great Depression, because it constrained the Fed's ability to expand the money supply to deal with insolvent banks and stimulate the economy. By the mid-1930s, all major economies were depleting their gold reserves and went off the gold standard, as it was proving to be a constraint on their economic recovery.

The importance of gold was rejuvenated after World War II. The major economies pegged their currencies to the U.S. dollar, and the U.S., in turn, fixed the price of gold at $35 per ounce. Thus, all currencies pegged to the dollar also had a fixed price relative to gold. This linkage of the major currencies to gold became unsustainable with rising trade imbalances in the late 1960s and was abandoned in the early 1970s.

Although a return to an explicit or implicit gold standard seems unlikely and inadvisable, could it play a role as a reserve asset that central banks can turn to in lieu of the dollar? There are reasons to be skeptical of the prospects of gold as a reserve asset that can be scaled up to meet the needs of international finance. It is not a convenient instrument for trade or financial transactions, and it does not have the liquidity of reserve currencies like the dollar.

The reality confronting those who favor a bigger role for gold is that its supply is inadequate and not rising fast enough to meet the needs of growing economies and an expanding international financial system. The liquidity provided by gold is ultimately limited by its production, the total stock that has been mined, and the remaining stock in the ground. The existing stock of gold in the world that is above ground is estimated to be about 165,000 metric tons, with a market value of about $7.5 trillion in May 2013. An interesting visual image, courtesy of the World Gold Council, is that the entire stock of gold mined since the beginning of civilization would amount to a cubic block with each edge measuring 20 meters. About half the world's stock of gold is held in the form of jewelry.

Official institutions, mainly central banks, hold 17 percent of the stock, with a market value of about $1.3 trillion. In contrast, total foreign exchange reserves at the end of 2012 amounted to $11 trillion. In other words, even if all the gold above ground in the world today were to replace other reserve assets, it would not be enough to meet the demand for world reserves across central banks at current prices. Furthermore, the stock of gold has been increasing at a rate of about 1.5 percent per year over the past decade. Underground reserves of gold are believed to be approximately 50,000 metric tons, but logistical constraints on mining operations have limited the amount of gold mined annually to

2,500–3,000 metric tons. Assuming future production does not grow at a dramatically higher rate, this pace is too slow to keep up with nongold reserve demand, which has grown at 16 percent per year since 2000. Given its inelastic supply, gold is unlikely to be a source of new liquidity for the international monetary system during times of high liquidity demand.

Because the supply of gold cannot easily be adjusted in response to shifting demand, the price of gold is subject to a high degree of volatility. The price of one ounce of gold surged to nearly $1,800 in the fall of 2012 before tumbling below $1,400 in May 2013. The high volatility of gold prices and uncertainty about their future trends is another reason central banks may be loath to make it a major component of their pool of reserves.

In aggregate, central banks were in fact selling rather than purchasing gold for most of the 1990s and 2000s. The financial crisis changed that. After having been a source of supply to the gold market, in 2010 central banks became net buyers of gold, with purchases amounting to 77 metric tons. In 2011 and 2012 together, central banks made net purchases amounting to nearly 1,000 metric tons. Still, the total quantity of gold held as official reserve assets was about 2,000 metric tons lower in 2012 than in 2000, when it stood at 33,000 metric tons. The U.S., the euro zone (including the ECB), the IMF, Switzerland, and Japan combined now account for about 23,000 metric tons or roughly three-quarters of all official gold holdings.

Reflecting their desire to seek any viable alternatives to the dollar for their reserve holdings, emerging market central banks have been accumulating gold over the past decade. Their accumulation picked up pace after the financial crisis, with their combined share of global gold reserves now at 15 percent. In particular, China has increased its official holdings of gold by 450 metric tons. Among the emerging markets, China and Russia, with about 1,000 metric tons apiece, and India with 550 metric tons are now the biggest holders of official gold reserves. Although these numbers are impressive, they should be viewed in relation to the overall stocks of these countries' international reserves. In March 2013, China's gold reserves had a total market value of about $55 billion, a significant amount but still accounting for less than 2 percent of its total international reserves. For the emerging markets as a group, gold reserves had a market value amounting to about 3 percent of their total international reserves.

The ability of central banks to shift a larger portion of their reserves into gold is limited by the thinness of that market relative to government bond markets. In January 2013, Yi Gang, the head of the agency that manages China's reserves—SAFE—was asked about the possibility of China adding a substantial amount of gold to its reserves. He rejected this notion:

> We need to take into account both the stability of the market and gold prices. . . . Compared with China's $3.3-trillion foreign exchange reserves, the size of the gold market is too small. More gold is always an option, but that requires profound judgment.

With a large share of the stock of gold tied up in jewelry and not actively traded, central banks simply cannot make large gold purchases without generating price spikes that could then come back to haunt them if their gold stocks were to subsequently fall in value.

To sum up, gold may well begin to play a more prominent role in the reserve portfolios of central banks than it has in the past few decades. However, limitations in gold's liquidity and the constraints on its supply continue to be impediments to its prospects as an important reserve asset.

Bitcoins and Electronic Money

The fascination with everything electronic has spawned various digital currencies, not just as a more convenient alternative to fiat money but also as a way of getting around the "system." These currencies are typically not backed by anything "real" or by the heft of a sovereign government with taxing authority. Of this group, bitcoins remain the most prominent digital currency. Others like DigiCash and CyberCash have disappeared or have been taken over.

The bitcoin network came into existence on January 3, 2009. Bitcoin is a decentralized digital currency that is not controlled by a single organization or government. Bitcoin has no central issuer; instead, the peer-to-peer network regulates bitcoin balances, transactions, and issuance according to consensus in network software. The system also provides anonymity for all transactions, as bitcoins are traded electronically and verified through multiple nodes. There is a predetermined fixed supply of 21 million bitcoins and a cost of production that is intended to keep the market in equilibrium. "Miners" are rewarded with a small number of bitcoins when they can solve a cryptographic problem using raw computing power. The difficulty level of the problem is automatically adjusted to limit the supply of new bitcoins each week. As with gold, there is a cost to production—measured in time and computational effort—that limits the elasticity of supply.

As of April 2013, BitPay reports having over 1,000 merchants accepting bitcoins under its payment processing service. At that date, there were about 11 million bitcoins in circulation. The exchange rate varies continuously and has fluctuated from $0.01 to more than $100. As an example of how volatile this market is, the exchange rate shot up from $14 per bitcoin in January 2013 to a high of $266 per bitcoin on April 10, 2013. It then crashed below $80 per bitcoin two days after it peaked.

Various hacking incidents reveal the vulnerability of this digital system. In June 2011, Mt. Gox, the largest bitcoin exchange, was hacked, causing the value of the bitcoin to temporarily drop from $17 to $0.01 per bitcoin credit. In September 2012, the Bitfloor currency exchange was hacked. The hackers reportedly made off with about 24,000 bitcoins, the equivalent of about $250,000 at the time. This was real money lost by those who had kept their bitcoin balances in online bitcoin wallets. The Mt. Gox exchange was hacked again in April 2013.

Given the conceptual and technical problems with electronic currencies, it is difficult to see them getting much traction, let alone posing a threat to existing currencies. The anonymity of transactions using the bitcoin network, touted as one of its main attractions, has spawned other issues as well. Concerns about the network being used for money laundering and tax evasion have tarnished the image of this digital currency, making it less likely that it will gain wide acceptance anytime soon.

Some academics have proposed the introduction of electronic versions of fiat monies. Like paper fiat money, electronic money issued by a central bank would have no intrinsic value but would generate more seigniorage revenue, as the cost of production would be much lower than that of paper money. More importantly, proponents say, it would allow a central bank to drive short-term nominal interest rates below zero. As things stand, it is difficult for a central bank to drive the nominal interest rate below zero, because there is always the alternative of holding on to paper money, which would yield a zero nominal rate of return. With electronic money, the central bank faces no such constraint, as it could simply trim down existing money holdings. This feature could be helpful in circumstances where a negative nominal rate would help push inflation-adjusted interest rates sufficiently low to stimulate economic activity.

Even if electronic money were to become prevalent, which should at least be technically feasible in the next few years, it will not affect perceptions of the safety of different currencies as stores of value or alter the balance among various reserve currencies.

Community Currencies

One wintry morning, while taking a break from writing this book, I went to browse the shelves at Autumn Leaves bookstore on the Ithaca Commons, a pedestrian mall in the town that is home to Cornell University. I then walked up to the Owl Café on the second floor and ordered a large cappuccino. When the frothy cup of sustenance arrived, I paid for it with a currency that you—dear reader—are unlikely to have encountered unless you happen to live in Ithaca, New York.

In 1991, a community activist named Paul Glover introduced a new currency called Ithaca Hours. The objective was to create

a local currency system that promotes local economic strength and community self-reliance in ways which will support economic and social justice, ecology, community participation and human aspirations in and around Ithaca, New York. Ithaca Hours help to keep money local, building the Ithaca economy. It also builds community pride and connections.

Other community currencies have similar objectives—to encourage locals to spend within the community and boost local pride. The list includes BerkShares (southern Berkshire region of Massachusetts), Bay Bucks (Traverse City, Michigan), and Madison Hours (Madison, Wisconsin). These bills are bought with U.S. dollars and can be traded with local shops for products or services. Toronto dollars, launched in 1998, trade at par with the Canadian dollar and are accepted by more than 100 merchants in the Toronto area. Ninety cents on every dollar go into a

Reserve Fund, which backs the Toronto dollars; the remaining 10 cents are used to fund community initiatives and projects.

Are such currencies legal? In fact, such a local currency is not illegal in the U.S. so long as it does not look like a dollar and is regarded as taxable income. In other words, a business accepting Ithaca Hours for a product or service that it provides must collect sales tax and pass that on to the government. Even though community currencies clearly do not have the scale to rival any of the major currencies, it is interesting to note that the objectives of their originators are in some ways similar to those of the major currency issuers—to use currency structures to achieve certain broader strategic objectives.

No Getting Away from Faith

Commodities or "real" things are seen as trustworthier than paper money, especially when considering the store-of-value function of money. Gold does have some intrinsic value, but its market value is far out of proportion to its intrinsic worth in industrial and other uses. Supporters of gold often advocate it as an effective hedge against lower confidence and declining value in international reserve currencies. Other commodities like silver arguably have an even stronger claim to intrinsic value, although silver lacks the allure of gold.

The crucial point is that all these alternatives to paper money issued by national central banks are also underpinned by faith. What sustains their value is that each person who accepts them as payment would do so with the expectation that others would in turn be willing to accept them. This principle is clearest in the case of community currencies that have no government or tax authority backing them but are built entirely on faith. Gold and other commodities provide some reassurance, because they have a tangible presence, but ultimately their roles as stores of value are also built on faith.

The SDR as Global Reserve Currency?

Perhaps what is needed is a broader level of coordination than what can be achieved at the level of one country. This requirement brings up one other candidate that was discussed in the previous chapter—the SDR of the IMF. According to the IMF,

The SDR is an international reserve asset, created by the IMF in 1969 to supplement its member countries' official reserves. Its value is based on a basket of four key international currencies, and SDRs can be exchanged for freely usable currencies.

The four currencies are the U.S. dollar, the euro, the Japanese yen, and the pound sterling. The stock of SDRs stands at roughly $300 billion (as of April 2013), accounting for 3 percent of global reserve assets.

In principle, SDRs can be exchanged for "freely usable" currencies but cannot be used directly in private transactions. Thus, increasing the stock of SDRs does not increase the total liquidity of the global monetary system. The IMF would simply act as an intermediary for a country to convert its holdings of SDRs into one of the reserve currencies.

The IMF can create SDRs out of thin air, though this happens only rarely, as this action needs the approval of a substantial majority of the institution's shareholders (who represent the member countries). The IMF then doles out the new SDRs to each country, based partly on a formula that incorporates factors—such as GDP and openness to trade—that also determine the country's share of voting rights at the IMF.

SDRs exist in virtual form on the books of the IMF and can only be used as a form of collateral that can be pledged by the country authority to borrow "real" money, such as dollars. Countries that borrow through the IMF using their SDR allocations pay an interest rate, and the country that lends some of its currency to the borrower receives an interest payment. What makes this different from other loans provided by the IMF is that there are no conditions attached, as a country would just be making a temporary conversion of SDRs into currencies that it could actually use to tide it over difficult times.

The IMF takes great pains to note that the SDR is not really money in the traditional sense but is mainly a unit of account. It is not to be seen as a reserve currency in itself but can be counted as a reserve asset, because "SDR holdings represent unconditional rights to obtain foreign exchange or other reserve assets from other IMF members." Moreover, there are other problems with making the SDR a reserve currency. As Maurice Obstfeld has pointed out, the SDR is not backed by a central fiscal authority that has the power to raise taxes and thereby generate real revenues. Furthermore, its distribution across countries would necessarily be a political matter, as it would ultimately be determined by the IMF's executive board rather than just through a mechanical formula.

Despite all its drawbacks, the notion of the SDR becoming a global reserve asset that challenges the dollar's prominence has never quite died down. The instrument that has been proposed for doing this is a substitution account. The idea is that a country could convert some portion of its hard currency reserves into SDRs through such a substitution account, thereby reducing the demand for dollars as a reserve asset and purportedly making the global financial system more stable as a consequence.

This idea is revived every time the dollar looks to be in trouble or, more recently, now that China and other emerging markets are confronting the unpleasant reality that they have no good alternatives for their stocks of foreign exchange reserves. One major stumbling block is that the IMF would have to take on a large amount of risk, as it would have to make up any losses from a decline in the value of the SDR relative to the dollar. These losses would eventually have to be borne by the IMF's shareholders, who in turn are the taxpayers of each country. Clearly, this political problem lacks an easy resolution. In any event, even such substitution accounts would not result in the net creation of global liquidity.

Notwithstanding all these problems and concerns, a concerted effort by a group, such as the BRICS, to put its collective weight behind a project to elevate the SDR's status could certainly have an impact. However, when the world needs a credible and trusted provider of liquidity, the IMF is likely to remain a poor substitute for the Fed. In sum, even a bulked-up SDR is unlikely to make much of a dent in the dollar's dominance as a global reserve asset.

Stuck

In principle, an asset whose supply cannot easily be expanded when demand for it rises—that is, an asset whose supply is inelastic—is best suited to play the role of a safe asset. The limited supply of the asset indicates that it is less likely to decline in value. Recent events in global financial markets have turned on its head this proposition that the safety of a "safe asset" is related to its inelastic supply. Indeed, many safe assets in present circumstances are precisely those that can be supplied elastically. The very fact that the supply of dollars can be expanded when there is a need for liquidity in international financial markets has led to the dollar becoming an even more prominent reserve asset. Even though the world's central bankers and investors in search of a safe haven are eager to shift away from the dollar, their choices are limited and are likely to remain so for the foreseeable future. The harsh reality is that at present, there are no obvious and viable alternatives to the dollar.

Stability can be ephemeral. History has taught us repeatedly that it is important to be prepared for the possibility of small trigger events setting off a cascade of large-scale changes that can rock civilization. A century ago, the assassination of Archduke Franz Ferdinand of Austria in 1914 sparked World War I. One does not even have to reach that far back in history for such examples. The self-immolation of Mohamed Bouazizi, a 26-year-old Tunisian street vendor, in December 2010 set off a chain of events culminating in the Arab Spring revolution that has dramatically transformed the political landscape in the Middle East.

In the next chapter, I examine the possibility that the realm of global finance may be no different when it comes to small events that can sometimes unexpectedly trigger cataclysmic changes.

14

Could the Dollar
Hit a Tipping Point and Sink?

*That one dramatic moment in an epidemic when everything can change
all at once is the Tipping Point.*

—Malcolm Gladwell

In 1987, Per Bak, Chao Tang, and Kurt Wiesenfeld published a paper in
Physical Review Letters on self-organized criticality in nature. In their
model, a system is spontaneously attracted to its critical state and, once it
reaches its critical state, the effects of small changes become unpredictable. A good example is a sandpile on which grains of sand are being
sprinkled in no specific order. Once it has reached its critical state, the
addition of one grain of sand either has no effect or causes large ava-
lanches that could lead to the collapse of the entire pile.

The principle is quite different from that of phase transitions, where
the critical point is attained by precisely tuning a particular parameter.
For instance, there are specific combinations of pressure and temperature points at which water turns into ice or into steam. These are big but
predictable changes and to some extent can be controlled. The insight in
the pathbreaking 1987 paper was the discovery of a mechanism by which
complexity could emerge spontaneously from simple local interactions,
without requiring careful fine-tuning of any parameters of the system.
To an ant on the sandpile, the system looks as stable before and after it
has reached its critical state, even just before the pile collapses.

The challenging question for those of us on the sandpile that is the
global monetary system is whether it is already in a critical state, vulnerable to collapse at the slightest tremor. There are some ominous signs. The
macroeconomic data paint a sobering picture of worsening public debt
dynamics and a sharply rising public debt burden in advanced economies, along with a high level of dependence on foreign investors in
search of a safe haven in the case of the U.S. These economies have had

the benefit of being able to issue sovereign debt in their own currencies, in effect allowing them to transfer currency risk to the foreign purchasers of their sovereign debt.

Advanced economies have not been subject to "original sin" (being able to issue debt only in foreign currencies), but their accumulated sins might eventually catch up with them. With low levels of population growth, rapidly aging populations, and rising costs of health care and other entitlement programs, the U.S. and other advanced economies could be in far worse shape beyond this decade if they do not bring their public finances under control.

High and rising public debt levels among advanced economies pose serious risks to global macroeconomic stability. At present, there is strong demand for government bonds of the reserve currency economies, but this is a fragile equilibrium. As demonstrated by recent events in the euro zone, bond investors—both domestic and foreign—can quickly turn against a weak country with high debt levels, leaving the country little breathing room on fiscal tightening and eventually precipitating a crisis. The U.S. is large, special, and central to global finance, but the tolerance of bond investors may have its limits. If so, where are the limits?

Research on Tipping Points: Handle with Care

Based on their extensive and pathbreaking research on debt crises, Carmen Reinhart and Kenneth Rogoff of Harvard University suggest that once public debt exceeds 90 percent of GDP, additional debt accumulation is associated with lower growth. Gross public debt in the U.S. is now over 100 percent of GDP, which puts the U.S. in the growth danger zone based on this criterion. In their academic writings, Reinhart and Rogoff were careful to point out that they had only detected a correlation, not a causal relationship between high debt and growth. These subtleties became blurred in translation to the world of public policy. The research proved influential during the fiscal austerity debates in the U.S. and Europe. It has subsequently come under fire, partly on account of some conceptual and data issues and partly because some policymakers and technocrats have used these findings to argue for fiscal austerity on the grounds that high debt levels *cause* lower growth. Still, these findings cannot entirely be dismissed, as other researchers have also found that high levels of government debt are associated with lower growth.

Even taken at face value, this research does not support the notion of a tipping point for the level of debt, beyond which bond markets would force the borrowing costs on public debt to increase sharply and threaten a country's solvency. Other recent research that directly tackles the question of whether there is such a tipping point suggests that countries with public debt above 80 percent of GDP and persistent current account deficits are vulnerable to a fiscal crunch. This could happen if investors get nervous about the level of debt, pushing up interest rates and making the debt problems more severe. It certainly has not been a problem for the U.S., even though all the danger signs identified by such researchers are flashing red. Whether this benign outcome is simply an artifact of the unconventional monetary policy actions of the Federal Reserve, which have included directly purchasing large quantities of government bonds and holding down long-term interest rates, remains to be seen.

The high level of U.S. debt, implying a large pool of debt securities, as well as the stability and liquidity of its government bond markets give the U.S. a tremendous advantage. But a tipping point could come if investors lose faith in the ability of the U.S. to honor its debt obligations without resorting to inflation. This does not mean that the U.S. will actually have to pay off its stock of outstanding debt, but the ability to roll over that debt will shrink as the level of debt rises. For now, foreign investors are locked into U.S. debt, but that could change over time as other economies' financial markets, especially those of emerging market economies, develop and offer a broader range of "safe assets." That nothing catastrophic has happened in U.S. debt markets so far despite rising debt levels is not, or ought not to be, much cause for complacency.

Although this logic is compelling, the reality appears quite different. Curiously, the available episodic evidence—some of which was discussed in Chapter 1—in fact suggests that there are more reasons to be sanguine than overly concerned. It is also possible that the research showing a correlation between higher levels of public debt and lower growth is less relevant for the U.S. compared to other economies, given the strong demand for safe assets and large official capital outflows from emerging markets.

So, is the dollar immune from a precipitous fall? History tells us that crises have a way of sneaking up on financial markets. One important lesson from past crises is that if something looks too good or too strange to last, it probably won't. More often than not, the longer the inevitable is postponed, the greater the likelihood that there will be an explosive burst rather than a painful but smaller pop.

What could trigger a tipping point that sends U.S. bond prices tumbling? There are many wild cards, with most of them seen as low probability events. But the global financial crisis should have made it clear that "black swans" are not just figments of the imagination but represent real risks of ignoring very low probability but extremely disruptive events.

A Red Wild Card

Take one potential tipping factor—China. Among the foreign purchasers of U.S. Treasury bonds, China has been a force to reckon with. Its reported purchases of U.S. Treasuries over the period 2008–12 amounted to about $750 billion, nearly a quarter of overall foreign investors' purchases of $3.2 trillion. During this period, rumors that China might be taking steps to increase the currency diversification of its foreign exchange reserves and shift away from the dollar were enough to cause tremors in currency markets. Even before that, the pronouncements of Chinese officials were being sifted carefully for evidence about China's intentions concerning its dollar reserves.

Yu Yongding, an Oxford-educated Chinese economist, has been on the frontlines of advocacy for greater liberalization of China's exchange rate. He was an academic member of the PBC's monetary policy committee from 2004 to 2006, a period when he made waves by pushing for further liberalization. On November 25, 2004, he was at an event in Shanghai, where he was quoted as saying that China had taken steps to reduce its holdings of U.S. Treasuries. Right after his speech was reported, the dollar fell against other major currencies. The next day, following reports that Yu said he had been misquoted, the dollar was back up. Although it is hard to know what drives currency movements day to day, these and other widely reported episodes of Chinese officials' statements rattling currency markets indicate how fragile sentiments in markets are.

An Atomic Weapon with a Nasty Recoil

Would China consider the use of its holdings of Treasuries as a weapon against the U.S.? In the Q&A posted on its website in 2011, China's State Administration of Foreign Exchange attempts to be clear that its investment decisions will be based only on rational economic factors and that its reserves will not be used as a weapon of international diplomacy:

Q: Will China use its foreign exchange reserves as a trump card or as an atomic weapon?

A: We have always emphasized our role as a responsible long-term investor. During the investment and operations of our foreign exchange reserves, we will strictly follow the rules of the market and the laws and regulations of the country concerned ... we will use the reserves as a financial investor and will not seek control over those investments ... we will actively cooperate with those countries that welcome our investment. But if any country is doubtful, we will slow down and try to reach agreement through communications.

As has been proven by the facts, the above concerns and worries are completely ungrounded.

Perhaps this response is meant more as a reassurance to the rest of the world rather than to Chinese citizens. The conventional wisdom is that China would be playing with fire if it tried to dump a significant portion of its dollar reserves. Attempting to sell even 10 percent of its reported holdings of U.S. Treasuries, which would amount to at least $130 billion, would probably be enough to set off panic in bond and currency markets. In ordinary circumstances, this amount would not be large enough to create tremors in such a deep and liquid market. But these are not normal times. With bond investors already nervous about the high and rising level of U.S. debt, such an action could act as a trigger around which negative market sentiments coalesce, especially if China's actions were seen as presaging similar moves by other foreign central banks.

The cost of U.S. government borrowing would rise, and the dollar would fall, which would certainly hurt the U.S. But China would hardly be immune and would itself stand to lose a lot. A fall in Treasury bond prices would result in a substantial drop in the capital value of China's existing holdings of U.S. government bonds. Moreover, if the dollar depreciated against the renminbi, then the renminbi value of those bonds would fall even more—in short, a bad deal for China in many respects. It is also not easy to envision what China could do with the money if it pulled significant sums out of U.S. Treasury bonds. Its sovereign wealth fund has enough challenges on its hands trying to find good investments, the gold market remains small, and other global bond markets simply do not have the capacity to absorb hundreds of billions of dollars.

This logic suggests that China cannot credibly threaten to disrupt U.S. financial markets without shooting itself in the foot. The logic is correct in purely economic terms. But politics sometimes overrides economics, and that may be the true wild card.

Geopolitics Takes Precedence over Economics

In early 2008, China cracked down hard on rioters in Tibet. These actions had a palpable effect on the presidential election campaign in Taiwan, which was heading into its critical phase. Before the riots in Tibet, a victory for Kuomintang party candidate Ma Ying-jeou, who favored stronger linkages with Beijing, looked like a sure bet. The events in Tibet shifted momentum toward Frank Hsieh, the candidate of the ruling Democratic Progressive Party, which preferred a harder line toward Beijing. As China made it clear that it was not happy with the way things were going, the U.S. dispatched two aircraft carriers for joint military exercises with Taiwan, further inflaming tensions in the region.

I made a trip to Beijing in March 2008 while these tensions were brewing. This was a few months before the city was to host the Olympic Games. China clearly viewed the Olympics as an opportunity to show the world that it had definitively established itself as a major sporting, economic, and political power. Beijing was being spruced up, and its grimier side was being sanitized, so no signs of poverty or disorder would be allowed to besmirch the reputation of a great power. Plans were even afoot to limit traffic on the streets and get factories around Beijing to shut down for a short period before the games started in order to alleviate concerns about pollution. Clearly, the games were a big deal, and no expense or effort was going to be spared to ensure their success.

Imagine then my surprise when, at virtually every meeting with senior officials during that visit, the one theme that inevitably came up was Taiwan. The officials made it clear that if Taiwan were to make any move to exert freedom from the Mainland, then China would have no choice but to intervene by force. They dismissed as being of little consequence any threat that military intervention could invite a boycott of the Olympics by certain countries, such as the U.S. The subtext was that national pride and sovereignty were far more important than any damage to China's moment in the sun as the host of the Olympics.

This approach is consistent with a pattern that China has demonstrated in its past actions, making it clear that it puts territorial sanctity above other political and economic considerations. A more recent example of this is the dispute with Japan over a string of barren islands in the East China Sea, referred to by China as the Diaoyu Islands and by Japan as the Senkaku Islands.

Barren Islands Become a Bone of Contention

These uninhabited islands are claimed by China, Japan, and Taiwan. The islands have no intrinsic value but are strategically valuable, because they are close to key shipping lanes and fishing grounds and there is also the prospect of oil reserves nearby. In September 2012, the Japanese government purchased three of the disputed islands from their private owner. The objective of the Japanese government was ostensibly to prevent the owner or others from using the islands for nationalistic expressions that would inflame tensions with China.

The action had the opposite effect. The Chinese saw the purchase as a provocative move by Japan to reinforce its territorial claim over the islands. Official condemnations from Beijing followed swiftly, along with street protests in many cities around China. Cars made by Japanese automakers were burned or smashed on the streets of many Chinese cities, and many Japanese manufacturers temporarily shut down their factories in China to avoid further damage.

China clearly did not feel the need to be subtle or nuanced in showing its displeasure about the escalation of the territorial dispute with Japan. In

October 2012, as Japan was preparing to host the prestigious IMF–World Bank annual meetings in Tokyo, Chinese banks started pulling out of events they had sponsored. At the last minute, China's senior officials also boycotted the meetings, which featured the senior-most officials—finance ministers and central bank governors—from practically every other country in the world. China's finance minister and central bank governor were conspicuous by their absence from the meetings. Governor Zhou had been slated to give the prestigious Per Jacobsson lecture on the last day of the meetings. His lecture was instead read out by another Chinese official.

China's actions were obviously intended as a slap in Japan's face, at a time when Tokyo was hoping to showcase its economic restoration after the March 2011 Sendai earthquake and tsunami. Chinese officials' no-show became one of the big stories of the meetings, which was certainly not what the hosts had hoped for.

An article published in an official newspaper, the *China Daily*, on October 26, 2012, summed up China's views on the matter. The article began on a gleeful note:

> Despite China not imposing any economic sanctions, the Japanese economy has been badly hit. The spontaneous anti-Japanese demonstrations in China, the cancellation of visits by Chinese nationals to Japan, and boycott of seminars held by business groups, the media and think tanks have dealt a blow to the Japanese economy.

The article then laid out the official view that China did not see the island purchase as a matter of negotiation but as a land grab by Japan that needed to be beaten back:

> China has used its diplomatic channels to make it clear to the international community that it wants to resolve the Diaoyu Islands dispute with Japan through diplomatic negotiations. China's State leaders, the Ministry of Foreign Affairs and other government agencies and civil organizations have declared time and again that the so-called nationalization of the Diaoyu Islands

by Japan is illegal and China will "make no concession" on issues concerning its sovereignty and territorial integrity.

The article then went on to make it clear, in case there were any remaining doubts, that China's actions, such as senior officials' boycott of the IMF–World Bank meetings, were intended to convey the government's displeasure with Japan's stance on the matter:

China has not only canceled many activities to commemorate the 40th anniversary of the normalization of its diplomatic relations with Japan and called off high-level governmental and military reciprocal visits, but also boycotted a series of international conferences and cultural activities in Japan, showing its determination to safeguard national sovereignty and territory.

The takeaway from these episodes is that, in line with a pattern demonstrated by its past actions, China is raising the stakes on geopolitical maneuvering. For the Chinese Communist Party, maintaining legitimacy is a tricky balance between delivering economic growth and stoking nationalistic pride. Given its unwillingness to entertain any serious moves toward an open democracy, unleashing nationalistic sentiments provides a safety valve for social restiveness. Perhaps one ought to be cautious about dismissing as impossible a situation in which, even at a short-term economic cost to itself, China might be willing to put the U.S. through the economic wringer.

How Big Would the Disruption Be?

The credibility of any threat to dump U.S. Treasury bonds depends on how disruptive such a move would be to those bond markets. Estimates by researchers at the Federal Reserve suggest that a decline in foreign official inflows into U.S. Treasuries of about $100 billion in a given month could push up five-year Treasury bond yields by about 40–60 basis points (100 basis points amounts to 1 percentage point). But such an increase in bond yields is also likely to pull in more foreign investors, dampening some of the initial rise and reducing the effect to about 20 basis points, which would be a more modest increase. In principle, these numbers suggest that it would take a big shift in foreign official inflows to raise interest rates by a full percentage point. It should be noted that the estimates are based on the effects of foreign inflows on Treasury bond yields in normal times, as the researchers' dataset ends in 2007 and excludes the crisis period.

With the financial crisis fresh in investors' minds, a significant shift in patterns of official inflows could have unpredictable effects on other investors and on bond markets. A big move away from U.S. Treasuries by the central banks of China or other emerging markets could spook private investors as well and set off more panic. This is uncharted territory, however, and any predictions about how investors will behave at a time of enormous stress in financial markets may have little to do with patterns of behavior in normal times.

Extrapolating from some aspects of what happened during the financial crisis, one cannot rule out the alternative possibility that turmoil in U.S. bond markets could spill over into even greater turmoil in other financial markets. The latter would eventually drive more money into U.S. bond markets on account of the safe haven effect, thereby more than offsetting the initial rise in bond yields.

Moreover, the Fed has left little doubt that it will step in and take extreme measures when necessary to stabilize the U.S. financial system. The Fed could easily mop up any debt sold by foreign official investors, given its demonstrated willingness to expand its balance sheet by buying Treasury bonds when it deems such a step to be necessary. This willingness substantially reduces the credibility of any foreign government's threat to destabilize U.S. bond markets by dumping even a portion of its holdings of those bonds.

In a report to Congress in July 2012, the U.S. Department of Defense examined the national security risks to the U.S. that China's ownership of its debt posed. The conclusion of the report was relatively sanguine:

attempting to use U.S. Treasury securities as a coercive tool would have limited effect and likely would do more harm to China than to the United States. As the threat is not credible and the effect would be limited even if carried out, it does not offer China deterrence options, whether in the diplomatic, military, or economic realms, and this would remain true both in peacetime and in scenarios of crisis or war.

The U.S. apparently does not view China's holdings of U.S. debt as a threat or as giving the Chinese any leverage in bilateral negotiations.

The Risk of an Own Goal

The U.S. Treasury bond market is vulnerable enough that one does not necessarily need to count on external agents to bring things to a tipping point. Even domestic investors may at some point start to have second thoughts about relying on U.S. Treasury bonds for safety or at least start demanding higher returns for investing more in those bonds. The high level of public debt is risky, because a small change in interest rates can have a large effect on debt financing costs. The U.S. Congressional Budget Office has warned that

> a growing level of federal debt would . . . increase the probability of a sudden fiscal crisis, during which investors would lose confidence in the government's ability to manage its budget, and the government would thereby lose its ability to borrow at affordable rates.

With the level of debt held by the public (excluding the Fed's holdings) equivalent to three-fifths of annual GDP, a 1 percentage point increase across the entire spectrum of interest rates could mean an increase of about 0.60 percentage points of GDP in government expenditure on debt financing. Such increases can quickly squeeze out other discretionary government expenditures.

In practice, the increase in financing costs is likely to be lower, as it depends on the maturity structure of government debt—the time profile for repayment or refinancing of that debt. Longer-term debt does not have to be refinanced as often, whereas short-term debt is more exposed to interest rate increases. The average maturity of U.S. Treasury debt had fallen steadily from a peak of 71 months in 2001 to 48 months in late 2008. This meant that the U.S. needed to refinance an amount equivalent to half its entire stock of debt roughly every two years.

After the crisis hit, even as the stock of U.S. net public debt was exploding, the maturity structure of debt was in fact turning more favorable. This happened because the U.S. Treasury wisely used to its advantage the rising global demand for longer-term bonds. By June 2013, the average maturity had risen to 66 months, well above the average of 58 months for 1980–2010. Part of the increase in the average maturity of Treasury debt was accounted for by the Fed's purchases of Treasury notes and bonds (securities with a maturity of more than one year) as part of its quantitative easing operations. From the end of 2008 to June 2013, the level of outstanding Treasury bonds and notes held by the public (including the Fed) rose by $5.5 trillion. Fed purchases of these securities accounted for $1.4 trillion or roughly one quarter of this increase. Thus, the increase in the average maturity of debt held by private investors is somewhat lower.

Nevertheless, the increase in the average maturity of Treasury debt provides a layer of security, as a rise in interest rates will not immediately feed through into a proportionate increase in debt financing costs. Still, the sheer volume of debt, the expected trajectory of future debt, and the prospect that market turmoil could lead to a sharp spike in rates leave little room for comfort. The amount of expected future accumulation of debt is enormous. The U.S. Office of Management and Budget forecasts that net borrowing from the public will amount to more than $4 trillion over 2013–17 and an additional $3 trillion or more over the following five years.

Mixed Signals

A complex balance of forces is at play in the market for U.S. Treasury debt. An increase in bond yields for the right reasons—a recovery in economic activity, a tighter labor market, and a modest increase in expectations of wage and price inflation—would not be such a bad thing. Interest rates typically rise and fall along with the business cycle, so higher bond yields relative to those that prevailed in 2012 and through the summer of 2013 would signal a return to normalcy. It could create the right incentives for fixed-income investors to come back into the bond market for the traditional reasons—the prospect of earning a modest rate of return with little risk. Their reappearance would be healthier than the force that is now driving investors into that market—the willingness to accept practically a zero rate of return to minimize risk in a highly volatile environment. In contrast, an increase in bond yields attributable to rising concerns about the level of debt and a possible surge in inflation without a strong recovery would be harmful. It could quickly spin out of control as investors rush for the exits.

The trouble is that these two outcomes are observationally equivalent in the short run, and investors who are unable to tell them apart could mistake one for the other, setting off a panic-driven dumping of U.S. Treasury bonds and dollars. Still, it is not easy to envision a scenario in which the dollar comes crashing down. Indeed, one small and somewhat dubious source of comfort is that such a situation of panic might again be self-correcting. Individual investors could find small supplies of other high-quality assets, such as investment-grade corporate paper, to shift their savings into. But larger institutional investors and the market as a whole simply lack viable alternatives either in the U.S. or abroad. Thus, in yet another irony, the panic set off by such an event would simply lead to money pouring back into the dollar.

A Blast from the Past

Although the dollar has been at the center of the international monetary system for decades, it has come under threat on many occasions in the past, and there have been times when the U.S. needed financing from abroad to support the dollar's external value. Those episodes might seem to provide an object lesson on how a dollar crisis might unfold. Instead, they actually illustrate how sticky the dollar trap is.

Roosa Bonds

In 1961, when the international monetary system was still on the gold standard, there were concerns that the dollar was vulnerable to a run by countries who wanted to convert their dollar holdings into gold. Many foreign central banks had built up large holdings of dollars, well beyond the levels needed to ensure their own currencies' convertibility into dollars. U.S. gold stocks, which in 1950 were enough to cover foreign central banks' dollar holdings many times over, had fallen by 1960 to a level barely sufficient to cover those holdings.

Robert Roosa, then the undersecretary for monetary affairs at the U.S. Treasury, went on the offensive on multiple fronts to protect the dollar's primacy in the international monetary system. He pushed for the creation of a "gold pool," a mechanism for merging gold reserves of major central banks to thwart speculation, helped create a new lending facility at the IMF called the General Arrangements to Borrow, and jawboned surplus countries like Germany and Japan to stimulate their economies to boost domestic demand.

The final arrow in his quiver was the creation of the Roosa bonds. These were nonnegotiable U.S. government bonds denominated in foreign currencies that were sold to foreign central banks. These bonds transformed a portion of dollar holdings of foreign central banks into longer-term debt that was protected from a fall in the dollar's value and were therefore designed to slow the conversion of foreign dollar holdings into gold. The bonds could be redeemed whenever their holders chose. Some central banks were reluctant to buy the bonds, but for others, these bonds made it easier to justify their large dollar holdings. From 1962 to 1974, the U.S. issued $4.7 billion worth of Roosa bonds, which were purchased by the central banks of Austria, Belgium, Germany, Italy, the Netherlands, and Switzerland.

Roosa bonds and currency swap lines that existed in the 1960s have been characterized as "bribes" in the form of a portfolio substitute for gold offered by the U.S. to other central banks. These facilities have served as a substitute for conversion of dollars into gold at times of crises. Such measures taken by the U.S. Treasury and Fed were designed to stabilize the international monetary system and, more importantly, to maintain the dollar's primacy. And it is worth noting how other countries reluctantly but eventually fell in line with these plans, as a precipitous fall in the dollar's value would have hurt them as well by causing turmoil in global financial markets.

That would not be the only time in recent history when the U.S. issued government bonds denominated in foreign currencies.

Carter Bonds

In the fall of 1978, there were growing concerns about weak U.S. macroeconomic policies, with inflation rising rapidly. Currency markets were in disarray, with the U.S. dollar under severe downward pressure and falling against other currencies, including the German deutsche mark and the Japanese yen.

On November 1 of that year, the Carter Administration announced a multipronged dollar defense package. The package included a sharp 1 percentage point increase in the main policy interest rate (the Fed's discount rate) and a $30 billion package of foreign currency resources to facilitate exchange market intervention. The $30 billion comprised $15 billion in currency swaps with foreign central banks, $5 billion from the IMF, and up to $10 billion in "Carter bonds." These bonds were to be denominated in foreign currencies, so the U.S. Treasury was encouraging foreign central banks to buy the bonds by taking upon itself the currency risk that would arise from a falling dollar. The issuance of these bonds could also be seen as signaling a commitment by the U.S. to take necessary steps to support the dollar's external value.

By January 1980, the U.S. had issued about $6.5 billion of Treasury securities denominated in deutsche marks and Swiss francs. The dollar defense package was an impressive one. Because it was backed up by strong monetary and other macroeconomic policy changes, it proved effective. The package quickly stabilized the dollar's value, and the dollar even rose in subsequent years, earning a tidy profit for the U.S. government when it retired the Carter bonds fully in July 1983. Because the dollar had appreciated relative to the currencies that the bonds were denominated in, the U.S. had to pay fewer dollars to redeem those bonds, hence the profits.

Obama Bonds?

In principle, the U.S. could issue similar instruments now if global demand for dollar-denominated assets were to decline and the economy needed financing for its large current account deficits. This action might temporarily prop up the value of the dollar, which would otherwise have to decline to bring down the current account deficit. Of course, the U.S. government would be unlikely to take such an action at a time when it has in fact been trying to guide the value of the dollar downward to boost exports. After all, the whole point of the ongoing currency wars is that other countries are doing all they can to prevent their own currencies from appreciating against the dollar, as that would hurt their export competitiveness.

Either way, the U.S. would be in a favorable position, even if it did issue such bonds. If the dollar stayed strong, the U.S. would continue getting cheap funding from foreign countries. If the dollar fell in value and U.S. inflation rose, the country would face a loss on its new foreign currency bonds but would foist on foreign central banks and other foreign investors an even larger loss on the enormous stock of dollar-denominated assets that they already hold. In short, any drastic changes to the dollar-centric system would be a lose-lose proposition for foreign countries, strongly favoring the perpetuation of the status quo.

An Unstable Foundation

One legacy of the global financial crisis is that it has stripped away the veneer of safety in a broad class of other financial assets, even as it has created greater demand for safe assets. This point, discussed in previous chapters, and the analysis in this chapter together bring us right back to the question we started with: *If not the dollar, and if not U.S. Treasury debt, then what?* The edifice of global financial stability seems to be built on this fragile foundation. Even if the world recognizes it is on an unstable sandpile, its only option seems to be to try to reinforce the foundations of that sandpile to avoid being hurt by its collapse.

Ultimate Paradox:
Fragility Breeds Stability

A fundamental reform of the international monetary system has long been overdue. Its necessity and urgency are further highlighted today by the imminent threat to the once mighty U.S. dollar.

Robert Triffin, November 1960

The U.S. economy is now too big and too important to stumble without pulling the rest of the world down with it. If it were to experience a fiscal or financial meltdown, the reverberations would be damaging for every country in the world. Just the fear of this devastation points to how central the U.S. economy is to the global financial system. The dubious promise of safety from this very devastation is the irresistible lure of the dollar trap.

The situation is rife with paradox. Fixing the global monetary system now requires that the U.S. put its domestic economic policies in order. This will entail getting a grip on long-term public finances instead of just relying on easy money policies that raise the risks of future financial instability. Until that happens, the rest of the world will be stuck in the trap of continuing to support U.S. fiscal profligacy. Remarkably, the U.S. will return the favor by extracting a cost from the rest of the world rather than paying a price for such support.

The present state of the international monetary system implies that the dollar is still mighty. The perceived imminence of the threat to the dollar's primacy —referred to by Triffin more than five decades ago—remains true to this day, although the nature of the peril has changed over time. History suggests that these threats might appear logical and compelling but, ultimately, prove evanescent. Practically in every decade in the postwar era, there are events that seem to spell the imminent doom of the dollar, with pundits warning of an impending dollar crash. The dollar has persevered through all these phases with its supremacy as the world's preferred store of value perhaps dented but never seriously challenged.

Spreading the Pain When the Going Gets Tough

The prospect, however remote, of China or other wild cards tipping U.S. public finances into a crisis should give U.S. policymakers abundant grounds for concern. However, for all the financial and economic destruction such a crisis would wreak, the U.S. is in a less vulnerable position than any other economy in this position would be. The exorbitant privilege that it has enjoyed in its role as the principal global reserve currency so far gives the U.S. a unique cushion.

There is a rich irony in that a dollar crisis could in fact be good for the U.S. in some respects. It would finally force the U.S. to enact better domestic policies but would buffer the pain from any short-term dislocations caused by those policies. For one, a cheaper dollar would be good for the U.S., as it would make its exports more competitive. Second, the U.S. would make a handsome profit on its external balance sheet position. As discussed in Chapter 6, most of its liabilities are denominated in U.S. dollars, so nothing changes on that side of the U.S. external balance sheet if the dollar's value declines. In contrast, most of the foreign assets the U.S. holds are denominated in foreign currencies. So their value, measured in terms of U.S. dollars, would actually rise when the dollar's value falls, as every unit of foreign currency would be worth more in dollars.

Of course, the U.S. would share in the pain as well. It would face higher borrowing costs on its public debt, which would squeeze the government budget even more. The U.S. would also find that printing money to pay off the debt would not work well. It would simply feed into higher domestic inflation, if the rest of the world were not keen to hold more dollars.

Still, the pain inflicted on the rest of the world would be even greater. Other countries would be forced to make a major adjustment by ramping up domestic demand if U.S. economic growth were to slow and the dollar were to depreciate sharply. As the global financial crisis showed, no country would escape the negative consequences of a U.S. meltdown.

Why America Rules

Given its fragile and in some ways frightening debt situation, why is the U.S. still in the position of being the world's liquidity provider of last resort? What accounts for the childlike faith of investors worldwide that the U.S. government will eventually settle its debt obligations in an orderly manner? The answer, in large part, rests on its robust and resilient institutions that, in some respects, might even prevail over sheer economic power.

Institutions Are Crucial

It has become an article of faith among academic economists that economic, legal, and political institutions, along with social norms, are important determinants of a country's long-term economic success. The seminal work of Nobel Laureate Douglass North of Washington University emphasized the growth-enhancing role of institutions that support private contracting arrangements but also limit the possibility of expropriation by the government or other politically powerful groups.

Daron Acemoglu, Simon Johnson, and James Robinson at MIT have built up a large body of empirical work strengthening the case for the primacy of institutions. In some of their work, they attempt to unbundle the roles of different types of institutions. They conclude that "property rights institutions," which protect ordinary citizens against expropriation by government or political elites, are essential for long-run economic growth, investment, and financial development. They find that "contracting institutions," which enable the enforcement of private contracts, have a greater influence on financial intermediation than on growth. Other researchers have found that participatory rights and democratic accountability are more important than property rights institutions for explaining cross-country outcomes of indicators of economic and social development.

These institutional factors are the core building blocks for the level of trust that the rest of the world has in the U.S. The trump card is an institutionalized system of checks and balances that operates among the executive, legislative, and judicial branches of its government. The emphasis on transparency of public institutions, the right to free expression, and an unfettered media are all necessary for building confidence. They accomplish this not by emphasizing strengths but by making weaknesses and faults in the system obvious, with the democratic process then providing a self-correcting mechanism.

The current dysfunctionality of the political system makes one wonder whether the above line of logic suggests a blind and misplaced faith in the United States. A reading of U.S. history indicates that the degree of political fragmentation is hardly a new phenomenon, and there have been many instances in this relatively young country's history when the degree of animus between the main political parties and the lack of bipartisanship have brought effective policymaking to a grinding halt. The country and its polity have survived these difficult times with relatively few scars to show for them, and smooth political transitions have remained the norm, even following pitched and divisive political battles.

The system of open and transparent democracy is crucial for explaining the confidence that foreign central banks and other investors have that the U.S. will not default on its debt, either directly or through indirect means, such as by allowing inflation to soar even temporarily. That about $4.5 trillion of Treasury debt is owned by U.S. investors, particularly by many groups—like retirees—who form potent voting blocks, is a comforting thought for foreign investors. Moreover, given how broadly the holdings of U.S. Treasury securities are dispersed, the notion of the U.S. targeting a specific country and reneging on its obligations to that country is unrealistic and unlikely to pass legal muster.

Indeed, the U.S. legal framework is another bedrock that is not only independent from the executive and legislative branches but is also seen as a fair and consistent interpreter of the rules. Although one may quarrel with the complexity of U.S. laws and regulations, their application and enforcement in a generally consistent and uniform manner is important for inspiring confidence among both domestic and foreign investors.

Many of the U.S. advantages reinforce one another. The strong regulatory and legal frameworks have led many foreign firms to seek listings on U.S. exchanges to "bond" themselves to the U.S. institutional framework. Foreign companies that register with the U.S. Securities and Exchange Commission subject themselves to stronger corporate governance standards and disclosure requirements. In return, they enjoy higher valuations, cheaper funding, and better long-run financial performance than similar companies that do not subject themselves to the discipline and scrutiny of U.S. markets and institutions.

Growth versus Institutions

Isn't economic performance an ace that should beat out any advantage conferred by superior institutions? The Chinese Communist Party has clearly done a skillful job of managing the economy, at least when considering GDP growth as the measure of success. China stands out as an anomaly in the context of the voluminous academic literature that well-developed legal and financial systems are important determinants of growth. The void in these dimensions in China has been filled to some extent by mechanisms based on reputation and relationships, as well as by informal financial intermediaries. These informal institutions have been able to support growth in ways that are still not clearly understood by researchers, but they offer little comfort to investors from other countries. Many of these investors may decide that the risks of expropriation or a weak legal framework to protect their rights are compensated for by the high growth potential of the Chinese economy. This assessment may explain the high levels of direct investment in China by foreign investors. However, it also suggests why foreign investors are unlikely to view the country as a predictable, low-risk destination for investment when safety matters more to them than yield.

Turning to the political framework, China's government remains opaque, and even the political decision making process at top levels is shrouded in secrecy. In the latest transition of power that took place during 2012–13, competing factions were battling fiercely for control of power, but all of this took place behind the scenes. It is certainly not the case that the Chinese Communist Party is a monolithic institution that speaks and acts fully in concert, brooking no internal dissent. Cheng Li of the Brookings Institution has characterized China as having two informal coalitions or factions that now check and balance each other's power in the Politburo, the country's highest political authority. However, these countervailing forces are no substitute for the sort of durable and institutionalized checks and balances that the U.S. system has.

In the summer of 2013, even as China's new leaders were escalating the battle against corruption and fostering expectations of significant economic reforms, they made it clear that major political and institutional reforms would not be tolerated. A document issued by the Party's Central Committee General Office, apparently with the approval of top leaders, surfaced in public in August. "Document No. 9" enumerated seven perils that the Party needed to guard against in order to maintain its authority. These included Western constitutional democracy; advocacy of Western concepts of freedom, democracy, and human rights; advocacy of freedom of the press; and advocacy of neoliberal free market concepts and the notion of civil society in which individual rights have supremacy. This was an unambiguous statement that economic reforms and liberalization would remain divorced from reforms in other spheres. Thus, even setting aside the issue of its low level of financial development, it is difficult to envision China as a safe haven, given the present form of its political and legal frameworks.

Flight to Liquidity Rather Than to Safety

In addition to the quality and resilience of its public institutions, another of the key characteristics that defines the U.S. is the depth of its financial markets. Thus, investments in U.S. government bonds are at least liquid and easily tradable. In some respects, the rush into U.S. Treasury bonds during times of global financial turmoil can be characterized more as a flight to liquidity and depth than as a flight to safety. Even if the prospect of an eventual dollar depreciation exposes foreign investors to a small loss in principal, they will still come flocking into U.S. Treasuries at stormy times in global financial markets. For they know that they can pull their money back by selling Treasuries without too much difficulty when the storms have passed and the skies have cleared.

Like many other asset markets, U.S. bond markets are perhaps being borne along by the "greater fool" theory. This concept, which became popular in the U.S. housing market boom in the 2000s, is that it makes sense to buy an asset even if it is regarded as overpriced, so long as one can be reasonably confident of finding another investor willing to pay an even higher price. The logic in many investors' minds may be that, given the enormous level of trading activity in the U.S. Treasury bond market, finding other fools may not be too difficult.

For all these reasons, at present the dollar remains the ultimate safe haven currency. But this is not necessarily a ringing testament to American exceptionalism. In global finance, everything is relative. What the continued dominance of the dollar shows is that the rest of the world simply cannot match the institutions and the financial markets that America has created. Despite their weaknesses, U.S. institutions and markets still remain the yardstick against which global investors measure other countries. Ronald McKinnon of Stanford University has nicely summed up the current state of affairs:

while nobody loves the dollar standard, the revealed preference of both governments and private participants in the foreign exchange markets since 1945 is to continue to use it . . . it is a remarkable survivor that is too valuable to lose and too difficult to replace.

Whether this is an encouraging or depressing prospect depends on where one sits.

What Lies Ahead

Monetary exchange has freed humanity from inefficient barter arrangements. It has boosted domestic and international trade, and it has paved the way for economic progress around the world. Fiat money is here to stay and, for all its flaws, there is no obvious superior alternative.

Notwithstanding its benefits, fiat money has also become a source of instability within countries and in their interactions with the rest of the world. If the current structure of the global monetary system is adding to this instability, the question is why a system with such a central role for a small set of reserve currencies persists. With a broader distribution of global economic power and worldwide financial market development, an increasing number of currencies will over time come to be used in international trade and financial transactions.

However, the flow of money across national borders has itself become a source of macroeconomic and financial instability. In particular, emerging market economies are unable to fully protect themselves against calamity wrought by the volatility of these flows using fiscal, monetary, and financial sector policies that are under their control. Hence, these economies are left with little choice but to accumulate certain fiat monies as reserve assets to protect themselves.

The scheme for country insurance outlined in Chapter 11 would reduce the need for large stocks of reserve assets but still leave in place an important role for the major central banks that can create liquidity in adequate amounts when the world's financial system needs it. The inertia in global finance and the lack of effective global governance mechanisms militate against the rapid adoption of any such scheme. The structure of reserve currencies, with the dollar at its core, is therefore unlikely to be dislodged anytime soon.

Hard Economic Power Shifts, Soft Power Does Not

Emerging markets now have enormous clout in the global economy, accounting for a substantial share of global growth. But their financial markets remain relatively underdeveloped. Conversely, advanced economies have well-developed financial markets but are groaning under the burden of high and rising debt levels, along with rapidly aging populations that will only make these problems worse. Over the next decade, advanced economies will remain vulnerable to debt and financial crises that could limit their already weak growth prospects. Emerging market economies are more exposed to domestic institutional and policy fragilities that could slow their growth momentum but are unlikely to derail it.

The U.S. and other advanced economies still enjoy many advantages over emerging markets. The major advanced economies have greater institutional and political stability, together with deeper and better-developed financial markets. Even when subject to political gridlock, they usually have more orderly political transitions. The strength of their public institutions remains a critical anchor of political and economic stability. Their central banks still have independence and credibility, which is crucial for having the ability to undertake conventional and unconventional monetary policy actions without inflation expectations becoming unanchored. However, the ongoing political fragmentation in many of these countries and the deteriorating trust in their public institutions are taking a toll. Central banks are also coming under increasing pressure to expand their mandates and toe the line of politicians.

The U.S. is the prime example of a rich country with enormous institutional advantages that has exploited its exorbitant privilege to the hilt. Those advantages cannot be relied on to compensate for all its policy foibles in perpetuity. The level of political dysfunctionality in the U.S. and its implications for financial stability have also become painfully apparent to the world at large. Nevertheless, given their own political and institutional weaknesses, other countries have not been able to extricate themselves from the dollar trap, and many have in fact become even more enmeshed in it.

A trenchant summary of the present situation comes from a private sector analyst, Steven Englander of Citi, in a comment on the 2011 monetary conference in Nanjing that was discussed in Chapter 12. He observed that all countries but one are trying to figure out how to get rid of the dollar as the world's major reserve currency, one country is trying to keep its currency as the world's major reserve currency but have it depreciate against all the others, and one country wants its currency to become a reserve currency but doesn't want anyone to buy it without permission. The intended outcome is reform of the international monetary system.

Fragility Breeds Stability

The world economy is in a fragile equilibrium. Although our imagination does not easily help us conceive of the scenario that could cause it to happen, it is possible that we are on a sandpile that is just a few grains away from collapse. The dollar trap might one day end in a dollar crash. For all its logical allure, however, this scenario is not easy to lay out in a convincing way.

This book has made the argument for a proposition to the contrary. The equilibrium in which the dollar remains the dominant global reserve currency is suboptimal but stable and self-reinforcing. This proposition seems to run counter to logic and is hard to fathom. At the same time, it is difficult to escape from this conclusion if one maps logic on to the existing state of the global monetary and financial systems.

The dollar trap has become a protective but prickly cocoon for a troubled world, which could do a lot worse than putting its money and trust in the U.S.

FIGURE A-1. Global Distribution of Gross Domestic Product

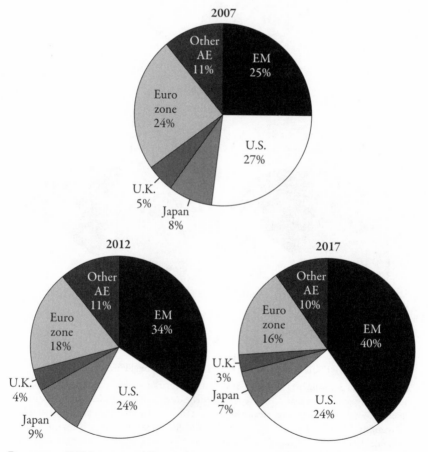

Data source: IMF International Financial Statistics.

Notes: Gross domestic product is measured at current prices and converted to a common currency at market exchange rates. Data for 2017 are based on IMF forecasts. "Other AE" denotes other advanced economies, and "EM" stands for emerging markets. All calculations in the appendix figures are based on the sample of 29 advanced economies and 29 emerging market economies listed in the box in Chapter 3, page 34.

FIGURE A-2. Global Distribution of Government Debt

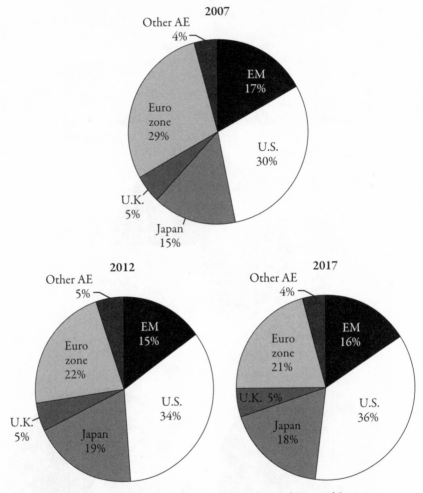

Data sources: IMF Fiscal Monitor, April 2013; IMF International Financial Statistics.

Notes: General government net debt is used in the calculations. Gross debt data are used for the following economies that do not report net debt: advanced economies—Czech Republic, Greece, Hong Kong, Singapore, Slovak Republic, and Slovenia; emerging market economies —Argentina, China, India, Indonesia, Malaysia, the Philippines, Romania, Russia, and Thailand. Data for 2017 are based on IMF forecasts. "Other AE" denotes other advanced economies, and "EM" stands for emerging markets. All debt data were converted to a common currency at market exchange rates before undertaking these calculations.

FIGURE A-3. Accounting for Changes in Global Government Debt and Gross Domestic Product

A. Contributions to changes in world net government debt

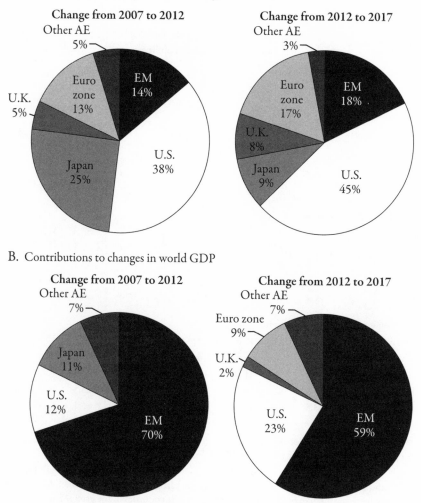

B. Contributions to changes in world GDP

Data sources: IMF Fiscal Monitor, April 2013; IMF International Financial Statistics.

Notes: The two charts in panel A show the contributions of different economies (or groups of economies) to the changes in the absolute levels of world general government net debt (measured in a common currency at market exchange rates). The two charts in panel B show the contributions of different economies (or groups of economies) to the changes in the absolute levels of world nominal gross domestic product (measured in a common currency at market exchange rates). From 2007 to 2012, the euro zone did not make a positive contribution to global GDP growth in dollar terms. Japan's contribution to global GDP growth in dollar terms from 2012 to 2017 is expected to be negative, even if the Japanese economy registers positive GDP growth, because of the sharp depreciation of the yen relative to the dollar at the end of 2012 and in early 2013. Data for 2017 are based on IMF forecasts. "Other AE" denotes other advanced economies, and "EM" stands for emerging markets.

TABLE A-1. Structure of External Liabilities
(percent)

	FDI / total liabilities			Portfolio equity / total liabilities			(FDI + PE) / total liabilities		
	2000	2007	2011	2000	2007	2011	2000	2007	2011
Advanced economies									
Median	20.0	20.8	22.4	15.0	12.7	7.4	40.3	38.1	29.5
Weighted mean	17.5	17.0	16.7	21.6	15.9	11.9	39.1	32.9	28.7
Emerging market economies									
Median	31.8	39.3	41.5	3.1	8.1	7.5	34.4	56.7	57.5
Weighted mean	34.8	42.8	47.5	7.2	18.6	12.8	42.0	61.4	60.3
Selected advanced economies									
Euro zone average	17.7	19.2	18.3	20.2	15.5	10.7	37.9	34.6	29.0
Germany	17.9	18.7	15.9	11.7	13.6	7.4	29.6	32.3	23.3
Japan	2.8	4.3	5.7	30.4	39.3	19.9	33.1	43.7	25.6
U.K.	10.2	7.6	6.9	22.2	10.4	7.5	32.5	18.0	14.4
U.S.	18.8	14.1	13.9	21.7	15.6	13.9	40.4	29.6	27.9
Selected emerging market economies									
Brazil	32.8	33.8	45.8	9.9	39.7	24.7	42.7	73.6	70.5
China	66.5	57.3	61.3	3.1	10.5	7.2	69.6	67.8	68.5
India	14.7	25.8	31.7	12.6	24.8	16.8	27.2	50.5	48.5
Russia	17.5	39.5	41.5	6.0	24.9	16.1	23.5	64.4	57.5
South Africa	43.5	38.9	40.9	22.6	38.8	31.6	66.1	77.8	72.5

Data sources: IMF's International Financial Statistics; Lane and Milesi-Ferretti (2007), using the 2012 updated dataset provided by Lane and Milesi-Ferretti.

Notes: "FDI" is foreign direct investment; "PE" stands for portfolio equity. The ratios of FDI liabilities and PE liabilities of a country relative to its total external liabilities are shown. Median refers to the cross-sectional median of the relevant ratio across the countries in the group. The weighted mean is the sum of the numerator variable for all countries in the group divided by the sum of the denominator variable for those countries. Economies not included in the euro zone are Cyprus, Luxembourg, and Malta. For some economies, 2001 or 2002 data are used when 2000 data are not available. Data for 2011 were not available for Kenya and Saudi Arabia. The figures for the medians in the third panel are not the sums of the figures for the medians in the first two panels.

TABLE A-2. International Investment Positions of Selected Economies, 2012
(billions of U.S. dollars)

	Germany	Japan	U.K.	U.S.	Brazil	China	India	Russia
Net position	1,394	3,554	−873	−4,416	−690	1,736	−282	138
A. Assets								
Total	9,543	7,705	16,115	21,489	788	5175	442	1241
1. FDI	1,790	1,055	1,808	5,673	231	503	118	362
2. Portfolio	2,760	3,620	3,556	7,211	24	241	2	44
Equity	747	723	1,220	4,920	15	130	2	6
Debt	2,013	2,898	2,336	2,292	9	111	0	38
3. Other investment	3,627	1,765	5,823	4,414	153	1,044	27	331
4. Reserve assets	249	1,265	98	571	379	3,388	296	499
Fx reserves	38	1,193	67	50	362	3,312	262	472
5. Financial derivatives	1,118	0	4,829	3,620	1	0	0	6
B. Liabilities								
Total	8,150	4,151	16,988	25,905	1,477	3,439	724	1,103
1. FDI	1,307	205	1,321	3,799	676	2160	226	457
2. Portfolio	3,505	2,065	4,201	13,653	606	336	170	226
Equity	707	927	1,435	4,178	345	262	129	178
Debt	2,798	1,138	2,766	9,475	261	74	41	49
3. Other investment	2,227	1,881	6,680	4,891	192	943	328	414
4. Financial derivatives	1,110	0	4,785	3,562	4	0	0	6

Data source: IMF's International Financial Statistics.

Notes: Provisional data for India for 2012 (except for foreign exchange reserves) come from the Reserve Bank of India. Data for Brazil and Russia are for 2012 Q3 and 2011 Q4, respectively. Data for all other economies are for 2012 Q4. Net position is given by total external assets minus total external liabilities. "FDI" stands for foreign direct investment. "Fx reserves" stands for foreign exchange reserves.

TABLE A-3. Changing Structure of Emerging Markets' External Balance Sheets, 2000–2011

Country	A. Liabilities			B. Assets
	Change in FDI liabilities / change in total liabilities	Change in PE liabilities / change in total liabilities	Change in FDI + PE liabilities / change in total liabilities	Change in foreign exchange reserves / change in total assets
Argentina	—	—	—	19.4
Brazil	51.3	29.3	80.5	53.7
Bulgaria	73.3	0.8	74.1	46.7
Chile	58.7	8.5	67.2	13.4
China	60.3	8.0	68.3	70.9
Colombia	64.7	3.5	68.2	30.8
Hungary	67.6	1.9	69.5	12.9
India	36.4	18.0	54.4	62.5
Indonesia	57.8	26.5	84.3	64.6
Jordan	73.2	5.7	78.9	61.8
Kazakhstan	58.6	1.8	60.4	17.0
Latvia	26.4	0.6	27.0	21.0
Lithuania	35.4	0.7	36.1	35.0
Malaysia	34.7	22.5	57.2	38.2
Mexico	44.5	19.1	63.6	34.1
Morocco	73.9	5.0	78.9	92.9
Nigeria	82.6	19.3	101.9	32.6
Pakistan	34.4	2.7	37.0	66.0
Peru	45.0	29.4	74.5	59.2
Philippines	29.7	40.2	69.8	66.2
Poland	45.1	5.0	50.1	40.5
Romania	40.8	1.0	41.7	65.5
Russia	47.2	18.5	65.7	43.1
South Africa	39.8	35.6	75.3	17.4
Thailand	59.4	30.2	89.6	59.0
Turkey	34.8	9.1	43.9	44.9
Ukraine	37.1	1.8	38.9	22.3
Median	45.1	8.0	67.2	43.1
Weighted mean	52.2	14.7	66.9	55.1
Weighted mean excluding China	49.0	17.3	66.4	40.9

Data sources: IMF's International Financial Statistics; Lane and Milesi-Ferretti (2007), using the 2012 updated dataset provided by Lane and Milesi-Ferretti.

Notes: "FDI" stands for foreign direct investment; "PE" is portfolio equity. The first column under Panel A shows the change in the stock of a country's FDI liabilities from 2000 to 2011 as a ratio of the change in that country's total external liabilities over the same period. The last column (Panel B) shows the change in the stock of a country's foreign exchange reserves from 2000 to 2011 as a ratio of the change in that country's total external assets over the same period. The weighted mean is the sum of the numerator variable for all countries in the group divided by the sum of the denominator variable for those countries. Argentina is excluded from the calculations in Panel A since its total foreign liabilities declined between 2000 and 2011.

TABLE A-4. Foreign Exchange Reserves Evaporate during the Crisis

Country	Reserves level (billions of U.S. dollars) High	Low	High month	Low month	Percentage drop	Number of months: high to low	March 2013 level (billions of U.S. dollars)
Brazil	206	186	September 2008	February 2009	9.6	5	366
Bulgaria	20	14	August 2008	February 2009	30.4	6	16
India	305	239	May 2008	November 2008	21.7	6	260
Indonesia	58	48	July 2008	February 2009	17.3	7	98
Malaysia	125	87	June 2008	April 2009	30.6	10	135
Mexico	98	79	September 2008	August 2009	19.0	11	158
Nigeria	62	42	September 2008	August 2009	32.7	11	48
Peru	35	28	June 2008	February 2009	17.9	8	65
Poland	82	56	July 2008	January 2009	31.6	6	101
Russia	582	367	July 2008	March 2009	37.0	8	464
S. Korea	264	200	March 2008	November 2009	24.3	8	317
Turkey	76	64	September 2008	April 2009	16.0	7	104
Ukraine	37	24	July 2008	April 2009	36.2	9	23
Median reserve losses					24.9	8	

Data source: IMF's International Financial Statistics.

Notes: Shown are the peak levels of foreign exchange reserves held by each country before the worst of the global financial crisis and the trough levels in the aftermath of the crisis. The economies selected for this table are relatively large emerging markets (along with one advanced economy—South Korea) that experienced significant reserve losses.

TABLE A-5. Central Bank Swap Arrangements with People's Bank of China, December 2008–June 2013

Bank	Date	Amount (billions of yuan)	U.S. dollar equivalent (billions)
1. Bank of Korea	*December 12, 2008*	*180*	*26.3*
	October 26, 2011	360	56.5
2. Hong Kong Monetary Authority	*January 20, 2009*	*200*	*29.2*
	November 22, 2011	400	62.9
3. Bank Negara Malaysia	*February 8, 2009*	*80*	*11.7*
	February 8, 2012	180	28.6
4. National Bank of the Republic of Belarus	March 11, 2009	20	2.9
5. Bank Indonesia	March 23, 2009	100	14.6
6. Central Bank of Argentina	April 2, 2009	70	10.2
7. Central Bank of Iceland	June 9, 2010	4	0.5
8. Monetary Authority of Singapore	*July 23, 2010*	*150*	*22.1*
	March 7, 2013	300	48.2
9. Reserve Bank of New Zealand	April 18, 2011	25	3.8
10. Central Bank of the Republic of Uzbekistan	April 19, 2011	1	0.1
11. Bank of Mongolia	*April 19, 2011*	*5*	*0.8*
	March 20, 2012	10	1.6
12. National Bank of Kazakhstan	June 13, 2011	7	1.1
13. Bank of Thailand	December 22, 2011	70	11.1
14. State Bank of Pakistan	December 23, 2011	10	1.6
15. Central Bank of the United Arab Emirates	January 17, 2012	35	5.5
16. Central Bank of the Republic of Turkey	February 21, 2012	10	1.6
17. Reserve Bank of Australia	March 22, 2012	200	31.7
18. National Bank of Ukraine	June 26, 2012	15	2.4
19. Banco Central do Brasil	March 26, 2013	190	30.6
20. Bank of England	June 22, 2013	200	32.6

Data source: People's Bank of China.

Notes: The local currency bilateral agreements listed above cover the years after 2008. The agreements shown in italics have been superseded by subsequent agreements between the PBC and the relevant countries. The dollar equivalents are calculated using the exchange rate on the date of each agreement. The total amount under the 20 open agreements as of June 2013 is about 2.2 trillion yuan, or roughly $360 billion based on the June 2013 exchange rate of 6.13 yuan per dollar. A number of bilateral agreements signed before 2008, mostly under the Chiang Mai Initiative, are not included in this table. Many of those agreements are not in the local currencies of the relevant countries.

NOTES

PREFACE

The U.S. Congressional Budget Office prepares forecasts of U.S. deficits and debt based on current policies. In May 2013, the budget office forecast that federal debt held by the public would be 76 percent of GDP in 2014, fall to 71 percent of GDP by 2018, then rise to 74 percent of GDP by 2023. See: "Updated Budget Projections: Fiscal Years 2013 to 2023." Washington, DC: U.S. Congressional Budget Office.

CHAPTER 1. PROLOGUE

The opening quote is taken from Twain (1897), Volume 2, Chapter XV. An online version of the text is available at the Gutenberg Project: http://www.gutenberg.org/files/5809/5809-h/5809-h.htm.

An earlier version of this quote can be found in Lord Byron's *Don Juan,* which has the following text: "'Tis strange, but true, for truth is always strange, Stranger than fiction. If it could be told, How much would novels gain by the exchange! How differently the world would men behold!" See the text near the end of Canto the Fourteenth in Byron (1819–1824).

Stage Set for Dollar Collapse

Jim Rogers's quote is reported in: Ambrose Evans-Pritchard. "Fears of Dollar Collapse as Saudis Take Fright." *The Telegraph.* September 19, 2007. The *Der Spiegel* editorial "A Pearl Harbor without War" was written by Gabor Steingart and appeared on November 13, 2007. Krugman's quote is taken from the abstract of Krugman (2007). Rogoff's quote is reported in: Carter Dougherty. "Dollar's Retreat Raises Fear of Collapse." *New York Times.* September 13, 2007.

Sakakibara's prediction appears in this story: Stanley White and Kazumi Miura. "Sakakibara Says Dollar May 'Plunge,' Forcing Response." *Bloomberg News.* October 18, 2007. The IMF warning of a disorderly adjustment of the dollar can be found in the *World Economic Outlook*, October 2007. The World Bank's *Global Development Finance 2007* report contains a similar warning.

317

Act One

The Reserve Primary Fund, one of the largest money market funds in the U.S. before the financial crisis, had about $65 billion in assets in August 2008. On September 17, 2008, the Fund announced that the net asset value of its shares had fallen below one dollar, partly as a result of having to mark down the value of its holdings of $785 million worth of Lehman Brothers debt to zero.

The data on U.S. cross-border securities flows in this chapter are from the Treasury International Capital (TIC) reporting system that is maintained on the U.S. Treasury Department's website. The TIC definition of foreign official investors includes central banks, government-sponsored investment funds, and other government institutions.

Net foreign financial inflows into U.S. securities markets amounted to $513 billion during September–December 2008, $499 billion of which was from foreign private investors. During this period, it appears that foreign official investors shifted their investments out of long-term Treasury securities (Treasury notes and bonds) and private securities (including bonds issued by government-sponsored enterprises, such as Fannie Mae and Freddie Mac) into short-term Treasury securities (Treasury bills).

Balance of payments data (not seasonally adjusted) from the U.S. Bureau of Economic Analysis indicate that the U.S. had overall net inflows of $407 billion in the second half of 2008, with most of these net inflows accounted for by U.S. investors retrenching from foreign investment destinations. In contrast, Germany and Japan had small net outflows in that period.

Bertaut and Pounder (2009) analyze U.S. cross-border financial flows during the financial crisis. Milesi-Ferretti and Tille (2011) provide a broader cross-country analysis of financial flows during the crisis. Fratzscher (2011) uses data on weekly flows of individual investment funds to document that, among the advanced economies, only the U.S. experienced little change in either equity flows or bond flows at the height of the crisis. Euro zone countries experienced strong outflows, including large bond outflows. Jackson (2013) documents that, for the full year 2008, foreign private inflows into U.S. assets other than Treasury securities fell, although foreign direct investment inflows did hold up well.

The negative interest rates on U.S. Treasury bills are reported in: Michael Mackenzie. "Interest Rate on U.S. T-Bills Turns Negative." *Financial Times*. December 9, 2008.

Act Two

See "Report on Greek Government Deficit and Debt Statistics." European Commission. January 8, 2010. The 2009 deficit and debt numbers for Greece were subsequently revised up to 15.4 percent of GDP and 127 percent of GDP, respectively. See "Information Note on Greek Fiscal Data." Eurostat. November 15, 2010.

Net foreign financial flows into U.S. securities markets in the third quarter of 2010 amounted to $179 billion, $110 billion of which was from private investors and $69 billion of which was from other foreign official investors.

Overall net balance of payments inflows in that quarter amounted to $241 billion. Source: Bureau of Economic Analysis. Non–seasonally adjusted data, June 2013 data release.

The data source for the yield on ten-year Treasury notes is the Federal Reserve Board.

Act Three

There is precedent for wrangling over the debt ceiling leading to a technical, even if very short-lived, "default." In late April 1979, the U.S. Treasury failed to redeem $122 million of Treasury bills on time. The reason was a delay in raising the debt ceiling, which led to the postponement of several securities auctions. This was compounded by technical problems related to the relocation of Treasury's check-issuance operations, noted in a memo sent to regional Federal Reserve banks that stated "It took considerable time and effort to reactivate all of the word processors." See: Edward P. Foldessy. "Treasury Hits Delays in Mailing Checks to the Holders of Its Maturing Securities." *Wall Street Journal.* May 9, 1979. Zivney and Marcus (2005) chronicle this event in detail and conclude that it resulted in a 60 basis-point interest premium on certain federal debt for several years afterward. They argue that this event, although modest and short-lived, made investors feel that the probability of a U.S. default was not as low as they had thought it was.

The U.S. Treasury quote is taken from "Debt Limit: Myth v. Fact." This document and others related to the debt limit are available at: http://www.treasury.gov/press-center/news/Pages/debt-limit.aspx.

The S&P August 5, 2011, press release "United States of America Long-Term Rating Lowered to 'AA+' Due to Political Risks, Rising Debt Burden; Outlook Negative" can be found at: http://www.standardandpoors.com/ratings/articles/en/us/?assetID =1245316529563.

The details of the debt deal are described in a fact sheet issued by the White House: "Fact Sheet: Bipartisan Debt Deal: A Win for the Economy and Budget Discipline." The deal raised the debt limit by $2.1 trillion, generated more than $900 billion in deficit reduction over a decade based on discretionary spending caps relative to the baseline deficit projections, and established a process to achieve an additional $1.5 trillion in other additional balanced budget deficit reductions. The document is available at: http://www.whitehouse.gov/fact-sheet-victory-bipartisan-compromise-economy-american-people.

The yield on ten-year Treasury notes fell from 3 percent in July 2011 to 2 percent in September 2011. Data source: Federal Reserve Board.

In August–September 2011, net foreign inflows into U.S. securities markets amounted to $176 billion, of which $156 billion was from private investors and $20 billion was from foreign official investors. Net balance of payment inflows were $168 billion in the third quarter of 2011.

A broad trade-weighted, inflation-adjusted index of the dollar's value relative to other currencies fell by about 25 percent from its peak in February 2002 through April 2008. It then rose by 15 percent by March 2009. From March 2009 to July 2011, the index fell by 16 percent, followed by a 5 percent upward spike in the last half of

2011 (July–December). The index was relatively stable in the last quarter of 2012. These calculations are based on the index constructed by the Bank for International Settlements (BIS). Calculations based on the BIS broad nominal effective exchange rate indexes yield similar results. See Elwell (2012) for a discussion of the factors driving these changes in the dollar's value.

Act Four

The Republican Party's reactions to the Obama Administration's proposals to avoid the fiscal cliff are summarized in: http://tv.msnbc.com/2012/11/30/boehner-obama-debt-proposal-not-serious/.

The Drama Goes On

For details on the budget cuts under "sequestration," see the White House Office of Management and Budget's March 2013 report "OMB Report to the Congress on the Joint Committee Sequestration for Fiscal Year 2013." The sequestration mandates cuts to defense and nondefense funding totaling $109 billion in each year from 2014 to 2021. For 2013, the mandated cuts are $85 billion. See: Richard Kogan. "Sequestration by the Numbers." March 2013. Washington, DC: Center on Budget and Policy Priorities.

In the Bizarro World series from DC Comics, most of the action takes place on the cube-shaped planet Htrae (Earth spelled backwards). The term was popularized in an episode of the American television comedy *Seinfeld* titled "The Bizarro Jerry."

CHAPTER 2. WHAT IS SO SPECIAL ABOUT THE DOLLAR?

The opening quote is from "The Country of the Blind," a short story by H. G. Wells, originally published in April 1904 in the *Strand Magazine* (see Parrinder 1990).

Demand for Safe Assets Rises and Supply Shrinks

The expression about China having enough reserves to cope with anything but apocalypse is a modified version of a sentence in Prasad and Rajan (2005).

It's All Relative

For a nice discussion of changes in the world economy, see El-Erian (2008) and O'Neill (2011).

No Room for Comfort

Dr. Pangloss, an inveterate optimist, espouses the view that "all is for the best" in this, "the best of all possible worlds." He is the mentor of Candide, the main character in the French philosopher Voltaire's satirical novel *Candide,* which was first published in 1759. The latter part of Dr. Pangloss's worldview was taken from the work of the German philosopher (and polymath) Gottfried Leibniz, whose views Voltaire felt were inconsistent with the harshness of reality. The precise phrasing above is taken from a 1991 republication (Dover Publications) of an anonymous English translation. See penultimate paragraphs of Chapters III and XXX.

A Brief History of the U.S. Dollar's Road to Dominance

The Federal Reserve is not the first central bank the U.S. has had. There were two central banks established earlier in the U.S.—the First Bank of the United States (1791–1811) and the Second Bank of the United States (1816–36). In both cases, the banks were set up with 20-year charters that were not renewed. See "A History of Central Banking in the United States." Federal Reserve Bank of Minneapolis. http://www.minneapolisfed.org/community_education/student/centralbankhistory/bank.cfm?

The U.S. was the only major economy to stay on the gold standard, both in principle and in practice, during and right after World War I. Friedman and Schwartz (1963) present an authoritative overview of the evolution of monetary arrangements in the U.S. economy from the mid-1800s to 1960.

For historical analysis of the dollar's rise, see Eichengreen (2005), Eichengreen and Flandreau (2009, 2010), and Frankel (2011). On the subject of the dollar's exorbitant privilege, see Eichengreen (2011a).

Under Attack

At its creation in 1999, the euro zone had 11 members—Austria, Belgium, Finland, France, Germany, Ireland, Italy, Luxembourg, the Netherlands, Portugal, and Spain. Greece joined in 2001. There are now 17 members—including Cyprus, Estonia, Malta, Slovakia, and Slovenia.

For early prognoses of the euro's future as a rival to the dollar, see Papaioannou, Portes, and Siourounis (2006) and Chinn and Frankel (2007, 2008). See Posen (2008) for a skeptical view of the euro's role as a reserve currency.

Figures on the currency composition of world foreign exchange reserves are from the IMF's Composition of Foreign Exchange Reserves (COFER) database (March 29, 2013, update). The reported figures are based on the share of "allocated" reserves, whose currency composition is reported by national authorities. The share of "unallocated" reserves, those held by countries that do not report the currency composition of those holdings, has risen from 22 percent in 2000 to 44 percent in 2012. China and India are among the countries that may not report the currency composition of their reserves (the IMF does not say which countries do not report). Both countries are believed to hold about two-thirds of their reserves in dollar assets.

The euro's reported share of allocated foreign exchange reserves was 18 percent in 1999–2000, rose to 25 percent in 2003–04, and peaked at 28 percent in 2009. It then fell to 24 percent in 2012. In fact, after adjusting for the changes in currency values, the share of the euro in global foreign exchange reserves has not changed much since its inception. The euro's share at market exchange rates rose from 18.3 percent in 2000 to 24.8 percent in 2004 (a 36 percent increase in the share), while the euro exchange rate (end of year) went from 1.08 per dollar to 0.73 per dollar, an appreciation of 32 percent. In other words, a large part of the increase in the euro's share of allocated reserves from 2000 to 2004 may have been the result of changes in currency values. Cohen (2009) discusses the impact of currency valuation adjustments on the euro's share of reserves.

Preliminary data from the IMF for March 2013 indicate little change in the share of allocated reserves in total foreign exchange reserves, or in the currency composition of alloted reserves.

Coup de Grâce Turns into Moment of Grace

For more details on the Chicago Board Options Exchange Volatility Index, see: www.cboe.com/vix.

The Relatively Short History of U.S. Fiscal Profligacy

Historical current account data for the U.S. (1870–1960) were graciously provided by Alan Taylor of the University of Virginia and are described in Taylor (2002).

A Delicate Political Equilibrium

As of June 2013, U.S. federal government gross debt was $16.8 trillion, and net debt was $12.0 trillion. At the end of 2008, these numbers were $10.7 trillion and $6.4 trillion, respectively. Net debt includes privately held debt ($10 trillion in June 2013) and Federal Reserve holdings ($2 trillion). The Fed is technically not part of the U.S. government. Its reported holdings exclude Treasury securities held under repurchase agreements. For more details, see the U.S. Treasury Bulletin. Daily data on U.S. public debt can be found at the Treasury Direct website: http://www.treasurydirect.gov/NP/debt/current. The current-dollar GDP figure for the second quarter of 2013 is from the U.S. Bureau of Economic Analysis.

Paradoxes Proliferate

Bizarro bonds are referred to in: Jerry Siegel and John Forte. July 1961. "Bizarro, Private Detective." *Adventure Comics* 1 (286). New York: National Comics Publications (DC Comics). Page 27.

The Dollar's Dominance Weakens—Except as a Store of Value

For some data on the dollar's role in various international trade and financial transactions, see Goldberg (2010) and references therein. The Society for Worldwide Interbank Financial Telecommunication (SWIFT) estimates that the euro has already overtaken the dollar as the currency for settling payments on international transactions intermediated through its platform. At the end of 2012, the euro accounted for 40 percent of world payments, whereas the dollar accounted for 33 percent. This information is based on the January 2013 issue of SWIFT's monthly *RMB Tracker* publications. Auboin (2012) examines the reasons for the dominance of the U.S. dollar and euro in the invoicing of international trade. He argues that it will take a number of years before the renminbi is in a position to challenge this duopoly.

Data on outstanding stocks of domestic debt securities as of December 2012 are taken from the Statistical Annex of the *BIS Quarterly Review*. June 2013. Basel, Switzerland: Bank for International Settlements. Data for the advanced economies are from Tables 3B and 3A (Table 3B has total debt securities, and Table 3A has international debt securities, which need to be subtracted from the figures in Table 3B).

Some Reserves Lose Their Luster

S&P's downgrades of Austria and France were both announced on January 13, 2012. The press releases can be found at: www.standardandpoors.com.

For Moody's November 19, 2012, announcement of the cut in France's government bond rating, see the document "Rating Action: Moody's Downgrades France's Government Bond Rating to AA1 from AAA, Maintains Negative Outlook." For Moody's February 22, 2013, announcement of the U.K. debt rating downgrade, see the document "Rating Action: Moody's Downgrades UK's Government Bond Rating to AA1 from AAA; Outlook Is Now Stable." Both documents are available at: www.moodys .com.

CHAPTER 3. THE PARADOX OF UPHILL CAPITAL FLOWS

The opening quote is from the 2009 movie *Pink Panther 2*. The lines are uttered about 25 minutes into the movie.

See Lucas (1990).

Theory Meets Reality

For examples of research attempting to explain the Lucas (1990) puzzle, see Tornell and Velasco (1992), Caselli and Feyrer (2007), and Alfaro, Kalemli-Ozcan, and Volosovych (2008).

For a catalogue of consumption booms and their causes, see Montiel (2000).

Uphill Flows

A country's current account balance is a summary measure of its capital imports or exports. A country's trade deficit, the excess of imports of goods and services over exports of goods and services, must be matched by a capital account surplus—net capital inflows—that enables financing of that trade deficit. So a current account deficit, which is roughly equivalent to the trade deficit, signals net imports of capital from the rest of the world. Similarly, a country with a current account surplus usually runs a matching capital account deficit—capital exports to the rest of the world.

It is also possible for a country to run a current account surplus and a capital account surplus simultaneously. It can happen if the country's central bank exports capital by accumulating foreign exchange reserves in an amount exceeding the inflows of capital. In this case also, the current account surplus captures the country's total capital exports—the capital exported by the central bank minus the amount of capital inflows reflected in the capital account surplus. In short, the current account balance captures all these scenarios and tells us whether a country is importing or exporting capital, depending on whether that balance is a deficit or surplus.

Aizenman, Pinto, and Radziwill (2007); Prasad, Rajan, and Subramanian (2007); and Gourinchas and Jeanne (2013) document uphill flows of capital in recent years.

Pradhan and Taylor (2011) note that capital generally flowed from richer to poorer economies during the nineteenth century. In the late nineteenth century, rich economies that were also financial centers—the U.K., France, and Germany—were the main providers of capital. The recipients included economies such as Argentina, Australia, Canada, Chile, New Zealand, and the U.S. that were rich in natural resources and had high per capita incomes but were short of capital.

At market exchange rates, China's per capita income in 2012 was $6,100, whereas U.S. per capita income was $49,900. Measured at purchasing power parity (PPP) exchange rates, China's per capita income in 2012 was $9,200. The U.S. per capita income remains the same, as it is the benchmark country for PPP exchange rate calculations. Source: IMF World Economic Outlook database, April 2013.

Capital Exporters and Importers

The picture of capital exports and imports looked similar before the global financial crisis. From 2000 to 2007, advanced economies—led by the U.S.—imported almost $2.8 trillion of capital, financed mostly by emerging markets' capital exports of about $1.6 trillion (capital exports of oil-exporting countries account for most of the difference).

The level of Germany's current account surplus now rivals that of China. See, for instance: Kemal Derviş. "Back to the Brink for the Eurozone?" *Project Syndicate.* October 10, 2012.

Are Uphill Flows a Problem?

For an analysis of China's saving and investment patterns and their implications, see Prasad (2009b, 2011b) and Lardy (2011). Chamon and Prasad (2010) and Chamon, Liu, and Prasad (2013) analyze the determinants of rising household savings rates in China. They find that the underdeveloped financial system—which makes it harder to borrow against future income or diversify financial assets—and an inadequate social safety net are important drivers of household savings rates.

Another Growth Conundrum

See Prasad, Rajan, and Subramanian (2007) and Gourinchas and Jeanne (2013).

Deficits as a Sign of Virtue

See Bernanke (2005) and Taylor (2008). For other critical perspectives on the savings glut hypothesis, see Borio and Disyatat (2011) and Shin (2012).

Supachai Panitchpakdi, the head of the United Nations Conference on Trade and Development and a former Thai government official, rejected the savings glut hypothesis:

> Asians financed cheap consumption in the rest of the world, this is what they say. This is something I just cannot understand. This is another theory we have to debunk. Asians have not been oversaving and underconsuming.

Zhou Xiaochuan, head of China's central bank, argued that focusing too much on "macro" issues like savings imbalances risks diverting needed attention from "micro" factors, such as financial regulation. He was quoted as saying:

The crisis originated from Wall Street and many indisputable facts have established that micro factors had played an overwhelmingly important role in causing this crisis.

See: Andrew Batson. "Asian Officials Reject Focus on Savings Glut." *Wall Street Journal.* July 6, 2009.

See: "Economic Report of the President, 2008" (prepared by the president's Council of Economic Advisors; available at: www.gpo.gov/fdsys/pkg/ERP-2008/pdf/ERP-2008.pdf).

Do Current Account Imbalances Matter?

Lawson put forward his argument at the IMF–World Bank Annual Meetings in September 1988. See: International Monetary Fund. 1988. *Summary Proceedings of the Forty-Third Annual Meeting of the Board of Governors.* Washington, DC; and Lawson (1992). The "consenting adults" view in the context of Australia is espoused by Pitchford (1989) and Corden (2007). See Blanchard (2007) for a formal analysis of these arguments. Wolf (2010) explicitly links the financial crisis to global macroeconomic imbalances. Obstfeld and Rogoff (2009) argue that imbalances and the crisis are both the products of bad policies in different groups of countries.

The IMF's Independent Evaluation Office notes that before the global financial crisis, the IMF management and staff were most concerned that global current account imbalances could precipitate a dollar crash, triggering a global recession. Other IMF publications pointed to financial system risks but, in the words of the evaluation office, "not emphatically enough and with critical omissions." See: Independent Evaluation Office. 2010. "IMF Performance in the Run-Up to the Financial and Economic Crisis: Multilateral Surveillance." Independent Evaluation Office Background Paper. Washington, DC: International Monetary Fund. December. Abstract.

For an analysis of macroeconomic developments in Chile from the mid-1970s to the early 1990s, see Laban and Larrain (1992).

What Explains Persistent Current Account Imbalances?

Obstfeld (2012) provides a nice survey of the analytical issues. Dooley, Folkerts-Landau, and Garber (2004); Caballero, Farhi, and Gourinchas (2008a,b); and Mendoza, Quadrini, and Ríos-Rull (2009) present different versions of the argument that differential levels of financial development between surplus and deficit countries account for global imbalances. Acharya and Schnabl (2010) contend that global banking flows, rather than global imbalances, determined how the crisis spread around the world. Rodrik (2008) argues that emerging markets are investment constrained rather than savings constrained.

CHAPTER 4. EMERGING MARKETS GET RELIGION

The opening quote is from a poem by the Indian poet Rabindranath Tagore, who won the Nobel Prize in Literature in 1913. See Tagore (1916) or the online version via Project Gutenberg at http://www.gutenberg.org/files/6522/6522.txt.

Lane and Milesi-Ferretti (2008) analyze the forces driving financial globalization. For an evaluation of financial globalization trends after 2007, especially the contrast between advanced and developing economies, see the March 2013 McKinsey Global Institute report "Financial Globalization: Retreat or Reset."

Kose and Prasad (2010) examine the relative resilience of emerging market economies during the global financial crisis and attribute this outcome to improved policies in these economies.

Country Balance Sheets Expand
Gross and Net

See Obstfeld (2010) on the importance of analyzing gross positions.

A standard dataset used in this literature is the one constructed by Lane and Milesi-Ferretti (2007). Most major economies now report their IIPs, although only for the past decade or so in many cases. For the empirical analysis in this chapter and elsewhere, I use official IIP data as the baseline source—this has an added advantage of helping me include 2011 data for many countries (the Lane and Milesi-Ferretti database has been updated through 2010). I use the Lane and Milesi-Ferretti data for historical comparisons and for countries that do not provide IIP data. Milesi-Ferretti, Strobbe, and Tamirisa (2010) discuss gross and net bilateral external asset and liability positions among major economies on the eve of the financial crisis.

Flows Also Matter

See Forbes and Warnock (2012) for an analysis of capital flow waves.

Good and Bad Capital

See Eichengreen and Hausmann (1999).

Corsetti, Pesenti, and Roubini (1999) present a nice overview of the dynamics and determinants of the Asian currency and financial crisis. For a broader analysis of the causes of banking and balance of payments crises, see Kaminsky and Reinhart (1999).

Sharing Rather Than Adding Risk

For evidence that FDI and portfolio equity flows promote international risk sharing, see Kose, Prasad, and Terrones (2009a).

Collateral Benefits

See Kose, Prasad, Rogoff, and Wei (2009) for a discussion of "collateral benefits" from capital account opening. Bekaert, Harvey, and Lundblad (2005) and Henry (2007) find that equity market liberalization has a positive effect on GDP growth.

The Chinese government imposes a 20 percent ownership limit on any single foreign investor in a Chinese bank, with a total foreign ownership of 25 percent. For a discussion of the structure and benefits of foreign investment in Chinese banks, see Dobson and Kashyap (2006), Leigh and Podpiera (2006), and Hope, Laurenceson, and Qin (2008).

Razin, Sadka, and Yuen (1998) argue that FDI is superior to debt and portfolio equity flows. Kose, Prasad, and Terrones (2009b) find that FDI and portfolio equity inflows are associated with higher growth in total factor productivity, whereas debt inflows have the opposite effect on productivity.

Emerging Markets Shed Risky Liabilities

See Prasad (2011a) for more details on the changes in countries' external liability positions.

Old Risks Fade, New Risks Emerge

India's exchange rate policy is summarized in the Reserve Bank of India Monetary Policy Statement 2010–11 by Dr. Subbarao, governor. Paragraph 36 notes that:

> Our exchange rate policy is not guided by a fixed or pre-announced target or band. Our policy has been to retain the flexibility to intervene in the market to manage excessive volatility and disruptions to the macroeconomic situation.

Capital Flows and Domestic Risks

In the last quarter of 2006 and first two quarters of 2007, gross external commercial borrowings by Indian firms surged to $7 billion per quarter, compared to an average of $2.5 billion per quarter in 2005 and the first three quarters of 2006 (based on data from the Reserve Bank of India). In August 2007, the Reserve Bank of India clamped down on external commercial borrowings. See: Reserve Bank of India. 2007. *Foreign Exchange Management (Amendment) Regulations, 2007.* Notification FEMA 157/2007-RB. August 30.

On the implications of financial openness for inequality, Ye (2011) reports preliminary evidence that greater financial openness is associated with greater wage inequality in emerging market economies. Ernst and Escudero (2008) report similar findings. Levchenko (2005) shows how households with limited financial access can be adversely affected in terms of domestic risk sharing possibilities as a consequence of capital account liberalization. Krueger and Yoo (2002) provide a detailed analysis of the role of crony capitalism in contributing to Korea's vulnerability to the Asian financial crisis. Rajan (2010) discusses how, even in the U.S., inequality and a feeble safety net led to distorted government policies that ultimately resulted in an unraveling of the financial system.

For some evidence on the role of rapid credit expansion in making countries more vulnerable to the aftershocks of the global financial crisis, see Kose and Prasad (2010), Frankel and Saravelos (2012), and Gourinchas and Obstfeld (2012).

Low deposit interest rates in advanced economies, which some authors have characterized as financial repression (e.g., Reinhart and Sbrancia 2011), are less of a concern from the perspective of generating inequitable outcomes. In these economies, there are other investment opportunities available to retail investors, making them less reliant on domestic banks.

CHAPTER 5. THE QUEST FOR SAFETY

The opening quote is from Adams (1982), Chapter 32 (Chapter 33 in some editions).

Data on emerging markets' foreign exchange reserves are taken from the IMF. The total stocks of foreign exchange reserves held by emerging and developing economies (the categorization used by the IMF) amounted to $0.60 trillion in 1998, $0.66 trillion in 1999, and $7.25 trillion in 2012 (all end-of-year data).

Shunning Appreciation
Building Up Reserves

Reinhart and Reinhart (2008) discuss how reserve accumulation is the by-product of one of the strategies used by emerging markets to cope with capital inflows.

The IMF is the arbiter of what assets on a central bank's balance sheet count as reserve assets. The IMF's *Balance of Payments Manual* defines reserve assets as follows: "These are foreign financial assets available to, and controlled by, the monetary authorities for financing or regulating payments imbalances or for other purposes." This definition points to an important role played by foreign exchange reserves, rather than their being just a by-product of policies to keep the domestic currency from appreciating.

At the end of 2012, global foreign exchange reserves stood at $10.9 trillion, official gold stocks at $1.7 trillion (with gold valued at market price), and Special Drawing Rights (SDRs) at $0.3 trillion. If gold stocks were valued at the IMF's book value (SDR 35 per ounce), the stock of gold reserves would amount to only $55 billion and foreign exchange reserves would account for 96 percent of international reserves.

Reserves as Insurance

See Frankel and Saravelos (2012) for evidence on how reserves reduced countries' vulnerability to the aftershocks of the financial crisis. In contrast, an earlier study by Blanchard, Das, and Faruqee (2010) concluded that there was no compelling evidence that international reserves played an important role as safety buffers in the crisis.

Corsetti, Pesenti, and Roubini (1999) analyze the Asian financial crisis. Haggard (2000) describes the politics of the affected countries in the lead-up to and following the crisis. He notes that the crisis contributed to the collapse of the Suharto regime in Indonesia, the installation of new governments in South Korea and Thailand, and political reforms in Malaysia.

Indonesia first signed a loan agreement with the IMF in October 1997. The January 1998 agreement was in some ways more significant, as it was then that Suharto agreed to undertake a number of important economic reforms. Suharto resigned from office in May 1998.

In a speech in 2002, Y. V. Reddy, then a deputy governor at the Reserve Bank of India, noted that he had been in charge of managing the tiny and dwindling pool of reserves in 1990–91, when he was at the Ministry of Finance. He said that "In such a predicament, the threat of national humiliation as well as discomforting relations with foreign agencies obviously touched on personal pride." Reddy went on to serve as Governor of the Reserve Bank of India from 2003 to 2008. See Reddy (2002), page 1.

Goldberg, Hull, and Stein (2013) note that advanced economies hold foreign exchange reserves for much the same reasons as emerging markets. These reasons are: managing the exchange rate, calming disorderly financial markets, and insuring against liquidity losses and disruptions to capital market access.

The Big Bazooka Principle
A Bazooka Fails but Sets a Standard

The Senate Committee hearing was on the subject of "Recent Developments in U.S. Financial Markets and Regulatory Responses to Them." Hank Paulson's bazooka comment was reported widely, including in: Andrew Ross Sorkin. "Paulson's Itchy Finger, on the Trigger of a Bazooka." *New York Times.* September 9, 2008.

How Much Is Enough?

The Guidotti-Greenspan rule is enunciated in Guidotti (1999) and Greenspan (1999).

The role of short-term external debt in balance of payments and financial crises is catalogued in Reinhart and Rogoff (2011) and Frankel and Saravelos (2012).

Various papers have tried to explain the increase in emerging markets' reserves. Obstfeld, Shambaugh, and Taylor (2010) estimate a model of reserve stocks that includes the monetary aggregate M2, financial openness, ability to access foreign currency through debt markets, and exchange rate policy. These variables do better at explaining emerging markets' reserve accumulation during the 2000s than traditional models that include only imports and external short-term debt. These authors note that countries with hard or soft currency pegs have reason to hold more reserves than if they were to have floating exchange rates. Jeanne (2007) presents a theoretical analysis of different motives for reserve accumulation—crisis prevention versus mitigation. For other analyses of accumulation motives and criteria for reserve adequacy, see Aizenman and Lee (2007) and Dominguez, Hashimoto, and Ito (2011). Also see the 2011 IMF Policy Paper "Assessing Reserve Adequacy." February 14. Washington, DC.

Game Changer

From 2000 to 2007, Chile experienced average annual real GDP growth of 4.7 percent and average annual CPI inflation of 3.1 percent. The Chilean peso fell from 508 pesos per U.S. dollar in November 2007 to 659 pesos per U.S. dollar in November 2008, a depreciation of about 30 percent. GDP growth was –0.9 percent in 2009 and then averaged 5.7 percent during 2010–12. Data source: IMF.

The quotes in the remainder of this section are from the following sources:

Chile: De Gregorio (2011a), pages 3–4. Nigeria: Reserve Management, Central Bank of Nigeria: http://www.cenbank.org/Intops/ReserveMgmt.asp. South Africa: "Management of Gold and Foreign-Exchange Reserves." South African Reserve Bank. See page 2. Colombia: "Administración de las Reservas Internacionales." Banco de la República, Colombia. March 2011. See page 9. Translation provided by Laura Ardila.

Bulking Up the Bazooka

See Prasad (2011a) for more details on the structure of emerging markets' external balance sheets.

Squirreling Away Nuts (or Bazooka Grenades) for the Winter
Safety First

China: State Administration of Foreign Exchange FAQs on Foreign Exchange Reserves (I), 2011/07/20. http://www.safe.gov.cn. Brazil, Hungary, Korea: "Guidelines for Foreign Exchange Reserve Management: Accompanying Document." Washington, DC: International Monetary Fund. March 26, 2003.

A description of results from the BIS survey of central banks' reserve management strategies can be found in Borio, Galati, and Heath (2008).

Risks Abound

India: "Half Yearly Report on Management of Foreign Exchange Reserves." Reserve Bank of India. October 2011–March 2012. See page 9.

Taking Some Modest and Considered Risks

Data on sovereign wealth funds are taken from the Sovereign Wealth Fund Institute's website: http://www.swfinstitute.org/fund-rankings.

The CIC was technically financed through the issuance of special government bonds worth 1.55 trillion yuan, which were then used to obtain foreign currency from the PBC's stock of international reserves. Data on CIC's balance sheet are taken from the *China Investment Corporation Annual Report 2011 Focusing on the Future*.

PBC reportedly acknowledged in 2008 that SAFE Investment Company had been set up in 1997. See: Jamil Anderlini. "China Investment Arm Emerges from Shadows." *Financial Times*. January 4, 2008. Estimates of SAFE Investment Company's assets are taken from the Sovereign Wealth Fund Institute.

On the announcement about SAFE's Co-Financing office, see: Zhou Xin. "China to Use Forex Reserves to Finance Overseas Investment Deals." *Bloomberg*. January 14, 2013. SAFE's 2011 annual report notes the existence of SAFE Co-Financing as an affiliated institution and describes the reason it was set up (see pages 8 and 75 of the annual report). It is possible that SAFE Investment Company and SAFE Co-Financing refer to the same entity.

For some evidence that sovereign wealth funds are stabilizing forces in global financial markets, see Sun and Hesse (2009) and references therein. This literature is in its early stages and is not conclusive.

The Price of Safety Goes Up

The discussion in this section draws extensively on Chapter 3 of the IMF's April 2012 *Global Financial Stability Report*.

The Basel Committee for Banking Supervision defines banks as systemically important on the basis of the following indicators: size, interconnectedness, complexity, cross-jurisdictional activity, and lack of substitutes for services they provide. See "Consultative Document: Global Systemically Important Banks: Assessment Methodology and the Additional Loss Absorbency Requirement." Basel, Switzerland: Bank for International Settlements. The liquidity coverage ratio will be introduced in 2015, with a minimum requirement set at 60 percent. The minimum requirement will rise to 100 percent by 2019. "Basel III: The Liquidity Coverage Ratio and Liquidity Risk Monitoring Tools." January 2013. Basel, Switzerland: Bank for International Settlements. For an update, see "Consultative Document: Liquidity Coverage Ratio Disclosure Standards." July 2013. Basel, Switzerland: Bank for International Settlements. All three documents cited here were prepared by the Basel Committee on Banking Supervision.

Caballero and Farhi (2012) and Gourinchas and Jeanne (2012) discuss the shortage of safe assets and argue that only public debt, supported by monetary policy, can play this role. For a discussion of collateral requirements and how they are altering the demand and supply of tradable safe assets, see Singh (2013). On this point, also see: Ralph Atkins. "Crunch Feared If Collateral Rules Enforced." *Financial Times*. February 5, 2013.

Supply of Private Safe Assets Shrinks

The quote is from the IMF's April 2012 *Global Financial Stability Report*. See page 86.

On the debt issuances by Amazon and Apple, see: Patrick McGee and Greg Bensinger. "Amazon Raises $3 Billion in a Rare Bond Offering." *Wall Street Journal*. November 26, 2012; and Katy Burne and Mike Cherney. "Apple's Record Plunge into Debt Pool." *Wall Street Journal*. April 30, 2013. Moody's and S&P rated Apple's debt offering one notch below AAA. An analyst for Moody's noted that it was in a "highly volatile industry." A report by S&P analysts said:

> While Apple will probably maintain "excellent" liquidity, most of its revenue is generated in highly competitive markets characterized by rapid technology evolution and short product life cycles.

See: Charles Mead, Victoria Stillwell, and Sarika Gangar. "Apple's $145 Billion in Cash Fails to Win AAA Debt Rating." *Bloomberg News*. April 24, 2013.

See Rajan (2005).

Public Debt Looks Less Safe

Chapter 3 of the IMF's April 2012 *Global Financial Stability Report* describes the changing fraction of AAA-rated government debt.

At the end of 2012, gross debt of the six core euro zone countries amounted to €4771 billion, 54.3 percent of total euro zone gross debt. Gross debt of the five euro zone periphery economies amounted to €3574 billion, 40.7 percent of the total. Gross debt of the remaining countries (Belgium, Cyprus, Estonia, Malta, Slovak Republic, and Slovenia) amounted to €453 billion. All data in this paragraph refer to government debt. The data source is: "Provision of Deficit and Debt Data for 2012—First Notification." Eurostat News Release. April 22, 2013.

For data on foreign net purchases of government debt of the euro zone and other advanced economies, see Figure 9 in Arslanalp and Tsuda (2012). The quote is taken from the foreword to the ECB's report: "The International Role of the Euro." July 2013. Frankfurt, Germany: European Central Bank.

Bazookas Can Be Costly Even If They Are Not Used

See Rodrik (2006) on the social costs of reserve accumulation by emerging markets.

Costly Sterilization

Estimates of the cost of reserve accumulation for Asian emerging markets can be found in Filardo and Grenville (2012).

The Colombian central bank governor's speech is in Uribe (2012). The translation is taken from this news report: Matthew Bristow and Christine Jenkins. "Colombia Weighs Fiscal Cost of FX Intervention, Uribe Says." *Bloomberg*. August 17, 2012.

Other Costs

The estimates of the costs of financial repression in China are from Lardy (2008). Also see Prasad (2009b) for a discussion of how the Chinese government maintains low interest rates and what the implications are for households.

For evidence on the motives for reserve accumulation, see Aizenman and Lee (2007). Based on an extensive cross-country empirical investigation, they conclude that the economic importance of variables associated with the mercantilist motive, such as export growth, in accounting for reserves hoarding is close to zero. They find that country characteristics, such as liberal capital account regimes and vulnerability to crises, play a far more important role in accounting for reserve accumulation. They argue that the results are equally valid for countries like China.

Backfiring Bazookas: Could Safe Assets Turn Risky?

The quote is from Summers (2006).

Caballero, Farhi, and Gourinchas (2008a, 2008b) argue that emerging markets' search for safe assets precipitated global macroeconomic imbalances. Mendoza, Quadrini, and Ríos-Rull (2009) make a related point that the greater financial depth of advanced economies attracts large inflows.

CHAPTER 6. A TRILLION DOLLAR CON GAME?

Warren Buffett, an avid poker player, included this quote in his 1987 report to the shareholders of Berkshire Hathaway (sent in March 1988). Various versions of this quote are apparently familiar to poker players. References to Buffett as the Sage of Omaha are widespread. See, for instance: Aline Sullivan. "Buffett, the Sage of Omaha,

Makes Value Strategy Seem Simple: Secrets of a High Plains Investor." *International Herald Tribune*. December 20, 1997. The headquarters of Berkshire Hathaway, which Mr. Buffett heads, is in Omaha, Nebraska.

A transcript of Geithner's speech is at: http://blogs.wsj.com/chinarealtime/2009/06/01/full-text-of-geithners-speech-at-peking-university/.

Zhang Boyang's question was reported in the Chinese media—the translation was provided by him. Geithner's response was reported in: Glenn Somerville. "Geithner Tells China Its Dollar Assets Are Safe." *Reuters*. June 1, 2009. A description of the event and a slightly different version of Geithner's response can be found in: Bill Powell. "Geithner's Asia Background Shows on His China Trip." *TIME Magazine*. June 1, 2009. http://www.time.com/time/world/article/0,8599,1902099,00.html.

At the end of 2012, total foreign exchange reserves in the world were $10.9 trillion, with advanced economies accounting for $3.7 trillion and emerging markets and other developing economies for $7.2 trillion. The assumption that two-thirds of global foreign exchange reserve accumulation goes into dollar-denominated assets is based on IMF data on the composition of foreign exchange reserves. See: http://www.imf.org/external/np/sta/cofer/eng/. At the end of 2012, the share of "allocated" foreign exchange reserves held in dollars amounted to 62 percent. This number is based on data from countries that report the currency composition of their foreign exchange reserves to the IMF. Some countries (possibly including China and India) do not report this composition to the IMF, so the share of "unallocated" reserves—those whose currency composition is not known—has risen sharply in recent years and accounted for 44 percent of global foreign exchange reserves ($4.9 trillion) in 2012.

According to data from the Treasury International Capital (TIC) reporting system, foreign holdings of U.S. Treasury securities rose from $1 trillion in December 2000 to $5.6 trillion in December 2012.

At market exchange rates, the mean per capita GDP in 2012 (based on country data, not weighted by country size) was $39,930 for advanced economies and $8,500 for emerging markets. The corresponding medians were $41,510 and $7,855, respectively. These calculations are based on the sample of advanced and emerging market economies listed in Chapter 3. U.S. per capita income in 2012 was $49,920. Data source: IMF's World Economic Outlook (April 2013 version of the database).

Safe Assets Balloon and Become More Fragile

In the U.S., gross debt is defined as total public debt, including intragovernmental holdings. For details on the social security trust funds and legal restrictions on what instruments those funds can be invested in, see the website of the Social Security Administration: http://www.ssa.gov/OACT/ProgData/fundFAQ.html.

Net debt excludes intragovernmental holdings but does include the Federal Reserve's holdings of government debt. Technically, the Federal Reserve is not part of the U.S. government; rather, it describes itself as "an independent entity within the government, having both public purposes and private aspects." See: http://www.federalreserveeducation.org/faq/topics/fed_basics.cfm. The U.S. Treasury defines debt held by other domestic and foreign investors, including foreign official investors, as debt that is "privately held." At the end of 2012, total U.S. public debt (gross) was $16.4 trillion, of which net debt was $11.6 trillion and intragovernmental holdings were $4.8 trillion. Of the net debt total, $1.6 trillion was accounted for by Federal Reserve holdings, and $10 trillion was privately held. Source: U.S. Treasury Bulletin, June 2013.

Japan's debt data were taken from the IMF and converted to U.S. dollars using the 2012 annual average exchange rate between the yen and the dollar.

Disturbing Debt Dynamics

The cross-country data on government debt used in this section come from the April 2013 update of the IMF's *Fiscal Monitor*. For more detailed data, including estimates of the burden of general government debt (debt per capita or per working-aged person), see Prasad and Ding (2011) and www.ft.com/debtburden. Note that, to ensure cross-country consistency of its data, the IMF adjusts official national data on debt levels according to its own definitions.

My book with M. Ayhan Kose is Kose and Prasad (2010).

Digging a Deeper Hole

Cross-country forecasts for population growth, labor force growth, the fertility rate, and dependency ratios are from the U.S. Census Bureau's International Data Base: http://www.census.gov/population/international/data/idb/informationGateway .php.

China's National Bureau of Statistics indicates that China's labor force, defined as the population aged 15 to 59, declined by 3 million to a level of 937 million. See: National Bureau of Statistics of China. 2013. "Statistical Communiqué of the People's Republic of China on the 2012 National Economic and Social Development." Beijing. February 22, 2013. Other estimates, such as those from the United Nations, suggest that growth of China's population in the 15–64 age range will turn negative between 2015 and 2020.

Cecchetti, Mohanty, and Zampolli (2010) present sobering projections of advanced economies' long-term debt levels under current policies in those countries. The April 2013 IMF *Fiscal Monitor* describes some challenges posed by high debt levels in advanced economies, including the large short-term financing needs implied by those debt levels.

Should Emerging Markets Fret over Their Foreign Bond Holdings?

Edwards (2005), Obstfeld and Rogoff (2005), and Feldstein (2007, 2011) make the case for a dollar depreciation to temper U.S. current account deficits.

For a more precise statement of the Balassa-Samuelson effect—the effects of relative productivity growth in the traded and nontraded goods sectors on the real exchange rate—see Chapter 4 in Obstfeld and Rogoff (1996). For evidence on the predictability of exchange rates in the long term, see Mark (1995) and Taylor and Taylor (2004).

For a comprehensive overview of the energy outlook for the U.S., including estimates of shale gas reserves and production, see the U.S. Energy Information Administration report "Annual Energy Outlook 2012, with Projections to 2035." June 2012.

Washington, DC: U.S. Department of Energy. For estimates of the potential impact of the shale gas revolution on U.S. GDP growth and the trade balance, see the following investment bank reports. "The U.S. Energy Revolution: How Shale Energy Could Ignite the US Growth Engine." September 2012. Goldman Sachs Asset Management. "Historic Opportunities from the Shale Gas Revolution." November 2012. New York: Kohlberg Kravis and Roberts & Co. For an analysis of the potential impact on global energy markets, and also a discussion of why factors specific to the U.S. have helped foster the shale gas revolution, see: Thomas Helbling. 2013. "On the Rise." *Finance and Development,* March 2013. Washington, DC: International Monetary Fund.

Uncomfortable Implications of Changing Currency Values

Labor productivity growth numbers for China and the U.S. are based on Bosworth and Collins (2008), Gordon (2010), and McMillan and Rodrik (2011). For a more pessimistic view about long-run growth and productivity in the U.S., see Gordon (2012).

The TIC is the source of official data on foreign investors' holdings of U.S. securities. Tables on portfolio holdings of U.S. long-term securities by foreigners, broken down by asset type and by country, can be found at: http://www.treasury.gov/resource-center/data-chart-center/tic/Pages/ticsec3.aspx. These data are collected primarily on the basis of custodial data but cannot attribute holdings of U.S. securities with complete accuracy. The TIC website notes:

> if a U.S. Treasury security purchased by a foreign resident is held in a
> custodial account in a third country, the true ownership of the security
> will not be reflected in the data. The custodial data will also not properly
> attribute U.S. Treasury securities managed by foreign private portfolio
> managers who invest on behalf of residents of other countries. In addition,
> foreign countries may hold dollars and other U.S. assets that are not captured
> in the TIC data. For these reasons, it is difficult to draw precise conclusions
> from TIC data about changes in the foreign holdings of U.S. financial assets
> by individual countries.

BIS data indicate that, against a smaller basket of 27 economies (nearly all of them advanced), the dollar index depreciated by an average of 1 percent per year in inflation-adjusted terms over 2000–2012. Comparing these figures with those shown in Figure 6-4 (1.2 percent depreciation per year in the broad index that includes most emerging market economies in addition to the countries in the narrow index) indicates that the dollar had a larger depreciation in inflation-adjusted terms over this period against emerging market currencies compared to its depreciation against other advanced economy currencies.

Diversification Does Not Help

In its 2013 "Productivity Brief," The Conference Board estimates that average annual labor productivity growth in 2012–13 will be 0.4 percent in the U.S. and the euro zone, zero percent in Japan, and 3.7 percent among the emerging and developing economies (see: http://www.conference-board.org/press/pressdetail.cfm?pressid=4702).

See Jorgensen and Vu (2010).

Just Bookkeeping?

The Q&A can be found on the English version of the SAFE website: http://www .safe.gov.cn/wps/portal/english/Home.

For a description of the bank recapitalization, which took place on December 31, 2003 but was actually implemented in January 2004, see Chapter VII by Steven Barnett in Prasad (2004).

Taking Creditors to the Cleaners

The U.S. debt default in 1933 occurred when the U.S. abrogated the gold clause attached to its debt, so the government would repay its debt in dollars but eliminated the option for owners of the debt to receive payment in gold. Reinhart and Rogoff (2008) catalog sovereign defaults on domestic debt.

Sharing the Pain with Foreign Investors

In Figure 6-5, for the U.S., the level of privately held debt and the share held by foreign investors (both official and private) are based on data from the Treasury Bulletin Table OFS-2 "Estimated Ownership of U.S. Treasury Securities" (columns 3 and 11). Column (3) shows the total amount of U.S. Treasury securities that is privately held. In this table, Federal Reserve holdings are clubbed in with other intragovernmental holdings in column (2). Column (11) shows holdings of foreign and international investors, both official and private. For Japan, net debt is based on the outstanding stock of Japanese Government Bonds (JGBs), from the Bank of Japan's Flow of Funds data (Chart 5-2 (2)). The following are then excluded: JGBs held by the Bank of Japan, general government, and public financial institutions (which includes pension funds). The share of overseas ownership of remaining JGBs is used to deduce net debt holdings by domestic and foreign investors. The data for Japan are converted to U.S. dollars using the end-2012 exchange rate of 86.2 yen per dollar. U.K. data are taken from the U.K. Debt Management Office's Gilt Market Data chart "Distribution of Gilt Holdings." Central government securities (gilts) held by public corporations, local governments, and the Bank of England are excluded from the measure of net debt. Overseas holdings (column K) are then used to deduce debt holdings by domestic and foreign investors. The data are converted to U.S. dollars using the end-2012 exchange rate of $1.62 dollars per British pound. Based on these calculations, the net debt figures at the end of 2012 and foreign investors' holdings of that net debt shown in Figure 6-5 are as follows. U.S.: $9.90 trillion, $5.57 trillion; Japan: $8.60 trillion, $0.97 trillion; U.K.: $2.19 trillion. $0.68 trillion.

Data for Switzerland are from: *Federal Treasury Activity Report 2012*. Bern: Federal Finance Administration, Swiss Confederation. See figure 14.

Foreign investors also hold some U.S. state and local government debt, but that figure, about $68 billion at the end of 2012, is dwarfed by foreign holdings of Treasury securities. See Tables L.106 and L.211 in: "Flow of Funds Accounts of the United States." Federal Reserve Statistical Release. March 7, 2013. Washington, DC: Board of Governors of the Federal Reserve.

Data on foreign ownership of sovereign debt for euro zone countries are taken from the IMF and the United Nations' European Intelligence Unit. See Andritzky (2012) for a more detailed analysis. Arslanalp and Tsuda (2012) estimate that about 80 percent of foreign holdings of Greek government debt are accounted for by other euro zone countries (see Figure 3 in that paper). The ECB figure is taken from the report: "The International Role of the Euro." July 2013. Frankfurt, Germany: European Central Bank. Table 1 indicates that foreign holdings of euro area debt denominated in euros, as a percentage of total euro-denominated debt, amounted to 17.3 percent in the second half of 2012. It is not clear from the table whether these calculations are based just on sovereign debt issued by euro zone countries.

A Calculated Risk: Domestic Investors Share in the Pain

The shares of U.S. public debt held by different categories of domestic investors can be found in Table OFS-2, "Estimated Ownership of U.S. Treasury Securities," available at: http://www.fms.treas.gov/bulletin/index.html.

Basu (2009) shows that, so long as the government is constrained to default equally on domestic and foreign holders of its debt, making the domestic economy vulnerable to default can help the government borrow more cheaply abroad. Default on domestic residents has a large economic cost, making default less likely.

The principal of a Treasury Inflation-Protected Security increases with inflation and decreases with deflation, as measured by the CPI. For more details on TIPS and other U.S. Treasury securities, see the Treasury Direct website: www.treasurydirect.gov.

Data on the composition of Treasury debt is taken from Table FD-2 of the September 2013 Treasury Bulletin.

Social Security benefits have a cost of living adjustment measured by the Consumer Price Index for Urban Wage Earners and Clerical Workers (CPI-W) prepared by the Bureau of Labor Statistics. See: http://www.ssa.gov/pressoffice/factsheets/colafacts2013.htm.

The U.S. Government Budget for 2014 proposed shifting from indexation of social security benefits based on the standard CPI to a chained CPI.

Auerbach and Gale (2009, 2012) provide an extensive discussion of how inflation may not be an effective approach to reducing the debt burden. They also note, for instance, that Medicare and Medicaid payments are implicitly linked to inflation.

Favilukis, Ludvigson, and Van Nieuwerburgh (2012) discuss the distributional consequences (within the U.S.) of foreign ownership of U.S. safe assets.

No Fear of Selective Default

Treasury debt may be held in custodial accounts of major banks, but the true ownership of those assets may be concealed, either intentionally or otherwise, through various layers of claimants to funds in those accounts.

See Mooney (2012) and the comments on that paper by Donald S. Bernstein and Steven L. Schwarz for a fascinating discussion about the legal issues surrounding a default on U.S. Treasury debt, including the legality of a selective default. The comments by Bernstein and Schwarz appear in the same volume as the Mooney paper.

See: Paul V. Kane. "To Save Our Economy, Ditch Taiwan." *New York Times.* November 10, 2011.

Must It End?

For a formal analysis of the debt dynamics formula and a framework for evaluating debt sustainability, see: Julio Escolano. 2010. "A Practical Guide to Public Debt Dynamics, Fiscal Sustainability, and Cyclical Adjustment of Budgetary Aggregates." IMF Technical Note. Washington, DC: International Monetary Fund.

Uncle Sam Is Very Special

Data on the composition of U.S. external assets and liabilities are based on the U.S. international investment position at the end of 2012. See Table A-2 in the Appendix.

See Gourinchas and Rey (2007a,b) and Curcuru, Dvorak, and Warnock (2008). The latter set of authors argues that estimates of the return differential between U.S. and foreign investors are biased upward by Gourinchas and Rey's use of revised Bureau of Economic Analysis data on U.S. international positions and flows. They contend that the flows data are only partially revised relative to original data releases, even if reporting errors become known, whereas data on positions (stocks) are fully revised. This leads to an upward bias in estimated capital gains on U.S. claims. The reverse bias exists for U.S. external liabilities.

Creditor Pays Up, Debtor Rakes It In

Data on investment incomes are from the IMF. Yu Yongding highlights the irony of China being a large creditor and simultaneously experiencing a large investment income deficit. See: Yu Yongding. "China's Flawed Balance-of-Payments Position." *Project Syndicate.* May 31, 2013.

Curcuru and Thomas (2012) calculate that the aggregate yield on U.S. cross-border assets was on average 1.4 percent per year higher than the yield on U.S. cross-border liabilities during 1990–2010. They conclude that the positive investment income balance despite the large net liability position of the U.S. can be explained largely by the return on U.S. direct investment abroad, which they estimate had an average yield 6.2 percent per year higher than direct investment in the U.S.

Hausmann and Sturzenegger (2006) contend that U.S. investments abroad are much larger than captured by official data, and that the U.S. is in fact a net creditor rather than net debtor. They refer to the difference between their estimates and official estimates of investments abroad as dark matter. Dark matter has three sources—mismeasurement of FDI, the unaccounted value of liquidity services provided by the U.S., and the insurance value of safe U.S. assets.

Some (Temporary) Compensation from the U.S.

See Gourinchas, Rey, and Truempler (2012).

We Hate You Guys

The Luo Ping quote was reported in: Henny Sender. "China to Stick with U.S. Bonds." *Financial Times.* February 11, 2009.

The Wen Jiabao quote and the assessment of the implications of China's concerns about its holdings of U.S. debt can be found in this cable available at the Wikileaks site: http://wikileaks.org/cable/2009/03/09BEIJING728.html.

The Chen Deming quote can be found in this cable: http://wikileaks.org/cable/2009/06/09BEIJING1500.html.

A Rhetorical Threat

U.S. views on China's threatened retaliation in response to tariffs imposed on tire imports from China can be found at: http://wikileaks.org/cable/2009/09/09BEIJING 2630.html.

The Q&A can be found on the English version of the SAFE website: http://www .safe.gov.cn/wps/portal/english/Home.

Data on CIC investments are taken from its annual report: China Investment Corporation. 2011. *Focusing on the Future.* Beijing. Page 28. Twenty-one percent of CIC's portfolio was in fixed-income securities, which included government bonds (62 percent of that total), agency bonds (7 percent), corporate bonds (21 percent), asset-backed securities (5 percent), and other structured products (5 percent). CIC does not report the exact country allocation or currency composition of its entire portfolio.

Lou Jiwei's remarks are taken from two news reports: Bei Hu. "China's CIC Seeks to Cut Reliance on U.S. Debt, Chairman Says." *Bloomberg News.* January 14, 2013. Daniel Kruger. "China's Treasuries Holdings Rise to One-Year High as Japan Adds." *Bloomberg News.* January 16, 2013.

A French Connection

The discussion in this section draws extensively on Accominotti (2009). The quotation from Émile Moreau is taken from a translation of his memoirs (Moreau 1991, page 288). Mouré (1991) describes in detail the difficult economic and political calculations the Banque de France faced at different points of this episode, but notes that the Banque de France was in communication with and in some instances provided direct support to the Bank of England. Belying such accounts of cooperation between these two central banks, Einzig (1931, 1932) argues that France's actions were motivated entirely by self-serving political considerations. He argues that France intentionally engaged in financial warfare aimed at weakening the sterling and improving the prospects of Paris becoming an international financial center.

CHAPTER 7. CURRENCY WARS

The opening quote is from Heller (1961), Chapter 8 (Lieutenant Scheisskopf).

Mantega's quote was reported widely. For instance, see: Jonathan Wheatley and Peter Garnham. "Brazil in 'Currency War' Alert." *Financial Times.* September 27, 2010.

The G-20 includes 19 economies (9 advanced economies, 10 emerging markets) plus the European Union. It was formally established in 1999 as a forum for economic cooperation among these economies. For more details, see: www.g20.org.

Timing Is Everything

G-20 finance ministers and central bank governors had been meeting since 1999. G-20 summits attended by national leaders originated during the financial crisis. The list of summits to date is as follows: Washington, DC (November 2008); London (April 2009); Pittsburgh (September 2009); Toronto (June 2010); Seoul (November 2010); Cannes, France (November 2011); Los Cabos, Mexico (June 2012); St. Petersburg, Russia (September 2013).

See Bernanke (2010a) for his speech presaging QE2. For a technical description of QE2, see "Statement Regarding Purchases of Treasury Securities." Federal Reserve Bank of New York Press Release. November 3, 2010.

Zhu Guangyao's comments are reported in: Michael Forsythe. "China Says Fed Easing May Flood World Economy with 'Hot Money.'" *Bloomberg News.* November 8, 2010.

Shifting Alliances

In 2012, German GDP was €2,365 billion, exports of goods and services amounted to €1,363 billion, and net exports of goods and services was €152 billion. Source: Statistiches Bundesamt.

For Schäuble's comments, see: Ralph Atkins. "Germany Attacks US Economic Policy." *Financial Times.* November 7, 2010. For an analysis of the European perspective on currency wars, see Darvas and Pisani-Ferry (2010).

Kick in the Backside Rather Than a Pat on the Back

The Seoul G-20 Summit communiqué (full version titled "Seoul Summit Document") can be found at: www.g20.utoronto.ca.

Fighting Back with Rhetoric

See Bernanke (2010b).

A Condensed History of Currency Wars

For brief outlines of the history of mercantilism, see Cannon (2002) and Ames (2004). Early proponents of mercantilism include Thomas Mun (see Mun 1664; this work was written in 1621) and Jean-Baptiste Colbert (see Sargent 1899). Detractors of mercantilism include Hume (1742) and Smith (1776). For the quoted text, see Keynes (1936, Chapter 23).

Sachs and Warner (2001) discuss the natural resource curse and the concept of Dutch Disease.

See Bhalla (2012) and Rodrik (2008) for a defense of currency undervaluation as a strategy for promoting growth in developing economies.

Are Currency Wars Overblown?
Unconventional Approach to Devaluation?

President Obama's 2010 State of the Union address can be found at: www.whitehouse .gov/briefing-room.

In 2012, goods exports amounted to 9.9 percent of U.S. GDP and services exports were 4 percent of GDP. Source: U.S. Bureau of Economic Analysis.

The Bernanke quote is from Bernanke (2002).

Much Ado about Nothing?

For a discussion of push factors and other determinants of capital flows to emerging markets in different parts of the world, see the studies in the volume edited by Edwards (2000).

For some evidence of spillovers from the Fed's quantitative easing programs to emerging market capital flows, currencies, and asset markets, see Bayoumi and Bui (2011), Chen et al. (2012), and Fratzscher, Duca, and Straub (2012).

Brazil's exports to GDP ratio for 2012 is taken from the IMF. Data on China's trade balance is from official balance of payments data obtained through the CEIC database.

The Bank of Thailand maintained a pegged exchange rate regime from right after World War II until June 1997. In 1997, Thailand had to seek assistance from the IMF to cope with the financial crisis that devastated its economy. Under the IMF program, it abandoned the exchange rate peg and switched to a floating exchange rate. At that time, it adopted a monetary targeting regime, where the target of monetary policy was the domestic money supply. This regime lasted from July 1997 through May 2000. In view of the increasingly unstable relationship between money supply and output growth, the Bank switched to an inflation targeting framework in May 2000. In addition to technical and practical considerations, the Bank offered this rationale for the change in monetary policy regime:

> Given the institutional reforms required for an inflation targeting framework to operate successfully, it was envisaged that inflation targeting would help rebulid [sic] confidence and credibility of the central bank and monetary [policy], going forward.

This quote and more information on the evolution of the Bank of Thailand's monetary policy framework are available at the Bank's website: http://www.bot.or.th/English/ MonetaryPolicy/Target/Framework/Pages/index.aspx.

Commodity Prices

For Chidambaram's remarks, see "Transcript: U.S. Treasury Secretary Geithner, Finance Minister Chidambaram Press Conference." October 9, 2012. Available at the website of the U.S. Embassy in New Delhi at: http://newdelhi.usembassy.gov/sr100913.html.

Based on an event study analysis, Kozicki, Santor, and Suchanek (2012) conclude that the announcements of the Fed's large scale asset purchase (LSAP) programs did not raise commodity prices but did lead to currency appreciation and equity market increases in some commodity-exporting countries. Chen et al. (2012) report some results consistent with those results. Glick and Leduc (2011) find that announcements about LSAPs in fact tended to lower commodity prices.

Currency Valuation and Volatility

One definition of the equilibrium exchange rate is that it is the level at which a country is in a state of internal and external balance. Those concepts are fuzzy at best, and they are made operational by looking at specific variables. For instance, an evaluation of external balance involves the current account. The next step is to make a judgment about what the right current account balance for a country is, given its level of development, demographic structure, and a host of other factors. Large current account balances, either surpluses or deficits, are sometimes interpreted as representing misalignments between actual and equilibrium currency values. Statistical models are of limited value in determining the right level of the current account balance, especially as every country is unique in its own way. See Cline (2008), Lee et al. (2008), and the IMF's 2012 *Pilot External Sector Report.* July 2. Washington, DC.

Feldstein (1989) makes an early argument against targeting domestic macroeconomic policies to try to attain stability of the dollar exchange rate. He notes that such stability, if attained in the course of pursuing prudent macroeconomic policies, is welcome but should not be viewed as a policy objective.

For recent evidence on exchange rate overshooting, see Bjørnland (2009). The overshooting hypothesis was set out by Dornbusch (1976). See Engel (2013) for a survey of theory and evidence on this topic.

Squaring Up Opposing Views: Scale Matters

The description of the King Canute (Cnut) episode and the translation of the quote were obtained from: *Henry, Archdeacon of Huntingdon: Historia Anglorum (History of the English People).* Edited and translated by Diana Greenway. Oxford Medieval Texts, 1996. Oxford: Oxford University Press. Pages 367–369. This source is believed to provide one of the first written accounts of the episode.

A reference to the phrase attributed to Edwin Truman can be found in: Sewell Chan. "Geithner Calls for Global Cooperation on Currency." *New York Times.* October 6, 2010.

Collateral Damage and More Irony

The SNB announcement was made in this press release: "Swiss National Bank Sets Minimum Exchange Rate at CHF 1.20 per Euro." Swiss National Bank. September 6, 2011.

Guns and Roses

A transcript of Indian Prime Minister Manmohan Singh's remarks at the G-20 summit can be found at: www.business-standard.com/india/news/textpms-speech-at-g20-summit/115713/on.

Strong Dollar Rhetoric

For Robert Rubin's quote about the desirability of a strong dollar, see: "A Talk with Robert Rubin." *BusinessWeek*. March 1997. For the Lawrence Summers quote, see: Rachel Koning. "Summers: Strong Dollar Desirable." *MarketWatch*. September 22, 2000. John Snow, who was Treasury secretary from 2003 to 2006, was quoted as saying "A strong dollar is in the national interest." See: Dan Ackman. "Is This a Strong Dollar or What?" *Forbes*. May 23, 2003.

Henry Paulson, Treasury secretary from 2006 to 2009, made this statement early in his tenure: "I believe that a strong dollar is in our nation's interest and that currency values should be determined in open and competitive markets in response to underlying economic fundamentals." See: "Treasury Secretary Says He Backs Strong Dollar." *Reuters*. August 2, 2006. The Paulson quote in the text can be found in: John Brinsley and Rich Mille. "Treasury's Paulson Says He Favors a 'Strong Dollar'." *Bloomberg News*. February 28, 2008.

Timothy Geithner, Treasury secretary from 2009 to 2013, said: "I believe deeply that it's very important to the United States, to the economic health of the United States, that we maintain a strong dollar." See: Rebecca Christie. "Geithner Says Strong Dollar 'Very Important' to U.S." *Bloomberg News*. November 10, 2009.

For Jacob Lew's statement, see: Ian Katz and Kevin Costelloe. "Lew Says He Will Maintain Strong Dollar Policy If Confirmed." *Bloomberg News*. February 13, 2013. Paul O'Neill is quoted in: Rhonda Schaffler and John Brinsley. "O'Neill Says U.S. 'Strong Dollar' Policy Is 'Vacuous Notion'." *Bloomberg News*. April 16, 2008. For Alan Greenspan's quote, see: "Greenspan 'Cringed' at Strong Dollar Talk." *CNNMoney*. May 15, 2007.

President George W. Bush said: "The policy of my administration is for there to be a strong U.S. dollar." See: "Bush Backs 'Strong Dollar,' Calls Currency 'Devalued'." *Bloomberg News*. May 31, 2006. President Obama does not seem to have made a strong dollar statement himself, perhaps leaving the job to his Treasury secretaries.

Bernanke's statement is taken from a transcript of his news conference available at: http://www.federalreserve.gov/monetarypolicy/fomcpresconf20110427.htm.

According to Section 613 of The Foreign Assistance Act of 1961 (as amended), the secretary of Treasury has the sole authority to establish exchange rates for all foreign currencies. The Act is available at: http://www.usaid.gov/sites/default/files/documents/1868/faa.pdf.

For a nice exposition of the history, evolution, and implications of the strong dollar policy, see the Citigroup Global Economics View research note by Willem Buiter and Ebrahim Rahbari. "The 'Strong Dollar' Policy of the U.S.: Alice-in-Wonderland Semantics vs. Economic Reality." May 26, 2011. Also see the trenchant op-ed article by Christina Romer. "Needed: Plain Talk about the Dollar." *New York Times.* May 21, 2011. Buiter and Rahbari discuss other examples of economies where the finance ministry or treasury department, rather than the central bank, has statutory responsibility for management of the currency's value.

More Battles to Come?

The Fed's announcement of QE3 can be found at: http://www.federalreserve.gov/newsevents/press/monetary/20120913a.htm.

The monetary policy actions of the Bank of Japan are listed on its website: www.boj.or.jp/en/mopo.

For details on the ECB's open market operations, see http://www.ecb.int/mopo/implement/omo/html/index.en.html.

The ECB indicated that it would sterilize euro zone government bonds purchased through its Securities Markets Programme. See "Technical Features of Outright Monetary Transactions." ECB Press Release. September 6, 2012.

Renewed Tensions

Mantega's quotes are reported in: Ana Nicolaci da Costa and Sujata Rao. "Brazil May Fire Up Tax Artillery in 'Currency War.'" *Reuters.* September 21, 2012.

The Bank of England did not provide an official transcript of Mervyn King's speech at the New York Economic Club. An unofficial transcript of the speech and the Q&A session that followed it can be found at: http://www.ritholtz.com/blog/2012/12/mervyn-king-bofe-governor-speech-at-economic-club-of-ny/. Many of the relevant quotes from his remarks appeared in various news sources, including: Catherine Rampell. "Britain's Departing Central Banker Is Troubled by Trade Imbalance." *New York Times.* December 10, 2012.

See Bergsten (2013).

Each Country for Itself

Weidmann's comments are reported in: Brian Blackstone. "Bundesbank Head Cautions Japan." *Wall Street Journal.* January 21, 2013.

The statements by Hollande and Rösler can be found in: Hugh Carnegy, Quentin Peel, and Alice Ross. "Hollande Calls for Managed Exchange Rate." *Financial Times.* February 5, 2013.

In 2012, Japan's nominal GDP was $5.9 trillion and merchandise exports were about $800 billion. Source: IMF.

See the press release: "Introduction of the 'Quantitative and Qualitative' Monetary Easing." Tokyo: Bank of Japan. April 4, 2013.

See: "Report to Congress on International Economic and Exchange Rate Policies." U.S. Department of the Treasury. Washington, DC. April 12, 2013.

For Hyun Oh Seok's statements, see: Cynthia Kim. "South Korea's Hyun Says Yen Bigger Issue Than North Korea." *Bloomberg News*. April 18, 2013. In a similar vein, David Li, a former monetary policy committee member of the PBC, noted in an op-ed that "Abenomics has simply generated expectations of further [yen] devaluation. This type of recovery is unfair since it comes at the expense of Japan's trading partners." See: David Li. "Abenomics Will Only Damage Japan's Neighbors." *Financial Times*. May 21, 2013.

A Grim Reality

Gerhard Schröder was the German chancellor from 1998 to 2005. He started his second term in 2002, when the economy recorded an unemployment rate of 8.7 percent and zero GDP growth. For a summary of the main reforms that were part of Agenda 2010, see "A Quick Guide to Agenda 2010." *Deutsche Welle*. October 17, 2003. http://dw.de/p/497W.

Schröder's political fate was emblematic of the tension that politicians face when it comes to doing the right thing. This dilemma was nicely summed up by Jean-Claude Juncker, Luxembourg's prime minister and the president of the eurogroup, the body that brings together the area's finance ministers. He is reported to have said, "We all know what to do. It's just we don't know how to get re-elected after we've done it." See: Jennifer Thompson. "Belt Tightening: Cuts to Save Economy May Anger Voters." *Financial Times*. December 15, 2011.

José De Gregorio's reference to "currency suicide" was made at this event: http://www.brookings.edu/events/2012/09/26-capital-flows#. Also see De Gregorio (2011b).

CHAPTER 8. SEEKING A TRUCE ON CURRENCY WARS

The opening quote is from the radio show *Gunsmoke* and is taken from an episode titled "The Gentleman" that aired on March 6, 1954. It was rebroadcast on the Washington, DC, radio station WAMU as part of its Sunday night Big Broadcast on November 18, 2012. The audio for the original episode can be found at: http://podbay.fm/show/288417316/e/1242719640?autostart=1. The quoted text appears around the 5:00 minute mark.

Is Peer Pressure the Right Prod for Better Policies?

For an interesting historical account of the Bretton Woods conference that led to the creation of the IMF, see Steil (2013).

The World Trade Organization, which was set up in 1995, mediates trade disputes among its members and has a well laid-out dispute resolution mechanism, with clear penalties for countries that are judged to have violated agreed-on rules. However, the World Trade Organization does not have either the direct mandate or the expertise to deal with currency issues, as those are seen as a matter of macroeconomic policy rather than trade policy.

See Bernanke (2005).

Trying to Make Peace

The announcement about the IMF's multilateral consultation can be found here: "IMF to Begin Multilateral Consultations with Focus on Global Imbalances." IMF Press Release 06/118. June 5, 2006. http://www.imf.org/external/np/sec/pr/2006/pr06118.htm.

The report "IMF Staff Report on the Multilateral Consultation on Global Imbalances" contains a description of each country's policy commitments and is available at: www.imf.org/external/np/pp/2007/eng/062907.pdf.

The report on the IMF executive board's assessment of the promised policy measures is: "IMF Executive Board Discusses Multilateral Consultation on Global Imbalances." Public Information Notice 07/97. August 7, 2007. http://www.imf.org/external/np/sec/pn/2007/pn0797.htm#P30_665.

The IMF Attacks China, Then Retreats

Official responses provided by the authorities to written questions submitted by the IMF's China team are based on personal records.

A Blow to the Chin

See: "IMF Executive Board Adopts New Decision on Bilateral Surveillance over Members' Policies." IMF Public Information Notice 07/69. June 21, 2007. http://www.imf.org/external/np/sec/pn/2007/pn0769.htm.

Beating a Retreat

See: IMF. 2009. "The 2007 Surveillance Decision: Revised Operational Guidance." Policy Paper. Washington, DC. The paper is available at: www.imf.org/external/np/pp/eng/2009/062209.pdf. Since this episode, the IMF has not stopped trying to forge a multilateral consensus for global rebalancing through channels such as the Mutual Assessment Process, "spillover reports" that assess the effects of each of the major countries' policies on the rest of the world, and various other reports. For instance, see: International Monetary Fund. *People's Republic of China: Spillover Report for the 2011 Article IV Consultation and Selected Issues.* IMF Country Report 11/193, July 2011; and International Monetary Fund. *United States: Spillover Report for the 2011 Article IV Consultation.* IMF Country Report 11/203, July 2011. Washington, DC. For the IMF's assessment of China's exchange rate regime in 2010, see: International Monetary Fund. *People's Republic of China: 2010 Article IV Consultation— Staff Report; Staff Statement; Public Information Notice on the Executive Board Discussion.* IMF Country Report 10/238, July 2010. Washington, DC.

CHAPTER 9. IT TAKES TWENTY TO TANGO

The opening quote is from the German playwright Bertolt Brecht's play *Life of Galileo*. These lines appear near the end of Scene 12 in the translation by Charles Laughton, available as an appendix in the Penguin Classics version. The lines appear in slightly different forms in other translations.

A transcript of Gordon Brown's speech and the subsequent Q&A can be found at: http://www.docstoc.com/docs/71422948/Prime-Minister-Gordon-Brown-at-the-G2o-London-Summit.

A transcript of President Obama's press conference, from which his statements are taken, is in: "The President's News Conference in London, England." In *Administration of Barack H. Obama*. April 2, 2009. Washington, DC: United States Government Printing Office.

"Kumbaya, My Lord" is a popular campfire song, and the expression itself is meant to evoke the warm image of campers sitting around the campfire in perfect companionship and harmony. The expression has come to be used to convey a sense of naïve optimism about harmony in a group.

The term "hosanna" is used as a cry of acclamation or praise (Merriam-Webster dictionary). It originated in the Jewish and Christian liturgical traditions, where it was used to signify praise for God or Christ.

The $750 billion boost to the IMF's resources was to include $500 billion in contributions from its member countries and an agreement by its members that the IMF could issue $250 billion in new SDRs.

Soon after Brown's speech, there was considerable skepticism about the accounting behind the headline number that he had announced. For instance, see: Chris Giles. "Large Numbers Hide Big G20 Divisions." *Financial Times*. April 2, 2009.

The communiqué from the Pittsburgh G-20 Summit, "Leaders' Statement, The Pittsburgh Summit, September 24–25 2009," is available at the U.S. Treasury Department's G-20 Resource Center: http://www.treasury.gov/resource-center/international/g7-g20/Pages/g20.aspx.

Global Policy Coordination in Good and Bad Times
Meeting of Minds at the Plaza

For the text of the Plaza Accord, see "Announcement of the Ministers of Finance and Central Bank Governors of France, Germany, Japan, the United Kingdom, and the United States." September 22, 1985. For the text of the Louvre Accord, see "Statement of the G6 Finance Ministers and Central Bank Governors." February 22, 1987. Both documents are available at the University of Toronto website: http://www.g8 .utoronto.ca/. Funabashi (2008) provides an interesting account of the circumstances and process leading up to the two accords, and describes how political dynamics played out within and among the countries involved in these accords. Jacquet and de Montbrial (1991) provide a cynical perspective on international cooperation under such accords. They discuss how the accord suited the interests of each country involved and conclude:

Although it is desirable that cooperation benefit every participant, the Plaza Accord stemmed from narrow national interests more than from a proper assessment of the need for collective management of the world economy for the common good.

See page 138.

An Attempt at Herding Cats

See page 37 in the 2011 report of the Committee on International Economic Policy and Reform titled "Rethinking Central Banking." Washington, DC: Brookings Institution. The Svensson quote is taken from Svensson (2011), page 37.

For an analysis of the impact of central bank press conferences that are held to explain monetary policy decisions, see Ehrmann and Fratzscher (2009).

The IMF Tries to Regain Its Mojo

For Sarkozy's statement of support of rules for capital flow management, see: Nathalie Boschat and William Horobin. "Sarkozy: G-20 Should Set Capital Flow Rules." *Wall Street Journal.* December 13, 2010.

A Rulebook for Capital Flows

The G-20 directive to the IMF was in paragraph 26 of the communiqué: "We asked the IMF to deepen its work on all aspects of the international monetary system, including capital flow volatility." See: *The Seoul Summit Document, November 2011.* Available at http://www.g20.utoronto.ca/.

The Rules Hit a Roadblock

The 2010 IMF report "The Fund's Role Regarding Cross-Border Capital Flows" is available at: www.imf.org. For a summary of the IMF executive board discussion, see: "IMF Executive Board Discusses the Fund's Role Regarding Cross-Border Capital Flows." IMF Public Information Notice 11/1. January 5, 2011. http://www.imf.org/external/np/sec/pn/2011/pn1101.htm.

For Sarkozy's speech, see: "Address by the President of the French Republic. Press Conference to Present the Presidency of the G20 and G8." Élysée Palace, Paris. January 24, 2011.

Setting Standards
Getting Markets to Work Better

Details on the Basel III framework are on the website of the Bank for International Settlements: http://www.bis.org/bcbs/basel3.htm.

For a critical evaluation of the progress made by the U.K. and the U.S. on Basel III, see: Brooke Masters. "Basel III Phase-In Lags Behind." *Financial Times.* April 4, 2013.

CHAPTER 10. THE SIREN SONG OF CAPITAL CONTROLS

The opening quote is from the radio show *Gunsmoke* and is taken from the episode "Gun Smuggler," which aired on January 30, 1954. It was rebroadcast on the Washington, DC, radio station WAMU as part of its Sunday night Big Broadcast on October 21, 2012. The audio for the original episode can be found at: http://podbay.fm/show/288417316/e/1239007260?autostart=1. The quoted text appears near the 10:00 minute mark.

Capital Controls Make a Comeback

For some evidence and a survey of the literature on the risks of premature capital account liberalization, see Kose, Prasad, and Taylor (2011).

Mixed Evidence on Effectiveness

There is a large literature on the effectiveness of capital controls. In a recent contribution, Magud, Reinhart, and Rogoff (2011) find that controls can shift the composition of inflows and in some cases can also affect the overall volume of capital flows. Klein (2012) argues that episodic controls do not reduce financial vulnerability, whereas long-standing controls on a broad range of assets have more benign effects; neither type of controls affects exchange rates. Forbes (2007) finds that the Chilean capital controls disproportionately hurt smaller firms' access to finance, whereas larger firms were less affected. Kose, Prasad, Rogoff, and Wei (2009) discuss how de facto financial integration is proceeding faster than de jure financial opening for many middle-income economies, making formal capital controls less relevant over time.

Balin (2008) notes that investors circumvented India's controls on debt inflows by bringing in capital disguised as other types of inflows and then using transactions, such as loan "barters" and reciprocal asset swaps. For a specific example cited in the press, see: Sugata Ghosh and Rajesh Unnikrishnan. "Curbs Go Kaput as Firms Brandish Put Options." *Economic Times*. July 31, 2007.

De Gregorio, Edwards, and Valdes (2000) describe the Chilean capital controls and analyze their effectiveness.

Patnaik, Gupta, and Shah (2012) look at the determinants of trade misinvoicing using a cross-country dataset. They conclude that it is a channel that increases de facto capital account openness. Beja (2008) has some estimates of misinvoicing on China's trade. For a recent story suggesting that Chinese exports may be overstated on account of misinvoicing intended to get around controls on capital inflows into China, and for an explanation of the mechanics, see: Yajun Zhang, Richard Silk, and Tom Orlik. "Doubts Cast on Chinese Exports." *Wall Street Journal*. April 3, 2013.

Worth a Try?

De Gregorio, Edwards, and Valdes (2000) describe how Chilean capital controls had to be revised frequently to stay ahead of investors who were finding ways around them. Carvalho and Garcia (2008) describe in detail the different strategies adopted by investors to circumvent Brazilian capital controls.

A Central Bank's Reputation Takes a Baht

In December 2006, the Thai baht was trading at 36 baht per U.S. dollar, a stronger level (fewer baht per dollar) than in any other month since 1998. The exchange rate in

December 2005 was 41 baht per dollar, implying a 12 percent appreciation of the baht between then and December 2006.

The original announcement of the capital controls in Thailand is described in: "The Reserve Requirement on Short-Term Capital Inflows." Bank of Thailand Press Release 51/2006. December 18, 2006. The relaxation of controls is detailed in: "Summary of the Reserve Requirements on Short-Term Capital Inflows." Bank of Thailand Press Release 52/2006. December 22, 2006.

The Thai capital control reversal and Pridiyathorn Devakula's statements are reported in: Thomas Fuller and Wayne Arnold. "Thailand Scraps Capital Controls after Stocks Plummet." *New York Times*. December 19, 2006. Subsequent comments from Central Bank Governor Tarisa Watanagase are reported in: Thomas Fuller and Wayne Arnold. "Thai Stock Market Rebounds from Plunge." *New York Times*. December 20, 2006.

Emerging Markets Act and the IMF Follows

For a description of Argentina's controls on outflows since 2011 (President Cristina Fernández de Kirchner was re-elected in October 2011), see: Eliana Raszewski. "Argentine President Tightens Foreign Exchange Controls: Timeline." *Bloomberg News*. March 20, 2013. Argentina's nationalization of its biggest oil company is described in: Hugh Bronstein. "Argentina Nationalizes Oil Company YPF." *Reuters*. May 4, 2012. For a summary of concerns about Argentina's inflation and other economic data and the censure it drew from the IMF, see: Sandrine Rastello and Eliana Raszewski. "IMF to Put Argentina on Path to Censure over Inflation Data." *Bloomberg News*. September 18, 2012.

The imposition of capital controls in Iceland and Ukraine is described in: "Liberalizing Capital Flows and Managing Outflows—Background Paper." IMF Background Paper. March 16, 2012. The IMF's assessment of how the controls worked in the two countries is as follows (see pages 29 and 39). Iceland:

Comprehensive capital controls were imposed following the onset of a severe crisis in 2007–08. The controls, complemented by other policies, ultimately provided Iceland with significant policy space. The authorities intend to lift controls gradually as conditions allow.

Ukraine:

The 2008 crisis hit Ukraine through a sharp deterioration in the terms of trade, a collapse of exports, and a reversal of capital flows. A number of capital controls were introduced to stem outflows and defend the exchange rate. The effectiveness of controls was mixed reflecting their design and a lack of fully supportive policies.

Cyprus faced a run on its banking system during its crisis in March 2013. As part of a loan program that it agreed to with the European Union and the IMF, Cyprus was allowed to impose tight but temporary controls on outflows to prevent a flight of deposits from the banking system. See: "Statement by the European Commission on the Capital Controls Imposed by the Republic of Cyprus." European Commission Press Release. March 28, 2013. The statement noted that the dire circumstances justified the use of capital controls but added that "Such exception to the principle of the free movement of capital must be interpreted very strictly and be non-discriminatory, suitable, proportionate and applied for the shortest possible period."

Labels Matter

The IMF report "The Liberalization and Management of Capital Flows: An Institutional View," dated November 14, 2012, is available at: www.imf.org.

The comments from Brazilian and Indian officials are reported in: Lesley Wroughton. "IMF Adopts View on Capital Controls, India Wary." *Reuters.* December 3, 2012.

A Better Approach but Not a Panacea

Mishkin (2008) makes the case for what emerging markets need to do to harness the benefits of financial globalization. See Burger, Warnock, and Warnock (2010) for an analysis of how local currency bond markets influence financial stability. This topic is also covered by the 2007 report "Financial Stability and Local Currency Bond Markets." Committee on the Global Financial System Paper 28. Basel: Bank for International Settlements.

For analysis and evaluation of corporate bond market development in Asia, see Bhattacharyay (2011), Goswami and Sharma (2011), and Kawai and Prasad (2011). An earlier analysis can be found in the 2006 report "Developing Corporate Bond Markets in Asia." BIS Paper 26. Geneva: Bank for International Settlements.

Data on India's general government debt levels are taken from the IMF. The debt levels for fiscal years 2011–12 and 2012–13 are both estimated at 67 percent of GDP. See: "IMF Executive Board Concludes 2013 Article IV Consultation with India." IMF Public Information Notice 13/14. February 6, 2013.

Reality Not Quite As Neat

See Singh (2011, pages 10–12). For a description of China's approach to liberalization of different types of capital flows, see Prasad and Wei (2007). For India, see Prasad (2009a).

No Place to Hide

See Williams (2005).

CHAPTER 11. SAFETY NETS WITH GAPING HOLES

The opening text appears in John Donne's *Devotions Upon Emergent Occasions*. It can be found in Devotion XVII, Meditation XVII. The phrase was of course popularized by Ernest Hemingway's 1940 novel *For Whom the Bell Tolls*.

Swap Lines
Swapping for Dollars

See Bernanke (2000).

For riveting accounts of the Fed's actions to save the domestic financial system in the midst of the financial crisis, see Sorkin (2010) and Wessel (2010). Irwin (2013) provides a broader account of the roles of the Fed, the ECB, and the Bank of England during the crisis.

Information about the various liquidity and credit facilities deployed by the Federal Reserve can be found on the Fed's website under the section "Credit and Liquidity Programs and the Balance Sheet": http://www.federalreserve.gov/monetarypolicy/bst.htm.

The Chosen Ones

For more details about the Fed's swap arrangements with other central banks, see Fleming and Klagge (2010) and Goldberg, Kennedy, and Miu (2010). Press releases and more information about the dollar and foreign currency liquidity swap lines can be found at the Federal Reserve Board's website: http://www.federalreserve.gov/monetarypolicy/bst_liquidityswaps.htm.

Detailed data on individual countries' use of the swap lines is provided at this link: http://www.federalreserve.gov/newsevents/reform_swaplines.htm. Aizenman and Pasricha (2009) evaluate the effects of the swap lines on emerging markets that received them from the Fed.

Self-Serving Charity Pays Off

See: Gerald O'Driscoll. "The Federal Reserve's Covert Bailout of Europe." *Wall Street Journal.* December 28, 2011, and William C. Dudley. "Dollar-Swaps Protect U.S. Markets." *Wall Street Journal.* January 5, 2012.

Dudley's testimony was delivered on March 27, 2012, at a hearing of the Subcommittee on Domestic Monetary Policy and Technology of the Committee on Financial Services of the U.S. House of Representatives. The hearing was on "Federal Reserve Aid to the Eurozone: Its Impact on the U.S. and the Dollar."

The Spurned

Details about requests for swap lines by Chile, the Dominican Republic, and Indonesia were obtained from Wikileaks cables and confirmed in off-the-record discussions with official sources. The relevant cables are available at:

Chile: http://wikileaks.org/cable/2008/10/08SANTIAGO976.html.

Dominican Republic: http://wikileaks.org/cable/2009/02/09
SANTODOMINGO155.html.

Indonesia: http://wikileaks.org/cable/2009/02/09PARTO22610.html.
http://wikileaks.org/cable/2009/03/09JAKARTA418.html.

The quote from Luis Valdivieso can be found in: "Peru Eyes Financing, but Fed Credit 'Unlikely.'" *Associated Press*. January 15, 2009.

The Spurned Seek Other Suitors

The State Department cable that describes the currency swap agreement between Indonesia and China is available at: http://wikileaks.org/cable/2009/03/09 JAKARTA542.html.

The quote from the *Jakarta Globe* is from this article: "Indonesia and China Signal Growing Ties." *Jakarta Globe*. March 23, 2009.

The cable from the U.S. embassy in Jakarta dated October 7, 2009 is available at: http://wikileaks.org/cable/2009/10/09JAKARTA1685.html.

The quote from Reserve Bank of India Governor Duvvuri Subbarao is reported in: Anoop Agarwal and Kartik Goyal. "U.S. Hesitant on India's Currency Swap Proposal." *Bloomberg News*. November 20, 2012. The $15 billion bilateral currency swap agreement between the Bank of Japan and the Reserve Bank of India was signed on December 4, 2012. See: "India, Japan Ink $15 Billion Currency Swap Arrangement." *Financial Express*. December 4, 2012. This agreement had been preceded by an earlier bilateral swap agreement for $3 billion that was in effect from June 2008 to June 2011. The terms of the swap arrangement are that it is to be activated "when an IMF-supported program exists or is expected to be established in the near future. Nevertheless, up to 20 percent of the maximum amount of drawing could be disbursed without an IMF-support program." See: "Signing of the Bilateral Swap Arrangement between Japan and India." Bank of Japan Press Release. June 30, 2008.

For details on the ECB's liquidity provision arrangements with European national central banks, see Darvas (2009) and Vergote et al. (2010). Darvas (2009) notes that the Swiss National Bank subsequently offered euro/Swiss franc swaps to Hungary and Poland, so they could get Swiss franc liquidity in exchange for euros. Loans denominated in Swiss francs had become popular in these countries before the crisis.

The BoJ's moves to expand and/or extend bilateral swap lines under the umbrella of the Chiang Mai Initiative can be found at: http://www.boj.or.jp/en/intl_finance/cooperate/index.htm/.

Pooling Up to a Bigger Bazooka

The ten members of ASEAN are Brunei, Cambodia, Indonesia, Lao People's Democratic Republic, Malaysia, Myanmar, the Philippines, Singapore, Thailand, and Vietnam.

The idea of an Asian Monetary Fund had been mooted by Japanese officials in 1997 but met strong opposition from China and the U.S. As a consequence, Japanese officials downplayed but did not entirely abandon the idea at the time of the Chiang Mai Initiative agreement. See: Thomas Crampton. "East Asia Unites to Fight Speculators." *New York Times*. May 8, 2000. Subsequently, the idea of setting up an Asian Monetary Fund has resurfaced. See Kawai (2010) and also: Keiko Ujikane and Tatsuo Ito. 2009. "Asia Needs Own Monetary Fund to Stem Crisis, ADB's Kawai Says." *Bloomberg News*. February 24, 2009.

For more on the Chiang Mai Initiative and its antecedents, see Kuroda and Kawai (2004) and Henning (2009).

Combined foreign exchange reserves of the ten ASEAN countries fell from $527 billion in April 2008 to $474 billion in October 2008.

For details on the CMIM, see Grimes (2011) and references therein. For a critical perspective on the CMIM, see: Hal Hill and Jayant Menon. "Asia's New Financial Safety Net: Is the Chiang Mai Initiative Designed Not to Be Used?" *Voxeu.org*. July 25, 2012. Also see: Pradumna B. Rana. "The Next Steps in ASEAN+3 Monetary Integration." *Voxeu.org*. May 27, 2012.

The CMIM came into effect on March 24, 2010. See: "Joint Press Release: Chiang Mai Initiative Multilateralization (CMIM) Comes into Effect." Bank of Japan. March 24, 2010. The doubling in size of the CMIM was agreed to on May 3, 2012. See: "Press Release: ASEAN+3 Finance Ministers and Central Bank Governor's Meeting Successfully Concludes." Ministry of Strategy and Finance, Korea. The bilateral arrangements among ASEAN countries China, Japan, and Korea take the form of bilateral swap and repurchase agreement facilities.

Under the CMIM, financial contributions of the big five ASEAN countries— Indonesia, Malaysia, the Philippines, Singapore, and Thailand—are about $9 billion. These economies can purchase up to 2.5 times their contributions. The contributions of the other five countries are smaller, but their purchasing multiples can be up to five times their contributions.

Firewall Made of BRICS

As of June 2013, foreign exchange reserves, in billions of U.S. dollars, were as follows: China, 3,497; Russia, 462; Brazil, 359; India, 255; South Africa, 39; total, 4,612. Source: IMF. Data were converted from SDRs into dollars using the end of period exchange rate (1 SDR = $1.54).

The statements released on March 27, 2013, at the conclusion of the BRICS summit in Durban, South Africa, can be found at the University of Toronto's BRICS Information Centre: www.brics.utoronto.ca. The relevant documents are "Fifth BRICS Summit, eThekwini Declaration" and "Statement by BRICS Leaders on the Establishment of the BRICS-Led Development Bank."

The initial scale of the proposal by the BRICS to pool some of their reserves is reported in: Lesley Wroughton and Alonso Soto. "BRICS Eye Forex Reserves Pool of up to $240 billion—Document." *Reuters*. November 9, 2012. For an article that illustrates, with quotes from relevant officials, some of the disagreements among the BRICS that became apparent at the Durban summit, see: Michelle Faul. "BRICS Plan Development Bank to Fund Infrastructure." *Associated Press*. March 27, 2013.

The IMF Gets Flexible

The documents referred to in this section are all available at the IMF's website: www .imf.org.

The FCL was a reincarnation of an earlier program called the Contingent Credit Lines that was introduced in 1999 and allowed to expire in 2003. It was never used. A postmortem of the program concluded that, among other factors, potentially eligible countries lacked confidence that

> a CCL [Contingent Credit Line] would be viewed as a sign of strength rather than weakness. These countries may also have been concerned about the risk of negative fallout if they were to be considered ineligible at a future date.

See: "Factsheet: The IMF's Contingent Credit Lines (CCL)." IMF. March 2004.

The revamp of the criteria for the IMF's FCL can be found in: "IMF Implements Major Lending Policy Improvements." IMF. March 2009. The revised criteria state that to be eligible a country would need to have: (1) a sustainable external position; (2) a capital account position dominated by private flows; (3) a track record of steady sovereign access to international capital markets at favorable terms; (4) a reserve position that is relatively comfortable when the FCL is requested on a precautionary basis; (5) sound public finances, including a sustainable public debt position; (6) low and stable inflation, in the context of a sound monetary and exchange rate policy framework; (7) the absence of bank solvency problems that pose an immediate threat of a systemic banking crisis; (8) effective financial sector supervision; and (9) data transparency and integrity.

Mexico signed up for the FCL in April 2009. Colombia and Poland did so in May 2009. Each of these programs was initially for a duration of one year but has since been extended to two years. All three countries have received renewals—the latest ones, all for two-year periods, being in December 2012 for Mexico ($73 billion), January 2013 for Poland ($34 billion), and June 2013 for Colombia ($6 billion). None of these countries has drawn on the FCL according to this document: "Factsheet: The IMF's Flexible Credit Line." IMF. April 2012 (footnote 1 in this factsheet indicates that the document was updated on March 20, 2013; it was retrieved on April 3, 2013).

Some evidence that the FCL reduces sovereign credit spreads is in an IMF report: "Review of the Flexible Credit Line and Precautionary Credit Line." November 2011. Washington, DC: International Monetary Fund. These spreads, the difference between yields on countries' sovereign bonds and the yields on government bonds issued by a benchmark country such as the U.S., serve as a gauge of investors' perceptions of the creditworthiness of the relevant countries.

For Those Good but Not Good Enough

The text about the Precautionary Credit Line can be found in: "Factsheet: The IMF's Precautionary Credit Line (PCL)." September 2011. Washington, DC: International Monetary Fund. The Flexible Credit Line, Precautionary Credit Line, and Global Stabilization Mechanism proposal are described, along with further references, in: "The Fund's Mandate—The Future Financing Role: Reform Proposals." June 2010. Washington, DC: International Monetary Fund.

A Simple Proposal to Fix a Big Problem
A Proposal for Global Liquidity Insurance

The global liquidity insurance proposal discussed here was first formally presented at the August 2011 Jackson Hole Symposium (see Prasad 2011a). It had earlier been sketched in a *Wall Street Journal Asia* op-ed article in 2009 (Prasad 2009c). The proposal has elements in common with other recent proposals for reform of the international monetary system. See, for instance: Palais-Royal Initiative. "Reform of the International Monetary System: A Cooperative Approach for the Twenty First Century." February 2011. Paris. This report argues for the establishment of norms for countries' policies. Also see: Centre for Economic Policy Research. 2011. "Reforming the International Monetary System." London. This report proposes institutionalizing central bank swap lines, but through the IMF.

One could also conceivably penalize countries (by charging them a higher premium) if they are accumulating large stocks of reserves or running persistent large current account surpluses. The logic would be that these countries' policies would be making themselves safer but increasing global risks.

Operation of the Insurance System

The mission statement of the BIS appears on its website: http://www.bis.org/about/.

Participation

The Financial Stability Board was established by the G-20 "to coordinate at the international level the work of national financial authorities and international standard setting bodies and to develop and promote the implementation of effective regulatory, supervisory and other financial sector policies." See: http://www.financialstability board.org/. It replaced the Financial Stability Forum, which was established in 1999 by the G-7 countries.

CHAPTER 12. IS THE RENMINBI READY FOR PRIME TIME?

The opening quotation is a selection from T. S. Eliot's poem "The Hollow Men." The full text of the relevant stanzas is as follows: "Between the idea / And the reality / Between the motion / And the act / Falls the Shadow / *For Thine is the Kingdom* / Between the conception / And the creation / Between the emotion / And the response / Falls the Shadow / *Life is very long.*"

The speed of the dollar's ascent as it vaulted past the pound sterling is documented by Eichengreen and Flandreau (2009).

Going Global—Cautiously

Prasad and Ye (2012) provide a systematic evaluation of China's progress in each of the dimensions of the renminbi's progress as an international currency. Chen, Peng, and Shu (2009) and Subramanian (2011) argue that the renminbi is well on its way to becoming a major, if not dominant, reserve currency. Dobson and Masson (2009), Eichengreen (2011b), and Kroeber (2011) offer more nuanced and skeptical views.

Angeloni et al. (2011) discuss probabilities of alternative scenarios, noting that the renminbi may gain more prominence if the euro does not mount a serious challenge to the dominance of the U.S. dollar.

Opening Up the Capital Account

For more details on measures taken by China in recent years to open up its capital account, see Prasad and Ye (2012) and the IMF's *Annual Reports on Exchange Arrangements and Exchange Restrictions.*

In 2007, the limit on foreign exchange purchases by residents for remittance abroad for personal reasons was increased to $50,000 a year per individual. In 2009, the government dropped review and approval requirements for outward remittances of funds for direct investment abroad by Chinese corporations and financial institutions.

The total quota for QFIIs was raised to $80 billion in 2012. The upper limit on portfolio investments by individual QFIIs was raised to $1 billion. The period for which these investments are "locked up" and cannot remit their principal abroad ranges from 3 to 12 months, depending on the type of institution. See: "QFII Investment Quota to Be Increased by 50 Billion US Dollars." China Securities Regulatory Commission. April 2012. See also: "Regulations on Foreign Exchange Administration of Domestic Securities Investments by Qualified Foreign Institutional Investors." SAFE circular. December 2012. The SAFE website is: http://www.safe.gov.cn/wps/portal/english/. By February 2013, the China Securities Regulatory Commission had granted QFII licenses to 215 foreign institutions, and SAFE had approved aggregate quotas amounting to $41 billion. In July 2013, China increased the overall quota under the QFII program to $150 billion, although the approved quota had reached only $43 billion. See the press release from the China Securities Regulatory Commission titled "QFII Quota Raised to USD 150 billion and RQFII Pilot Expanded in Singapore and London." July 12, 2013. Available at http://www.csrc.gov.cn/pub/csrc_en/newsfacts/release/201308/t20130815_232696.htm.

The Exchange Rate Regime

Before 2010, renminbi-related activities in the offshore market were quite limited, which contributed to a marked deviation of the CNH exchange rate from that of the CNY—the renminbi was typically more valuable offshore, reflecting strong demand. The two exchange rates became more closely linked after a series of developments in the last quarter of 2010 boosted renminbi-denominated financial transactions. The main developments include the approval granted to financial institutions and banks in Hong Kong to open renminbi accounts and for Hong Kong banks to access the onshore interbank market, activation of a swap line between the PBC and the Hong Kong Monetary Authority, and a flurry of renminbi-denominated bond issuance activities.

The structure of these markets sometimes results in quirky outcomes. For instance, in mid-2011, the renminbi was briefly worth more on onshore than on offshore markets.

In addition to these spot rates, other renminbi-related exchange rates are the dollar-settled nondeliverable forward rate (NDF) and the trade settlement exchange rate. The NDF market predates the CNH market and precludes participation by

Mainland residents. However, the NDF is linked to the onshore CNY exchange rate, because its value is derived from expected future CNY spot rates. The trade-settlement exchange rate is the one that prevails for cross-border trade transactions, for which the CNH rate does not apply.

Putting the Cart before the Horse

For a discussion of the issue of sequencing capital account liberalization in the context of China, see Prasad, Rumbaugh, and Wang (2005) and references therein. A burgeoning literature looking at specific aspects of China's exchange rate management and capital account liberalization includes Frankel (2005, 2011), Eichengreen (2011b), Lardy and Douglass (2011), Yam (2011), and Yu (2012).

Goodfriend and Prasad (2007) discuss the implications of China's exchange rate regime for monetary policy formulation and implementation.

For a description of the challenges facing China's financial system, see Lardy (2011) and Prasad and Ye (2012). Walter and Howie (2011) paint a dire picture of the Chinese financial system. For a brief summary of the range of estimates of local government debt and related concerns, see: Simon Rabinovitch. "China Local Authority Debt 'Out of Control'." *Financial Times*. April 16, 2013.

In July 2013, the PBC removed the floor on banks' lending rates but retained the ceiling on deposit rates. See: Jamil Anderlini and Leslie Hook. "China Takes Step to Financial Reform." *Financial Times*. July 19, 2013.

Could Stepping Stones Turn Slippery?

Deng Xiaoping became China's paramount leader following Mao's death in 1976. He helped open up China's economy and set the country on a course of reform and liberalization, but he was firmly opposed to political liberalization. Deng—who never officially served as the Communist Party chief or head of government—was the Chairman of the Central Military Commission of the Communist Party of China from 1981 to 1989. In 1992, he emerged from retirement to promote more radical economic reforms that launched China's high growth era. See Vogel (2011).

See Prasad, Rumbaugh, and Wang (2005), and Prasad and Rajan (2006, 2008). The Prasad and Rajan (2006) article was cited favorably, for instance, by: Martin Wolf. "China Should Risk Bolder Trials." *Financial Times*. June 6, 2006.

Capital Account Liberalization with Chinese Characteristics

The official Chinese name for the "through-train" program is "港股直通车." For more details on the nature and timing of China's moves to open its capital account, including the QDII program, see Prasad and Ye (2012).

Promoting International Use of the Currency

Based on data from CEIC, in 2012, renminbi settlement of trade in goods was $327 billion, which was 9 percent of China's total trade in goods. In these calculations, renminbi amounts were converted to U.S. dollars using annual average exchange rates taken from CEIC.

It is estimated that Hong Kong banks handled about 73 percent of China's renminbi trade settlement in 2010 and that this proportion rose to 93 percent in the first ten months of 2012. See: "Hong Kong: The Premier Offshore Renminbi Business Center." Hong Kong Monetary Authority Publications and Research Reference Materials. December 2012.

During 2012, remittances of renminbi used for cross-border settlement in Hong Kong averaged roughly $35 billion per month, compared to $9 billion per month in the second half of 2010 (source: CEIC). Cross-border renminbi settlement is not confined exclusively to Hong Kong, but its banks play a dominant role. Renminbi clearing transactions were virtually zero until mid-2010, when financial institutions in Hong Kong were allowed to open renminbi-denominated accounts. Since then, both the volume and value of transactions have increased dramatically.

The issuance of dim sum bonds rose sharply from 2007 to 2011 before leveling off at about RMB 110 billion ($18 billion) in 2012, according to the same Hong Kong Monetary Authority report cited above.

Some caveats are in order when assessing the renminbi's rapid growth in offshore transactions. First, dim sum bond issuance remains somewhat narrow in scope, in that such issuance is still heavily confined to banking and financial institutions. Second, a large portion of the issuance currently comes from the Mainland. Third, various reports suggest that a significant portion of cross-border renminbi settlement is used mainly for cross-border arbitrage between Mainland companies and their Hong Kong subsidiaries. These factors imply that the influence of offshore renminbi use still has some ways to go to reach its full potential. See Prasad and Ye (2012) for more discussion and references.

Settling Accounts Directly

The renminbi-ruble trading is described in: Andrew E. Kramer. "Sidestepping the U.S. Dollar, a Russian Exchange Will Swap Rubles and Renminbi." *New York Times.* December 14, 2010. The agreement between the Chinese and Russian central banks can be found in: "China and Russia Signed New Bilateral Local Currency Settlement Agreement." People's Bank of China Press Release. June 23, 2011.

See Christine Kim. "China, South Korea Agree to Boost Yuan, Won Use in Trade." *Reuters.* December 4, 2012.

Julia Gillard, the Australian prime minister, announced the initiation of direct currency trading between the Australian dollar and the renminbi in April 2013. See: Josh Noble. "China Opens Aussie Dollar Direct Trading." *Financial Times.* April 8, 2013.

For details on the China-Japan agreement, see: "Enhanced Cooperation for Financial Markets Development between China and Japan." People's Bank of China Press Release. December 25, 2011. China has also given permission for the Japan Bank for International Cooperation to issue a yuan-denominated bond, and Japan has indicated that it will buy some Chinese government bonds, presumably to add to its reserve portfolio.

In 2012, Japan's exports to China were valued at $145 billion and imports at $189 billion. FDI flows between the two countries amounted to $13.6 billion, with most of this being FDI from Japan to China. Source: Japan External Trade Organization. In 2011, China increased its portfolio investment in Japan by $107 billion, mostly through purchases of debt securities. Other categories of flows seem rather modest. Source: Coordinated Portfolio Investment Survey, IMF.

Financial Markets—A Weak Link in the Renminbi as Reserve Currency Project

On the importance of home country financial market development for a currency to become a reserve currency, see Tavlas (1991), Chinn and Frankel (2007), Forbes (2009), and Obstfeld (2011b).

Banks and Equity Markets

See Prasad and Ye (2012) for details.

More Debt Needed

Data on outstanding stocks of domestic debt securities as of December 2012 are taken from the Statistical Annex of: *BIS Quarterly Review*. June 2013. Basel: Bank for International Settlements. Data for the advanced economies are from Tables 3B and 3A (Table 3B has total debt securities, and Table 3A has international debt securities, which need to be subtracted from the figures in Table 3B). For emerging markets, Table 3B has data on domestic debt securities. See Prasad and Ye (2012) for further discussion of the concepts and data.

The turnover ratio on government bonds—the ratio of transactions in a given year relative to the outstanding stock of bonds—is about 1 for China, compared to a ratio of about 14 for the U.S. In addition to the limited turnover, China restricts foreign investors' participation in its government bond markets, which could affect its currency's scope to become a reserve currency. However, China has a relatively high turnover ratio in its corporate bond market, which is consistent with the rapid growth of the corporate debt market. That market is about one-sixth the size of the U.S. corporate bond market.

Data on foreign exchange market turnover, derivatives markets, and currency denomination of international debt securities are taken from the Bank for International Settlements. See Prasad and Ye (2012) for further discussion of the concepts and data.

Other emerging markets' currencies also have low shares of global foreign exchange turnover. The U.S. dollar accounts for 87 percent of turnover. The five major reserve currencies combined account for 160 percent of total turnover (the total is 200 percent, as each transaction involves two currencies). Moreover, the spot and derivatives markets for trading in the renminbi remain underdeveloped. The renminbi's foreign exchange derivatives trading volume is far smaller than that of the major reserve currencies. These data are taken from the September 2013 Triennial Central Bank Survey conducted by the Bank for International Settlements.

China does have a major presence in markets for commodity futures. Based on the number of futures/options traded, three of China's commodity futures exchanges are among the top 20 derivatives exchanges in the world. This ranking is encouraging, but a large commodity derivatives market may be of limited use from the perspective of promoting international use of a currency.

Another indicator of the currency's potential use in international financial transactions is the relative size of international debt securities (i.e., debt issued outside the home country) in different currencies of issuance. The existing reserve currencies clearly dominate, with the U.S. dollar and the euro accounting for about 80 percent of outstanding international bonds and notes. The top five reserve currencies combined account for 94 percent of these instruments. Only a negligible fraction of international debt is denominated in renminbi and other major emerging market currencies. Source: *BIS Quarterly Review,* September 2013.

Other steps to broaden China's financial markets can also be traced back to the mid-2000s. In 2005, China lifted prohibitions against banks trading in equity and commodity-based derivative products. The development of the over-the-counter interest rate derivative market followed, with interest rate swaps first issued in 2006. As of April 2012, the gross notional amounts outstanding of over-the-counter interest rate derivatives denominated in euros and U.S. dollars were $172 trillion and $173 trillion, respectively. The same measure for the renminbi is about $435 billion, just over half the comparable figures even for Brazil and India. Source: TriOptima.

For more details on the data presented in this section, see Prasad and Ye (2012).

The Reserve Currency Scorecard

Although having large trade flows is neither a necessary nor sufficient condition for a country to have an international currency, it does boost the potential for the economy's currency to serve as an invoice currency. Krugman's (1995) triangle model of currency invoicing implies that economies are more likely to use the currency of the large nation, as measured by trade, because of economies of scale.

Another important criterion is the degree to which an economy is interconnected with other economies through trade linkages, which influences the incentives of traders in other countries to settle their transactions in the home country's currency. Errico and Massara (2011) conclude that China is now the second-most interconnected country in terms of its trade flows. China ranks second in terms of the size of its trade, giving it the top rank in terms of overall systemic trade importance. The U.S. ranks first in size and nineteenth in terms of interconnectedness, giving it the rank of sixth in systemic trade importance. The Netherlands has the highest rank in terms of interconnectedness; it is a small but very open economy with extensive trade linkages. The systemic trade importance ranks of some other countries are: Germany (2), Korea (7), Japan (9), India (14), Russia (19), and Brazil (20).

About 40 percent of China's trade is accounted for by processing trade, wherein most of the inputs are imported from other countries and only some assembly and packaging is done in China. The Chinese portion of value added in these products is small, but the full values of imported inputs and exported goods are included in the trade statistics. Based on value added measures, China's contribution to world trade would look a lot smaller than the official figures indicate. For data on adjusted measures of trade, see: "Measuring Trade in Value Added: An OECD-WTO Joint Initiative." The data and methodology are described in more detail on the Organisation for Economic Co-operation and Development website: http://www.oecd.org/industry/ind/measuringtradeinvalue-addedanoecd-wtojointinitiative.htm.

Čihák et al. (2012) have constructed alternative indicators of financial market development and financial access. China actually looks quite good in a cross-country comparison of some of those indicators. One measure of financial market development in this study is the sum of stock market capitalization and outstanding domestic private debt securities expressed as a ratio to GDP. The average of this ratio over the years 2009–11 was 110 percent for China, compared to 75 percent for Germany, 114 percent for Japan, 127 percent for the United Kingdom, and 220 percent for the United States.

Angeloni et al. (2011) note that, in addition to strong financial markets, a reserve currency should be backed up by: (1) the reliability of rules and institutions, (2) the quality and predictability of fiscal and monetary policies, (3) the ability of policymakers to respond to unexpected shocks, and (4) political cohesion.

Some authors also argue that network externalities are important, as they generate economies of scale and scope. The more countries that use a particular reserve currency, the easier it is for others to do so as well. See, for instance, Chinn and Frankel (2008). There is related empirical evidence on strong persistence effects in international investment patterns, which benefit the dollar in its status as the incumbent global reserve currency. See Appendix C of the report: "The International Role of the Euro." July 2013. Frankfurt, Germany: European Central Bank.

The Renminbi Takes Off
Currency Swaps with China Proliferate

The PBC had arranged six currency swap lines with other ASEAN+3 economies under the Chiang Mai Initiative in the early 2000s. Although China established bilateral local currency swap agreements with the Philippines, South Korea, and Japan, most of the other swap arrangements (e.g., the one with Thailand) were dollar-renminbi swaps. The swap lines with Korea and Japan were established in 2002 and are "two-way"—either party can provide liquidity. The swap with the Philippines was established in 2003 and, though denominated in local currency, it is a one-way swap such that China would provide renminbi liquidity in return for Philippine pesos should the Philippines need to draw on the credit line (see Henning 2009; Ito 2011).

See: "Remarks Given by Chris Salmon, Executive Director for Banking Services and Chief Cashier, at the London Money Market Association Executive Committee Meeting." Bank of England. January 24, 2013. For the announcement about the agreement between the Bank of England and the PBC, see the news release: "People's Bank of China Swap Line." June 22, 2013. London: Bank of England.

Christian Noyer's opinions are taken from this interview: Li Xiang. "Paris Vies to be Yuan Hub." *China Daily.* April 19, 2013. His remarks are also quoted in: Langi Chiang and Ben Blanchard. "France Plans Currency Swap Line with China: Paper." *Reuters.* April 12, 2013.

A Red-Tinged Bazooka

Foreign central banks that want to buy Chinese bonds for their reserve portfolios have to get permission from the Chinese government through the QFII scheme. Sovereign wealth funds have to do the same. By November 2012, the Hong Kong Monetary Authority, Norges Bank, Government of Singapore Investment Corporation, and Temasek Holdings Fullerton Management had reached their $1 billion quotas. Responding to strong demand for higher access limits, in December 2012, SAFE removed the ceiling on inward investments by sovereign wealth funds, central banks, and monetary authorities. See: "Regulations on Foreign Exchange Administration of Domestic Securities Investments by Qualified Foreign Institutional Investors." SAFE circular. December 2012. After this announcement, Qatar's sovereign wealth fund was reported to have applied for a QFII license and a $5 billion quota. See: Zhang Dingmin. "China Scraps QFII Limit on Sovereign Funds, Central Banks." *Bloomberg News.* December 16, 2012.

Bank Negara Malaysia's renminbi purchases are reported in: Kevin Brown, Robert Cookson, and Goeff Dyer. "Malaysian Bond Boost for Renminbi." *Financial Times.* September 19, 2010. Bank Indonesia's purchases are reported in: Lingling Wei. "Indonesia Joins Yuan Bandwagon." *Wall Street Journal.* July 23, 2012. For statements by a Bank of Korea official, see: Song Jung-a and Robert Cookson. "South Korea Seeks to Shift Reserves to China." *Financial Times.* May 4, 2011. The Bank of Thailand's intentions to buy renminbi assets can be found in a speech of Governor Prasarn Trairatvorakul: "Economic and Financial Cooperation between China and Thailand." Opening remarks at the luncheon to inaugurate the Bank of Thailand Beijing Representative Office, Beijing. April 6, 2012.

The Austrian central bank's announcement is in: "People's Bank of China and Oesterreichische Nationalbank Sign Important Agreement Today." Oesterreichische Nationalbank Press Release. November 10, 2011. On Nigeria's decision to buy renminbi for its reserve portfolio, see: "Nigeria Approves Inclusion of Chinese Renminbi in External Reserves." Central Bank of Nigeria press release. September 5, 2011. Governor Sanusi's statement about the extent of planned diversification into renminbi assets is reported in: Tim Cocks. "Nigeria to Put 5–10 Percent of FX Reserves into Yuan." *Reuters.* September 5, 2011. Figures for the currency composition of Nigeria's reserves appear in "Central Bank of Nigeria Annual Report—2011." Appendix B2. Central Bank of Nigeria. February 2013. The figures for the Chilean central bank's holdings of renminbi-denominated assets in its investment portfolio are taken from: "Monetary Policy Reports." Banco Central de Chile. September 2011 (Table B.6) and September 2012 (page 42). Table B.6 in the 2012 report indicates that the share of renminbi assets in the internally managed investment portfolio is 1.64 percent; the text on page 42, which seems to refer to the entire investment portfolio, mentions that the benchmark share is 1.95 percent.

For examples of other central banks considering adding renminbi assets to their reserves, see: Vinjeru Mkandawire. "Africa: New Frontier for the Renminbi." *Finan-*

cial Times. August 22, 2012. This article notes that Nigeria and Tanzania together bought bonds worth RMB 500 million from the China Development Bank, a state-owned bank. The Philippines Finance Secretary Cesar Purisima is quoted as favoring buying some yuan assets in this story: Fion Li. "Nigeria Buys 'Well-Managed' Yuan, Thailand Poised: China Credit." *Bloomberg News.* September 9, 2011. Venezuelan Central Bank President Nelson Merentes is quoted in this story as saying that it would be logical to diversify the country's reserves into renminbi: Diego Laje. "China's Yuan Moving Towards Global Currency." *CNN.* September 29, 2011.

In April 2013, Deputy Governor Philip Lowe of the Reserve Bank of Australia revealed the intention to hold about 5 percent of Australia's foreign currency assets in China. See: Philip Lowe. "The Journey of Financial Reform." Address to the Australian Chamber of Commerce in Shanghai. April 24, 2013.

Matchmaking for the Renminbi and Special Drawing Rights
See Zhou (2009).

Sarkozy Cozies Up to Beijing
Remarks made by Sarkozy at the opening of the Nanjing conference can be found at: http://www.g20.utoronto.ca/2011/sarkozy-110331-en.html. Timothy Geithner's prepared remarks at that conference are posted at: http://www.treasury.gov/press-center/press-releases/Pages/tg1122.aspx. I attended this conference and some of the remarks about the atmosphere at the conference are based on my observations.

Xia Bin's comment is reported in: "Nations Discuss Monetary Reform." *China Daily.* April 1, 2011.

Li Daokui's comments are reported in: "RMB Convertibility Process Should Be Decoupled from SDR Reform (人民币可自由兑换进程应与SDR改革脱钩)." *Caijing.* March 31, 2011. Translated from the Chinese by Yuhui Jiang.

The final communiqué from the Cannes G-20 meeting, as well as the near-final draft of the communiqué with the language about broadening the SDR basket of currencies, can be found at the website of the University of Toronto's G-20 Information Centre: http://www.g20.utoronto.ca/.

A transcript of Nicolas Sarkozy's press conference is available at: http://www.ambafrance-uk.org/President-Sarkozy-s-G20-summit.

Beijing Cool, IMF Warm to Sarkozy's Overtures
For the Yi Gang quotes, see: Lu Jianxin and Kazunori Takada. "China FX Head Proposes Adding BRICS Currencies to SDR." *Reuters.* May 4, 2011.

The documents summarizing the IMF's official positions are: "IMF Executive Board Completes the 2010 Review of SDR Valuation." IMF Public Information Notice 10/149; "IMF Executive Board Discusses Criteria for Broadening the SDR Currency Basket." IMF Public Information Notice 11/137. For more details on the underlying analysis, see: "Criteria for Broadening the SDR Currency Basket." IMF. September 2011.

The IMF's definition of a freely usable currency is one that is liquid, convertible, and used for the settlement of international transactions. The composition of the SDR basket is governed by operational rather than technical criteria, so the lack of convertibility is not a hindrance to including the renminbi (or other emerging market currencies) in the basket.

Not Quite a Safe Haven

The article on capital flight is: Alex Frangos, Tom Orlik, and Lingling Wei. "In Reversal, Cash Leaks out of China." *Wall Street Journal.* October 15, 2012.

A transcript of Draghi's speech to the Global Investment Conference in London is available at the ECB website: http://www.ecb.int/press/key/date/2012/html/sp120726.en.html.

For a description of the ECB's Outright Monetary Transactions program, see: "Technical Features of Outright Monetary Transactions." ECB press release. September 6, 2012.

The End Game
What's in It for China's Own Economic Development?

See: Eswar Prasad. "Will China's Yuan Rival the Dollar?" *Wall Street Journal.* February 8, 2012. I later became aware that the Trojan horse metaphor had been used earlier in a news report in the same newspaper. See: Bob Davis. "Were China's Leaders Conned?" *Wall Street Journal.* June 1, 2011.

Prasad (2009b) argues that capital account opening, especially if accompanied by greater exchange rate flexibility, could also strengthen China's domestic economic structure. It would facilitate financial sector reforms, allowing for a rebalancing of growth away from reliance on exports and investment-driven growth to a more balanced model of growth, with higher private consumption.

Widening the Field of Play

On April 18, 2012, the City of London Corporation launched its London-RMB initiative. At that time, the U.K. bank HSBC sold the first ever dim sum bond in London. In November, China Construction Bank became the first Chinese bank to issue a renminbi-denominated bond in London. See: Alice Ross. "CCB Issues 'Dim-Sum' Bonds in London." *Financial Times.* November 30, 2012.

For a discussion of China's outward investment strategy, see Rosen and Hanemann (2009) and Scissors (2011).

A Slow Move toward the End Game

See Yam (2011).

The Impact on the World

Yi Gang's quote from an interview at the World Economic Forum in Davos, Switzerland, is taken from: "China to Pursue RMB Internationalization." *Xinhua* and *China Daily.* January 28, 2013.

CHAPTER 13. OTHER CONTENDERS NIPPING AT THE DOLLAR'S HEELS

The opening lines are from one of the early scenes in the 1942 movie classic *Casablanca*.

Is a System with More Reserve Currencies Better?

For a discussion about multiple reserve currencies and some of the other topics covered in this chapter, see Eichengreen (2011a).

Benefits of Being a Reserve Currency

For a clear and accessible explanation about how the concepts of seigniorage and the inflation tax are related, see Woodward (2005). For a comprehensive technical explanation, see Buiter (2007a).

Estimates of inflation during the hyperinflationary episodes in Germany and Zimbabwe are taken from Hanke and Kwok (2009). Information about the price of a loaf of bread in Zimbabwe in January 2009 is taken from: "Zimbabwe to Print First $100 Trillion Note." *CNN.com*. January 16, 2009. Also see: "Zimbabwe Rolls Out Z$100tr Note." *BBC News*. January 16, 2009. The BBC article indicates that the Zimbabwe dollar 100 trillion note would be worth only $30, unlike the CNN article, which pegs its value at $300. Both articles were published on the same day.

Figures on U.S. currency in circulation are from the Federal Reserve Board website and estimates of the share of U.S. banknotes held outside the U.S. are from Goldberg (2010). Based on estimates by Judson (2012), Williams (2012) calculates that the share of U.S. currency held abroad rose from 56 percent in 2007 to nearly 66 percent in 2012. Williams (2012) also makes the interesting observation that demand for $100 bills has increased sharply during the recent period of global financial turmoil; these high-denomination notes now account for more than three-quarters of the value of U.S. currency in circulation (based on Federal Reserve data). He argues that this phenomenon, in addition to Judson's result, shows that U.S. banknotes are an important safe asset both at home and abroad. Of course, large denomination bills are also preferred by those engaged in illegal activities and money laundering. Feige (2012) argues that the share of U.S. banknotes held outside the U.S. is lower than other authors' estimates and is in the range of 30–37 percent.

Figures on euro banknotes and coins in circulation and estimates of euro banknotes in circulation outside the euro zone are from the European Central Bank website.

Haunted by Triffin

Tavlas (1991) discusses the deutsche mark's role in international finance. Also see Ungerer (1997). Emminger's views have been quoted by many authors and were reported in an article in the *Frankfurter Allgemeine Zeitung* newspaper, September 27, 1979.

Obstfeld (2011a) has argued that the Triffin dilemma is really a fiscal issue rather than one about the current account. Lago, Duttagupta, and Goyal (2009) make the point that the Triffin dilemma does not necessarily apply in a world with large gross capital flows. For a nice description of the context in which the Triffin dilemma was a real concern for the international monetary system, see Bordo (1993). Bini Smaghi (2011) provides a nuanced view of the contemporary relevance of the dilemma.

Is a Single Currency or World Currency the Solution?

The Single Global Currency Association has a number of articles on its obvious pet topic: http://www.singleglobalcurrency.org/.

Robert Mundell has argued for a world currency and notes on his website that "My ideal and equilibrium solution would be a world currency (but not a single world currency) in which each country would produce its own unit that exchanges at par with the world unit." See: http://robertmundell.net/economic-policies/world-currency/.

Do Emerging Market Currencies Have a Place in Global Finance?

See Aziz, Dunaway, and Prasad (2006) for a comparative evaluation of financial market development in China and India. Maziad et al. (2011) discuss the pros and cons of internationalization of emerging market currencies.

Data on outstanding stocks of domestic debt securities as of December 2012 are taken from the Statistical Annex of the *BIS Quarterly Review*. June 2013. Data for the U.S. come from Tables 3B and 3A (Table 3B has total debt securities, and Table 3A has international debt securities, which need to be subtracted from the figures in Table 3B). For emerging markets, Table 3B has data on domestic debt securities.

Other Faith-Based Alternatives
Gold

See Eichengreen (1996). The role of gold in the international monetary system is also discussed by Bordo and Eichengreen (1998).

The data in this section are taken from the World Gold Council (www.gold.org), including some data not on the public website that the Council graciously provided.

Yi Gang's quotes concerning China's holdings of gold reserves are reported in: "China's Gold Reserves Stand at 1,054 Tons." *Xinhua*. March 14, 2013.

At a price of $1,500 for a troy ounce, the market value of a metric ton of gold is $48.2 million (1 metric ton = 32,151 troy ounces). The price of gold hit a peak of $1,883 per troy ounce in August 2011. At the end of 2012, the price was $1,687 per troy ounce. It then fell to about $1,419 on May 31, 2013. The price fell further to just over $1,200 per troy ounce in late June 2013, before rebounding to $1,400 by late August 2013.

Bitcoins and Electronic Money

More information on bitcoins is at: www.bitcoin.org.

The exchange rate relative to the dollar is based on data for April 2, 2013. Bitcoin exchange rates quoted on different exchanges and against various currencies can be found at: http://bitcoincharts.com/markets/.

A report on the hacking of bitcoin currency exchanges is: "Bitcoin Theft Causes Bitfloor Exchange to Go Offline." *BBC News*. September 5, 2012. For more details on the Mt. Gox hack, see: James Ball. "LulzSec Rogue Suspected of Bitcoin Hack." *Guardian*.

June 22, 2011. The April 2013 hack of Mt. Gox is reported in: "Hack Attacks Hit Bitcoin Exchange Rates." *BBC News*. April 4, 2013.

The U.S. is applying money-laundering rules to bitcoin and other virtual currencies. See: Jeffrey Sparshott. "Web Money Gets Laundering Rule." *Wall Street Journal*. March 21, 2013. U.S. prosecutors filed money-laundering charges against the operators of the digital currency exchange Liberty Reserve in May 2013. See: Emily Flitter. "U.S. Accuses Currency Exchange of Laundering $6 Billion." *Reuters*. May 29, 2013.

For a description of how bitcoins constitute a decentralized currency without a central authority, and why some people place their trust in such a currency, see: Paul Ford. "Bitcoin May Be the Global Economy's Last Safe Haven." *Bloomberg News*. March 28, 2013.

Buiter (2007b) and Kimball (2013) discuss the benefits of electronic currency and also provide an exposition of some technical issues involved in their introduction. For a less technical introduction to this issue, see Matthew Yglesias. "Mo Money, Mo Problems: How Eliminating Paper Money Could End Recessions." Slate.com. December 12, 2011. http://www.slate.com/articles/technology/technology/2011/12/how _eliminating_paper_money_could_end_recessions_.html.

Community Currencies

For more on community currencies in the U.S., see Solomon (1996) and Collom (2005). Information on Ithaca Hours is at: http://ithacahours.info/.

The SDR as Global Reserve Currency?

The value of the SDR was defined at its creation in 1969 as equivalent to 0.888671 grams of fine gold. At that time, its value was also equivalent to one U.S. dollar (the dollar had a fixed price against gold). After the collapse of the Bretton Woods system, the SDR was redefined as a basket of currencies comprising the 16 leading currencies in international trade. In 1981, the basket was pared down to five currencies—the U.S. dollar, the French franc, the deutsche mark, the Japanese yen, and the pound sterling. See: "The Role of the SDR in the International Monetary System." Occasional Paper 51. Washington, DC: IMF. 1987. When the euro came into being, it replaced the deutsche mark and the French franc, shrinking the basket to four currencies.

The figure on the stock of SDRs in April 2013 is based on a stock of 204 billion SDRs converted to U.S. dollars at the April 30 exchange rate of 0.66 SDRs per $1. For more details on the SDR, see: "IMF Factsheet: Special Drawing Rights (SDRs)." IMF. March 2013.

The discussion of the SDR's conceptual definition is from the IMF's *Balance of Payments Manual*. August 2011.

For a discussion of the role of the SDR as a reserve asset, see Eichengreen and Frankel (1996) and Obstfeld (2011c).

Boughton (2001, pages 936–943) describes the economic and political reasons due to which the proposal for an SDR substitution account did not gain traction. Kenen (2010a) advocates an SDR-based reserve system, and Kenen (2010b) discusses the mechanics of a substitution account, including calculations of the potential cost to the U.S. if, for instance, the U.S. dollar were to depreciate against the SDR. For other recent advocacy of the idea of a substitution account, see: C. Fred Bergsten. "How to Solve the Problem of the Dollar." *Financial Times.* December 11, 2007.

Stuck

For an emerging market policymaker's perspectives on this state of affairs, see Sheel (2011).

CHAPTER 14. COULD THE DOLLAR HIT A TIPPING POINT AND SINK?

The opening quote is from Gladwell (2002), page 9.

See Bak, Tang, and Wiesenfeld (1987). A more detailed explanation of the concept of self-organized criticality, along with a number of examples from nature, can be found in Bak (1996). Scheinkman and Woodford (1994) apply the concept to an economic model of production and inventory dynamics.

The physics of phase transitions is in fact more complex than suggested in the text. There is a boundary line (determined by different combinations of temperature and pressure) between different phases where a material will coexist in two of three states of matter: as solid and liquid, as liquid and gas, or as solid and gas. There is also a specific combination of pressure and temperature at which a material reaches a thermodynamic equilibrium and matter can exist in all three states simultaneously. This balancing point, where the boundary lines between different phases intersect, is called the "triple point." For a simple explanation, see: http://chemwiki.ucdavis.edu/Physical_Chemistry/Physical_Properties_of_Matter/Phase_Transitions/Phase_Diagrams.

Research on Tipping Points: Handle with Care

See Reinhart and Rogoff (2009, 2010). For a critique of their work, see Herndon, Ash, and Pollin (2013). Cecchetti, Mohanty, and Zampolli (2011, page 1) are less circumspect than Reinhart and Rogoff about the causal effects of high debt levels, asserting that "beyond a certain level, debt is a drag on growth. For government debt, the threshold is around 85% of GDP." For some illustrations of how senior policymakers in the U.S. and Europe invoked the Reinhart-Rogoff threshold of 90 percent of GDP, see: Alicia P. Q. Wittmeyer. "How Influential Was That Reinhart-Rogoff Paper, Exactly?" *ForeignPolicy.com.* April 16, 2013.

Greenlaw et al. (2013) provide evidence for the 80 percent of GDP threshold. Their preferred measure of debt in these calculations is gross debt to GDP.

A Red Wild Card

Data on China's and all foreign investors' purchases of U.S. Treasury securities from December 2007 to December 2012 are taken from the Treasury International Capital System (www.treasury.gov/tic) and the "Report on Foreign Portfolio Holdings of

U.S. Securities" (as of May 2013), available at that website. Foreign investors' holdings of U.S. Treasuries rose from $2.35 trillion in December 2007 to $5.57 trillion in December 2012. China's holdings of U.S. Treasuries at these two dates were $0.48 trillion and $1.22 trillion, respectively.

Yu Yongding's comment, the market reaction, and Yu's clarification are reported in: Chris Giles. "Chinese Whispers Frighten Currency Markets." *Financial Times.* November 27, 2004.

An Atomic Weapon with a Nasty Recoil

The quoted text is taken from: "State Administration of Foreign Exchange FAQs on Foreign Exchange Administrative Policies" (3), July 7, 2010. http://www.safe.gov.cn.

Geopolitics Takes Precedence over Economics

See: Keith Bradsher. "China Tensions Could Sway Vote in Taiwan." *New York Times.* March 21, 2008.

Even before 2008, China had made it clear that it was willing to risk the Olympics if Taiwan forced its hand into military intervention by taking steps toward asserting its independence. For instance, Major General Peng Guangqian of the Academy of Military Science of the People's Liberation Army explicitly listed loss or boycott of the 2008 Olympics among the "six prices" China was ready to pay to uphold national unity and territorial integrity. See: Joseph Kahn. "Chinese Officers Warn that Taiwan Referendum Could Lead to War." *New York Times.* December 3, 2003. Similarly, Taiwan President Chen Shui-bian's proposal, ahead of the 2004 elections, to hold a referendum on independence from the Mainland prompted a strong response from Chinese Premier Wen Jiabao. Wen said that such a move would not be acceptable and that "The Chinese people will pay any price to safeguard the unity of the motherland." See: John Pomfret. "China Warns U.S. About Taiwan." *Washington Post.* November 23, 2003. Following Chen Shui-bian's successful re-election bid, China raised the pressure on him to avoid pro-independence statements in his inauguration speech. The government-owned *China Daily* newspaper had an article that included this quote from Xu Bodong, a Chinese academic:

> the mainland is ready to afford to a slow-down in its modernization bid, a reversion in Sino-US ties and the boycott of the Olympic Games. Nothing can override the importance of protecting part of the Chinese territory from being split from the motherland.

See: Xing Zhigang. "Taipei Urged Not to Misjudge Beijing's Resolve." *China Daily.* May 18, 2004.

Barren Islands Become a Bone of Contention

The Japanese government bought three of the disputed islands from a private landowner to preempt their purchase by Tokyo's nationalist governor. A Japanese newspaper summarized the situation as follows: "Sources in the Noda administration have said one purpose of the government's plan was to prevent friction from heightening with Beijing and Taipei. Central government officials feared that diplomatic ties would unravel if Tokyo Governor Shintaro Ishihara carried out the metropolitan government's plan to buy the islands from the Saitama landowner." See: "Noda Government to Buy Senkaku Islands for 2 Billion Yen." *Asahi Shimbun.* September 5, 2012.

The *China Daily* quotes are from: Wang Xingyu. "Good Move on Diayou Islands." *China Daily.* October 26, 2012.

How Big Would the Disruption Be?

Beltran et al. (2012) estimate the bond market reaction to a decline of inflows from foreign investors.

The Department of Defense report "Assessment of the National Security Risks Posed to the United States as a Result of the U.S. Federal Debt Owed to China as a Creditor of the U.S. Government" was prepared at the request of the U.S. Congress and was completed in July 2012.

The Risk of an Own Goal

See: "Federal Debt and the Risk of a Fiscal Crisis." CBO Economic and Budget Issue Brief. July 27, 2010. Washington, DC: Congressional Budget Office. The quoted text appears on page 1.

Data on the maturity structure, financing costs, and other aspects of U.S. federal debt financing, including forecasts of the Office of Management and Budget, can be found on the U.S. Treasury Department's website in the section related to the Treasury Borrowing Advisory Committee: http://www.treasury.gov/resource-center/data-chart-center/quarterly-refunding/Pages/TBAC-Discussion-Charts.aspx. The reported data on the weighted average maturity of marketable debt outstanding are from the fiscal year 2013 Q3 report, downloaded on September 28, 2013. Cochrane (2012) notes some pitfalls in using these numbers. Hamilton and Wu (2011) and Cochrane (2012) make the case for a more aggressive shift toward long-maturity debt to take advantage of a low interest rate environment.

The outstanding stock of Treasury bonds and notes held by the public (including the Fed) rose from \$3.38 trillion in December 2008 to \$8.89 trillion in June 2013. During this period, the Fed's holdings of Treasury bonds and notes rose from \$0.41 trillion to \$1.85 trillion. Sources: U.S. Treasury Bulletin (Table FD-2, columns 4 and 5), September 2013. Factors Affecting Reserve Balances: Federal Reserve Statistical Release. Available at: http://www.federalreserve.gov/releases/h41/.

A Blast from the Past
Roosa Bonds

For a discussion of the Roosa bonds and their provenance, see Block (1977, pages 179–180). Bordo (1999) and Meltzer (2010) offer interesting historical narratives of the events surrounding that period. The aggregate Roosa bonds issuance figure is taken from Meltzer (2010, page 215).

Bordo, Humpage, and Schwartz (2012) track a specific Roosa bonds transaction that took place in 1964. At that time, the Fed owed $75 million worth of Swiss francs to the Swiss National Bank and $145 million worth of Swiss francs to the Bank for International Settlements. It had obtained the Swiss francs through bilateral short-term currency swaps with the two institutions. The Swiss franc was trading above par, and the Fed could not acquire sufficient amounts of that currency to meet its commitments. In May 1964, the Treasury issued $70 million worth of Swiss franc–denominated Roosa bonds to the BIS and sold the Swiss franc proceeds to the Fed, which in turn repaid an equivalent amount of Swiss franc debt to the BIS. Thus, the BIS obtained long-term foreign currency–denominated debt in return for its dollar holdings. These positions were eventually unwound through gold sales and then purchases of francs with dollars when the franc came under depreciation pressures in the next two years.

Makin (1971) demonstrates an empirical connection between pressures on the swap and Roosa bond facilities on the one hand and an index of concern about the gold value of the dollar on the other.

Carter Bonds

Events surrounding the issuance of the Carter bonds are described in Marston (1988) and Henning (1999). The $5 billion from the IMF was meant to include drawings on the U.S. position in the IMF as well as sales of U.S. holdings of SDRs. Information on the exact amount of Carter bonds sold can be found in: "Transcript of the Federal Open Market Committee Meeting." Federal Reserve Board. July 9, 1980. Page 2. It is also mentioned in: John C. Given. "Could 'Reagan Bonds' Help Ease the Nation's Economic Ills?" *Associated Press.* January 9, 1988.

Bergsten (1996) offers an interesting insider account of the economics and politics of U.S. international monetary policy.

CHAPTER 15. ULTIMATE PARADOX: FRAGILITY BREEDS STABILITY

The opening quote is taken from the IMF's website: http://www.imf.org/external/np/exr/center/mm/eng/mm_sc_03.htm. See Triffin (1960) for a more detailed exposition of his views.

Why America Rules
Institutions Are Crucial

See North (1982), Acemoglu and Johnson (2005), and Acemoglu and Robinson (2012). Bardhan (2005) discusses the importance of participatory democratic institutions.

Mayhew (2005) attempts to debunk the notion that the American national government functions effectively only when one party controls the presidency and Congress. He argues that, when it comes to productivity in terms of important legislative actions, divided government is no less effective than a unified government. In subsequent work, he argues that, despite heated partisan conflicts over the past two centuries, the system has developed a self-correcting impulse that tends to nudge institutions back toward the median voter, accounting for the government's success and long-standing vitality (Mayhew 2013). Connelly (2010) documents that partisanship and polarization have long been a feature of U.S. congressional politics. Dionne (2012) offers a tour of America's fractious political past, highlighting the ability of the American system to self-correct.

For evidence to support the bonding hypothesis, see Doidge, Karolyi, and Stulz (2007, 2009).

Growth versus Institutions

Allen, Qian, and Qian (2005) discuss the roles of formal and informal financial and legal institutions in China. Lin (2011) provides a nice overview of China's development model.

See Li (2012) for a discussion of China's political structure. For a critical evaluation of China's legal and judicial frameworks, see He (2012) and Lubman (2012). Shih (2009) shows how the management and operation of major financial institutions in China are interwoven with factional struggles in the Chinese Communist Party.

Document No. 9 lists the following seven perils: advocating Western constitutional democracy; advocating universal values; advocating civil society; advocating neoliberalism; advocating Western notions about the press; disseminating historical nihilism; and questioning the reform and opening up, and the socialist nature of socialism with Chinese characteristics. See http://www.mingjingnews.com/2013/08/9.html (in Mandarin). For a summary, see Chris Buckley. "China Takes Aim at Western Ideas." *New York Times*. August 19, 2013.

Flight to Liquidity Rather Than to Safety

The quote at the end of this section is from McKinnon (2012, page 4).

What Lies Ahead
Hard Economic Power Shifts, Soft Power Does Not

The Steven Englander quote is taken from: Alan Wheatley. "G20 Keeps Up Snail's Pace of Global Monetary Reform." *Reuters*. April 1, 2011.

REFERENCES

Accominotti, Olivier. 2009. "The Sterling Trap: Foreign Reserves Management at the Bank of France, 1928–1936." *European Review of Economic History* 13(3): 349–376.

Acemoglu, Daron, and Simon Johnson. 2005. "Unbundling Institutions." *Journal of Political Economy* 113(5): 949–995.

Acemoglu, Daron, and James A. Robinson. 2012. *Why Nations Fail: The Origins of Power, Prosperity, and Poverty.* New York: Crown Business Publishing.

Acharya, Viral V., and Philipp Schnabl. 2010. "Do Global Banks Spread Global Imbalances? Asset-Backed Commercial Paper during the Financial Crisis of 2007–2009." *IMF Economic Review* 58(1): 37–73.

Adams, Douglas. 1982. *Life, the Universe and Everything.* New York: Harmony.

Aizenman, Joshua, and Jaewoo Lee. 2007. "International Reserves: Precautionary versus Mercantilist Views: Theory and Evidence." *Open Economies Review* 18: 191–214.

Aizenman, Joshua, and Gurnain Kaur Pasricha. 2009. "Selective Swap Arrangements and the Global Financial Crisis: Analysis and Interpretation." NBER Working Paper 14821. Cambridge, MA: National Bureau of Economic Research.

Aizenman, Joshua, Brian Pinto, and Artur Radziwill. 2007. "Sources for Financing Domestic Capital: Is Foreign Saving a Viable Option for Developing Countries?" *Journal of International Money and Finance* 26(5): 682–702.

Alfaro, Laura, Sebnem Kalemli-Ozcan, and Vadym Volosovych. 2008. "Why Doesn't Capital Flow from Rich to Poor Countries? An Empirical Investigation." *Review of Economics and Statistics* 90(2): 347–368.

Allen, Franklin, Jun Qian, and Meijun Qian. 2005. "Law, Finance and Economic Growth in China." *Journal of Financial Economics* 77: 57–116.

Ames, Glen. 2004. "Mercantilism." *Europe, 1450 to 1789: Encyclopedia of the Early Modern World.* New York: Charles Scribner's Sons.

Andritzky, Jochen R. 2012. "Government Bonds and Their Investors: What Are the Facts and Do They Matter?" IMF Working Paper WP/12/158. Washington, DC: International Monetary Fund.

Angeloni, Ignazio, Agnès Bénassy-Quéré, Benjamin Carton, Zsolt Darvas, Christophe Destais, Jean Pisani-Ferry, André Sapir, and Shahin Vallée. 2011. *Global Currencies for Tomorrow: A European Perspective.* CEPII Research Report. Paris, France: CEPII.

Arslanalp, Serkan, and Takahiro Tsuda. 2012. "Tracking Global Demand for Advanced Economy Sovereign Debt." IMF Working Paper WP/12/284. Washington, DC: International Monetary Fund.

Auboin, Marc. 2012. "Use of Currencies in International Trade: Any Changes in the Picture?" Staff Working Paper ESRD-2012-10. Geneva: World Trade Organization.

Auerbach, Alan J., and William G. Gale. 2009. "The Economic Crisis and the Fiscal Crisis: 2009 and Beyond." *Tax Notes* (October 5): 101–130.

———. 2012. "The Federal Budget Outlook: No News Is Bad News." *Tax Notes* (September 24): 1597–1607.

Aziz, Jahangir, Steven Dunaway, and Eswar S. Prasad, editors. 2006. *China and India: Learning from Each Other: Reforms and Policies for Sustained Growth.* Washington, DC: International Monetary Fund.

Bak, Per. 1996. *How Nature Works: The Science of Self-Organized Criticality.* New York: Copernicus.

Bak, Per, Chao Tang, and Kurt Wiesenfeld. 1987. "Self-organized Criticality: An Explanation of the $1/f$ Noise." *Physical Review Letters* 59(4): 381–384.

Balin, Bryan J. 2008. "India's New Capital Restrictions: What Are They, Why Were They Created, and Have They Been Effective?" Manuscript. Washington, DC: Johns Hopkins University School of Advanced International Studies.

Bardhan, Pranab. 2005. "Institutions Matter, but Which Ones?" *Economics of Transition* 13(3): 499–532.

Basu, Suman. 2009. "Sovereign Debt and Domestic Economic Fragility." Manuscript. Cambridge, MA: Massachusetts Institute of Technology.

Bayoumi, Tamim, and Trung Bui. 2011. "Unforeseen Events Wait Lurking: Estimating Policy Spillovers from U.S. to Foreign Asset Prices." IMF Working Paper 11/183. Washington, DC: International Monetary Fund.

Beja, Edsel L. 2008. "Estimating Trade: Misinvoicing from China: 2000–2005." *China and the World Economy* 16(2): 82–92.

Bekaert, Geert, Campbell R. Harvey, and Christian Lundblad. 2005. "Does Financial Liberalization Spur Economic Growth?" *Journal of Financial Economics* 77: 3–55.

Beltran, Daniel O., Maxwell Kretchmer, Jaime Marquez, and Charles P. Thomas. 2012. "Foreign Holdings of U.S. Treasuries and U.S. Treasury Yields." International Finance Discussion Papers (January) 2012-1041. Washington, DC: Board of Governors of the Federal Reserve System.

Bergsten, Fred C. 1996. *Dilemmas of the Dollar: The Economics and Politics of United States International Monetary Policy.* Second edition. New York: Council on Foreign Relations.

———. 2013. "Currency Wars, the Economy of the United States and Reform of the International Monetary System." Stavros Niarchos Foundation Lecture delivered on May 16. Washington, DC: Peterson Institute for International Economics.

Bernanke, Ben S. 2000. "Japanese Monetary Policy: A Case of Self-Induced Paralysis." In *Japan's Financial Crisis and Its Parallels to U.S. Experience,* edited by Adam S. Posen and Ryoichi Mikitani. Special Report 13 (September). Washington, DC: Institute of International Economics.

———. 2002. "Deflation: Making Sure 'It' Doesn't Happen Here." Speech to the National Economists Club, Washington, DC, November 21.

————. 2005. "The Global Saving Glut and the U.S. Current Account Deficit." Sandridge Lecture, Virginia Association of Economists, Richmond, VA, March 10.

————. 2010a. "The Economic Outlook and Monetary Policy." Speech at the Federal Reserve Bank of Kansas City Economic Symposium, Jackson Hole, WY, August 27.

————. 2010b. "Rebalancing the Global Recovery." Speech at the Sixth European Central Bank Central Banking Conference, Frankfurt, November 19.

Bertaut, Carol, and Laurie Pounder. 2009. "The Financial Crisis and U.S. Cross-Border Financial Flows." *Federal Reserve Bulletin* 93: A147–A167.

Bhalla, Surjit S. 2012. *Devaluing to Prosperity: Misaligned Currencies and Their Growth Consequences.* Washington, DC: Peterson Institute for International Economics.

Bhattacharyay, Biswa Nath. 2011. "Bond Market Development in Asia: An Empirical Analysis of Major Determinants." ADBI Working Paper 300. Tokyo: Asian Development Bank Institute.

Bini Smaghi, Lorenzo. 2011. "The Triffin Dilemma Revisited." Speech at the Triffin International Foundation. October 3. Frankfurt, Germany: European Central Bank.

Bjørnland, Hilde C. 2009. "Monetary Policy and Exchange Rate Overshooting: Dornbusch was Right After All." *Journal of International Economics* 79(1): 64–77.

Blanchard, Olivier J. 2007. "Current Account Deficits in Rich Countries." *IMF Staff Papers* 54(2): 191–219.

Blanchard, Olivier J., Mitali Das, and Hamid Faruqee. 2010. "The Initial Impact of the Crisis on Emerging Market Countries." *Brookings Papers on Economic Activity* Spring: 263–307.

Block, Fred L. 1977. *The Origins of International Economic Disorder: A Study of United States International Monetary Policy from World War II to the Present.* Berkeley: University of California Press.

Bordo, Michael D. 1993. "The Bretton Woods International Monetary System: A Historical Overview." In *A Retrospective on the Bretton Woods System: Lessons for International Monetary Reform,* edited by Michael D. Bordo and Barry Eichengreen. Chicago: University of Chicago Press.

————. 1999. *The Gold Standard and Related Regimes: Collected Essays.* Cambridge: Cambridge University Press.

Bordo, Michael D., and Barry Eichengreen. 1998. "The Rise and Fall of a Barbarous Relic: The Role of Gold in the International Monetary System." NBER Working Paper 6436. Cambridge, MA: National Bureau of Economic Research.

Bordo, Michael D., Owen F. Humpage, and Anna J. Schwartz. 2012. "Bretton Woods, Swap Lines, and the Federal Reserve's Return to Intervention." Working Paper 12-32. Cleveland, OH: Federal Reserve Bank of Cleveland.

Borio, Claudio, and Piti Disyatat. 2011. "Global Imbalances and the Financial Crisis: Link or No Link." BIS Working Paper 346. Basel, Switzerland: Bank for International Settlements.

Borio, Claudio, Gabriele Galati, and Alexandra Heath. 2008. "FX Reserve Management: Trends and Challenges." BIS Working Paper 40. Basel, Switzerland: Bank for International Settlements.

Bosworth, Barry, and Susan M. Collins. 2008. "Accounting for Growth: Comparing China and India." *Journal of Economic Perspectives* 22(1): 45–66.

Boughton, James M. 2001. *Silent Revolution: International Monetary Fund, 1979–1989.* Washington, DC: International Monetary Fund.

Buiter, Willem H. 2007a. "Seigniorage." NBER Working Paper 12919. Cambridge, MA: National Bureau of Economic Research.

———. 2007b. "Is Numérairology the Future of Monetary Economics?" *Open Economies Review* 18(2): 127–156.

Burger, John D., Francis E. Warnock, and Veronica Cacdac Warnock. 2010. "Investing in Local Currency Bond Markets." NBER Working Paper 16249. Cambridge, MA: National Bureau of Economic Research.

Byron, Lord [George Gordon]. 1819–1824. *Don Juan.* London: Penguin Classics (2004 reprint edition).

Caballero, Ricardo J., and Emmanuel Farhi. 2012. "A Model of the Safe Asset Mechanism (SAM): Safety Traps and Economic Policy." Manuscript. Cambridge, MA: Massachusetts Institute of Technology.

Caballero, Ricardo J., Emmanuel Farhi, and Pierre-Olivier Gourinchas. 2008a. "Financial Crash, Commodity Prices, and Global Imbalances." *Brookings Papers on Economic Activity* Fall: 1–55.

———. 2008b. "An Equilibrium Model of 'Global Imbalances' and Low Interest Rates." *American Economic Review* 98(1): 358–393.

Cannon, John. 2002. "Mercantilism." In *The Oxford Companion to British History,* edited by David Dabydeen, John Gilmore, and Cecily Jones. New York: Oxford University Press.

Carvalho, Bernardo S. de M., and Márcio G. P. Garcia. 2008. "Ineffective Controls on Capital Inflows Under Sophisticated Financial Markets: Brazil in the Nineties." In *Financial Markets Volatility and Performance in Emerging Markets,* edited by Sebastian Edwards and Márcio G. P. Garcia. Chicago: University of Chicago Press for National Bureau of Economic Research.

Caselli, Francesco, and James Feyrer. 2007. "The Marginal Product of Capital." *Quarterly Journal of Economics* 122(2): 535–568.

Cecchetti, Stephen G., M. S. Mohanty, and Fabrizio Zampolli. 2010. "The Future of Public Debt: Prospects and Implications." BIS Working Paper 300. Basel, Switzerland: Bank for International Settlements.

———. 2011. "The Real Effects of Debt." Conference proceedings of the Jackson Hole Symposium *Achieving Maximum Long-Run Growth*, Federal Reserve Bank of Kansas City, Jackson Hole, WY, August 25–27.

Chamon, Marcos, and Eswar S. Prasad. 2010. "Why Are Saving Rates of Urban Households in China Rising?" *American Economic Journal: Macroeconomics* 2(1): 93–130.

Chamon, Marcos, Kai Liu, and Eswar S. Prasad. 2013. "Income Uncertainty and Household Savings in China." *Journal of Development Economics,* forthcoming.

Chen, Hongyi, Wensheng Peng, and Chang Shu. 2009. "The Potential of the Renminbi as an International Currency." BIS Asian Research Program Research Papers. Basel, Switzerland: Bank for International Settlements.

Chen, Qianying, Andrew Filardo, Dong He, and Feng Zhu. 2012. "International Spillovers of Central Bank Balance Sheet Policies." BIS Paper 66. Geneva: Bank for International Settlements.

Chinn, Menzie, and Jeffrey A. Frankel. 2007. "Will the Euro Eventually Surpass the Dollar as Leading International Reserve Currency?" In *G7 Current Account Imbalances: Sustainability and Adjustment,* edited by Richard Clarida. Chicago: University of Chicago Press.

———. 2008. "Why the Euro Will Rival the Dollar." *International Finance* 11(1): 49–73.

Chinn, Menzie D., and Hiro Ito. 2008. "A New Measure of Financial Openness." *Journal of Comparative Policy Analysis* 10(3): 309–322.

Čihák, Martin, Aslı Demirgüç-Kunt, Erik Feyen, and Ross Levine. 2012. "Benchmarking Financial Systems around the World." Policy Research Working Paper 6175. Washington, DC: World Bank.

Cline, William R. 2008. "Estimating Consistent Fundamental Equilibrium Exchange Rates." PIIE Working Paper 08-6. Washington, DC: Peterson Institute for International Economics.

Cochrane, John H. 2012. "Having Your Cake and Eating It Too: The Maturity Structure of U.S. Debt." Manuscript. Chicago: University of Chicago.

Cohen, Benjamin J. 2009. "Dollar Dominance, Euro Aspirations: Recipe for Discord?" *Journal of Common Market Studies* 47(4): 742–766.

Collom, Ed. 2005. "Community Currency in the United States: The Social Environments in Which It Emerges and Survives." *Environment and Planning* 37(9): 1565–1587.

Connelly, Jr., William F. 2010. *James Madison Rules America: The Constitutional Origins of Congressional Partisanship.* Lanham, MD: Rowman and Littlefield.

Corden, W. Max. 2007. "Those Current Account Imbalances: A Sceptical View." *World Economy* 30(March): 363–382.

Corsetti, Giancarlo, Paolo Pesenti, and Nouriel Roubini. 1999. "What Caused the Asian Currency and Financial Crisis?" *Japan and the World Economy* 11: 305–373.

Curcuru, Stephanie E., Tomas Dvorak, and Francis E. Warnock. 2008. "Cross-Border Returns Differentials." *Quarterly Journal of Economics* 123(4): 1495–1530.

Curcuru, Stephanie E., and Charles P. Thomas. 2012. "The Return on U.S. Direct Investment at Home and Abroad." International Finance Discussion Paper 1057. Washington, DC: Board of Governors of the Federal Reserve System.

Darvas, Zsolt. 2009. "The EU's Role in Supporting Crisis-Hit Countries in Central and Eastern Europe." Bruegel Policy Contribution 2009/17. Brussels: Bruegel.

Darvas, Zsolt, and Jean Pisani-Ferry. 2010. "The Threat of 'Currency Wars': A European Perspective." Bruegel Policy Contribution 2010/12. Brussels: Bruegel.

De Gregorio, José. 2011a. "Chile: Policy Responses to the Global Crisis." Presentation delivered at the conference *Monetary Policy and Central Banking in the Post Crisis*

Environment, Central Bank of Chile and Global Interdependence Center, Santiago, Chile, January 17.

De Gregorio, José. 2011b. "International Reserve Hoarding in Emerging Economies." Economic Policy Paper 40. Santiago: Central Bank of Chile.

De Gregorio, José, Sebastian Edwards, and Rodrigo Valdes. 2000. "Controls on Capital Inflows: Do They Work?" *Journal of Development Economics* 63(1): 59–83.

Dionne, Jr., E. J. 2012. *Our Divided Heart: The Battle for the American Idea in an Age of Discontent*. New York: Bloomsbury.

Dobson, Wendy, and Anil K. Kashyap. 2006. "The Contradiction in China's Gradualist Banking Reforms." *Brookings Papers on Economic Activity* Fall: 103–162.

Dobson, Wendy, and Paul R. Masson. 2009. "Will the Renminbi Become a World Currency?" *China Economic Review* 20(1): 124–135.

Doidge, Craig, G. Andrew Karolyi, and René M. Stulz. 2007. "Why Do Countries Matter So Much for Corporate Governance?" *Journal of Financial Economics* 86: 1–39.

———. 2009. "Has New York Become Less Competitive than London in Global Markets? Evaluating Foreign Listing Choices over Time." *Journal of Financial Economics* 91: 253–277.

Dominguez, Kathryn, Yuko Hashimoto, and Takatoshi Ito. 2011. "International Reserves and the Global Financial Crisis." Paper presented at the NBER Global Financial Crisis Conference, Bretton Woods, NH, June 3–4.

Dooley, Michael P., David Folkerts-Landau, and Peter Garber. 2004. "The Revived Bretton Woods System." *International Journal of Finance and Economics* 9(4): 307–313.

Dornbusch, Rudiger. 1976. "Expectations and Exchange Rate Dynamics." *Journal of Political Economy* 84(6): 1161–1176.

Edwards, Sebastian, editor. 2000. *Capital Flows and the Emerging Economies: Theory, Evidence, and Controversies*. Chicago: University of Chicago Press.

———. 2005. "Is the U.S. Current Account Deficit Sustainable? And If Not, How Costly Is Adjustment Likely to Be?" NBER Working Paper 11541. Cambridge, MA: National Bureau of Economic Research.

Ehrmann, Michael, and Marcel Fratzscher. 2009. "Explaining Monetary Policy in Press Conferences." *International Journal of Central Banking* 5(2): 41–84.

Eichengreen, Barry. 1996. *Golden Fetters: The Gold Standard and the Great Depression, 1919–1939*. New York: Oxford University Press.

———. 2005. "Sterling's Past, Dollar's Future: Historical Perspectives on Reserve Currency Competition." NBER Working Paper 11336. Cambridge, MA: National Bureau of Economic Research.

———. 2011a. *Exorbitant Privilege: The Rise and Fall of the Dollar and the Future of the International Monetary System*. Oxford: Oxford University Press.

———. 2011b. "The Renminbi as an International Currency." Manuscript. Berkeley: University of California, Berkeley.

Eichengreen, Barry, and Marc Flandreau. 2009. "The Rise and Fall of the Dollar, or

When Did the Dollar Overtake Sterling as the Leading Reserve Currency?" *European Review of Economic History* 13: 377–411.

———. 2010. "The Federal Reserve, the Bank of England and the Rise of the Dollar as an International Currency, 1914–39." BIS Working Paper 328. Basel, Switzerland: Bank for International Settlements.

Eichengreen, Barry, and Jeffrey Frankel. 1996. "The SDR, Reserve Currencies, and the Future of the International Monetary System." In *The Future of the SDR in Light of Changes in the International Financial System,* edited by Michael Mussa, James Boughton, and Peter Isard. Washington, DC: International Monetary Fund.

Eichengreen, Barry, and Ricardo Hausmann. 1999. "Exchange Rates and Financial Fragility." Conference proceedings from Jackson Hole Symposium *New Challenges for Monetary Policy,* Federal Reserve Bank of Kansas City, Jackson Hole, WY, August 26–28.

Einzig, Paul. 1931. *The Fight for Financial Supremacy.* London: Macmillan and Co.

———. 1932. *Behind the Scenes of International Finance.* London: Macmillan and Co.

El-Erian, Mohamed. 2008. *When Markets Collide: Investment Strategies for the Age of Global Economic Change.* New York: McGraw-Hill.

Elwell, Craig K. 2012. "The Depreciating Dollar: Economic Effects and Policy Response." Washington, DC: Congressional Research Service.

Engel, Charles. 2013. "Exchange Rates and Interest Parity." In *Handbook of International Economics* 4, edited by Gita Gopinath, Elhanan Helpman, and Kenneth Rogoff. Amsterdam: Elsevier.

Ernst, Ekkehard, and Veronica Escudero. 2008. "The Effects of Financial Globalization on Global Imbalances, Employment and Inequality." Discussion Paper DP/191/2008. Geneva, Switzerland: International Institute for Labour Studies.

Errico, Luca, and Alexander Massara. 2011. "Assessing Systemic Trade Interconnectedness—An Empirical Approach." IMF Working Paper 11/214. Washington, DC: International Monetary Fund.

Favilukis, Jack, Sydney C. Ludvigson, and Stijn Van Nieuwerburgh. 2012. "Foreign Ownership of U.S. Safe Assets: Good or Bad?" Manuscript. New York: New York University.

Feige, Edgar. 2012. "New Estimates of U.S. Currency Abroad, the Domestic Money Supply and the Unreported Economy." *Crime, Law and Social Change* 57(3): 239–263.

Feldstein, Martin. 1989. "The Case Against Trying to Stabilize the Dollar." *American Economic Review* 79(2): 36–40.

———. 2007. "Why Is the Dollar So High?" *Journal of Policy Modeling* 29(5): 661–667.

———. 2011. "Why the Dollar Will Weaken Further." *The International Economy* Summer 2011: 15–17, 79.

Filardo, Andrew, and Stephen Grenville. 2012. "Central Bank Balance Sheets and Foreign Exchange Rate Regimes: Understanding the Nexus in Asia." BIS Paper 66. Basel, Switzerland: Bank for International Settlements.

Fleming, Michael J., and Nicholas J. Klagge. 2010. "The Federal Reserve's Foreign Exchange Swap Lines." *Current Issues in Economics and Finance* 16(4): 1–7.

Forbes, Kristin. 2007. "One Cost of the Chilean Capital Controls: Increased Financial Constraints for Smaller Traded Firms." *Journal of International Economics* 71(2): 294–323.

———. 2009. "Financial Deepening and Global Currency Usage." In *The Euro at Ten: The Next Global Currency?* edited by Jean Pisani-Ferry and Adam Posen. Washington, DC: Peterson Institute of International Economics.

Forbes, Kristin J., and Francis E. Warnock. 2012. "Capital Flow Waves: Surges, Stops, Flight and Retrenchment." *Journal of International Economics* 88(2): 235–251.

Frankel, Jeffrey. 2005. "On the Renminbi: The Choice between Adjustment under a Fixed Exchange Rate and Adjustment under a Flexible Rate." NBER Working Paper 11274. Cambridge, MA: National Bureau of Economic Research.

———. 2011. "Historical Precedents for the Internationalization of the RMB." Paper prepared for the workshop organized by Council on Foreign Relations and China Development Research Foundation, Beijing, November 1, 2011.

Frankel, Jeffrey, and George Saravelos. 2012. "Are Leading Indicators Useful for Assessing Country Vulnerability? Evidence from the 2008–09 Global Financial Crisis." *Journal of International Economics* 87(2): 216–231.

Fratzscher, Marcel. 2011. "Capital Flows, Push versus Pull Factors and the Global Financial Crisis." Working Paper 1364. Frankfurt: European Central Bank.

Fratzscher, Marcel, Marco Lo Duca, and Roland Straub. 2012. "A Global Monetary Tsunami? On the Spillovers of U.S. Quantitative Easing." CEPR Discussion Paper 9195. London: Centre for Economic Policy Research.

Friedman, Milton, and Anna J. Schwartz. 1963. *A Monetary History of the United States: 1867–1960*. Princeton, NJ: Princeton University Press.

Funabashi, Yoichi. 2008. *Managing the Dollar: From the Plaza to the Louvre*. Washington, DC: Institute for International Economics.

Gladwell, Malcolm. 2002. *The Tipping Point: How Little Things Can Make a Big Difference*. New York: Back Bay Books.

Glick, Reuven, and Sylvian Leduc. 2011. "Are Large-Scale Asset Purchases Fueling the Rise in Commodity Prices?" Economic Letters 2011–10. San Francisco, CA: Federal Reserve Bank of San Francisco.

Goldberg, Linda. 2010. "Is the International Role of the Dollar Changing?" *Federal Reserve Bank of New York Current Issues* 16(1): 1–7.

Goldberg, Linda, Cindy E. Hull, and Sarah Stein. 2013. "Do Industrialized Countries Hold the Right Foreign Exchange Reserves?" *Federal Reserve Bank of New York Current Issues* 19(1): 1–9.

Goldberg, Linda, Craig Kennedy, and Jason Miu. 2010. "Central Bank Dollar Swap Lines and Overseas Dollar Funding Costs." Staff Report 429. New York: Federal Reserve Bank of New York.

Goodfriend, Marvin, and Eswar S. Prasad. 2007. "A Framework for Independent Monetary Policy in China." *CESifo Economic Studies* 53(1): 2–41.

Gordon, Robert J. 2010. "Revisiting U.S. Productivity Growth over the Past Century with a View of the Future." NBER Working Paper 15834. Cambridge, MA: National Bureau of Economic Research.

———. 2012. "Is U.S. Economic Growth Over? Faltering Innovation Confronts the Six Headwinds." NBER Working Paper 18315. Cambridge, MA: National Bureau of Economic Research.

Goswami, Mangal, and Sunil Sharma. 2011. "The Development of Local Debt Markets in Asia." IMF Working Paper WP/11/132. Washington, DC: International Monetary Fund.

Gourinchas, Pierre-Olivier, and Maurice Obstfeld. 2012. "Stories of the Twentieth Century for the Twenty-First." *American Economic Journal: Macroeconomics* 4(1): 226–265.

Gourinchas, Pierre-Olivier, and Olivier Jeanne. 2012. "Global Safe Assets." Manuscript. Baltimore: Johns Hopkins University.

———. 2013. "Capital Flows to Developing Countries: The Allocation Puzzle." *Review of Economic Studies*, forthcoming.

Gourinchas, Pierre-Olivier, and Hélène Rey. 2007a. "From World Banker to World Venture Capitalist: The U.S. External Adjustment and the Exorbitant Privilege." In *G7 Current Account Imbalances: Sustainability and Adjustment,* edited by Richard Clarida. Chicago: University of Chicago Press.

———. 2007b. "International Financial Adjustment." *Journal of Political Economy* 115: 665–703.

Gourinchas, Pierre-Olivier, Hélène Rey, and Kai Truempler. 2012. "The Financial Crisis and the Geography of Wealth Transfers." *Journal of International Economics* 88(2): 266–283.

Greenlaw, David, James D. Hamilton, Peter Hooper, and Frederic S. Mishkin. 2013. "Crunch Time: Fiscal Crises and the Role of Monetary Policy." Manuscript. San Diego: University of California, San Diego.

Greenspan, Alan. 1999. "Currency Reserves and Debt." Remarks at the World Bank Conference on Recent Trends in Reserves Management, Washington, DC, April 29.

Grimes, William W. 2011. "The Asian Monetary Fund Reborn? Implications of Chiang Mai Initiative Multilateralization." *Asia Policy* 11: 79–104.

Guidotti, Pablo. 1999. Remarks to the G-33 Seminar, Bonn, Germany, March 11.

Haggard, Stephen. 2000. *The Political Economy of the Asian Financial Crisis.* Washington, DC: Institute for International Economics.

Hamilton, James D., and Jing Cynthia Wu. 2011. "The Effectiveness of Alternative Monetary Policy Tools in a Zero Lower Bound Environment." *Journal of Money, Credit, and Banking* 44(1): 3–46.

Hanke, Steve H., and Alex K. F. Kwok. 2009. "On the Measurement of Zimbabwe's Hyperinflation." *Cato Journal* 29(2): 353–364.

Hausmann, Ricardo, and Federico Sturzenegger. 2006. "Why the US Current Account Deficit Is Sustainable." *International Finance* 9(2): 223–240.

He, Weifang. 2012. *In the Name of Justice: Striving for the Rule of Law in China.* Washington, DC: Brookings Institution Press.

Heller, Joseph. 1961. *Catch-22.* New York: Simon & Schuster.

Henning, C. Randall. 1999. *The Exchange Stabilization Fund: Slush Fund or War Chest?* Washington, DC: Institute for International Economics.

———. 2009. "The Future of the Chiang Mai Initiative: An Asian Monetary Fund?" Policy Brief 09-5. Washington, DC: Peterson Institute for International Economics.

Henry, Peter. 2007. "Capital Account Liberalization: Theory, Evidence, and Speculation." *Journal of Economic Literature* 45(4): 887–935.

Herndon, Thomas, Michael Ash, and Robert Pollin. 2013. "Does High Public Debt Consistently Stifle Economic Growth? A Critique of Reinhart and Rogoff." Manuscript. Amherst: University of Massachusetts.

Hope, Nicholas C., James Laurenceson, and Fengming Qin. 2008. "The Impact of Direct Investment by Foreign Banks on China's Banking Industry." Working Paper 362. Stanford, CA: Stanford Center for International Development.

Hume, David. 1742. *Essays Moral, Political, Literary, Part II, Book V: Of the Balance on Trade.* Edited and with a foreword, notes, and glossary by Eugene F. Miller. Indianapolis: Liberty Fund, 1987.

Irwin, Neil. 2013. *The Alchemists: Three Central Bankers and a World on Fire.* New York: Penguin Press.

Ito, Takatoshi. 2011. "The Internationalization of the RMB: Opportunities and Pitfalls." Working Paper. New York: Council on Foreign Relations.

Jackson, James J. 2013. "Foreign Ownership of U.S. Financial Assets: Implications of a Withdrawal." Washington, DC: Congressional Research Service.

Jacquet, Pierre, and Thierry de Montbrial. 1991. "Central Banks and International Cooperation." In *International Money and Debt: Challenges for the World Economy,* edited by Rudiger Dornbusch and Steve Marcus. San Francisco: ICS Press.

Jeanne, Olivier. 2007. "International Reserves in Emerging Market Countries: Too Much of a Good Thing?" *Brookings Papers on Economic Activity* Spring: 1–79.

Jorgenson, Dale W., and Khuong M. Vu. 2010. "Potential Growth of the World Economy." *Journal of Policy Modeling* 32(5): 615–631.

Judson, Ruth. 2012. "Crisis and Calm: Demand for U.S. Currency at Home and Abroad from the Fall of the Berlin Wall to 2011." International Finance Discussion Paper 1058. Washington, DC: Board of Governors of the Federal Reserve.

Kaminsky, Graciela, and Carmen M. Reinhart. 1999. "The Twin Crises: The Causes of Banking and Balance-of-Payments Problems." *American Economic Review* 89(3): 473–500.

Kawai, Masahiro. 2010. "From the Chiang Mai Initiative to an Asian Monetary Fund." Manuscript. Tokyo: Asian Development Bank Institute.

Kawai, Masahiro, and Eswar S. Prasad, editors. 2011. *Financial Market Regulation and Reforms in Emerging Markets.* Washington, DC: Brookings Institution Press.

Kenen, Peter B. 2010a. "An SDR Based Reserve System." *Journal of Globalization and Development* 1(2): Article 13.

———. 2010b. "Reforming the Global Reserve Regime: The Role of a Substitution Account." *International Finance* 13(1): 1–23.

Keynes, John Maynard. 1936. *The General Theory of Employment, Interest and Money.* London: Palgrave Macmillan (reprinted in 2007).

Kimball, Miles. 2013. "Breaking through the Zero Lower Bound." Manuscript. Ann Arbor: University of Michigan.

Klein, Michael. 2012. "Capital Controls: Gates and Walls." *Brookings Papers on Economic Activity* Spring: 317–355.

Kose, M. Ayhan, and Eswar S. Prasad. 2010. *Emerging Markets: Resilience and Growth amid Global Turmoil.* Washington, DC: Brookings Institution Press.

Kose, M. Ayhan, Eswar S. Prasad, and Ashley D. Taylor. 2011. "Thresholds in the Process of International Financial Integration." *Journal of International Money and Finance* 30(1): 147–179.

Kose, M. Ayhan, Eswar S. Prasad, and Marco E. Terrones. 2009a. "Does Financial Globalization Promote Risk Sharing?" *Journal of Development Economics* 89(2): 258–270.

———. 2009b. "Does Openness to International Financial Flows Raise Productivity Growth?" *Journal of International Money and Finance* 28(4): 554–580.

Kose, M. Ayhan, Eswar S. Prasad, Kenneth Rogoff, and Shang-Jin Wei. 2009. "Financial Globalization: A Reappraisal." *IMF Staff Papers* 56(1): 8–62.

Kozicki, Sharon, Eric Santor, and Lena Suchanek. 2012. "Large Scale Asset Purchases: Impact on Commodity Prices and International Spillover Effects." Manuscript. Ottawa: Bank of Canada.

Kroeber, Arthur. 2011. *The Chinese Yuan Grows Up Slowly: Fact and Fiction about China's Currency Internationalization.* Policy Paper. Washington, DC: New America Foundation.

Krueger, Anne O., and Jungho Yoo. 2002. "Chaebol Capitalism and the Currency-Financial Crisis in Korea." In *Preventing Currency Crises in Emerging Markets,* edited by Sebastian Edwards and Jeffrey Frankel. Cambridge, MA: National Bureau of Economic Research.

Krugman, Paul. 1995. *Currency and Crises.* Cambridge, MA: MIT Press.

———. 2007. "Will There Be a Dollar Crisis?" *Economic Policy* 22(51): 435–467.

Kuroda, Haruhiko, and Masahiro Kawai. 2004. "Strengthening Regional Financial Cooperation in East Asia." In *Financial Governance in East Asia: Policy Dialogue, Surveillance and Cooperation,* edited by Gordon de Brouwer and Yunjong Wang. London: Routledge.

Laban, Raul, and Felipe Larrain. 1992. "Continuity, Change, and the Political Economy of Transition in Chile." In *Reform, Recovery, and Growth: Latin America and the Middle East,* edited by Rudiger Dornbusch and Sebastian Edwards. Chicago: University of Chicago Press.

Lago, Isabelle Mateos, Rupa Duttagupta, and Rishi Goyal. 2009. "The Debate on the International Monetary System." IMF Staff Position Note 09/26. Washington, DC: International Monetary Fund.

Lane, Philip R., and Gian Maria Milesi-Ferretti. 2007. "The External Wealth of Nations Mark II: Revised and Extended Estimates of Foreign Assets and Liabilities, 1970–2004." *Journal of International Economics* 73(2): 223–250.

Lane, Philip R., and Gian Maria Milesi-Ferretti. 2008. "The Drivers of Financial Globalization." *American Economic Review (Papers and Proceedings)* 98(2): 227–332.

Lardy, Nicholas R. 2008. "Financial Repression in China." Policy Brief 08-8. Washington, DC: Peterson Institute for International Economics.

———. 2011. *Sustaining China's Growth after the Global Financial Crisis.* Washington, DC: Peterson Institute for International Economics.

Lardy, Nicholas R., and Patrick Douglass. 2011. "Capital Account Liberalization and the Role of the Renminbi." Working Paper 11-6. Washington, DC: Peterson Institute for International Economics.

Lawson, Nigel. 1992. *The View from No. 11: Memoirs of a Tory Radical.* London: Bantam Press.

Lee, Jaewoo, Gian Maria Milesi-Ferretti, Jonathan David Ostry, Alessandro Prati, and Luca Antonio Ricci. 2008. "Exchange Rate Assessments: CGER Methodologies." Occasional Paper 261. Washington, DC: International Monetary Fund.

Leigh, Lamin, and Richard Podpiera. 2006. "The Rise of Foreign Investment in China's Banks—Taking Stock." IMF Working Paper 06/92. Washington, DC: International Monetary Fund.

Levchenko, Andrei. 2005. "Financial Liberalization and Consumption Volatility in Developing Countries." *IMF Staff Papers* 52(2): 237–259.

Li, Cheng. 2012. *The Political Mapping of China's Tobacco Industry and Anti-Smoking Campaign.* Washington, DC: Brookings Institution Press.

Lin, Justin Y. 2011. *Demystifying the Chinese Economy.* Cambridge: Cambridge University Press.

Lubman, Stanley B, editor. 2012. *The Evolution of Law Reform in China: An Uncertain Path.* London: Edward Elgar.

Lucas, Robert E. Jr. 1990. "Why Doesn't Capital Flow from Rich to Poor Countries?" *American Economic Review* 80(2): 92–96.

Magud, E. Nicholas, Carmen Reinhart, and Kenneth Rogoff. 2011. "Capital Controls: Myth and Reality—A Portfolio Balance Approach." Working Paper 11-7. Washington, DC: Peterson Institute for International Economics.

Makin, John H. 1971. "Swaps and Roosa Bonds as an Index of the Cost of Cooperation in the 'Crisis Zone.'" *Quarterly Journal of Economics* 85(2): 349–356.

Mark, Nelson C. 1995. "Exchange Rates and Fundamentals: Evidence on Long-Horizon Predictability." *American Economic Review* 85(1): 201–218.

Marston, Richard C. 1988. "Exchange Rate Policy Reconsidered." In *International Economic Cooperation,* edited by Martin Feldstein. Chicago: University of Chicago Press for National Bureau of Economic Research.

Mayhew, David R. 2005. *Divided We Govern: Party Control, Lawmaking, and Investigations, 1946–2002.* Second edition. New Haven, CT: Yale University Press.

———. 2013. *Partisan Balance: Why Political Parties Don't Kill the U.S. Constitutional System.* Princeton, NJ: Princeton University Press.

Maziad, Samar, Pascal Farahmand, Shengzu Wang, Stephanie Segal, and Faisal Ahmed. 2011. "Internationalization of Emerging Market Currencies: A Balance between Risks and Rewards." IMF Staff Discussion Note 11/17. Washington, DC: International Monetary Fund.

McKinnon, Ronald I. 2012. *The Unloved Dollar Standard: From Bretton Woods to the Rise of China.* New York: Oxford University Press.

McMillan, Margaret S., and Dani Rodrik. 2011. "Globalization, Structural Change and Productivity Growth." NBER Working Paper 17143. Cambridge, MA: National Bureau of Economic Research.

Meltzer, Allan H. 2010. *A History of the Federal Reserve, Volume 2, Book 1, 1951–1969.* Chicago: University of Chicago Press.

Mendoza, Enrique G., Vincenzo Quadrini, and José-Víctor Ríos-Rull. 2009. "Financial Integration, Financial Development, and Global Imbalances." *Journal of Political Economy* 117(3): 371–416.

Milesi-Ferretti, Gian-Maria, and Cedric Tille. 2011. "The Great Retrenchment: International Capital Flows during the Global Financial Crisis." *Economic Policy* 26(66): 289–346.

Milesi-Ferretti, Gian-Maria, Francesco Strobbe, and Natalia Tamirisa. 2010. "Bilateral Financial Linkages and Global Imbalances: A View on the Eve of the Financial Crisis." IMF Working Paper 10/257. Washington, DC: International Monetary Fund.

Mishkin, Frederic S. 2008. *The Next Great Globalization: How Disadvantaged Nations Can Harness Their Financial Systems to Get Rich.* Princeton, NJ: Princeton University Press.

Montiel, Peter J. 2000. "What Drives Consumption Booms?" *World Bank Economic Review* 14(3): 457–480.

Mooney, Charles W., Jr. 2012. "United States Sovereign Debt: A Thought Experiment on Default and Restructuring." In *Is U.S. Government Debt Different?* edited by Franklin Allen, Anna Gelpern, Charles Mooney, and David Skeel. Philadelphia: FIC Press.

Moreau, Emile. 1991. *The Golden Franc, Memoirs of a Governor of the Bank of France: The Stabilization of the Franc (1926–1928).* Translated by Stephen D. Stoller and Trevor C. Roberts. Boulder: Westview Press. [Original published in 1954.]

Mouré, Kenneth. 1991. *Managing the Franc Poincaré: Economic Understanding and Political Constraint in French Monetary Policy, 1928–1936.* Cambridge: Cambridge University Press.

Mun, Thomas. 1664. *England's Treasure by Forraign Trade.* London: J. G. for Thomas Clark.

North, Douglass C. 1982. *Structure and Change in Economic History.* New York: W. W. Norton.

Obstfeld, Maurice. 2010. "Expanding Gross Asset Positions and the International

Monetary System." Proceedings of the 2010 Jackson Hole Symposium, Federal Reserve Bank of Kansas City, Jackson Hole, WY, August 26–28.

Obstfeld, Maurice. 2011a. "International Liquidity: The Fiscal Dimension." Keynote speech at Bank of Japan, Institute of Monetary and Economic Studies, International Conference, Tokyo, June 2–3.

———. 2011b. "The International Monetary System: Living with Asymmetry." Manuscript. Berkeley: University of California, Berkeley.

———. 2011c. "The SDR as an International Reserve Asset: What Future?" Manuscript. Berkeley: University of California, Berkeley.

———. 2012. "Does the Current Account Still Matter?" *American Economic Review* 102(3): 1–23.

Obstfeld, Maurice, and Kenneth S. Rogoff. 1996. *Foundations of International Macroeconomics.* Cambridge, MA: MIT Press.

———. 2005. "Global Current Account Imbalances and Exchange Rate Adjustments." *Brookings Papers on Economic Activity* Spring: 67–123.

———. 2009. "Global Imbalances and the Financial Crisis: Products of Common Causes." Paper prepared for the Federal Reserve Bank of San Francisco Asia Economic Policy Conference, Santa Barbara, California, October 18–20.

Obstfeld, Maurice, Jay C. Shambaugh, and Alan M. Taylor. 2010. "Financial Stability, the Trilemma, and International Reserves." *American Economic Journal: Macroeconomics* 2(2): 57–94.

O'Neill, Jim. 2011. *The Growth Map: Economic Opportunity in the BRICs and Beyond.* New York: Penguin.

Papaioannou, Elias, Richard Portes, and Gregorios Siourounis. 2006. "Optimal Currency Shares in International Reserves: The Impact of the Euro and the Prospects for the Dollar." NBER Working Paper 12333. Cambridge, MA: National Bureau of Economic Research.

Parrinder, Patrick. 1990. "Wells's Cancelled Endings for 'The Country of the Blind.'" *Science Fiction Studies* 17(1): 71–76.

Patnaik, Ila, Abhijit Sen Gupta, and Ajay Shah. 2012. "Determinants of Trade Misinvoicing." *Open Economies Review* 23(5): 891–910.

Pitchford, John D. 1989. "A Sceptical View of Australia's Current Account and Debt Problem." *Australian Economic Review* 86(Winter): 5–14.

Posen, Adam S. 2008. "Why the Euro Will Not Rival the Dollar." *International Finance* 11(1): 35–100.

Pradhan, Manoj, and Alan M. Taylor. 2011. "Current Accounts and Global Adjustment: The Long and Short of It." *Journal of Applied Corporate Finance* 23(1): 32–42.

Prasad, Eswar S., editor. 2004. *China's Growth and Integration into the World Economy: Prospects and Challenges.* IMF Occasional Paper 232. Washington, DC: International Monetary Fund.

———. 2009a. "Some New Perspectives on India's Approach to Capital Account Liberalization." *Brookings India Policy Forum* 5(2008/09): 125–178.

———. 2009b. "Is China's Growth Miracle Built to Last?" *China Economic Review* 20: 103–123.

———. 2009c. "The Insurance Solution." *Wall Street Journal Asia,* March 11.

———. 2011a. "Role Reversal in Global Finance." Conference proceedings of the Jackson Hole Symposium *Achieving Maximum Long-Run Growth,* Federal Reserve Bank of Kansas City, Jackson Hole, WY, August 25–27.

———. 2011b. "Rebalancing Growth in Asia." *International Finance* 14(1): 27–66.

Prasad, Eswar S., and Mengjie Ding. 2011. "Debt Burden in Advanced Economies Now a Global Threat." *Financial Times,* July 31.

Prasad, Eswar S., and Raghuram G. Rajan. 2005. "Controlled Capital Account Liberalization: A Proposal." IMF Policy Discussion Paper 05/7. Washington, DC: International Monetary Fund.

———. 2006. "Modernizing China's Growth Paradigm." *American Economic Review* 96(2): 331–336.

———. 2008. "A Pragmatic Approach to Capital Account Liberalization." *Journal of Economic Perspectives* 22(3): 149–172.

Prasad, Eswar S., and Shang-Jin Wei. 2007. "China's Approach to Capital Inflows: Patterns and Possible Explanations." In *Capital Controls and Capital Flows in Emerging Economies: Policies, Practices, and Consequences,* edited by Sebastian Edwards. Chicago: University of Chicago Press for National Bureau of Economic Research.

Prasad, Eswar S., and Lei Ye. 2012. *The Renminbi's Role in the Global Monetary System.* Brookings Report. Washington, DC: Brookings Institution.

Prasad, Eswar S., Raghuram G. Rajan, and Arvind Subramanian. 2007. "Foreign Capital and Economic Growth." *Brookings Papers on Economic Activity* Spring: 153–230.

Prasad, Eswar S., Thomas Rumbaugh, and Qing Wang. 2005. "Putting the Cart before the Horse? Capital Account Liberalization and Exchange Rate Flexibility in China." IMF Policy Discussion Paper. Washington, DC: International Monetary Fund.

Rajan, Raghuram G. 2005. "Has Financial Development Made the World Riskier?" Conference proceedings from Jackson Hole Symposium *The Greenspan Era: Lessons for the Future,* Federal Reserve Bank of Kansas City, Jackson Hole, WY, August 25–27.

———. 2010. *Fault Lines: How Hidden Fractures Still Threaten the World Economy.* Princeton, NJ: Princeton University Press.

Razin, Assaf, Efraim Sadka, and Chi-Wa Yuen. 1998. "A Pecking Order of Capital Inflows and International Tax Principles." *Journal of International Economics* 44(1): 45–68.

Reddy, Yaga V. 2002. "India's Foreign Exchange Reserves—Policy, Status and Issues." Special Lecture at the National Council of Applied Economic Research, New Delhi, India, on May 10, 2002.

Reinhart, Carmen M., and Vincent R. Reinhart. 2008. "Capital Inflows and Reserve Accumulation: The Recent Evidence." NBER Working Paper 13842. Cambridge, MA: National Bureau of Economic Research.

Reinhart, Carmen M., and Kenneth Rogoff. 2008. "The Forgotten History of Domestic Debt." NBER Working Paper 13946. Cambridge, MA: National Bureau of Economic Research.

Reinhart, Carmen M., and Kenneth Rogoff. 2009. *This Time Is Different: Eight Centuries of Financial Folly.* Princeton, NJ: Princeton University Press.

———. 2010. "Growth in a Time of Debt." *American Economic Review* 100(2): 573–578.

———. 2011. "From Financial Crash to Debt Crisis." *American Economic Review* 101(5): 1676–1706.

Reinhart, Carmen M., and M. Belen Sbrancia. 2011. "The Liquidation of Government Debt." Working Paper 16893. Cambridge, MA: National Bureau of Economic Research.

Rodrik, Dani. 2006. "The Social Cost of Foreign Exchange Reserves." Working Paper 11952. Cambridge, MA: National Bureau of Economic Research.

———. 2008. "The Real Exchange Rate and Economic Growth." *Brookings Papers on Economic Activity* Fall: 365–439.

Rosen, Daniel H., and Thilo Hanemann. 2009. "China's Changing Outbound Foreign Direct Investment Profile: Drivers and Policy Implications." Policy Brief 09-14. Washington, DC: Peterson Institute for International Economics.

Sachs, Jeffrey D., and Andrew M. Warner. 2001. "The Curse of Natural Resources." *European Economic Review* 45(4–6): 827–838.

Sargent, Arthur John. 1899. *The Economic Policy of Colbert.* London: Longmans, Green, and Company.

Scheinkman, Jose A., and Michael Woodford. 1994. "Self-Organized Criticality and Economic Fluctuations." *American Economic Review* 84(2): 417–421.

Schindler, Martin. 2009. "Measuring Financial Integration: A New Data Set." *IMF Staff Papers* 56(1): 222–238.

Scissors, David. 2011. "Chinese Outward Investment: More Opportunity than Danger." Heritage Foundation Backgrounder 2579. Washington, DC: Heritage Foundation.

Sheel, Alok. 2011. "Challenges in IMS Reforms: A Global and Emerging Markets' Perspective." ICRIER Policy Series 11. New Delhi, India: Indian Council for Research and International Economic Relations.

Shih, Victor C. 2009. *Factions and Finance in China: Elite Conflict and Inflation.* Cambridge: Cambridge University Press.

Shin, Hyun Song. 2012. "Global Banking Glut and Loan Risk Premium." *IMF Economic Review* 60(2): 155–192.

Singh, Manmohan. 2013. "The Changing Collateral Space." IMF Working Paper 13/25. Washington, DC: International Monetary Fund.

Singh, Sukudhew. 2011. "Monetary Policy Challenges for Emerging Markets in a Globalized Environment." In *Asian Perspectives on Financial Sector Reforms and Regulation,* edited by Masahiro Kawai and Eswar S. Prasad. Washington, DC: Brookings Institution Press.

Smith, Adam. 1776. *The Wealth of Nations, Book IV: Of the Principle of the Commercial or Mercantile System.* London: Methuen and Co.

Solomon, Lewis D. 1996. *Rethinking Our Centralized Monetary System: The Case for a System of Local Currencies.* Westport, CT: Praeger.

Sorkin, Andrew Ross. 2010. *Too Big to Fail: The Inside Story of How Wall Street and Washington Fought to Save the Financial System—and Themselves.* New York: Viking Press.

Steil, Benn. 2013. *The Battle of Bretton Woods: John Maynard Keynes, Harry Dexter White, and the Making of a New World Order.* New York: Princeton University Press.

Subramanian, Arvind. 2011. *Eclipse: Living in the Shadow of China's Economic Dominance.* Washington, DC: Institute of International Economics.

Summers, Lawrence H. 2006. "Reflections on Global Account Imbalances and Emerging Markets' Reserve Accumulation." L. K. Jha Memorial Lecture, Reserve Bank of India, Mumbai, India, March 24.

Sun, Tao, and Heiko Hesse. 2009. "Sovereign Wealth Funds and Financial Stability— An Event Study Analysis." Working Paper 09/239. Washington, DC: International Monetary Fund.

Svensson, Lars E. O. 2011. "Monetary Policy after the Crisis." In *Asia's Role in the Post-Crisis Global Economy,* edited by Reuven Glick and Mark M. Spiegel. San Francisco: Federal Reserve Bank of San Francisco.

Tagore, Rabindranath. 1916. *Fruit-Gathering.* New York: Macmillan.

Tavlas, George. 1991. "On the International Use of Currencies: The Case of the Deutsche Mark." Essays in International Finance 181. March. Princeton, NJ: Princeton University.

Taylor, Alan M. 2002. "A Century of Current Account Dynamics." *Journal of International Money and Finance* 21: 725–748.

Taylor, Alan M., and Mark P. Taylor. 2004. "The Purchasing Power Parity Debate." *Journal of Economic Perspectives* 18(4): 135–158.

Taylor, John B. 2008. "The Financial Crisis and the Policy Responses: An Empirical Analysis of What Went Wrong." In *A Festschrift in Honour of David Dodge's Contributions to Canadian Public Policy.* Ottawa: Bank of Canada.

Tornell, Aaron, and Andrés Velasco. 1992. "Why Does Capital Flow from Poor to Rich Countries? The Tragedy of the Commons and Economic Growth." *Journal of Political Economy* 100(6): 1208–1231.

Triffin, Robert. 1960. *Gold and the Dollar Crisis.* New Haven, CT: Yale University Press.

Twain, Mark. 1897. *Following the Equator: A Journey Around the World.* Hartford, CT: American Publishing Company.

Ungerer, Horst. 1997. *A Concise History of European Monetary Integration: From EPU to EMU.* Santa Barbara, CA: Praeger.

Uribe, José Darío. 2012. "En Defensa del Marco Actual de Política Cambiaria." Bogotá, Colombia: Banco de la República.

Vergote, Olivier, Werner Studener, Ioannis Efthymiadis, and Niall Merriman. 2010. "Main Drivers of the ECB Financial Accounts and ECB Financial Strength over the First 11 Years." Occasional Paper Series 111. Frankfurt: European Central Bank.

Vogel, Ezra F. 2011. *Deng Xiaoping and the Transformation of China.* Cambridge, MA: Belknap Press of Harvard University Press.

Walter, Carl E., and Fraser J. T. Howie. 2011. *Red Capitalism: The Fragile Financial Foundation of China's Extraordinary Rise.* New York: Wiley.

Wessel, David. 2010. *In Fed We Trust: Ben Bernanke's War on the Great Panic.* New York: Crown Publishing.

Williams, John C. 2012. "Cash Is Dead! Long Live Cash." In *2012 Annual Report of the Federal Reserve Bank of San Francisco.* San Francisco: Federal Reserve Bank of San Francisco.

Williams, Marion V. 2005. "Foreign Exchange Reserves: How Much Is Enough?" Speech at the Twentieth Adlith Brown Memorial Lecture, Central Bank of the Bahamas, Nassau, November 2.

Wolf, Martin. 2010. *Fixing Global Finance.* Baltimore: Johns Hopkins University Press.

Woodward, Thomas G. 2005. "Inflation Tax." In *The Encyclopedia of Taxation and Tax Policy,* edited by Joseph J. Cordes, Robert D. Ebel, and Jane G. Gravelle. Washington, DC: Urban Institute Press.

Yam, Joseph. 2011. "A Safe Approach to Convertibility for the Renminbi." Working Paper 5. Hong Kong: Institute for Global Economics and Finance, Chinese University of Hong Kong.

Ye, Lei. 2011. "Financial Integration and Wage Inequality." Manuscript. Ithaca, NY: Cornell University.

Yu, Yongding. 2012. "Revisiting the Internationalization of the Yuan." ADBI Working Paper Series 366. Tokyo: Asian Development Bank Institute.

Zhou, Xiaochuan. 2009. "Reform the International Monetary System." Beijing: People's Bank of China.

Zivney, Terry L., and Richard D. Marcus. 2005. "The Day the United States Defaulted on Treasury Bills." *Financial Review* 24(3): 475–489.

ACKNOWLEDGMENTS

This book incorporates work I have done over the past few years with a number of distinguished co-authors, who have helped shape my understanding of the issues discussed here. I am particularly grateful to Marcos Chamon, Menzie Chinn, Marvin Goodfriend, M. Ayhan Kose, Raghuram Rajan, Kenneth Rogoff, Arvind Subramanian, Marco Terrones, and Shang-Jin Wei, some of whom also offered helpful comments on parts of the material in this book. Julian Berengaut, Eduard Brau, Zsolt Darvas, Basia Kamińska, M. Ayhan Kose, and Alok Sheel read through early drafts of the entire manuscript and provided many thoughtful comments and suggestions. I also thank Kemal Derviş, Andrew Karolyi, Don Kohn, and Paweł Stefański for their suggestions. Numerous other friends and colleagues were generous with their time in reading parts of various chapters and offering helpful comments.

Cornell University and the Brookings Institution have been wonderful places to do research, and my colleagues at both institutions have sharpened and deepened my understanding of the subjects explored in this book. I am particularly grateful for the encouragement and support I have received over the years from Deans Susan Henry and Kathryn Boor at Cornell and Lael Brainard, Kemal Derviş, and Strobe Talbott at Brookings.

I spent the first (17-year) phase of my career as an economist at the International Monetary Fund. There are few better places to encounter high-quality research tangling with policy issues of immediate relevance across the world. I owe a considerable intellectual debt to my colleagues at the Fund and particularly to the string of top-notch Research Department directors that I had the privilege to work with—Jacob Frenkel, Michael Mussa, Kenneth Rogoff, and Raghuram Rajan. They have all been an inspiration, with their disciplined and rigorous approach to research and translation of that research into policy advice.

The excellent research assistance of a number of students and research collaborators helped me write this book. Kushagra Aniket, Laura Ardila, Mengjie Ding, Karim Foda, Yuhui Jiang, Ratish Malhotra, Mariana Olaizola, Arnav Sahu, Parul Sharma, Kirat Singh, Abigail Warren, Lei (Sandy) Ye, and Boyang Zhang all spent many tireless hours helping me compile data and do background research. Some of them also read through various parts of the manuscript and offered many helpful comments. Carol Thomson and Quynh Tonnu provided administrative support for my research. William Barnett helped with proofreading.

Seth Ditchik was the editor for this book and helped shepherd it through to its publication. Peter Strupp and his colleagues at Princeton Editorial Associates efficiently handled the copyediting and production of the book.

Finally, but most importantly, I owe an enormous debt to my family —my wife Basia and my daughters Berenika and Yuvika—for supporting me every step of the way and tolerating my obsession with getting this book done.

INDEX

Page numbers for entries occurring in figures are followed by an *f,* those for entries in notes, by an *n,* and those for entries in tables, by a *t.*